Y0-CSR-929

CISTERCIAN STUDIES SERIES: NUMBER EIGHT

THE ELEVENTH-CENTURY BACKGROUND
OF CÎTEAUX

CISTERCIAN STUDIES SERIES

Board of Editors

Louis Bouyer OF THE ORATORY
Louis Lekai S O CIST
Anselm Hoste OSB
Luke Anderson S O CIST
Edmund Mikkers OCSO
Mary Paul Macpherson OCSO

Jean Leclercq OSB
Charles Dumont OCSO
Teresa Ann Doyle OSB
Mary Gertrude Ballew OCSO
Basil De Pinto OSB
James Wicksteed OCSO

Jeremiah F. O'Sullivan

Managing Editor

M. Basil Pennington OCSO

CS 1: *The Climate of Monastic Prayer*
CS 2: *The Theology of Aelred of Rievaulx: An Experiential Theology*
CS 3: *The Cistercian Spirit: A Symposium*
CS 4: *The Praktikos, Chapters on Prayer*
CS 8: *The Eleventh-Century Background of Cîteaux*
CS 10: *William of St Thierry: the Man and his Works*
CS 11: *The Cistercian Sign Language: A Study in Non-verbal Communication*
CS 12: *Rule and Life: An Interdisciplinary Symposium*
CS 13: *Studies in Medieval Cistercian History*
CS 14: *The Abbot in Monastic Tradition*
CS 15: *The Golden Chain: The Theological Anthropology of Isaac of Stella*

CISTERCIAN STUDIES SERIES: NUMBER EIGHT

THE ELEVENTH-CENTURY BACKGROUND OF CÎTEAUX

Bede K. Lackner s o cist

CISTERCIAN PUBLICATIONS
CONSORTIUM PRESS
Washington, D.C.
1972

Cistercian Studies Series: ISBN 0-87907-800-6
This volume: ISBN 0-87907-808-1
Library of Congress Catalog Card Number: 70-152484

© Copyright, Cistercian Publications, Inc., 1972
Spencer, Mass. 01562

Printed in the Republic of Ireland by
Cahill & Co. Limited, Parkgate Printing Works, Dublin.

CONTENTS

Foreword by Jeremiah F. O'Sullivan — vii

Preface — xxi

1 Benedict of Aniane and Post-Carolingian Monachism — 1

2 Cluny (909–1100) — 40

3 The Crisis of Cenobitism — 92

4 Monastic Reform: Conciliar Legislation in Eleventh-Century France — 113

5 The Eleventh Century: Renewal in Earnest — 131

6 The Eleventh Century: New Religious Orders — 167

7 Molesme, the Home of Cîteaux — 217

Conclusion — 274

Bibliography — 277

Index — 297

ABBREVIATIONS

AS	*Acta Sanctorum* (Bollandiana). Paris, 1863–1867.
CE	*Catholic Encyclopaedia.* New York, 1908–1914.
CCSL	*Corpus Christianorum. Series Latina.* Turnholt, 1953ff.
CMH	*Cambridge Medieval History.* New York, 1911–1938.
CSEL	*Corpus Scriptorum Ecclesiasticorum Latinorum.* Vienna, 1866ff.
DACL	*Dictionnaire d'archéologie chrétienne et de liturgie.* Paris, 1907ff.
DDC	*Dictionnaire du Droit Canonique.* Paris, 1935ff.
DHE	*Dictionnaire d'Histoire Ecclésiastique.* Paris, 1912ff.
DOR	H. Hélyot, *Dictionnaire des ordres réligieux.* Paris, 1847–1859.
DSAM	*Dictionnaire de Spiritualité Ascétique et Mystique.* Paris, 1937ff.
DTC	*Dictionnaire de Théologie Catholique.* Paris, 1912ff.
EC	*Enciclopedia Cattolica.* Città del Vaticano, 1948–1954.
GCh	*Gallia Christiana.* Paris, 1715ff.
JL	*Regesta pontificum Romanorum ab condita Ecclesia ad annum post Christum natum MCXCVIII.* Edited by P. Jaffé and S. Loewenfeld. Leipzig, 1885–1888.
LTK	*Lexikon für Theologie und Kirche.* Freiburg, 1957–1965.
Mansi	*Sacrorum conciliorum nova et amplissima collectio.* Paris, 1901ff.
MGH. SS	*Monumenta Germaniae Historica. Scriptores.* Hannover, 1826ff.
PG	*Patrologiae cursus completus. Series Graeca.* Paris, 1857–1886.
PL	*Patrologiae cursus completus. Series Latina.* Paris, 1844ff.
RHE	*Revue d'Histoire Ecclésiastique.* Louvain, 1900ff.
RHF	*Recueil des historiens des Gaules et de la France.* Paris, 1868ff.

FOREWORD

FOREMOST AMONG THE PROBLEMS confronting monasticism during the Middle Ages was how to retain its identity in a society which was evolving from barbarism to feudalism.

St Benedict of Nursia had provided monasticism with an organization which was a renewal of all the then existing monastic practices and a code into which that renewal was incorporated. The next renewal was in 1098, the foundation date of Cîteaux. Between those two dates, many were the reforms, but no renewal. What is the distinction between reform and renewal?

Reform shores up and patches the structure, leaving unchanged the latter. It tightens up the incidentals to the structure, i.e., by imposing stricter discipline, etc. No attempt is made to change the foundations of the system. Renewal goes much deeper; it examines the structure and reconstructs it anew from the foundations up, if time and circumstances so demand. Renewal is, of necessity, interconnected with contemporary exigencies. This was the case in 540 and again in 1098.

The *Rule of St Benedict* is neither an end nor a beginning in itself. Many rules had been written prior to its redaction. St Benedict was a student of rules; from Pachomius, Basil, Augustine, Cassiodorus, Cassian and others he extracted what served his purpose. To this he added what was relevant to contemporary monastic exigencies. The monastic profession had come into disrepute in the West because many who wore the habit of the monk did not live in conformity with their calling. St Benedict's *Rule* was a restructuring of contemporary monasticism's constituent components, expressed in a positive legal code characterized by moderation and discretion. The Benedictine monk's life revolved around three basics: prayer, through the performance of the *Opus Dei*; manual labor, which gave the monk the dignity inherent in ministering to the community and through it to God and himself; and reading the Sacred Scriptures, which were the foundation of his spiritual discipline.

The *Rule* was written at a time when the population of the Western Roman Empire was experiencing the disastrous effects of German tribal invasions. Italy was the battleground between Justinian's armies and the Ostrogoths; the unstable Merovingians in Gaul were engaged in their ever recurrent fratricidal wars; beyond the Rhine was the *terra incognita*. The remnant population of the old Western Empire who had lived under the universal law of Rome were now subject to local tribal law which changed when masters changed. The Ostrogoths were Arian in faith; the ferocious Lombards who replaced them were also of that faith; the Merovingian kings were nominally Catholic but their behavior as Catholics may well cast doubt on their Christianity.

All institutions suffer loss during periods of political turmoil and concomitant social upheaval. Thus, retrogression in Christian practice in both Italy and Gaul is quite evident in the sixth and seventh centuries. This was so in spite of the efforts of many good bishops who, though nominated by the secular powers (instead of the then current canonical procedure of election by clergy and people), provided for the social and religious well-being of their flocks, yet often in very difficult circumstances. Historically, Western Europe was being Germanized but not barbarized because the sub-soil of Roman culture was cultivated by the Church and its agencies, chiefly Benedictine monasticism. Being Germanized meant the introduction of Germanic institutions. These in time evolved into feudalism where loyalties were pledged on a man to man basis. The Germans had no experience with the abstract concept of office independent of the holder; they did not accept the

Roman concept of the corporation and its separate entities. This latter was most important for the Church and canon law. The resulting German attitude toward the Church led to the *Eigenkirche*; private appointment of abbots to rule over communities; private appointment of archbishops and bishops to archbishoprics and dioceses; private expropriation of parish churches, monasteries and their properties. It also led to the struggle on the part of the Church to free itself from feudal entanglements so that it could govern itself according to its own canons instead of being governed by local feudal custom.

In 595, Pope Gregory I (590–604) reached a decision, momentous in its consequences for the formation of Western Christian Society. He took the Benedictine from his monastic enclosure and confided to him the task of evangelizing the German tribes of England, Frisia and Germany itself. In 597, the Benedictine, St Augustine, arrived in England and converted King Ethelbert and his *witan*; two years later Ethelbert redacted the first code of Anglo-Saxon law which incorporated into its *dooms* social place and legal status for the Christian clergy who were henceforth protected by law. In less than a century the conversion of England was complete. Institutionally and organizationally it was bound ecclesiastically to the center in Rome.

The Anglo-Saxon monks of St Benedict then turned their attention, with full papal approval and backing, to Frisia and Germany. Germany's apostle, St Boniface, carried on a full correspondence with the papacy on his missionary activities, in addition to making several journeys to the Holy City. Everything was done in close collaboration with Rome. Instead of the loose organizational ties which connected the Church in Frankland with Rome, the Benedictine-founded churches in England, Frisia and Germany were firmly bound to the center of Christendom.

Even though the last of the long-haired *rois fainéants* still reigned, at least in name, and was pulled around the countryside in a cart drawn by two white oxen, Carlmann and Pepin, sons of Charles Martel, enjoyed a relatively independent rule. Later, when Pepin sought papal approval of his actions in dethroning Chilperic, the request was made on the basis of his being king *de jure* but not *de facto*. Both brothers took cognizance of the sorry state of the Church in Frankland and called on Boniface to undertake the task of reformation. He, in turn, applied to Rome for permission before acceding to the request. As justification for the necessity of reform he painted, in a letter to Pope Zachary, a picture of woes which bears no color of the spectrum but black. According to him ecclesiastical councils had not been convoked in Frankland over the last eighty years—actually, it was forty-six years. Clerical life from top to bottom needed to be reformed. The old organizational bonds with Rome had fallen into desuetude and were discontinued. Both monastic and ecclesiastical property was being appropriated, sometimes with the connivance of local ordinaries who were men of the sword rather than men of the spirit. The impression conveyed by Boniface is of a church in chaos.

The councils convoked by Carlmann and Pepin are of particular interest because their procedures reveal much about the position of ecclesiastics vis-à-vis their Frankish lords. In this respect what is true of Frankland is true of Europe in general.

For a great part of the Middle Ages, major church councils were convoked not by ecclesiastical but by secular authorities. The affairs treated were both secular and ecclesiastic, so much so that it is difficult to determine where either the secular or ecclesiastical ends or begins. Thus, it is not surprising to find both Carlmann and Pepin summoning and presiding over the reforming councils in the eighth century.

Carlmann's council met at an unknown location somewhere in Austrasia in 742. It is known as the *Concilium Germanicum*. Though a church council, its decrees were promulgated by Carlmann and thus became the law of the land. In other words, conciliar decrees were only proposals submitted to Carlmann; through publication by him they achieved the force of law. According to these decrees, organizational ties with Rome should be reestablished by constituting archbishops over provinces and bishops over dioceses. As for the reformation of the lives of the clergy, bishops who were drunkards, warriors, hunters and thieves of diocesan revenues should henceforth act as bishops should. The majority of the clergy were married, henceforth they were to live lives of celibacy.

The next council met at Soissons in 744. Here the archbishoprics of Rouen, Rheims and Sens, which had been early foundations but had fallen by the wayside in the general turmoil of the invasions, were reconstituted in fulfillment of the decrees of 742. Two years later, Pepin sent a list of twenty-two queries on canon law to Pope Zachary, thereby acknowledging the authority of the Pope in such matters. Another council was held in 747. According to its decrees, monks and "maids of God" should observe the *Rule of St Benedict*. This too became the law of the land. At this Council, Boniface fought hard and tenaciously for the restoration of appropriated church property to its rightful owners; he had to be satisfied with less than half a measure. Only a small portion was to be restored but, "care must be taken that churches and monasteries whose properties have been granted to others as a *precarium* be not reduced to poverty and want." Actually, the councils left the legal status of appropriated monastic property very much as it had been prior to 742; appropriated monastic land had become the cash payment of the secular powers for service rendered by warriors on the battlefield.

What did these councils accomplish?

On the positive side, the reforming councils reconstituted the former archbishoprics of Rouen, Rheims and Sens, thus linking the Church in Frankland organizationally with Rome. Though the councils decreed Benedictine observance for all Frankland the effect was minimal if we judge by the task confronting St Benedict of Aniane. Probably one of the most important consequences of the councils was the initiation of the Reform Movement which is a medieval continuum. They also mark the occasion for the first Carolingian Renaissance—ecclesiastical, to be sure— the work of Anglo-Saxon Benedictines. Alcuin was a worthy successor to Boniface.

The continuation of the Anglo-Saxon—induced Carolingian ecclesiastical renaissance now became the concern of the Frankish native born. The task was undertaken by St Benedict of Aniane under the aegis of Louis the Pious, King of Aquitaine and later emperor. St Benedict operated through royal power just as St Boniface had acted through Carlmann and Pepin. Louis appointed him the canonical visitor of all monasteries in Aquitaine, with the official royal injunction to enforce the *Rule of St Benedict* of Nursia in accordance with the earlier decrees of Carlmann and Pepin. Benedict's idea was to put the monk back in his monastery where he was to observe the *Rule*. How successful he was in this is difficult to estimate. He did, however, reform several monastic establishments and founded others anew, retaining direct jurisdiction over observances in the latter. This was a departure from one of the basic structures of the *Rule* wherein each monastery was autonomous. In this one respect, he laid the groundwork for the lordship of Cluny's abbot over most of that Congregation's houses.

When Louis became emperor, Benedict accompanied him to Aachen. Here again he was appointed canonical visitor—this time for the empire at large, with the exception of Italy.

In 817, a council of abbots and monks met with Louis and Benedict at Aachen to deal with monastic observances. Its decrees are called the *capitulare monasticum*. The title is worth noting. It was a capitulary, which means that its decrees were modeled on the Carolingian imperial law. It was promulgated, not by Benedict or the abbots and monks present, but by the emperor Louis. The decrees are worthy of closer study both from the viewpoint of what they tell of the monastic state and what they also tell about the complex and complicated personality of Benedict. Their impact on western monasticism was momentous.

Benedict's early life parallels that of Ignatius Loyola in many aspects. Both were soldiers, both were wounded and while recuperating, their thoughts turned to God. Something of the convert's fervor remained with Benedict all his life. His first objective was to live the solitariness of the Egyptian hermit coupled with the austerity of an Irish Columbanus. The *Rule of St Benedict* was of second choice for him. Actually, its acceptance was forced upon him by the rebellion of his monks at Seine against all his unaccustomed austerity. It seems he never did fully accept the *Rule of St Benedict* or at least never quite understood its spirit. Many of his ascetical pronouncements remind one of La Grande Chartreuse; others are suggestive of Pachomius. The concepts of solitariness and separateness find echo in the *capitulare monasticum* of 817.

The Council of 817 concerned itself directly with certain aspects of the *Rule*. Evidently, many monasteries did not even possess a copy of it. This was true in the archdiocese of Rouen as late as the thirteenth century when very few houses possessed a copy. However, such a condition is quite understandable because the houses' *customs*, while embodying the structure of the *Rule*, tended to make its presence unnecessary.

Benedict opened the sessions by explaining the *Rule* at some length. When the abbots and monks returned to their respective monasteries their task was to explain the *Rule* to their brethren. The Council placed a certain stress on liturgy and cult; no less than fifteen canons dealt with the subject. Emphasis was also placed on the vow of obedience to the abbot; this was to be obedience in the original Benedictine sense, not the contemporary Germanic concept of fealty.

In the last month of 818 another council was convoked and met at Aachen. The agenda concerned free elections of abbots by their communities. About all Benedict could extract from Emperor Louis was free election in certain designated imperial monasteries. On the death of the abbots of these monasteries the communities were to apply to the emperor for the *congé d'élire*. Lip service was given to the plight of the appropriated houses; the laymen who had taken possession of them were reminded that adequate division of agricultural products should be made, lest the monks starve or suffer from want. This had already been decreed in 747.

On the whole, the actual results hardly compensated for the expenditure of so much energy by Benedict. The reforming decrees carried within them an aspect of coercion and were regarded as coercive by the communities of religious. This was confirmed when Benedict dispatched *missi* to oversee their implementation and to report back to him at Inde [Cornelimünster] on the progress being achieved. But no amount of legislation can overcome passive resistance; acquiescence does not necessarily mean compliance. Thus, for the most part, were Benedict's decrees treated in the ninth century.

The question now arises, what were the most likely sources of Benedict's ideas on reform? In general, they are to be found in the contemporary monastic practices then current in Frankland.

Irish monks had been a potent force on the continent of Europe both in mission and monastic efforts for at least two centuries prior to St Benedict of Aniane. Where they went, they carried the *paruchia* method, i.e., the priest-abbot ruled the mother house and *praepositi,* appointed by him, governed its daughter houses; a system strongly reminiscent of Pachomius. Very likely Irish practices influenced Benedict; he remained the abbot-in-chief of his own congregation while the abbots of subordinate houses exercised a function not unlike that of the Irish *praepositi* and, later on, of the Cluniac priors. In liturgy, the profuse bowing, genuflecting and prostrating of the Irish monks became the norm in reciting the *Opus Dei* in Benedict's monasteries. Also there was the *Laus perennis* or recitation of the Office by relays of monks. Many houses copied this Irish practice.

Irish monasteries such as Luxeuil, Annegray, Fountains, St Riquier, Bregenz, Bobbio, etc., exerted a tremendous influence on Frankish monasticism. Many Irish monks were raised to the episcopate—at least six from Luxeuil in the eighth century. Again, several houses adopted a mélange of Benedict's and Columbanus' rules. In the seventh century, fifty-three houses in Frankland followed the *Rule of Columbanus.* Furthermore, in the eighth century, the *laura* of St Martin of Tours, the Egyptian tradition of Cassian, the hermitical tendencies of Lerins and the *Rule of St Caesarius of Arles* still had adherents, not to mention the canons who followed the *Rule of Chrodegang of Metz.*

From out of this St Benedict set about the task of establishing a single order. He accepted the Benedictine *Rule* as a framework but grafted thereon so many contemporary practices that the former was almost lost in the latter. His reform was a compromise between the *Rule* and the then current monastic usages, with the result that it was neither the one nor the other. To the original *Rule* were attached so many appending liturgical accretions that the recitation of the *Opus Dei* practically consumed the whole day, leaving very little time for reading the Scriptures and for manual labor. When his reform was promulgated by imperial decree some, especially the German monks from beyond the Rhine, must have felt that some of the spirit of the *Capitulare de Partibus Saxoniae* had found its way into the *Capitulare Monasticum*. Monasticism, just as the State, was now administered from the center at Aachen.

In the light of what has been stated above regarding the distinction between reform and renewal, Benedict's legislation must be considered a reform, at the most. We may even question whether it was a real reform if the *Rule of St Benedict* is the accepted criterion. Be that as it may, Benedict of Aniane had a profound effect, not only on the monasticism of his own day, but even on monasticism of today.

The eleventh and twelfth centuries are unique in the history of western monasticism and of religion in general. The desire for a simpler spirituality, for a way of relating directly to Christ in a manner capable of harmony with human understanding, gradually took shape and expression. They were years of spiritual hunger and enthusiasm. Men turned to monastic rules. Rich and poor, learned and unlearned, lay and cleric took "to the stump," going from pulpit to open air meetings. From market-day gatherings to lonely byways, a greater number of laymen than clerics preached, exhorted and propounded their own understanding of spirituality. Europe's population as a whole seems to have been preoccupied with reform in religious practices. Everywhere audiences eagerly listened and were given what they wanted to hear. What they heard sometimes bordered on the fantastic: one preacher attacked the *Book of Joshua* because Joshua lacked humility; another communicated with the Holy Spirit by means of a swarm of bees in his stomach. The louder they buzzed the more vocal was the Holy Spirit. A traveling charlatan proclaimed himself a living saint. He ordained priests, consecrated bishops and archbishops even though he himself was not in Holy Orders. Preachers such as these abounded. In one instance a group built a medium-sized ship, pushed it overland over sixty miles, all the while "evangelizing" the crowds gathered from the countryside, and finished each night in orgy and debauchery. Groups, led by a preacher or preachers, "took to the road" and wandered from place to place: one such group moved from Italy across the Alps and reached Liége and Arras whose bishops they irritated no end.

This movement is not as simple as it appears; actually, it has yet to be studied and presented in all its interrelationships. For the poor, the unlearned, the layman suddenly gave voice to their spiritual longings. There had been very little place for them in a feudalized church. At the same time we find some of the most brilliant and creative minds of the Middle Ages, such as St Peter Damian, Lanfranc, St Victor, St Anselm, St Aelred of Rievaulx, St Bernard, William of St Thierry, St Bruno, Anselm of Lucca, Deusdedit, Ivo of Chartres, Gratian—to mention only a few. These were men of great learning but of spiritual simplicity. The learned and the unlearned spoke of the same subject but in different ways. What was in the hearts of both was the same; the unlearned erred not out of intent but only out of ignorance. In addition to seeking relationship to the Person of Christ, all sought devotion to the Virgin Mary, to the Cross; they sought the love of God and man, a spiritual union and spiritual affection, which was expressed more elegantly by the learned as *adhesio mentis* and *affectus mentis,* but wanted just as longingly by the unlearned.

These were the years when hermits came individually and in small groups from Constantinople, Italy and Ireland to Frankland. A bandit group mended their ways and became hermits at Afflingen in Belgium. They opened their hermitage to every passerby who sought solitude. In time there had gathered there nuns, priests and laymen, learned and unlearned, rich and poor.

The hermit mystique resulted in a renaissance of interest in the writings of the Desert Fathers, in Jerome, John Chrysostom,

Augustine and Cassian. Some groups became more consolidated and followed a version of the *Rule of St Benedict* but retained strong emphasis on the heremitical life; such were Tiron, Savigny, Hambye, Colan and Molesme, among the many. These sincere men felt that the only way to reform was a return to the desert; it was the only way to a real living of the *paupertas Christi* and the simplicity and brotherhood of the *ecclesia primitiva*. Such also were the ideals of Romuald of Ravenna, one of whose hermitages developed into the Order of Camaldoli, and John Gualbert, founder of Vallombrosa (both in Italy). Camaldoli still lives with us today. But the greatest, best known and most successful of this type was La Grande Chartreuse founded by St Bruno of Rheims. Its success is based on the fact that it was a complete retreat into the hills which served *in lieu* of the deserts of Egypt. All of these retained elements of St Benedict's *Rule*, but their emphasis was on the eremitical, rather than on the coenobitical.

What is the result of the almost universal seeking after God in western Europe in the eleventh and twelfth centuries? In the first place, groups develop, without prompting, a common understanding of a situation to the extent that the interpretation by the individual and by the whole tend to be uniform. In these two centuries there seems to have developed a common denominator, a consensus among the population at large regarding the ideal monastic order they would like to see come into being.

Cluny, the hitherto great name in monastic circles, was being looked at askance. It is not that its discipline was lax but, rather, that it had grown rich in lands, powerful in international politics, and thoroughly immersed in contemporary feudal society; so much so that it was a far cry from the ideal of those who hankered after *paupertas Christi* and the *ecclesia primitiva*. Cluny's physical establishments were not a good example of either. Renewal, not reform, was wished for, almost like the longing for the coming of the Messiah. Renewal is a slow-moving process; it evolves rather than revolves, but the evolutionary series of steps had been in the making for some time. The solution would be found in a new order which responded to the contemporary spiritual aspirations.

The Order which embodied within itself this longing of the populace came into being at the New Monastery—Cîteaux. Its founders returned to the original *Rule of St Benedict* and sought to observe it as had been done at Monte Cassino in the sixth century, with its day divided between the *Opus Dei,* manual labor and reading. But beyond the observance of the original *Rule,* the *paupertas Christi* was an actuality at Cîteaux. All its *ornamenta* attest to this; there were no cloth of gold vestments, no processional copes and capes, no golden chalices too heavy to lift—all was plain and poor without being shabby. Mass was the simple liturgical Mass stripped of its pomp and ceremonial accretions so dear to Cluny. Devotion to the Virgin Mary was featured prominently; the *Salve Regina* was sung after Compline each night; each monastery was dedicated to Mary, whose Office came to be recited daily. With Cîteaux, simplicity and poverty returned to monasticism and in a way the ordinary layman could understand.

Essentially the spirit of the New Monastery was a mirror of the contemporary layman's spiritual aspirations. In this lies the great importance of Cîteaux and accounts for its acceptance by rich and poor alike. Its monks, given to silence and contemplation, represented true monasticism. The writings of St Bernard and St Aelred stressed affective love of God and neighbor.

To contemporaries, the monk of Cîteaux lived the ideal of monastic poverty with his main meal of beans unsupplemented by the fulsome *pittanciae, generalia* and *pigmenta* of Cluny. Though poor himself, he willingly gave of what he had to those who were poorer.

The *Exordium Parvum* sets forth the constitutional base of the New Monastery. For its age, it is an unique document. It contains only two indirect references to Scripture instead of the many which were used in contemporary literature. The objective of the New Order is stated clearly and unequivocally in the very first sentence— the observance of the *Rule of St Benedict* as it was originally observed. This was a return in actuality to the balance between prayer, reading and manual labor—the *moderatio* and *discretio* of St Benedict of

Nursia. It was, furthermore, a community of silence in which each carried within himself his own solitude.

Keeping in mind the distinction between reform and renewal, Cîteaux was a renewal because it was a complete return to the substance and spirit of Monte Cassino, with the addition of incidentals to accommodate contemporary spiritual longings. Society did not fail to sense that this was indeed the fact.

Jeremiah F. O'Sullivan

PREFACE

FROM ITS BEGINNINGS IN 1098, Cîteaux has occupied a place of prominence in monastic annals and in western history. The causes of this distinction are not only St Bernard of Clairvaux and the radiance of subsequent Cistercian ventures, but, in a very real sense, the greatness of its Founders, eminent in both mind and spirit. A right understanding of Cîteaux, therefore, presupposes a familiarity with its origins—with the lives, the ideals and the untiring labors of its pioneers recorded in truly remarkable contemporary documents. Long convinced of this, historians have produced a number of ground-breaking studies on the subject. But, because they restricted themselves to early Cîteaux, the outcome of their efforts has been, inevitably, an incomplete picture, a *Kleingeschichte*, lacking dimension and depth.

For, while the program of Cîteaux was defined by its great Founders, its components came from a variety of sources: the contemporary milieu and monastic developments dating back at least to Carolingian times. The aim of this volume is to consider precisely this aspect of the question. In the absence of works dealing with the subject, it proposes to provide the necessary focus and perspective for the events surrounding the Cistercian beginnings.

An undertaking of this kind simply cannot do justice to everyone. It was not possible, for instance, to explain every monastic term or to pay adequate attention to early medieval monasticism; nor could all the desired material or the critical editions of the sources be obtained. For these and other obvious reasons the following investigation should not be construed as being the final word on the subject, but rather as an incentive to further study in a continuing search for increasingly clearer historical views. Such clarity will result in a growing appreciation of the great creation of the Cistercian pioneers and point out ways to benefit from their example.

B. K. L.

BENEDICT OF ANIANE AND
POST-CAROLINGIAN MONACHISM

IT HAS OCCASIONALLY BEEN STATED, though never sufficiently demonstrated, that Benedict of Aniane was in some respects a fore-runner of Cîteaux. For the birth of the latter could never be fully understood without a probing of Cluny, nor could the role of this great monastic center be sufficiently explained without reference to Benedict of Aniane whose influence on the destinies of monasticism in the West ranks second only to that of the great Patriarch of Monte Cassino.[1] Benedict of Aniane's aim of restoring the Benedictine Rule to its proper place in the monastic life was also the ideal of the Founders of Cîteaux, and his ideas on liturgical uniformity, centralization and seclusion—to

---

1. The monastic reforms of Benedict of Aniane found a wide acceptance in the various religious houses of western Europe. Foremost among these were the twelve monasteries which had come under the direct jurisdiction of Aniane. One of the latter, Saint Savin, Poitiers, preserved the reform of Benedict of Aniane and restored the abbey of Saint Martin, Autun, around 870 AD. Some six years later Berno, one of its monks, was sent to revive the monastery of Baume in the Jura region, and in time became the abbot of Baume. As such he introduced the usages of Saint Martin, Autun, which in turn had come from Saint Savin and Benedict of Aniane. This Berno became the monastic founder of Cluny when during the first decade of the tenth century William of Aquitaine made his historic foundation. "Thus through Baume, Saint Martin, and Saint Savin, the usages of Cluny are traceable, directly and in an unbroken tradition, to the usages which the great abbot of Aniane had personally introduced at Saint Savin." Othon Ducourneau, *Les origines cisterciennes* (Ligugé: E. Aubin et fils, 1933), 29.

mention only the most obvious—certainly influenced the thinking of the Cistercian pioneers. Hence the importance of Benedict and the need for a discussion of his impact on monastic history.

Benedict of Aniane, really Witiza (Euticius),[2] was born around the middle of the eighth century, of noble Visigothic parents in Aquitaine.[3] In his youth he was at the court of King Pepin where he received his first education under the supervision of the queen. Entering afterwards the king's service, he became Pepin's attendant and accompanied his master into battle. After Pepin's death he transferred his allegiance to Charlemagne and, in 774, took part in the latter's Italian campaign. On the lookout, for some three years, for the best way to serve God, he now decided to become a monk and entered the monastery of St Seine (Sequanus) in the vicinity of Dijon. Here he led for some time a life which included all kinds of

2. Benedict's baptismal name was Witiza; this became *Euticius* in Latin. See DHE 8:177 and Marquard Herrgott, *Vetus disciplina monastica seu Collectio Auctorum ordinis S. Benedicti* (Parisiis: Typis Caroli Osmont, 1726), 14. According to P. Schmieder, Euticius is simply a translation of Witiza. Cf. Bruno Albers, *Untersuchungen zu den ältesten Mönchsgewohnheiten. Ein Beitrag zur Benediktinergeschichte des X.-XII. Jahrhunderts* (München: Lentner, 1905), 20 n. 3. The monk John of Salerno, biographer of Odo of Cluny, writes of Baume, the motherhouse of Cluny: "*Fuerunt autem institutores ejusdem loci imitatores cujusdam patris Eutici.*" PL 133:53. Baume however followed the usages of Benedict of Aniane. See above, n. 1 and ch. II, n. 9. John of Salerno further mentions that Euticius wrote a concordance of various rules and that he was a friend of Louis the Pious who had a monastery built for him near the imperial palace: "*Fuit idem vir temporibus Ludovici magni videlicet imperatoris carus regi omnibus quia amabilis. Nam cum esset laicus et peregrinis studiis eruditus, deserens ea unde superbire solet humana fragilitas, totum se dedit beatorum patrum regulis et institutionibus, ex quibus nempe auctoritatibus diversis consuetudines sumpsit unoque volumine colligavit. Deinde non multo post monachus est effectus et in tanto amore apud regem habitus, ut infra palatium illi construeret monasterium.*" PL 133: 53f. A comparison of John and Ardo, Benedict's biographer, reveals further similarities; hence Mabillon felt safe in stating: "From all this I would not hesitate to assert that Benedict of Aniane is one and the same with Abbot Euticius." And B. Albers concludes, "In fact every reasonable doubt should be excluded." *Untersuchungen*, 19f. See also *ibid.*, 18.

3. Benedict's *vita*, the work of his disciple Ardo, is found in PL 103:353-384 and in MGH, SS, 15:200-220. Ardo, also called Smaragdus, was a monk, priest and teacher at Aniane, where after a saintly life he died at the age of sixty, in 843. Cf. Josef Narberhaus, *Benedikt von Aniane Werk und Persönlichkeit. Beiträge zur Geschichte des alten Mönchtums und des Benediktinerordens*, Heft 16

mortifications, fasts, vigils, prayers, silence and the cheapest clothes. He took no baths and found no work degrading, whether this meant polishing his confreres' shoes or cleaning the house.[4] Convinced of the superiority of eastern asceticism, he spurned his abbot's orders to relax his practices and exercises.[5] As Ardo, his biographer, records, Benedict "constantly strove after impossible things."[6] He discarded the Benedictine Rule as one meant for beginners and weaklings and followed oriental rules instead, particularly those of Pachomius and Basil.[7] Eventually, however, he was appointed cellarer and, five years after his entrance, chosen to succeed the deceased abbot of the monastery. But since he knew that his attempts to restore the *ordo regularis* were ill appreciated by his monks, he refused the office, loath to govern such subjects, and retired to his paternal grounds in Aquitaine. There, in 779, or in the following year, he founded a monastery at Aniane located in what is today the diocese of Montpellier.[8] The chapel of the new establishment was "dedicated in honor of Mary the Holy Mother of God," a practice that will find imitators in Cluny, Molesme and Cîteaux.[9]

(Münster in W.: Aschendorffsche Verlagsbuchhandlung, 1930), 6–8. See also MGH, SS, 15:198. The *vita* itself was completed in 822 or in the following year. Cf. J. Narberhaus, *op. cit.*, 12f. A French translation was procured by M. Classan, *Vie de saint Benoît d'Aniane* (Montpellier, 1876). Short accounts of Benedict's life can be found in DTC 2:708; DHE 8:178ff.; DSAM 1:1438 ff.; LTK 2:179f.; and J. Narberhaus, *op. cit.*, 15ff.

4. PL 103:356f.

5. "*Cum cogeretur ab abbate parcius erga semetipsum exercere rigorem, assensum minime praebuit.*" PL 103:357.

6. "*Jugiter impossibilia rimabat.*" Ibid.

7. "*Regulam quoque beati Benedicti tironibus seu infirmis positam fore contestans, ad beati Basilii dicta nec non Pachomii regulam scandere nitens....*" PL 103:357. According to Cuthbert Butler, "He had even a contempt of St Benedict's Rule." *Benedictine Monachism. Studies in Benedictine Life and Rule* (New York: Barnes & Noble, 1961), 357. Cf. also Edmund Bishop, *Liturgica Historica. Papers on the Liturgy and Religious Life of the Western Church* (Oxford: At the Clarendon Press, 1918), 212.

8. PL 103:358.

9. "*Domus enim in eo erat loco quo fundare moliebantur monasterium, quam auctam in honore Dei genitricis consecrarunt Mariae.*" PL 103:360.

At first, Benedict did not introduce the full Benedictine life, for the monks accepted no property or serfs, but worked with their hands, lived by alms and took only bread and water for nourishment,[10] as was done by the monks of the East. Eastern austerity prevailed also in the liturgy: all their chalices were made of wood, later of glass and tin, and the vestments they used for Mass were without silk.[11] This enthusiasm for eastern monasticism, which was certainly connected with the Origenist revival of the ninth century,[12] did not however prove lasting. By the year 787 Benedict became fully convinced that eastern practices were too difficult for the majority of his monks and that therefore the rule most suited for westerners—if not the only one—was that of St Benedict, noted for its moderation. He therefore constructed an abbey, a *coenobium*, and—having undergone a complete change in his liturgical outlook —a new church noted for the splendor of its columns, altars, lights, costly vestments and silver vessels.[13] He introduced the full Benedic-

10. "*Solo viventes pane et aqua.*" PL 103:359. To this may be added their strict asceticism. "*Certabant siquidem quis eorum esset . . . in abstinentia ardentior, in vigiliis anterior . . . in vestitu vilior, in charitate ferventior: quibusdam etiam revelationes fiebant.*" Ibid., 361. One should also note their collective poverty: "*Non enim ornatis parietibus tegulisque rubentibus, vel pictis laquearibus, sed stramine vilique maceria cooperire vel facere domos decreverat.*" Ibid., 360.

11. "*Vasa autem ad Christi conficiendum corpus nolebat sibi esse argentea: siquidem primum ei fuerunt lignea, deinceps vitrea; sic tandem conscendit ad stannea; planetam vero refutabat habere sericeam, et si aliquis illi dedisset, mox aliis ad utendum praestabat.*" PL 103:360. Cf. also E. Bishop, *op. cit.*, 212 and Rose Graham, *English Ecclesiastical Studies* (London: Society for Promoting Christian Knowledge, 1928), 11.

12. "Indications point to the conclusion that in every period or place where there was a monastic renewal, there was a revival of Origen. It is true of the Carolingian reform. . . . The Origenist revival of the ninth century coincided with the monastic revival connected with the name of St Benedict of Aniane." Jean Leclercq, *The Love of Learning and the Desire For God*, trans. Catharine Misrahi (New York: New American Library, 1960), 100. See also "Origène, précurseur du monachisme," *Théologie de la vie monastique* (Études publiées sous la direction de la faculté de théologie S. J. de Lyon-Fourvière, 49; Lyon: Aubier, 1961), 16.

13. "*A rigore vero suae primae conversationis paululum declinarat, quoniam impossibile opus assumpserat.*" PL 103:368. Cf. ibid., 358: "*Coopitulante gratia divina, ut multorum fieret documentum salutis, in amorem praefati viri Benedicti*

tine life in his abbey and from then on devoted all his energies to the study of the Rule, consulting experts whenever in doubt.[14] He now saw his vocation in a faithful observance of the Rule, which called for the elimination of contrary standards and a separation from the outside world. He came to realize that the observance of the integral text of the Rule was a strict moral obligation of every monk and wrote his *Concordia Regularum* with such a view in mind.[15]

Benedict was a model abbot. Strict with himself, he showed mildness and consideration to others and was fatherly to all. In

---

regulae accenditur et veluti de singulari certamine novus athleta ad campum publicae pugnaturus accessit." According to P. Schmitz, this marked the fourth stage in Benedict's monastic evolution. Cf. DHE 8:178. Ardo further records on the subject, "*nunc, opitulante Christo . . . quibus modis aliud in eodem loco coenobium aedificaverit, evidenti ratione pandamus.*" By now Aniane had a vast and splendid church, a cloister with marble pillars and fine altar vessels. "Seven lamps were suspended above the principal altar, dedicated in honor of the Trinity, and a hoop of silver lamps lighted the choir. There were silver chalices and costly vestments and beautiful service books . . . There were vast monastic buildings and Aniane was intended to set an example for other monasteries." *Ibid.*, 363f. See also J. Narberhaus, *op. cit.*, 19; R. Graham, *op. cit.*, 11; Guy de Valous, *Le monachisme clunisien dès origines au XVe siècle. Vie intérieure des monastères et organisation de l'ordre*, 2 vols. (Archives de la France monastique, vol. 39; Paris, A. Picard, 1935), 1:13; and Henry-Bernard DeWarren, "Le monachisme à l'apparition de saint Bernard," in *Bernard de Clairvaux*, edited by the Commission d'Histoire de l'Ordre de Cîteaux (Paris: Éditions Alsatia, 1953), 46.

14. "*Omne quippe desiderium suum in observationem Regulae converterat, suumque hoc permaxime erat studium.*" PL 103:380. *Ibid.*, we are told, "*quos peritos esse compererat, attente sciscitabatur circa longeque positos, eos etiam qui istis in partibus ad montem Casinum accederent.*" The same appears from *ibid.*, 365: "*Dedit autem cor suum ad investigandam beati Benedicti Regulam, eamdemque ut intelligere possit satagere circumiens monasteria, peritos quosque interrogans quae ignorabat.*" One detects here a response to Charlemagne's capitulary of the year 789 which urged monks to correct their liturgical books in the interest of meaningful services. PL 97:177. Cf. also Columban Spahr, *De fontibus constitutivis primigenii juris constitutionalis Sacri Ordinis Cisterciensis* (Romae: Universitas Lateranensis, 1953), 32.

15. Stephanus Hilpisch, *Benedictinism Through Changing Centuries*, trans. Leonard Doyle (Collegeville: St. John's Abbey Press, 1958), 34. See also Ursmer Berlière, "L'étude des réformes monastiques des Xe et XIe siècles, *Académie Royale de Belgique, Bulletin de Classe de Lettres*, 5e série, 18 (1932), 138.

the words of Ardo, he instructed the chanters, taught the readers, had grammarians and Scripture experts around himself, collected a multitude of books[16] and performed works of charity even outside the monastery. His interests soon began to take on wider proportions and ripened into one single ambition, the reform of contemporary Benedictine monasticism. This made him a natural ally of Charlemagne and Louis the Pious who also cherished ideas of renewal and reform.

Already Charlemagne granted immunity and the right of free election to the monastery of Aniane. When building his larger monastery in 782, Benedict enlisted "the help of dukes and counts." On its completion he went "to the most glorious emperor (sic) Charles on behalf of the monastery . . . lest after his own death the surviving monks should suffer any inconvenience from his relatives or kinsmen." To assure the survival of the monastery and of its way of life which—in the words of Charlemagne—was "in accordance with the Rule of St Benedict," the future emperor at once granted immunity, i.e., freedom from all interference and exaction and the right of freely electing the local abbot, a favor otherwise sparingly given by Charlemagne. In his charter Charlemagne also indicated that the petitioner

> has seen fit, after mature deliberation, to entrust to us the aforesaid monastery, with all its internal and external property and church ornaments, and to commit the holy place itself to our rule, protection and patronage.[17]

Louis the Pious soon made Benedict the superior of all Benedictine houses in Aquitaine so that he might reform them along the model usages of Aniane.[18] The program rested on Benedict's cooperation

---

16. "*Instituit cantores, docuit lectores, habuit grammaticos et scientia Scripturarum peritos, de quibus etiam quidam post fuere episcopi, aggrevagit. Librorum multitudinem congregavit.*" PL 103:365. See also Watkin Williams, *Monastic Studies* (Manchester: University Press, 1938), 88f.

17. See the text in PL 103:365f.

18. "*Ludovicus rex Aquitanorum . . . omnibus in suo regno monasteriis praefecit ut norman salutiferam cunctis ostenderet.*" PL 103:372. Cf. ibid., 367: "*Omnium denique monasteriorum, tam in Provincia quam in Novempolitania provincia consistentium erat quasi nutrix fovens juvansque.*"

with his royal patron and was furthered by such allies as Leidrad, Theodulph and Alcuin.[19] Its success rested on the example of Benedict who went from monastery to monastery, to explain the Rule and to work for free elections and immunity; "to correct alien practices, to reproach the slothful, to encourage the young, to urge the experienced to go on advancing, and to pressure the stagnant into correcting their ways."[20]

The influx of vocations brought the number of monks at Aniane eventually to more than a thousand. This made new foundations a necessity. The latter—Ardo calls them "new cells"—were established in solitary places, in order to keep the monks separated from the world; their superiors were appointed by Benedict himself.[21]

Even as emperor, Louis the Pious frequently sought the advice of Benedict who on that account had to undertake long journeys to distant Aachen. To improve the situation Benedict was made abbot of Maursmünster (Marmoutier) in Alsace and shortly thereafter, i.e. between 815 and 816, abbot of Inde, today's Cornelimünster, built by Louis the Pious some six miles from the imperial palace. This monastery, settled by thirty observant monks well known to and carefully chosen by Benedict from various monasteries, was to be a model for all other houses in the Frankish empire.[22]

The emperor had the renewal of religious life very much at heart. Already in 816 he sponsored a synod at Aachen, for the purpose of improving the life of the canons regular. This meeting also drafted some twenty-seven temporary rules known today as *Statuta Murbacensia* which paved the way for the great legislation that was

---

19. PL 103:369f. See also E. Bishop, *op. cit.*, 213; J. Narberhaus, *op. cit.*, 40 and M. Mourre, *op. cit.*, 279.

20. "*Coepit aliorum corrigere mores, negligentes arguere, exhortari tirones, ut proficerent admonere probos, ut corrigerentur increpare improbos.*" PL 103:358. On Benedict's activities as visitator in Aquitaine, see *ibid.*, 372.

21. "*Constituit locis congruis cellas, quibus praefectis magistris posuit fratres.*" PL 103:369. Cf. also J. Narberhaus, *op. cit.*, 37.

22. PL 103:376. See also J. Narberhaus, *op. cit.*, 46.

to come.[23] This was enacted in 817, by another synod of Aachen where, with imperial support, Benedict devised rules for a uniform monastic observance throughout the empire. These are, cumulatively, the so-called *capitulare monasticum,* made up of some eighty canons defining matters not regulated or specified by the Rule, adding a number of new regulations, and dispensing from practices which in the circumstances could not be well observed. These canons were to be introduced in all Frankish monasteries and visitors (*missi*) were to see to their execution. The usages of Inde were to serve as the authentic norm to be copied by all other houses. Benedict himself supervised the reform program as general superior, appointed by the emperor "that as he had instructed Aquitaine and Gothia in the norm of salvation so he should also imbue Francia with his salutary example."[24] He worked with untiring zeal until death ended his labors—too soon after 817—on February 11, 821, in the monastery of Inde.[25]

While E. Sackur perceived in Benedict "the stubbornness of fanatical natures,"[26] Ardo characterized his hero as a highly talented man of action: "quick and practical in all things," with clear ideas

23. The main provisions are these: Abbots should read, discuss and carry into effect the provisions dealing with monastic reform. Everyone should therefore memorize the Rule of St Benedict, and every monastery which hitherto followed the Roman liturgy should restore the Benedictine usages. In accordance with the Rule, no difference should prevail any longer between abbots and monks with regard to food, drink, sleep and other matters. All should have a clearly specified wardrobe. Similarly, all were to engage once more in manual labor, i.e., work in the kitchen, the bakery, the laundry and in the various workshops; this undoubtedly also to safeguard the all-important principle of seclusion. The statutes are reprinted in Bruno Albers, *Consuetudines monasticae,* 5 vols. (Stuttgart: Joseph Roth and Monte Cassino: Typis Montis Casini, 1900–1912), 3:79–93 and in Mansi 14:439f. See also DHE 8:180.

24. "*Praefecit eum quoque imperator cunctis in regno suo coenobiis: ut sicut Aquitaniam Gothiamque norma salutis instruxerat, ita etiam Franciam salutifero imbueret exemplo.*" PL 103:577.

25. "*Obiit autem septuagenarius, tertio Idus Februarii, anno ab incarnatione Domini octingentesimo vigesimo primo, indictione decima quarta.*" PL 103:384. The letter of the monks of Inde announcing Benedict's death is found in MGH, SS 15 (1):129.

26. Ernst Sackur, *Die Cluniacenser in ihrer kirchlichen und allgemeingeschichtlichen Wirksamkeit* (Halle: Max Niemayer, 1892), 1:4f.

Benedict of Aniane and Post-Carolingian Monachism 9

and sure working habits indicating obvious qualities of leadership. To this must be added a firm bearing and winning manners, exclusively apostolic and pastoral concerns, and a love of erudition.[27] A man of letters, his writings include the *Liber ex regulis diversorum patrum collectio*, or *Codex Regularum*, as it is commonly called, a collection of eastern and western monastic rules; the handier *Concordia Regularum*, a concordance of some twenty-six rules and their comparison with the Rule of St Benedict; a treatise on the Incarnation; a pamphlet against Adoptianism—Benedict went twice to Spain to combat this heresy—and letters.[28]

Benedict's reforming activity reached its peak in the great abbots' meeting of Aachen in 817 which began its deliberations, on imperial orders, on July 10 and met for several days. The assembly, composed entirely of abbots and monks, held its sessions in the sacristy of the dome.[29] The soul of the synod was Benedict. "To the assembly," writes Ardo, "Benedict explained the Rule in its entirety. He cleared up difficulties, resolved doubts, exposed errors, approved customs and made useful additions."[30] Then he drafted a capitulary which

---

27. "*Velox et ad omnia utilis.*" PL 103:355. "*Nihil intellectui ejus excederet.*" Ibid., 380. Cf. J. Narberhaus, *op. cit.*, 16. Ibid., 73, we find a pertinent quotation from Ermollus Nigellus (Carm. II): "*Dulcis, amatus erat, blandus placidusque modestus.*" See also Stephan Hilpisch, *Geschichte des benediktinischen Mönchtums in ihren Grundzügen dargestellt* (Freiburg: Herder & Co., 1929), 121.

28. PL 103. Ibid., 380 is Ardo's reference to the *Codex Regularum* and the *Concordia Regularum*. Lists of Benedict's works are also found in DTC 2: 708; DHE 8:186f.; DSAM 1:1439; and LTK 2:179. See also Otto Seebass, "über das Regelbuch Benedikts von Aniane," *Zeitschrift für Kirchengeschichte*, 15 (1895), 245-257; Ernst Tomek, *Studien zur Reform der deutschen Klöster im XI. Jahrhundert* (Wien Mayer & Co., 1910), 177; U. Berlière, "L'étude des réformes monastiques," *loc. cit.*, 138; Philibert Schmitz, *Histoire de l'Ordre de Saint-Benoît*, 2nd ed. (Maredsous: Les Éditions de Maredsous, 1948), 1:107.

29. "*Jubente imperatore aggregatis coenobiorum Patribus una cum quam pluribus monachis perplures resedit dies.*" PL 103:377. Among the participants was Arnulf, Abbot of Noirmoutier, Apollinarius of Monte Cassino, Alvens of St Hubert's in the Ardennes, Agiulph of Solignac and Joshua of St Victor's (Volturno). Cf. M. Mourre, *op. cit.*, 280. See also Mansi 14:393-400; MGH, LL Sec. II, *Capitularia Regum Francorum*, 1:343-349 and PL 103:381-394.

30. "*Regulam ab integro discutiens, cunctis obscura dilucidavit, dubia patefecit, priscos errores abstulit, utiles consuetudines affectusque confirmavit.*" PL 103:377. Cf. also J. Narberhaus, *op. cit.*, 51.

was discussed for several days and subsequently submitted to the emperor so that he might order its uniform observance in all of Frankland. The canons of the capitulary are brief enunciations, reiterations of laws and customs, a careful summary of ancient and recent written and oral tradition, a task that had not been undertaken since the great Patriarch of Monte Cassino wrote his Rule. They are precise regulations, dealing with the liturgy, the care of the body (food and clothing) and claustral discipline.[31] They answered an absolute need in a world where, to use Ardo's remark, "regular life had nearly vanished."[32] The fact is that until the ninth century the Rule had not been in general use and few abbeys practiced regular Benedictine life. There were still monasteries which retained their ancient statutes, while others had become dependencies of bishops or were transformed into canonries. In the liturgy there were hardly any differences between the regular and the secular clergy. And last but not least, a great many monasteries came under lay influence or fell completely into secular hands. Princes, treating monasteries as if they were their personal benefices, often gave them *in commendam* to their followers for services rendered, or exploited them, as their *advocati*, to their own advantage instead of protecting and safeguarding them, their rights and their interests. Thus a great many monasteries became destitute and their members, lacking the barest necessities, were often compelled to disband.[33]

Since there are a number of *lacunae* in the Benedictine Rule—many details and safeguards remain unmentioned; there are gaps in the horarium, customs and rubrics; and several items are simply left to the abbot's discretion—Benedict of Aniane perceived the need for

---

31. "*Judicia igitur Regulae cunctaque dubia ad proficuum deducta effectum, assentientibus omnibus protulit.*" PL 103:377. See also Jean-Berthold Mahn, *L'ordre cistercien et son gouvernement dès origines au milieu du XIII siècle (1098–1265)* (Paris: E. deBoccard, 1945), 22; E. Bishop, *op. cit.*, 218; M. Mourre, *op. cit.*, 280 and J. Narberhaus, *op. cit.*, 51.

32. "*Regularis pene deperierat ordo.*" PL 103:377.

33. PL 103:373 and 377. See also J. Narberhaus, *op. cit.*, 2f.; P. Schmitz, *op. cit.*, 1:108; K. Spahr, *De fontibus constitutivis*, 91; Herbert Workman, *The Evolution of the Monastic Ideal from the Earliest Times Down to the Coming of the Friars* (London: Charles H. Kelly, 1913), 225.

additional legislation.³⁴ This resulted in the *capitulare monasticum* of Aachen, characterized by Ardo as "judgments on the Rule and on doubtful matters and customs not specified therein."³⁵ It was to be a standard for all monks, through the establishment of a personal spiritual bond between the individual monk and the Rule of St Benedict.

The first forty canons of the synod recall, without major alterations, the essence of the Rule. From now on every monk was to observe with the greatest fidelity the Rule alone. The keynote of the *capitula* is given in the first two canons:

> 1. Let the abbots, as soon as they have returned to their monasteries, read the Rule in full. Considering it word by word, and by the help of the Lord profitably understanding it, let them together with their monks study to observe it completely.
>
> 2. Let all monks, who can do so, learn the Rule by heart.³⁶

This means that henceforth abbots were to govern their houses according to the Rule of St Benedict and that monks were to observe the Rule without the least delay in every situation.³⁷ The capitulary also stresses that the divine office and the readings should be in conformity with the provisions of the Rule,³⁸ i.e. that the Roman *cursus* should be discontinued.³⁹ No reference is made, however, to

---

34. U. Berlière, "L'étude des réformes monastiques," *loc. cit.*, 138. See also S. Hilpisch, *Benedictinism*, 34.

35. "*Judicia ... Regulae cunctaque dubia ... quas minus pandit Regula consuetidines ... protulit.*" PL 103:377.

36. PL 97:381. These measures are clearly foreshadowed by the legislation of the preceding years. Cf. PL 97:225ff., 242, 248 and Mansi 14:349f. See also W. Williams, *op. cit.*, 97 and G. de Valous, 1:10. The second edition of this fundamental work was published in 1970.

37. C. (for canon) 22. PL 97:385.   38. C. 3, *ibid.*, 381.

39. C. 29, *ibid.*, 386. According to G. de Valous, "The only important ordinance of the council of 817 is the one which prescribes that henceforth all monasteries of the empire must follow the Benedictine Rule and liturgy. For it thus consecrated the unity of western monachism." *Le monachisme clunisien*, 1:10.

chapter seventy-three of the Rule where St Benedict calls his work a "rule for beginners;" the expression obviously did not suit Benedict of Aniane in his attempts at monastic uniformity.[40]

In general, the eighty-odd canons of Aachen can be grouped around three main headings: (1) seclusion and peace; (2) restoration of discipline and regular observances; and, (3) moral conversion.[41]

Seclusion is a basic postulate of the monastic life. To restore it, the capitulary decreed that things of the world which could disturb the inner peace and quiet of the monastery should be banished. This is why monks were no longer to leave their monastery, and when abbots undertook a journey they were to go without monk-companions, except when attending a Church council.[42] As a rule, they should leave their monastery only in case of necessity and return as quickly as possible. Unauthorized leaves called for strict punishments: all kinds of penances, incarceration and even ejection from the community.[43] Similarly, monks could no longer accept obligations in the world, not even the supervision of their manors.[44] If by some necessity a monk had to travel outside the monastery, he was to have a companion and if the journey was long, both were to make halts at monasteries where they were not to disturb the monks of the place or make contacts with other guests, but sleep in a special dormitory situated in the vicinity of the oratory.[45] Visiting monks, as a rule, were to be cared for by *docti fratres* seeing to it that all

---

40. Georg Grützmacher, *Die Bedeutung Benedikts von Nursia und seiner Regel in der Geschichte des Mönchtums* (Berlin: Mayer & Müller, 1892), 16 n. 4.

41. Cf. J. Narberhaus, *op. cit.*, 52ff. Authors disagree on the actual number of canons. Following B. Albers (*Consuetudines monasticae*, 3:115ff.) P. Schmitz and J. Narberhaus mention 75 (*op. cit.*, 1:181 and 51 respectively), E. Bishop 80 (*op. cit.*, 218) and G. de Valous 83 (*Le monachisme clunisien*, 1:10).

42. C. 59. PL 97:391. Cf. also *Regula*, Prologue (*in fine*), and chs. 1, 4 (*in fine*), and 66, as well as J. Narberhaus, *op. cit.*, 52.

43. Cc. 40, 64, 80. PL 97:388, 391 and 393. Cf. also cc. 13 and 14. *Ibid.*, 382f. See also G. de Valous, *Le monachisme clunisien*, 1:13 and S. Hilpisch, *Benedictinism*, 33.

44. Cc. 16 and 26. PL 97:383 and 385. See also J. Narberhaus, *op. cit.*, 53.

45. Cc. 15 and 58. PL 97:383 and 390. Cf. J. Narberhaus, *op. cit.*, 53.

worldliness was kept from the inmates of the monastery.[46] Like their abbots, monks could no longer be travelling companions of canons, for the freer life would inevitably lead to a decline of the religious spirit. Such considerations also motivated the rule that monks should not kiss women.[47] If guests came to the monastery, they were to eat in a special dining room and not in the monks' refectory for there they might cause commotion.[48] Laymen of lower rank could no longer be permanent guests of the monks[49] nor were outsiders to receive instruction in the monastery.[50] To do away with the practice of accepting unworthy recruits in order to secure their property for the monastery, the decision was taken that the newcomer should be poor and his possessions should not be given to the monastery but be returned to his parents.[51] If several of the brethren had to stay away from the monastery on a habitual basis or whenever a new foundation was made, the size of the group was to include at least six monks, and this number could not be filled with canons.[52] During work both inside the monastery and in the fields each monk had a religious supervisor or senior who saw to the preservation of seclusion.[53] Laymen could no longer be appointed superiors or hold any other offices.[54]

Worldliness was to be avoided also in matters of food and clothing. From now on monks were to wear only clothes befitting a religious.[55] They were to keep the law of abstinence strictly. Not even oblates could eat meat, and fowl was allowed only on certain

---

46. Cc. 53 and 16. PL 97:391 and 383.
47. J. Narberhaus, *op. cit.*, 53. Cf. cc. 16 and 59. PL 97:383 and 390.
48. Cc. 52 and 27. PL 97:390 and 385f.
49. C. 42. PL 97:388. 50. C. 45. *Ibid.*, 389.
51. Cc. 34 and 75. *Ibid.*, 386f. and 392.
52. C. 44. *Ibid.*, 389. 53. C. 33. *Ibid.*, 386.
54. "*Ut monachis, non nisi monachus constituatur praepositus.*" C. 32, PL 97:386. This was to put an end to the system of commendatory abbots, as is evidenced also from Ardo. "*Assensum praebet gloriosissimus imperator, monasteria in Regno suo cuncta praenotata, in quibus ex his Regulares Abbates esse queant decernit.*" PL 103:381. Cf. also DSAM 1:1440.
55. Cc. 20 and 22. PL 97:384.

days during the Christmas and Easter season.[56] The monks were to abstain from talking in a loud voice and from taking oaths, the former because it could lead to quarrels and the latter because it could end in perjury.[57] Any disturbance of the peace, as when someone hits another with a stick or even with his bare fist, will be punished. Not even the smallest noise should disturb the quiet and peace of the monks whose every movement and action should be performed with recollection. In the refectory they must eat at some distance from one another to forestall possible conversations or communications. This is also why a reader was appointed for the servers who ate after the community.[58] All this shows, as J. Narberhaus has pointed out, that "there are no mitigations with regard to enclosure and discipline, for herein lies the . . . *raison d'être* of the Benedictine life."[59]

To continue the list, abbots were enjoined not to squander the goods of the community during travels and similar occasions, and, in accordance with the Rule, to provide the monks with all the food, drink and clothing they needed, without any exception.[60] They could no longer act in an arbitrary manner and depose a monastic official without the consent of the community. This meant a circumscription of the abbot's power and a corresponding increase of community responsibility.[61] On the other hand Benedict redefined the concept of obedience which had received a Germanic interpretation and became something like an oath of allegiance, of fealty or submission, as in the case of French capitularies, with their stipulations guaranteeing a greater or lesser degree of personal

---

56. Cc. 37 and 78. *Ibid.,* 387 and 392. Also 392 n. 10.

57. Cc. 41 and 43. PL 97:388.

58. Cc. 76 and 28. *Ibid.,* 392 and 386.

59. *Loc. cit.,* 64. Cf. also DSAM 1:1441: "To Benedict of Aniane the Benedictine is the monk who lives exclusively for God, who leads his monastic life with all the purity required by the Rule; he is not a missionary, nor a teacher or cleric . . . in preference to the letter [of the Rule]."

60. Cc. 53 and 25. PL 97:390 and 385. See also E. Sackur, *op. cit.,* 1:51f. and G. de Valous, *Le monachisme clunisien,* 1:63.

61. C. 56. PL 97:390.

freedom. (This, as can easily be seen, fomented the spirit of individualism and actually hampered a uniform interpretation of the Rule.) The capitulary of 817 eliminated this anomaly, by proscribing these exceptions (*excusationes*); Germanic law had to bow before Roman discipline and submit to the Benedictine monastic ideal.[62] In this connection Benedict also revived the *decanatus* system of the Rule where always ten confreres were placed under a dean, addressed by his charges as *nonnus*.[63] Also here, transgressions called for adequate sanctions. Benedict enlarged the existing penal code so that certain infringements led to excommunication or, in serious cases, to incarceration. But, even on this point, Benedict was for moderation: he wished that these dungeons should be heatable and that they have a yard where the inmates could do some work.[64]

Benedict must also be credited with the re-introduction of the second part of the Benedictine profession, the so-called conversion of manners. This had fallen into disuse, through its fusion with the vow of *stabilitas in congregatione*, which in turn had replaced the old Benedictine *stabilitas loci*. Benedict studied the question and restored the middle part of the Benedictine vows to its proper place, though he employed the term *conversatio* for *conversio*.[65]

A dominant feature of the *capitulare monasticum* is the prominence it gives to the liturgy. As has been mentioned, Benedict had by now given up his preference for liturgical simplicity;[66] as a result he developed a great passion for elaborate or minutely regulated ceremonies. At least sixteen canons deal with the office alone, a fact which has led to charges of ritualism in modern times.[67] Also, not

62. Cc. 34 and 75. *Ibid.*, 386f. and 392.
63. Cc. 33 and 61. *Ibid.*, 386 and 390.
64. Cc. 14, 40, 71 and 72. *Ibid.*, 383, 388, and 392.
65. J. Narberhaus, *op. cit.*, 60.   66. See *above*, n. 13.
67. Cc. 23, 24, 30, 39, 46, 48, 50, 51, 60, 62, 66, 67, 68, 70 and 74. See also Ardo, PL 103:363–365; J. Mahn, *L'ordre cistercien*, 22 and J. Narberhaus, *op. cit.*, 2 and 29f. The same author concludes, "Now it becomes clear to us why Benedict introduces art into the monastery. It was to serve for a deepening and an intensification of the religious spirit and for the solemn execution of the divine service, as Ardo himself indicates: '*Quicquid operi Dei necessarium esse conspexit, summo cum studio adquisivit.*' (PL 103:365)." *Op. cit.*, 31.

content with prescriptions regulating minute details, Benedict increased the monks' daily *pensum* by adding prayers not prescribed by St Benedict, among them special psalms for the *eleemosynarii* and the Office of the Dead.[68] In the capitulary he also described the daily proceedings in the chapter room which were to include readings from the Martyrology and the Rule, and a homily.[69]

A great many ordinances are devoted to the care of the body. Here, again, Benedict tried to steer a middle course between extremes in regard to food and drink, and thus gave once more evidence of his moderation. For instance, whenever the monks spent the day in hard work or added to the regular choir the Office of the Dead, they were entitled to an extra portion before Compline.[70] On fast days work was to be less strenuous, and during the summer months it was permissible to take a siesta on such occasions.[71] Benedict also opposed regular bleeding because of its weakening effect, unless it had to be done for reasons of health; but in that case the patient was given better food.[72] Food, as a rule, was to have the ingredients needed for nourishment, except on Fridays, the eight days before Christmas and the period between Quinquagesima Sunday and Easter.[73] In all, seventeen ordinances legislate for the monk's diet.[74] This diet should not include fowl, whether in the

---

68. PL 103:378–380. Cf. PL 97:389 c. 50; J. Narberhaus, *op. cit.*, 43f. and M. Herrgott, *op. cit.*, 21. For the Office of the Dead see the report of Tatto and Grimalt, two monks of Reichenau who spent some time at Inde, in Albers, *op. cit.*, 3:110f. and 118. According to the two visitors, "As soon as Vespers of the day are over, they immediately say Vespers of the Dead, with antiphons, and after Compline, Matins of the Dead with antiphons and responsories, sung with full and sonorous voice and with great sweetness; next morning, after Matins of the day, Lauds of the Dead." E. Bishop, *op. cit.*, 217. The psalms said for the *eleemosynarii* and the *familiares* are specified in B. Albers, *op. cit.*, 3:171.

69. C. 69, PL 97:391. The regulations on the chapter room are practically borrowed from the so-called *Ordo qualiter* which definitely predates Benedict of Aniane; B. Albers, *op. cit.*, 3:30f.

70. C. 12. PL 97:382.

71. Cc. 12, 18, 46 and 71. *Ibid.*, 382, 383, 389 and 392.

72. C. 11. *Ibid.*, 382.   73. C. 77. *Ibid.*, 392.

74. Cc. 8, 9, 10, 12, 18, 22, 25, 26, 37, 46, 47, 51, 57, 71, 76, 77 and 78.

monastery or outside it, except in the case of illness and on four specified days during the Christmas and Easter season, if such a supply should be at hand.[75] Bishops were told not to dispense monks from this obligation.[76] Other meat was completely banished, even for oblates if they were in good health.[77] Wednesdays and Fridays were fast days, and on Good Friday only bread and water was taken.[78] There was no fast during the octave of Pentecost, unless called for by a special reason.[79] Abbots and monks were to have the same portion of food and drink.[80] To avoid the extremes of too much or too little, Benedict introduced a new standard weight for the pound.[81] Every monk was given his individual portion with no permission to give part of it to someone else.[82] Apples and lettuce could only be eaten with other food, not outside meals.[83] On great solemnities and feasts of saints there were two meals, and whenever guests came to the monastery the abbot could increase the measure of food and drink in their honor. If there was no wine, a double measure of beer was given instead.[84]

In matters of clothing, Benedict introduced new articles and increased, for several reasons, the number of garments allowed by the Rule. Because the climate in Gaul is considerably colder than in Italy where the Rule had been drawn up, the Frankish monks definitely needed more and warmer clothes than what had been granted by the Rule. In the absence of adequate legislation on the subject, some northern monks had taken matters into their own hands by increasing their wardrobe long before, thus presenting Benedict of Aniane with a *fait accompli*. Considering these additions legitimized through age-old practice, they not only resisted attempts to return to the stricter provisions of the Rule, but in some instances even called for more allowances. An additional problem was the

75. Cc. 8 and 78. PL 97:382 and 392f.   76. C. 9. *Ibid.*, 382.
77. "*Ut volatilia intus, forisve, nisi pro infirmitate, nullo tempore comedant.*" PL 97:382. Cf. also c. 37; *ibid.*, 387.
78. Cc. 18 and 47. *Ibid.*, 383 and 389.
79. C. 51. *Ibid.*, 390.   80. C. 25. *Ibid.*, 385.   81. C. 57. *Ibid.*, 390.
82. C. 76. *Ibid.*, 392.   83. C. 10. *Ibid.*, 382.
84. C. 46. *Ibid.*, 389. Cf. also cc. 22 and 26. *Ibid.*, 384f.

case of negligent abbots who failed to provide their charges with the necessary items of clothing.[85] To remedy the situation Benedict ordained in seven canons[86] that garments should neither be extremely cheap nor overly expensive, but of average quality.[87] The canons specify the length of the *cuculla* and prohibit all discrimination between the abbot's and the monks' wardrobe.[88] The latter should receive clothes, shoes and whatever of this sort they may need, including flannel capes and warm muffs on account of the climate.[89] Canon twenty-two details the monks' wardrobe, as follows: two undershirts, tunics, *cucullae* and capes—even three of each in case of necessity; four pairs of stockings; two underdrawers; a mantle; two pelisses, i.e. long fur-lined outer garments; two belts (*fasciolae*)— four in case of necessity or when traveling; and, finally, two kinds of gloves (muffs), i.e. for summer and winter use; two pairs of day shoes; two night gowns, and a sufficient quantity of soap and oils.[90]

The Rule of St Benedict assigns an important place to daily manual labor. By the early ninth century this practice had nearly disappeared since the monks as a rule had all come from the ranks of the non-working feudal nobility. Benedict now revived manual labor. He himself engaged in regular physical and field work and prescribed that "the brethren work in the kitchen, in the bakery and in other workshops with their own hands, and that they also

85. Tomek, *op. cit.*, 248f.

86. Cc. 20, 21, 22, 25, 53, 61 and 79. Of these cc. 53 and 25 seem to be somewhat contradictory. Cf. E. Tomek *op. cit.*, 249 and E. Sackur, *op. cit.*, 1:58f.

87. C. 20. PL 97:384. See also E. Tomek, *op. cit.*, 248.

88. Cc. 21 and 25. PL 97:384f.   89. Cc. 53, 61 and 79. *Ibid.*, 390 and 393.

90. "*Abbas . . . hoc omnino provideat, ut camisias duas, et tunicas duas, et cucullas duas, et cappas duas unusquisque monachorum habeat; quibus vero necesse est, addatur et tertia; et pedules quatuor paria, et femoralia duo paria, roccum unum, pellicias usque ad talos duas, fasciolas duas; quibus autem necesse est itineris causa, alias duas; manicas quas vulgo wantos appellant, in aestate, et in hieme muffulas vervecinas; calciamenta diurna paria duo, subtalares per noctem in aestate duas, in hieme vero soccos; saponem sufficientem et uncturam.*" C. 22, PL 97:384. Ardo similarly reports, "*Concessit etiam necessitatis causa, propter quam Regula jubet, duas scilicet stamineas, et femoralia, pelliceas, quaecunque necessaria prospexit, ut omnem amputaret occasionis ambagem, tribuit et concessit.*" PL 103:380.

wash their laundry."[91] Intellectual labor was done in intern schools for oblates.[92] In this instance, too, Benedict called for moderation. He wished that work should cease with the office of None during Lent, and that it should be lighter on Wednesdays and Fridays, because of the fast.[93] The provisions on manual labor thus never exceed the demands of the Rule; they prescribe that house work must be done by the monks themselves, while field labor was undertaken only by way of exception.[94]

The capitulary provided also that tithes be given to the poor. In

91. Cc. 4, 17 and 39; PL 97:381, 383 and 388. Cf. B. Albers, *op. cit.*, 3:83. Even if, on occasions, there was field work and the gathering of fruit, this involved no contact with the world, for the monks were enjoined to work in silence and recite psalms in the meantime. *"Nec laborantium quis fabulis perstrepere audebat, sed manus opere, linguae occupabantur psalmodiis."* PL 103:368. Ibid., 379 we read, *"Expleta Prima in unum aggregati solvant capitulum; quo expleto, cum silentio, aut psalmos decantando exeant ad opus sibi injunctum."* According to Albert Hauck, the rule of silence simply mirrors the regulations of St Columba on this subject. *Kirchengeschichte Deutschlands* (Leipzig: J. C. Hinnrichs'sche Buchhandlung, 1906), 2:592. See also B. Albers, *op. cit.*, 3:91.

92. *"Ut scola in monasterio non habeatur, nisi eorum qui oblati sunt."* PL 97:389 c. 45. P. Schmitz asks here, "Should the accent be placed on *scola* or on *monasterio?"* His answer is: "The first interpretation seems the more obvious one: It is also the general view. In this case every external school is rejected." "L'influence de Saint-Benoît d'Aniane dans l'histoire de l'Ordre de Saint-Benoît," *Il Monachesimo nell'alto medioevo e la formazione della civiltà occidentale* (Settimane di Studio del Centro Italiano di Studi Sull'Alto Medioevo, IV; Spoleto: Presso la Sede del Centro, 1957), 412. This meant a discontinuation of monastic instruction for outsiders. According to A. Hauck, the characteristic feature of Benedict's innovation lies in the fact "that no theological studies are prescribed while silent manual labor, discontinued in many monasteries, is restored and that the monks are forbidden to have a school within the monastery unless it was for oblates." *Op. cit.*, 2:596. See also B. Albers, *op. cit.*, 3:128; DSAM 1:1440; G. de Valous, *Le monachisme clunisien*, 1:10; and David Knowles, *The Monastic Order in England, A History of Its Development from the Time of St Dunstan to the Fourth Lateran Council, 954-1216*, 3rd ed., (Cambridge: Cambridge University Press, 1950), 27.

93. Cc. 39 and 18. PL 97:388 and 383.

94. J. Narberhaus, *op. cit.*, 64. See also S. Hilpisch, *Geschichte*, 125; D. Knowles, *The Monastic Order in England*, 27 and Charles Dereine, "Odon de Tournai et la crise du cénobitisme au XIe siècle," *Revue du Moyen Age Latin*, 4 (1948), 149.

this concern Benedict anticipated subsequent ecclesiastical and monastic legislation.[95]

Considering the provisions of Aachen as a whole, one has to admit that they do not offer strikingly original or new ideas. Quite frequently they are but a repetition of ordinances contained in the capitularies of previous rulers and synodal decrees of Church councils. Still, by assimilating and coordinating all this material they brought about a reform that went deeper and reached wider proportions in their fundamental thoroughness than preceding particular endeavors.[96]

There can be no doubt that the capitulary of 817 was basically the work of Benedict of Aniane, a man quite capable of such an undertaking, in view of his personality, his studies, the experiences he gathered from visiting monasteries and, last but not least, his friendship with Louis the Pious.[97] The emperor, who liked to listen to his advice,[98] quickly approved the draft accepted by all the participants of the synod. He thus made it an official capitulary of the realm and expressed his wish that the execution of the reform decrees should start within a year in all monasteries. The movement received additional impetus from the provision that representatives from other monasteries should spend—*imperiali censura*—some time at Inde to acquaint themselves with its model usages, and from the appointment of *missi dominici*, taken from the *ordo regularis*, for the purpose of visiting the monasteries. These *missi* were to ascertain whether the provisions of Aachen were faithfully carried out, and to remedy possible failings by denouncing uncooperative and negligent

---

95. "*Ut de omnibus in eleemosynam datis, tam ecclesiae quam fratribus, decimae pauperibus dentur.*" PL 97:389 c. 49.

96. J. Narberhaus, *op. cit.*, 51.

97. *Ibid.*, 4f., and 39. See also E. Tomek, *op. cit.*, 178; R. Graham, *English Ecclesiastical Studies*, 2; Ursmer Berlière, *Ascèse bénédictine dès origines à la fin du XIIe siècle* (Paris: P. Lethielleux, 1927), 27f.; G. de Valous, *Le monachisme clunisien*, 1:12; D. Knowles, *The Monastic Order in England*, 26; and H. DeWarren, "Le monachisme à l'apparition de saint Bernard," *loc. cit.*, 46f.

98. "*Ludovicus . . . ejus consilium libenter obtemperabat.*" PL 103:372.

abbots to the local bishop or, if this should not suffice, to the metropolitan and his synod.[99] Guided with the same objectives and encouraged by Benedict of Aniane, Louis the Pious held a new synod at Aachen between December, 818, and January, 819, during which he reduced the services owed by monasteries, granted the right of free (abbatial) elections to some royal monasteries, made provisions for monasteries which had lay abbots, and appointed Benedict the superior of all the monasteries in his kingdom.[100]

Since all monks had one *professio*, Benedict wished that they should also have one *salubris consuetudo*, i.e. identical customs and practices in the liturgy, in vigils, in chanting, in food, drink, and similar matters. He felt, "since all took the same vows, all monasteries should have the same salutary usages."[101] And, as Ardo reports, "one Rule is given to all and observed by all. All monasteries were brought into such a unity that they seemed to have been taught by the same master and in the same place. The same observance con-

---

99. "*De quibus etiam capitulare institutum imperatori confirmandum praebuit, ut omnibus in regno suo positis monasteriis observare praeciperet . . . Cui protinus imperator assensum praebuit, inspectoresque per singula posuit monasteria . . . Suos in Inda degentes ita omni intentione instruxit, ut ex diversis regionibus adventantes monachi . . . imbuerentur.*" PL 103:377f. These *missi* were from the *ordo regularis*. Cf. *ibid.*, 385, and B. Albers, *op. cit.*, 3:94. The literature attesting the existence of these inspectors is found in DHE 8:181. See also J. Narberhaus, *op. cit.*, 64f; B. Albers, *Consuetudines Monasticae*, 3:90 and 93; C. Butler, *Benedictine Monachism*, 236f.; P. Schmitz, *op. cit.*, 1:106; S. Hilpisch, *Benedictinism*, 36 and M. Mourre, *op. cit.*, 280. Louis' total dedication to the monastic idea was in marked contrast with Charlemagne's rather one-sided promotion of monasticism. For details see A. Hauck, *op. cit.*, 2:578ff.

100. "*Praefecit eum quoque imperator cunctis in regno suo coenobiis.*" PL 103:377. The *Vita* also talks about Benedict's "*sollicitudo omnium monasteriorum circa longeque positorum*" (*ibid.*, 368). Cf. P. Schmitz, *op. cit.*, 1:106f. For the grant of free elections see *Ludovici I et Lothari capitula*, PL 97:397: "*Monachorum siquidem causam qualiter Deo opitulante ex parte disposuerimus, et quomodo ex se ipsis sibi eligendi abbates licentiam dederimus, et qualiter Deo opitulante quiete vivere propositumque suum indefesse custodire valerent ordinaverimus, in alia scedula diligenter adnotari fecimus et ut apud successores nostros ratum foret et inviolabiliter conservetur, confirmavimus.*"

101. "*Ut autem, sicut una omnium erat professio, fieret quoque omnium monasteriorum salubris una consuetudo.*" PL 103:377.

cerning drink, food, fasting and chanting was prescribed for all."[102] According to his biographer, Benedict also wished that all should have the same monastic habit,[103] and "that there be no variety in anything, anywhere in the realm, among those who made the monastic profession."[104] To him the best way to maintain and safeguard regular life was to set up uniform practices protected by the canons of Aachen and the alertness of the *missi* who were to preclude arbitrary interpretations.

Since there was to be a uniform observance, the need for establishing close bonds between monasteries and for placing an authority over them to supervise their discipline could not be overlooked. Uniform observances were to effect a certain union among monasteries, something unknown before the end of the eighth century in western monachism. Until that time each monastery formed a separate, distinct and independent unit, with its local particularism in prayers, usages and interpretation of the Rule. Any rapport that existed between monasteries rested on a purely spiritual basis as is, for instance, a prayer association. Benedict of Aniane now

---

102. "*Una cunctis generaliter posita observatur regula, cunctaque monasteria ita ad formam unitatis redacta sunt ac si ab uno magistro et in uno imbuerentur locoa Uniformis mensura in potu, in cibo, in vigiliis, in modulationibus cunctis, observand. est tradita.*" PL 103:377.

103. "*In habitu quoque dissimilis fecerat multorum consuetudo. Siquidem nonnullis usque ad talos cucullae pendebant. Quam ob rem vir Dei uniformem cunctis tenendum monachis instituit modum, ut non amplius duobus cubitis excederet mensura, vel usque ad genua pertingere posset.*" Ibid., 379f.

104. "*Imprimis ut nulla in ullis rebus inter hujus professionis viros in toto regno suo . . . inveniatur varietas.*" *Capitula novitiarum*, by Tatto and Grimalt, composed before the great synod of Aachen; B. Albers, *op. cit.*, 3:95.—Mabillon, using the *Vita Ludovici Pii*, writes in this connection, "*Peracto concilio constituit idem Deo amabilis imperator Benedictum abbatem et cum eo monachos strenuae vitae, qui per omnia monasteria monachorum euntes redeuntesque uniformem traderent cunctis monasteriis tam viris quam monialibus feminis vivendi secundum Regulae sancti Benedicti incommutabilem morem.*" PL 103:385. Cf. also C. Butler, *Benedictine Monachism*, 236 and 357; U. Berlière, "L'étude des réformes monastiques," *loc. cit.*, 138; O. Ducourneau, *op. cit.*, 24; S. Hilpisch, *Benedictinism*, 34; W. Williams, *op. cit.*, 94 and 96f.; G. de Valous, *Le monachisme clunisien*, 1:10 and Vincent Hermans, *Spiritualité monastique* (Roma: O. Cist. Ref., 1954), 115.

went one step further. He took twelve monasteries under his special supervision, and assumed the right to transfer monks from one place to another.[105] One may well see in this the outline of a monastic congregation, as a basic component of the unity envisioned by our reformer. But it was far from being a perfect congregation, for royal and episcopal power was still too strong and the concept of land as the source of power too ingrained. Still, Benedict saw in the multitude of scattered and isolated houses a real family;[106] hence his endeavor to replace the multi-colored particular observances of individual monasteries with uniform practices. This uniformity, with its fixed customs, was to produce a *forma unitatis*, a stable way of life and put an end to the chaos of preceding centuries. There was no more need for formal organization: the example of the mother-house, the work of the inspectors and Benedict's personal influence proved sufficient for the moment.[107]

The idea of grouping the monasteries into a federation based on the broad foundations of the Rule was strongly supported by Louis the Pious. This is why he agreed to send imperial inspectors to every monastery and why he had built the model monastery of Inde in the vicinity of the imperial palace at Aachen where all could learn the authentic monastic practices. This is also why he prescribed that

---

105. "*Habuit sub regimine suo monasteria duodecim, id est Anianum, Gellonem, Casam-Novam, Insulam-Barbaram, Menatem, Sanctum Savinum, Sanctum Maximinum, Massiacum, Cormariacum, Cellam-Novam in Tolosano, Monasterium-Maurum in Alsatz, Indam.*" PL 103:383. These are the monasteries of Aniane, Gellone, Cazaneuve, Ile-Barbe, Ménat, Saint-Savin, Micy, Massay, Cormery, Celleneuve, Marmoutier and Inde. Cf. DHE 8:179. See also J. Narberhaus, *op. cit.*, 43, and C. Butler, *Benedictine Monachism*, 236.

106. According to P. Schmitz, "Here we have already the blueprint of a congregation, an element of the unity envisioned by our reformer." *Op. cit.*, 1:103. See also S. Hilpisch, *Benedictinism*, 33; U. Berlière, "L'étude des réformes monastiques," *loc. cit.*, 138; V. Hermans, *op. cit.*, 115, and Anselme Le Bail, "La paternité de Saint Benoît sur l'Ordre de Cîteaux," *Collectanea Ordinis Cisterciensium Reformatorum*, 9 (1947), 111.

107. J. Narberhaus, *op. cit.*, 43. *Ibid.*, 74f. the author concludes that the reform of Benedict of Aniane marks the beginning of an inner process leading to a greater centralization in the Church. It was another attempt to integrate a unified French church into the universal Church. "The Church awakened in souls. The idea of the *universalitas Ecclesiae* became alive."

each monastery send one or two of its members to Inde, to be instructed by Benedict himself, and then, upon their return, to acquaint everyone with the usages of Inde. According to C. Butler, "Such were the plans of Benedict . . . a rigid uniformity among the monasteries of the empire, secured by the appointment of himself as General."[108]

Benedict was no fanatic for the law. While he enforced the Benedictine Rule, he also modified several of its prescriptions and supplied many regulations of his own. Ardo clearly explained Benedict's reasoning on this point:

> Many things are [explicitly] prescribed by the Rule. But there are other details of the daily schedule which one would expect it to regulate, but it is silent about them. These also are needed for without them the monk's life becomes dissolute, fickle and unstable. The Rule prescribes certain things to promote harmonious unity, others to encourage what is right or advisable in view of human frailty. Therefore, whatever the venerable abbot of blessed memory found explicitly ordained by the Rule, that he prescribed to be done without any hesitation or subterfuge. Whatever he found could be dispensed or changed for legitimate reasons, he still prescribed for his disciples, insofar as it was better for the place in view of its means and actual situation. Where the Rule was less clear or remained in complete silence, he supplied his own decisions, with moderation and competence.[109]

The capitulary of Aachen mitigated the provisions of the Benedictine Rule in more than ten different instances, where it judged its observance too difficult for the time and place. Thus Benedict

---

108. *Benedictine Monachism*, 237. See also PL 103:377f.

109. "*Propter plurimorum . . . indiscretum fervorem et quorundam ineptum teporem minusque capacium sensum obtunsum . . . ordinemque observandum cunctis tradidit: illos retrahens ne superflua peterent, hos imperans ut torporem excuterent, alios nihilominus admonens ut saltem visa implere expeterent . . . Quapropter piae recordationis venerabilis abbas, quaeque observanda comperit, absque ulla cunctatione vel excusationis fuco implere decrevit: ea vero quae certis pro causis aut dimittenda cognovit aut commutanda inspexit, nihilominus, prout rectius et secundum posse locique positionem dirimere quivit, suis observanda discipulis tradidit.*" PL 103:378.

granted more and better clothing to his monks, subjected the abbot to the common rule, gave the community a voice in the selection of the most important monastic officials, increased the powers of the prior, appointed local and external (*missi*) supervisors, expanded and changed the liturgy and the various monastic usages, made disciplinary innovations and discontinued the teaching of outsiders.

From an ascetical point of view, these regulations breathe moderation rather than restriction; they are not in conflict with the Rule nor with its spirit. Their purpose was much broader than an introduction of mitigations for the sake of compromise. Actually, the primary concern of Benedict of Aniane was to prescribe uniform customs for all monasteries in order to establish greater bonds of monastic unity.[110]

Ardo preserved for us the basic features of the daily schedule at Inde. He reports that the monks rose at the sound of a bell which was placed in the dormitory. (It seems the custom was that the outside or church bell was used only when the monks were ready to start the community prayers. Thus guests entering the church would find the monks already in their respective stalls.) Rising swiftly, as the Rule of St Benedict demands, the monks hastened to the church where they took holy water and made visits to its various altars. Then, going to their places, they recited the so-called *trina oratio* made up of the fifteen gradual psalms. Five psalms were said for all living Christians, five for all the deceased, and the remaining five for those who died recently. After each of the three groups of five psalms there was a prostration during which the monks could say private prayers for the persons included in their general intention. Then, i.e. after the *trina oratio*, the priest in charge started the regular office of Matins.

110. J. Narberhaus, *op. cit.*, 64. H. DeWarren, "Le monachisme à l'apparition de saint Bernard," *loc. cit.*, 50; O. Ducourneau, *op. cit.*, 25f.; W. Williams, *op. cit.*, 95ff.; and G. de Valous, *Le monachisme clunisien*, 1:13, n. 3. In contrast to S. Hilpisch (*Geschichte*, 125) J. Narberhaus concludes: "His (Benedict's) ordinances are nowhere in conflict with the Rule or with its spirit; nowhere are the ascetical demands of the Rule overstepped. On the contrary, every ordinance breathes the spirit of mildness and represents a relaxation rather than a restriction of the Rule." *Op. cit.*, 64.

In summertime the monks left the church immediately after Lauds, *propter somnolentiam*, i.e. so as not to fall asleep. Then they exchanged their night slippers for day shoes (*calcei diurni*), washed themselves, and returned to the church in the manner already described, i.e. they took holy water and made the usual altar visits.

Next followed the recitation of Prime, the first hour of the day office (*officium diurnum*). The latter was not said in the Benedictine sequence but followed, beginning with Psalm 118, the Roman *cursus*. Or it is also possible that Psalm 118 was simply added to the regular Benedictine office. The bell rang again, as before Matins, so that upon the completion of the altar rounds the hebdomadary could start the office at the end of the signal. To enable all to finish their visits, the bell was rung *prolixe*, i.e. for some time. Prime itself consisted of the *Deus in adjutorium meum intende* (*Lord, come to my aid*), a hymn, three psalms, a short reading, a versicle, the *Kyrie eleison* (*Lord, have mercy*), and the concluding prayers.

As Ardo laconically tells us, Prime was followed by the office of the chapter (*officium capituli*): "After Prime they gathered to have the chapter," without explaining of what this office consisted. Fortunately, we have sufficient data—for instance, the capitulary of Aachen and the report of the Reichenau monks—to reconstruct it with a great deal of accuracy. According to these the chapter services began with a reading from the Martyrology. This was followed by the versicle *Pretiosa*, the thrice repeated *Deus in adjutorium*, the doxology, Kyrie and a reading from the Rule or a homily which was concluded by the versicle *Tu autem Domine*. Then, it seems, they had the chapter of faults. At the end of this each monk received his daily work assignment, in the kitchen, the bakery, the storage rooms or fields, to which he proceeded in silence or reciting psalms.

The *Vita* mentions no other supererogatory prayers until the office of Compline, indeed it actually seems to exclude them by its silence.

Ordinarily, at the end of each canonical hour the monks were free to remain in the church for private prayers. Community prayers were prescribed for some occasions. These were the already mentioned altar visits before Matins and Prime and after Compline. After Compline, the monks had to stay in church and say ten psalms in winter and five psalms in summer, before making the usual altar rounds. It is at this juncture that Ardo specifies what prayers were said at the altars. Before the first altar the monk had to recite the Our Father and the Creed, elsewhere he was to say the Our Father and the *Confiteor* (*I Confess*). After this everyone retired for the night to get sufficient rest, so as not to be overcome by sleep or troubled by drowsiness during the night office.

In his description of the *ordo diurnus* Ardo does not mention the evening reading (*collatio vespertina*) prescribed by the Rule of St Benedict. But when speaking of the writings of his hero, he tells us that the saint had written a book of homilies to be read in community—an obvious reference to the *collatio*.[111]

Ardo's account is supplemented by the information of the already mentioned Reichenau monks who spent some time at Inde and recorded their observations. They noted the dignified and peaceful bearing of the monks who walked about with gravity and downcast eyes, in strict silence, and who did everything in accordance with the regulations and without delay.[112] According to Ardo, Benedict instructed his monks in such a way that visiting monks had no need for words—to him distracting noises—to satisfy themselves about the monastery's way of life; from the actions and from the recollection of the individual monks they could see everything in practice.[113]

111. PL 103:378–380. Cf. Clemente Molas, "A propósito del Ordo diurnus de San Benito de Aniano," *Studia Monastica*, 2 (1960), 207ff.

112. PL 103:378ff. Tatto and Grimalt found the monks of Inde dignified, peaceful, walking with gravity and downcast eyes in strict silence and performing everything *"secundum ordinem"* and *"absque tarditate."* B. Albers, *op. cit.*, 3:112ff. Cf. MGH, Ep. 5:303ff.

113. *"Suos in Inda degentes ita omni intentione instruxit ut ex diversis regionibus adventantes monachi non, ut ita dixerim, perstrepentia, ut imbuerentur, indigerent verba: quia in singulorum moribus, in incessu habituque formam disciplinamque regularemque pictam cernerent."* PL 103:377. Cf. J. Narberhaus, *op. cit.*, 65. *Ibid.*, 60–63, is a discussion of the third group of ordinances aimed at strengthening the monk's interior recollection.

Benedict felt that the monk's main obligation was prayer, or, better, the divine office. If he did not actually say the characteristic *"Propter chorum fundati sumus"* as it is believed he did,[114] it is nevertheless a true expression of his sentiments and explains why he considerably augmented the daily prayer life of Inde. Besides the already mentioned additions he also introduced the Office of All Saints which at the time had only Vespers and Lauds. Thus he set the trend for the future so that the list eventually included the Offices of the Blessed Virgin Mary, of the Holy Cross, the Incarnation, the Holy Trinity and the Holy Spirit. The reason for this multiplication was not—as is often suggested—Benedict's delight in colorful church services, but a genuinely felt need to withdraw the monks from the world and from outside activities, in order to lead them to a more spiritual interior life, to a life worthy of their profession.[115] This is also why monks were told to recite psalms during work, or while proceeding to their assignments.[116]

Since the divine office was considerably expanded, the monks

---

114. Pius Halász, "Die geistliche Schule der Zisterzienser," trans. Bede Lackner, *Anima*, 8 (1953), 54.

115. PL 103:378–380. Cf. also E. Bishop, *op. cit.*, 214, U. Berlière, "L'étude des réformes monastiques," *loc. cit.*, 148f.; DSAM 1:1440f.; André Louf, *The Message of Monastic Spirituality*, trans. Luke Stevens (New York: Desclée Co. (1964), 168 and C. Molas, "A Propósito del Ordo díurnus de san Benito de Aniano," *loc. cit.*, 205ff. In this author's belief one should not attribute too much to Benedict of Aniane, for a number of practices described in Ardo's c. 52 (altar visits, prayers for the deceased, recitation of psalms during work) are of earlier origins. Cf. A. Louf, *op. cit.*, 168f.; M. Herrgott, *op. cit.*, 21, and DSAM 1:1440 where the divine office is described *"oeuvre primordiale du Bénédictine."* See also S. Hilpisch, *Benedictinism*, 35.

116. *"In monasterio quoque remanentes non fabulis occupentur otiosis, sed bini et bini, aut certe singuli in coquina, in pistrino, in cellario psalmos canent."* PL 103:379. It is of interest to see how authors disagree in their interpretation of Ardo's fifty-second chapter. According to P. Schmitz, "If one reads Ardo's description of the monk's daily schedule at Inde, he will no longer recognize in it the daily routine prescribed by St Benedict in his Rule." DHE 8:184. On the other hand one reads in DSAM 1:1441, "It suffices to compare the daily schedule prescribed by the Rule with the life of Benedict of Aniane's monk as it appears from the documents preserved . . . in order to see that their tasks are identical, that the spirit is the same, and that only questions of detail separate them."

had no time for field labor which came to be regarded as an extraordinary occupation. Work became more domestic and was done, for the most part, in workshops. In this situation the conviction could easily take root that, like the cleric, the monk was entitled to live from the altar. The consequence of it was that monasteries began to accept fixed revenues, tithes, altars and landed property cultivated by serfs. Thus a situation was created in which monastic property did not essentially differ from clerical and lay possessions. It implied the recognition of the manorial system with its serfs and laborers and led to involvements in the feudal world—the very thing Benedict sought to avoid.[117]

In the field of education, the Carolingian program had been to place teaching into the hands of the clergy. Benedict, convinced that his monasteries would suffer from such contacts with the world, prohibited institutional teaching, permitting only the training of oblates, i.e. of future monks.[118]

To evaluate Benedict's impact on monasticism, one must look to his admirers as well as to his critics. The latter are quite vocal, especially in more recent times. They point, first of all, to the fact that he upset the traditional balance between prayer, work and spiritual reading (study) set up so wisely by the Father of Western monasticism.[119] For with Benedict of Aniane a tradition set in according to which the office was no longer just the most important activity in monastic life, as St Benedict wished it to be, but practically the only occupation of the monks.[120] This overemphasis and extension of community prayer, regulated in all its details, led to the

117. C. Dereine, "Odon de Tournai," *loc. cit.*, 149, and LTK 2:179.

118. C. 45. PL 97:389. CF. also DSAM 1:1440; B. Albers, *Consuetudines Monasticae*, 3:128; D. Knowles, *The Monastic Order in England*, 27, and J. Narberhaus, *op. cit.*, 2 and 31. About this sensitive point A. Hauck remarks, "The more monasteries became institutions of culture, the less they remained representatives of the ascetical way of life. The latter denies the legitimacy of the former; the former obstructs the practice of the latter. It is simply impossible to combine the two." *Op. cit.*, 3:343.

119. E.g. P. Schmitz, *op. cit.*, 1:109.

120. Ursmer Berlière, *L'ordre monastique dès origines jusqu' au XXIe siècle* (Paris: P. Lethielleux, 1924), 129.

charge that Benedict ritualized the liturgy at the expense of simplicity.[121] This could happen, because field labor had practically ceased, because the contemporary feudal world was quite different from the realities of the sixth century, and because the monks had no extraclaustral activities. The "additions and accretions to the canonical office that set in with him and held their ground until almost modern times modified the character of Benedictine life for a period of eight centuries or more" (C. Butler)[122] and led to catastrophic results (U. Berlière).[123] Equally alien to the Rule were Benedict's attempts to force upon his monasteries a rigidly uniform and centralized organization, with its inspectors and its "General"—Benedict himself. "The centralization of monasteries was certainly contrary to the letter and even to the spirit of the Rule of St Benedict" (V. Hermans).[124] According to C. Butler, "The essential antagonism of spirit between Benedict of Aniane and the great Benedict" lies in the former's aim at a "cast-iron system of uniformity"[125] demanding an "almost mechanical will" (H. Workman).[126] This "scheme of rigid uniformity among the monasteries of the empire, secured by the appointment of himself as General, aided by an agent or inspector in each house—an ideal wholly alien to the most elementary conception of Benedictine life—met with the fate it deserved" (C. Butler).[127] It failed to effect a meaningful union of monasteries already in Benedict's own time.[128] Absolute uniformity, as envisioned by Benedict, was not only a "fatal mistake" (H. Workman),[129] but actually "a utopia" (U. Berlière).[130]

C. Butler also observed that the regulations Benedict had adopted at the synod of Aachen as a basis of a common observance, prove

121. See *above*, n. 13.
122. *Benedictine Monachism*, 295.
123. See *above*, n. 120.
124. V. Hermans, *op. cit.*, 115.
125. *Benedictine Monachism*, 237. See also DHE 8:184.
126. H. Workman, *op. cit.*, 227.
127. *Benedictine Monachism*, 237. See also DHE 8:184.
128. Georg Schreiber, *Gemeinschaften des Mittelalters* (Münster: Regensberg, 1948), 409.
129. *Op. cit.*, 220f.
130. U. Berlière, *Ascèse Bénédictine*, 47.

disappointing on examination. "Certainly such provisions were not the touchstone between observance and inobservance in monasteries, much less the test of religious spirit."[131] The provisions of Aachen are, in many respects, not an original creation, but the codification of existing practices, as found in the *Statuta Murbacensia*, in Paul the Deacon and others, especially in Italy. Their lack of inspiration is also apparent from the treatment of irrelevancies—a case in point is the regulation on shaving—and from seeming contradictions. An illustration of the latter is the great organization conceived by Benedict which created bonds between monasteries, set up various forms of control, brought outside responsibilities, necessitated trips and contacts with laymen—all measures that were "ill-conducive to seclusion and stability taken in a strict sense."[132] Moreover the capitulary of 817 in some ways altered the Rule, with its additions, modifications, eliminations and restrictions.[133] These may in part have been inspired by Benedict's exposure to eastern monachism and by his dealings with Origenism.[134] The fact is that in his *Concordia Regularum* Benedict sought to point out common elements in Eastern rules and the Rule of St Benedict. The multiplication of liturgical and monastic services, the minute prescriptions regulating daily tasks, the monastic government and material needs (such as shaving, the length of the cuculla and the standard weight of the pound) and the introduction of and stress on fasting and seclusion, are definitely indicative of Eastern monastic influences. Authors like U. Berlière and P. Schmitz still see in

131. *Benedictine Monachism*, 357.

132. Pierre Salmon, "Monastic Asceticism and the Origins of Cîteaux," *Monastic Studies*, 3 (1965), 122. In the words of P. Schmitz, "the famous capitula of Aix-la-Chapelle arouse little genuine interest. What does it matter, for instance, that the monks should shave every fifteen days and that they should not follow such practices during Lent?" *Op. cit.*, 1:108. Inconsequential regulations are also found in cc. 6–8, 10f., 21 and 76. Cf. M. Mourre, *op. cit.*, 282.

133. PL 103:378–380. See also J. Narberhaus, *op. cit.*, 64 and E. Bishop, *op. cit.*, 213.

134. PL 103:361. See also DTC 2:708; LTK 2:179; M. Mourre, *op. cit.*, 280 and J. Leclercq, *The Love of Learning*, 100.

Benedict more a disciple of the Eastern Fathers than a genuine son of the Patriarch of Western monasticism. This may also be deduced from Benedict's opposition to monastic schools and teaching which, of course, implied a disinterest in an intellectual and cultural self-improvement and in the intellectual formation of society. The re-introduction of Egyptian monastic elements and the return—at least, in part—to decidedly oriental practices unmistakably indicate a return to a tradition from which the Father of Benedictinism had moved three centuries before.[135]

Yet in another respect, Benedict was representative of the contemporary world, with its fixed revenues, its manors and proprietary churches. This was the result of accepting donations, of discontinuing field labor and of Benedict's centralizing efforts.

Benedict unquestionably spared no effort in the promotion of monastic reform; yet its actual success remains questionable. It was, for all practical purposes, a one-man reform, the brainchild of a man who was not thinking in the perspective of future centuries, who seemed more interested in accidentals and details than in cultivating a universal outlook.[136] "He was simply a monk—A. Hauck concludes—too interested in externals and small matters. He was exclusively and excessively reactionary as a reformer, without any new or forward-looking concept. In this regard he stands behind other monastic giants."[137]

But this is only one side—the negative side—of the picture; for

---

135. *"A rigore vero suae primae conversionis paululum declinarat, quoniam impossibile opus assumpserat: sed voluntas eadem permanebat."* PL 103:368. Benedict's admiration for eastern monasticism is also evidenced from his *Codex regularum* and the *Concordia regularum* written for the purpose of proving that the Benedictine Rule clearly followed oriental monastic traditions. See also P. Schmitz, *op. cit.,* 1:99, 108f.; U. Berlière, *L'ordre monastique,* 127; H. DeWarren, "Le monachisme à l'apparition de saint Bernard," *loc. cit.,* 46; V. Hermans, *op. cit.,* 115 and Bernard Bligny, "Un aspect de la vie réligieuse au Moyen Age. La concurrence dans les Alps aux XIe siècle," *Bulletin Philologique et Historique,* 1951–1952 (Paris: Imprimérie Nationale, 1953), 281.

136. J. Narberhaus, *op. cit.,* 75.   137. Albert Hauck, *op. cit.,* 2: 608f.

Benedict of Aniane and Post-Carolingian Monachism 33

Benedict also has a host of supporters. These praise his success in bringing about a reform from within, without any outside force (*sic*), and this with such an impact that he ranks second only to the great Patriarch of Monte Cassino.[138] To quote P. Schmitz:

> When Benedict started his reform around 785, it was a rarity to find abbeys where the Benedictine life was observed. Equally rare were abbeys that had a regular abbot for their superior. Disorder prevailed almost everywhere. Benedict restored regular discipline in a great many houses, from the Pyrenees to the Rhine. In these regions he has saved Benedictine monachism from an illness which could have become fatal. Hence he cannot be sufficiently praised for such an impressive accomplishment.[139]

According to Josef Semmler, later medieval monachism adopted from Benedict of Aniane

> the *una consuetudo* principle, an undeniable ritualism, a definite expansion of the monastic prayer *pensum*, and—all his openness to culture and regard for learning notwithstanding—a certain world-fleeing ascetical trait. Also the idea of making the *monasterium* a part of the *Eigenkirche* system and of the feudal domain.[140]

Moreover, Benedict realized and insisted that the Rule of St Benedict was a code of law, and thus saved it from becoming simply an inspirational spiritual directory. In the process he helped the Rule to achieve exclusive supremacy in the West and thus assured the future of Benedictinism.[141] While championing an integral and uniform observance of the Rule, he adapted the latter to the needs of the time, and this long before the advent of Cluny. He strength-

---

138. J. Narberhaus, *op. cit.*, 3. Some see in him "Benedict II." DSAM 1: 1441. P. Schmitz thinks the era is a turning point in monastic history. DHE 8:177. Of the same opinion is E. Bishop, *op. cit.*, 213.

139. *Op. cit.*, 1:108.   140. LTK 2:179.

141. Benedict of Aniane made the ninth-century monk a true Benedictine and helped the Benedictine Rule to victory over rival rules (DSAM 1:1441). See also G. de Valous, *Le monachisme clunisien*, 1:13, and J. Narberhaus, *op. cit.*, 4 and 72. By saving the Benedictine Rule as a code of law, he actually saved monasticism. S. Hilpisch, *Geschichte*, 120ff.

ened the monastic vows, settled questions not decided by the Rule and suppressed outdated and impracticable usages. In the process he authored, what may be called the first set of "declarations" on the Rule.[142] He was also the first monastic leader to work for an effective monastic unity, convinced that Benedictine houses actually constituted a monastic family. Midway between Monte Cassino and Cluny, he prepared the way for the latter, for imperial monachism and for the monastic reforms of the tenth and eleventh centuries. In fact, his reform became the basis for future legislation and usages.[143] In striving for beauty in the house of God and in the liturgy and in stressing the need for a genuine separation from the world, he was responsible for a spiritual regeneration in French monasteries.[144] This in turn had its effect on medieval piety and that type of humanism which is a bridge between the religious and the secular element in the field of culture.[145]

Benedict's pastoral concern was not restricted to monasteries. He improved the lot of the lower clergy, sought to raise its standards and gave a helping hand to the order of canons.[146] Defending the Roman concept of the Church against the Germanic view, he raised the Church to greater heights.[147] In his concern for the laity, he worked for peace, law and justice in the realm and cared for the poor and the needy.[148] Hence even C. Butler had to admit that Benedict produced "some good."[149] But any evaluation of

142. P. Schmitz, *op. cit.*, 1:105. See also G. de Valous, *Le monachisme clunisien*, 1:11 and 13; J. Narberhaus, *op. cit.*, 4 and H. DeWarren, "Le monachisme à l'apparition de saint Bernard," *loc. cit.*, 47.

143. E. Bishop, *op. cit.*, 213; S. Hilpisch, *Benedictinism*, 33; U. Berlière, "L'étude des réformes monastiques," *loc. cit.*, 139; G. de Valous, *Le monachisme clunisien*, 1:10 and 13; V. Hermans, *op. cit.*, 115 and J. Narberhaus, *op. cit.*, 74.

144. The monks of Inde wrote: "*Hic est Benedictus, per quem Dominus Christus in omni regno Francorum regulam sancti Benedicti restauravit.*" PL 103:383. Cf. also *ibid.*, 361 and J. Narberhaus, *op. cit.*, 72f.

145. J. Narberhaus, *op. cit.*, 75f.

146. *Ibid.*, 68f. and 78f.   147. *Ibid.*, 74. See also DHE 8:184f.

148. "*Erat quippe miserorum advocatus, sed monachorum pater; pauperum consolator.*" PL 103:377. See also J. Narberhaus, *op. cit.*, 26 and 73, and G. de Valous, *Le monachisme clunisien*, 1:13.

149. *Benedictine Monachism*, 237.

Benedict and his work will remain a matter of the examiner's *Weltanschauung,* if one may use the term. It will depend on the appreciation—or lack of appreciation—one has for monasticism and on one's own definition of the term. One can understand that A. Hauck calls Benedict a reactionary opposed to culture,[150] for he broke with Charlemagne's policy. Yet such a verdict is incorrect, for monasteries are, first of all, houses of God and in Charlemagne's time this was the case in only a very few instances. A purely external and secularized Christianity needed an intensification of the religious spirit, a religious and monastic renaissance. A religious and early Christian—perhaps oriental?—ingredient had to permeate the Carolingian world, in order to purify it and place it in the service of higher ideals.[151] And this undoubtedly was part of the contribution made by the reform of Benedict of Aniane.

In concluding these remarks a few words seem to be in order about the relationship between Benedict of Aniane and the reform of the early Cistercians. One reason is that such a comparison has never been seriously undertaken; secondly, the existence of ties between the two has either not even been suspected or else been hotly denied. Yet the preceding discussion has furnished a sufficient basis for considering such a relationship. For it clearly shows that Benedict of Aniane had a great influence on the thinking of the Cistercian pioneers. It indicates that their movement was partly an implementation of the measures advocated by Benedict of Aniane—both reforms, for instance, stressed the *una regula* and *una consuetudo* principle—and at the same time a more or less direct reaction to and transformation of his ideas.

Endowed with a unique authority and extraordinary powers by his monarch, Benedict had conceived and set in motion a compre-

---

150. According to this author Benedict "simply wanted to be a monk, and he was nothing but a monk: an upright religious, with no trace of self-righteousness. His whole life was in the service of the monastic idea. He may have been abrupt and without a vision, yet he had the wisdom to make concessions in small matters in order to save his greater projects." *Op. cit.,* 2:608.

151. J. Narberhaus, *op. cit.,* 73f.

hensive reform program which envisioned the union of all Frankish monasteries. He gave appropriate supervisory organs to this union and strengthened it through such bonds as (1) the Rule of St Benedict, (2) a uniform observance, (3) prayer associations for the living and the dead, (4) the protection and support of the secular power, and, finally, (5) a regular and uniform inspection of all monasteries.[152]

Thus Benedict "taught his followers that only the strict and narrow way (*arcta et angusta via*) will lead to (eternal) life." This is also what the preface of the *Exordium Parvum,* a near-contemporary account of the origins of Cîteaux, urges the Cistercians to follow: to "labor on the straight and narrow way (*arcta et angusta via*) prescribed by the Rule."[153] This way was, of course, the Rule of St Benedict which Benedict of Aniane sought to restore to its rightful place in his own and all other monasteries. This is why he turned all his attention to the study of the Rule; he wished to penetrate it, to ascertain its true meaning, and to observe it in full measure. Hence he discussed it and explained it to others and had it prescribed by the assembly of Aachen (817) for monasteries as well as for individuals. Similar aims animated also the Cistercian pioneers. In the face of widespread contemporary digressions, they, too, chose "the straight and narrow path prescribed by the Rule." They left Molesme, where the Rule was observed "poorly and neglectfully," and migrated to Cîteaux in order to serve God "in a wholehearted manner," i.e. "more strictly and more perfectly according to the Rule of St Benedict." Thus they strove to become worthy of their profession, as did Benedict of Aniane.[154]

To help this one Rule (*una regula*) to victory, Benedict set up the necessary bonds of unity (*forma unitatis*). One of these was the

---

152. C. Spahr, *De fontibus constitutivis,* 93.

153. "*Docens arctam et angustam viam esse quae ducit ad vitam*" (Benedict). PL 103:359. "*In arta et angusta via quam regula demonstrat usque ad ex(h)al(a)tionem spiritus desudent.*" *Exordium Parvum,* Preface; Joannes-B. Van Damme (ed.), *Documenta pro Cisterciensis Ordinis historiae ac juris studio.* (Westmalle: Typis Ordinis Cisterciensis, 1959), 5.

154. *Exordium Parvum,* II; J. Van Damme, *op. cit.,* 6.

principle of uniformity (*una consuetudo*): uniform customs in food, drink and clothing and other observances. Accordingly, he prevailed on Louis the Pious in 817 or shortly thereafter to tolerate "no diversity whatsoever in his kingdom among those who took the monastic vows." To make this possible he established his model monastery—Inde—whose usages were to be copied and followed by all other monasteries. These measures are also reflected in the legislation of the early Cistercians. They are a clear anticipation of the third ordinance of the original Charter of Charity (*Carta Caritatis prima*) which states, "We wish and ordain that they—i.e. the Cistercians—observe the Rule of St Benedict in all its particulars, as it is observed in the New Monastery (Cîteaux)," and that "all should live in the bond of charity under one Rule and in the practice of the same observances."[155]

For the same reason the Cistercians also adopted, *via* Cluny, but in a qualified sense—i.e. without doing violence to particular rights and local independence—Benedict's centralizing ideas. The assembly of 817 may well be considered the first general chapter of its kind in western monastic history, an idea Benedict may have borrowed from St Pachomius with whose rule he was well acquainted. Some three centuries later the Cistercians took up and perfected this idea of a "general" chapter and produced that admirable document, the Charter of Charity, to regulate the workings of this constitutional innovation. Also the *missi*, sent out by Benedict to supervise the implementation of the reform decrees of Aachen found counterparts in the Cistercian order where the fathers-immediate paid annual visits to their daughter-houses for similar purposes.[156]

But there are still other similarities between the two reforms. At least in his earlier years, Benedict advocated the need for great simplicity in the liturgy. He rejected silver chalices and used vessels of wood, glass and tin and kept only simple vestments. This is also what the Cistercians did. They retained only iron and copper vessels (candelabra, thuribles) in their services and banished vestments of

---

155. See *above*, n. 104 and *Carta Caritatis*, II, III; J. Van Damme, *op. cit.*, 16f.
156. *Carta Caritatis*, (5), (6), (7); J. Van Damme, *op. cit.*, 17.

silk, gold, or silver weave.[157] They also followed Benedict's example in heeding Charlemagne's capitulary issued in 789 which gave the monks a bold liturgical program:

> Correct carefully the Psalms, the notations, the songs, the calendar, the grammar in each monastery . . . and the catholic books. Because often some desire to pray to God properly, but they pray badly because of the incorrect books . . . If there is need of writing the Gospel, Psalter and Missal, let men of mature age do the writing with all diligence.[158]

In their quest for authenticity the Cistercians undertook a number of similarly inspired liturgical projects. Soon after the foundation of Cîteaux they began to copy and revise their liturgical books, prepared a new edition of the Bible, produced a new breviary, reformed their chant in several stages and composed their customary soon after 1119.[159]

If according to the great Patriarch of Monte Cassino, Benedictine life meant a "complete separation from the outside world, a life exclusively dedicated to prayer and work" (U. Berlière),[160] then Benedict of Aniane and the founders of Cîteaux wholly agreed with such a definition. Both accepted donations, but rejected serfs. Both said daily prayers for the deceased but excluded direct pastoral ministrations to the laity. And both of them needed safeguards. In the absence of a strong papacy Benedict solicited the support of secular princes; for this he had to pay the price of indebtedness to the realities of the contemporary world. The Cistercians had strong feelings about seclusion and monastic independence. They

---

157. *Exordium Parvum*, XVI; J. Van Damme, *op. cit.*, 14.

158. "*Psalmos, notas, cantus, compotum, grammaticam per singula monasteria [habeant] et libros catholicos bene emendatos; quia saepe dum bene aliqui Deum rogare cupiunt, sed per inemendatos libros male rogant . . . Et si opus est evangelium psalterium et missale scribere, perfectae aetatis homines scribant cum omni diligentia.*" *Capitulare ecclesiasticum*, March 23, 789. PL 97:177.

159. Bede K. Lackner, "The Liturgy of Early Cîteaux," *Studies in Medieval Cistercian History* (Spencer, Mass.: Cistercian Publications, 1970), 1–34.

160. DSAM 1:1440.

were always anxious to keep themselves free from feudal entanglements in order to ensure the survival of their monastic ideals. Instead of turning to the secular power for protection, they sought and obtained this support from the pope or from his legate.[161]

These few observations hopefully furnish sufficient evidence in proof of the fact that Benedict of Aniane is a greater figure in monastic history than is generally realized and not only paved the way for early Cluny but also for Cîteaux. He anticipated and traced the outlines of a number of ideas and practices which the first Cistercian generations adopted and transformed into genuinely Cistercian ways.

---

161. *Exordium Parvum*, II, VI, X, XII, XIV; J. Van Damme, *op. cit.*, 6, 8, 9. 10, 11, 12. See also *below*, chapter VII, nn. 144–148, pp. 270–271.

CLUNY (909–1100)

IT HAD BEEN THOUGHT for some time that Cîteaux came into being as a reaction to Cluniac decadence. The fact, however, is that in 1098, when Cîteaux made its appearance, Cluny was *in floribus*; hence it would be wrong to see the *raison d'être* of Cîteaux in the decline of Cluny. One must rather say that Cluny represented the epitome of traditional monachism in the second half of the eleventh century, a way of life Cîteaux will greatly alter in the direction of what its Founders felt to be the ideals of the Father of Western monachism. Thus, without Cluny there is no Cîteaux, and without a thorough-going knowledge of the former it would not be possible to understand the latter.

The abbey of Cluny in Burgundy, some twelve miles north-west of Mâcon,[1] rose at a time of general confusion when the Rule of St Benedict almost ceased to be observed.[2] The foundation was the result of an understanding reached between duke William of Aquitaine and Berno, abbot of Baume, in the diocese of Besançon, around the year 908. Both men were aware of the fact that one of the main reasons for the sad state of both Church and monasteries

---

1. "Protected by her gently swelling hills, she lay near one of the pilgrim routes to Rome, and close to the highways of the Saône and Rhône." Lucy Margaret Smith, *Cluny in the Eleventh and Twelfth Centuries* (London: Philip Allen & Co., 1930), xiiif. See also R. Graham, *English Ecclesiastical Studies*, 30. For the vast literature on Cluny see Max Heimbucher, *Die Orden und Kongregationen der Katholischen Kirche*, 3rd ed. (Paderborn: F. Schöningl., 1933), 1:183–188 and G. de Valous, *Le monachisme clunisien*, 1: Bibliography.

2. "At the beginning of the tenth century, the Rule had almost completely ceased to be observed." A. Hauck, *Kirchengeschichte Deutschlands*, 3:344.

was the latters' inability to defend themselves against lay and ecclesiastical interference. Thus when they formulated the charter of foundation in 909,[3] they agreed that Cluny should have its *libertas*, i.e. that it should be a free abbey, with full liberty to elect its own abbots, and with complete freedom from feudal, both episcopal and lay, jurisdiction. To ensure this the abbey was placed under direct papal protection. Equally important was the stipulation "that in Cluny a monastery shall be constructed in honor of the holy Apostles Peter and Paul, and that there the monks shall congregate and live according to the Rule of St Benedict."[4]

Led successively by such outstanding abbots as Berno (910–927), Odo (927–942), Aymard (942–954), Majolus (954–993), Odilo (993–1048) and Hugh the Great (1049–1109)—noted for their piety and erudition—Cluny prospered from its beginning.[5] Already

3. *Testamentum Willelmi cognomento Pii*, PL 133:843–854. Its highlights are 'I give and deliver to the Apostles Peter and Paul the village of Cluny, on the river Grôsne... with no reservations... I give it on condition that a regular monastery be established at Cluny in honor of the Apostles Peter and Paul, that monks shall form a congregation there, living under the rule of St Benedict . . . The monks have the power and liberty to elect as abbot and ruler the monk of their order whom they shall prefer, according to the good pleasure of God and the rule laid down by St Benedict, with no contradiction or impediment to this election from our part or that of any man. May they have as protectors the Apostles themselves, and for defender the Pontiff of Rome . . . from this day forward the monks united in congregation at Cluny shall be wholly freed from our power, from that of our kindred and from the jurisdiction of royal domain and shall never submit to the yoke of any earthly power." Cf. Joan Evans, *Monastic Life at Cluny 910–1157* (Oxford: Oxford University Press, 1931), 5f. See also E. Sackur, *op. cit.*, 1:40; R. Graham, *English Ecclesiastical Studies*, 30; U. Berlière, *L'ordre monastique*, 188; W. Williams, *Monastic Studies*, 20ff.; M. Mourre, *op. cit.*, 302f.; LTK 2: 1240; EC 3:1883ff., esp. 1887.

4. "*Eo siquidem dono tenore, ut in Cluniaco honore sanctorum apostolorum Petri et Pauli monasterium regulare construatur, ibique monachi juxta regulam beati Benedicti viventes congregentur.*" PL 133:849. Cf. EC 3:1887. On the history of the *libertas* ideal see Kassius Hallinger, "Zur geistigen Welt der Anfänge Klunys," *Deutsches Archiv*, 10 (1954), 437f.

5. Dijon, MS fonds Baudot, 1018, p. 114, corrected by J. Evans, *op. cit.*, xix. See also Gerd Tellenbach (ed.), *Neue Forschungen über Cluny und die Cluniacenser von Joachim Wollasch, Hans-Erich Mager und Hermann Diener* (Freiburg: Herder, 1959), 230ff. (Hereafter this work is cited whenever reference is made to Tellenbach, unless explicitly specified otherwise.)

Berno had jurisdiction over several monasteries, among them Déols, founded in 917. In March, 931, upon the request of Odo, Pope John XI solemnly confirmed the rights and possessions of Cluny as specified in the charter of foundation and subsequent charters drawn up when donations were made. Odo also secured the privilege of placing decadent monasteries permanently under the jurisdiction of the abbot of Cluny.[6] In 937 the Congregation of Cluny already numbered seventeen monasteries; this figure rose to thirty-seven in 994, to sixty-five in 1048 and reached the one-thousand mark during the twelfth century.[7]

The first abbots of Cluny—"better" than the popes of the period —were able to make their influence felt far beyond the confines of their monastery. Thus Cluny automatically became a center of monastic and ecclesiastical reform, advocating a renewal based on a combination of old and new principles of the religious life. The basis of this reform was the Rule of St Benedict, fidelity to the tradition of Benedict of Aniane, the already mentioned *libertas* ideal, a concern for the needy, and a strong stand against the evils of the *Eigenkirche* system exploited by feudal lords, both lay and ecclesiastic. Its success rested, in part, on the favorable geographical situation of the abbey—one could say Cluny was really in the center of the contemporary western world—on the quality of its customs and statutes, on its organization, uniform leadership, independence from local laws and the support of the papacy. The

---

6. "*Convenit apostolico . . . Quia petistis a nobis quatenus praedictum monasterium in illo statu, quo a Guillelmo duce per testamentum manere decretum est, nostra apostolica auctoritate in perpetuum constare decernemus . . . tibi ad regendum concedimus. Itaque sit illud monasterium cum omnibus rebus . . . liberum ab omni dominatu.*" PL 132:1046. Cf. ibid., 1057: "*Si autem coenobium aliquod ex voluntate illorum, ad quorum dispositionem pertinere videtur, in sua ditione ad meliorandum suscipere censeritis, nostram petimus licentiam ex hoc habeatis . . . Et quia, sicut nimis compertum est, jam pene cuncta monasteria a suo proposito praevaricantur, concedimus ut si quis monachus ex quolibet monasterio ad vestram conversationem solo dumtaxat meliorando vitae studio transmigrare voluerit cui videlicet suus abbas regularem sumptum ad depellendam proprietatem habendi ministrare neglexerit, suscipere vobis liceat, quousque monasterii sui conversatio emendetur.*" See also G. Tellenbach, *op. cit.*, 110.

7. Cf. E. Sackur, *op. cit.*, 1:300, 2:517ff. and LTK 2:1238.

times were really working for Cluny which soon became one of the most powerful monasteries in the West, the center of a truly great monastic congregation.[8]

At the beginning Cluny had no other norms to regulate its monastic life than the Rule of St Benedict and the eighty canons of the capitulary of Aachen (817), brought along from the monastery of Baume. Baume itself had escaped the general decline, largely because it had remained faithful to the reform of Benedict of Aniane.[9] According to John of Salerno, Odo's biographer:

> Those who dwelt in this place [Baume] were the followers of a certain Euticius . . . This Euticius lived at the time of the great Emperor Louis, and was well-loved by him, as he was by all, for he had an attractive personality. As a layman he was learned in unusual studies, but giving up all those things in which human weakness is accustomed to take pride, he devoted himself entirely to the rules and institutions of the holy Fathers; and from these authorities he took various customs and collected them into one volume. After a short time he became a monk, and he was so esteemed by the king that a monastery was built for him in the palace.[10]

This Euticius is Benedict of Aniane, the author of the *Concordia Regularum* and co-worker of Louis the Pious; hence the customs introduced by the monks of Baume in their new foundation (Cluny) were really the usages of Benedict of Aniane.[11] Also, as

---

8. Cf. LTK 2:1238f. and EC 3:1887.

9. E. Tomek, *op. cit.*, 179; E. Sackur, *op. cit.*, 36ff.; R. Graham, *English Ecclesiastical Studies*, 3; J. Mahn, *L'ordre cistercien*, 22 and G. de Valous, *Le monachisme clunisien*, 1:19, n. 2. Baume itself is in the diocese of Besançon (Jura). Cf. M. Mourre, *op. cit.*, 305.

10. "*In ea [Balma] namque erat monasterium nuper a Bernone abbate constructum. . . . Fuerunt autem institutores ejusdem loci imitatores cujusdam patris Eutici.*" PL 133:53. Cf. ibid., 54, "*Ipse enim pater Euticius institutor fuit harum consuetudinum, quae hactenus in nostris monasteriis habentur.*" See also R. Graham, *English Ecclesiastical Studies*, 2; and Gerard Sitwell, *St Odo of Cluny by John of Salerno and the Life of St Gerard of Aurillac by St Odo* (London: Sheed and Ward, 1958), 25f.

11. See ch. I, n. 1. Cf. B. Albers, *Untersuchungen*, 17f. and O. Ducourneau, *op. cit.*, 27. E. Sackur, *op. cit.*, 1:36 and 50n. 4; R. Graham, *English Ecclesiastical*

B. Albers noted, "In the life of Berno, the first abbot of Baume-Cluny, there are several facts which clearly show that Berno definitely followed or, at least, attempted to carry out the aims of Benedict of Aniane."[12]

Additional information about the early usages of Cluny may be gathered from Berno's will, from the instrument drawn up when Aymard abdicated in favor of Majolus,[13] and from the charters of the new foundations, such as of Déols and Romainmoutier. In his will, Berno exhorted his fellow superiors and monks, "to keep staunchly united, to observe, with the same exactness as before, the established usages in chanting psalms, in keeping silence, in the quality of food and raiment, and above all in the contempt of personal property."[14] Even more specific is the charter of a vassal of William of Aquitaine, who in 917 founded an abbey in his castle of Déols. It called for the recitation of the same number of psalms, the practice of hospitality, abstinence from flesh meat (excluding fish), the wearing of clothes in their natural color, the same obedience toward abbot and brethren, the avoidance of taking oaths, the practice of silence and contemplation, the total elimination of private property and other observances of this nature:

> We ask and implore the monks in the name of our whole religion and by the authority of the holy Rule, that they live in accordance with their calling, i.e., their monastic profession ... by keeping the same number of psalms, the same generous hospitality and the same total abstinence from flesh meat, excluding fish. Let their

---

Studies, 2; O. Ducourneau, *op. cit.*, 27; J. Evans, *op. cit.*, 9; and J. Mahn, L'ordre cistercien, 22.

12. Untersuchungen, 21.
13. PL 137:707f, n. 1.
14. *Testamentum Domni Bernonis abbatis*, PL 133:853–858. Cf. *ibid.*, 857: "*De caetero tam praelatos quam et omnes fratres, praesentes videlicet et futuros, per misericordiam Dei qui praesens respicit, deposco, ut inter vos unanimitas ita perseveret, quatenus modum conversationis huc usque retentum, tam in psalmodia, quam in observatione silentii, sed et in qualitate victus et vestitus et insuper in contemptu rerum propriarum.*" Cf. J. Evans, *op. cit.*, 9.

clothing be only of the natural color. Let them give the same obedience to the abbot and to each other, and let them completely abstain from oath-taking. Let them practice silence and meditation, and not have anything whatsoever that could be said or considered their own possession. Let them have identical usages also in other matters.[15]

This was also the program of Romainmoutier, founded by Agnes, countess of Burgundy, in 929. It called upon the monks of the new establishment to imitate always their confreres in the motherhouse [Cluny] in their way of life, the practice of abstinence, the chanting of psalms, the keeping of silence, the practice of hospitality, mutual love, humility, and obedience.[16]

Odo of Cluny saw in world-weary monasticism a fulfillment of the first Pentecost, a return to man's original state and the actual beginning of his future glory. Yet in a hymn which he composed in honor of St Martin, he described the contemporary monastic

15. *"Adiuro, ut nullus unquam aut praedicto loco aut rebus nostra vel aliorum donatione ad eum pertinentibus aut monachis ibidem consistentibus aliquam laesionem aut invasionem sive diminutionem per qualemcumque occasionem inferre praesumat, neque aliquis tanquam de nostra propinquitate praesumens ei quasi muniburdus aut advocatus per eandem propinquitatem existere nitens, hospitalitatem aut aliquod munusculum exigat, sed nec sub iure quidem commutandi aut comparandi de his, quae vel ad sepulturam vel in donariis quocunque pacto delata fuerint seu arte ad eundem locum quolibet ordine pertinuerit, aliquid exposcat, sed sicut unusquisque vestrum suas haereditates, portionem absque alterius inquietudine possidere voluerit, vel sic genetrici Dei et apostolis partem quae eis delegata est, tenere liceat. . . . Monachos autem ipsos per nomen totius religionis et sanctae regulae auctoritatem deprecamur et obtestamur, ut secundum propositum monasticae professionis vivant, et si non melius vel ad exempla istorum, quos ibi Berno venerabilis et reverendus abbas primitus posuit quique successores conversentur, eandem psalmodiae quantitatem, eandem hospitalitatis humanitatem, eandem ab omni carne praeter piscium perpetuam abstinentiam teneant. Sed et in vestitu nativum colorem solummodo habeant, eandem obedientiam vel abbati vel sibimet ipsis impendant, ab omni iuramento penitus abstineant, silentio et meditationi studeant, et nihil omnino, quod dici vel nominari potest, proprium habeant, sed et in caeteris consuetudinibus eundem modum observent."* E. Sackur, *op. cit.*, 1:380f. Cf. *ibid.*, 50, 52 and 63. See also G. Tellenbach, *op. cit.*, 89 and 95. If Déols was not actually a replica of Cluny, it at least complemented it. *Ibid.*, 96.

16. E. Sackur, *op. cit.*, 1:50. *Ibid.*, 51, the author, comparing the practices of Benedict of Aniane with the usages of early Cluny, as gathered from the life of Odo (PL 133:53), discovered a close affinity between the two reforms.

order as being near ruin.[17] To remedy the situation, he undertook many journeys, through France, Aquitaine, parts of Spain and to Rome in order to convince his contemporaries that their only salvation lay in a return to the ideals of St Benedict. Thus he became if not the founder, then certainly the moving spirit of the Cluniac reform movement in France and in Italy. He stressed that the Rule of St Benedict must once more be kept in its entirety. To gain his objective, he often restricted the ordinances of the Rule as interpreted in the tradition of Benedict of Aniane, seeing the essence of Benedictinism in a life of silence, prayer, work and frugality.[18] Accordingly, we read in his biography, "On ferial days in the day and night office together they sang 138 psalms" from which they subtracted fourteen "for the sake of the weaker brethren." And "during the other octaves, i.e. of the saints they sang seventy-five psalms only in the day and night offices together."[19] Knowing that no recollection is possible without silence, Odo insisted that it be strictly observed and made it a basic feature of his monastic ideal. He believed that "without silence . . . the life of a monk is of no purpose," that it "is of value as long as he takes pains to keep silence."[20] Yet no one should think that the cultivation of silence

---

17. "*Monastico nunc ordini Iam pene lapso subveni. Amen.*" Cf. E. Sackur, *op. cit.*, 2:331. Odo's basic monastic convictions—actually a reflection on early Cluny—are discussed in K. Hallinger, "Zur geistigen Welt der Anfänge Klunys," *loc. cit.*, 417–445.

18. "*Odo, inquam primus Cluniacensis Ordinis Pater qui emortuum iam, et pene ubique sepultum monastici propositi fervorem resuscitare suo conamine aggressus est. Defecerat suo tempore Sanctus: diminutae sunt veritates a filiis hominum. In cunctis pene Europae nostrae finibus, de Monacho, praeter tonsuram et habitum, nihil. Instituit ille divino operi fere tunc solus, et Cluniaci prima iaciens fundamenta, post, huc illucque Religionis semina, quandiu advixit, serere non cessavit.*" Petrus Venerabilis, *Ep.* VI, 17; PL 189:425 and PL 182:569f. Cf. also PL 133:71f.; U. Berlière, *L'Ordre monastique*, 194; J. Evans, *op. cit.*, 9f.; Augustin Fliche, *La réforme grégorienne*, 3 vols. (Paris: E. Champion, 1924–1937), 1:40f. and 47 and LTK 2:1240.

19. "*In quotidianis diebus inter diei noctisque cursus CXXXVIII canebant psalmos: ex quibus XIV nos dempsimus propter pusillanimorum animos . . . In octavis quas diximus, LXXV tantum canebant inter praedictos cursus.*" PL 133:57.

20. "*Quia de actu silentii sermo se intulit, sine quo videlicet ducenda est pro nihilo vita monachi . . . Vita enim monachi usque adeo est aliquid, donec sub silentio esse studuerit.*" PL 133:67.

is a "modern" invention, as some say in error, for there are the long-standing examples of Isaiah, David, and the Apostle Paul, and their imitators Anthony, Hilarius, John (Cassian) and Benedict.[21] All this may also account for the use of a sign language introduced, possibly, already in the times of Berno.[22] Odo worked with equal zeal for frugality in the monk's diet; to him it was a vice to eat flesh meat. Then he insisted that monks should live "sparingly . . . possess nothing of their own and . . . what they possessed they should renounce before all in the manner of the Apostles."[23] Nor should they exchange "their proper and accustomed dress," for "colored and flowing cowls and tunics" or "adorn themselves with a cloak."[24] To obtain effective and lasting results, he even thought of grouping the diverse abbeys into a strongly centralized congregation whose head would have absolute and unlimited authority.[25] J. Narberhaus, perhaps too strongly, speaks of a "world conquest" in this connection.[26]

21. *"Nullus arbitretur hoc silentium modernis temporibus fuisse inventum, sicut quidam male suspicantes fantentur. Hos namque et Novi Testamenti Patres, Paulus, Antonius, Hilarion, Joannes, ac postremum beatissimus pater Benedictus imitati sunt, et alii quamplurimi."* PL 133:68.

22. E. Sackur, *op. cit.*, 1:54.

23. *"Coepit eis suadere, ut ab esu carnium recederent, parceque viverent, nihilque proprium possiderent: id ipsum quod occulte habebant apostolorum more coram omnibus renuntiarent."* PL 133:81. Cf. *ibid.*, 79f., *"Non quibamus eis subtrahere ab esu carnis. Ordinavit autem pater noster in eodem coenobio praepositum unum ex nostris fratribus nomine Theodardum. Videns autem ille eo quod virtute nec sanctitate ab eodem vitio eos posset cohibere, coepit ex finitimis regionibus pisces emere."*

24. *"Ante hos itaque annos, persistente monastica congregatione apud ecclesiam beati Martini Turonis, coeperunt modum suum, consuetudinesque relinquere, ac propriis voluntatibus vitam suam propositumque corrumpere. Relinquentes namque nativa et assueta vestimenta, coeperunt fucatas, atque fluxas pallioque ornatas circumferre cucullas."* PL 133:75f. For an English translation of these texts see Gerard Sitwell, *op. cit.*, Odo even threatened with excommunication everyone who *"sive detrahenda vel impedienda conversatione, quam novelli fratres tenere visi sunt, contrarius existiterit."* PL 132:1076.

25. J. Evans, *op. cit.*, 10. *Ibid.*, 11 we read, "there was no question of real affiliation."

26. J. Narberhaus, *op. cit.*, 75 n. 1. Cf. PL 133:17, *"Odone praesertim abbate Cluniacum super omnia coaenobia cput extulit."*

The merit of Berno and Odo lies, then, in their successful labors to reinvigorate and spread the Benedictine Rule as interpreted by Benedict of Aniane and by themselves. (This "editing" of the Rule obviously contained the seeds of a further evolution which, sooner or later, had to lead to a confrontation with the old Rule.) On the whole, the early statutes of Cluny endeavored to help the monk remain devoted to a life within the monastery, i.e., detached from secular and even diocesan affairs; this means that the *desertum* and *solitudo* were present, at least as an ideal, at the beginning of Cluny.[27]

According to Peter the Venerable, every abbot of Cluny, from Odo to Hugh, made changes in the customs of the monastery, when the situation required it.[28] Yet Cluny had no official book of usages until the second half of the eleventh century. This, possibly, because in the age of heroes, when love, fervor and enthusiasm prevailed, there was no need for a code (which is more for the benefit of the lukewarm), and because the long reign of eminent abbots guaranteed enough stability and adherence to accepted standards. In time, however, disciplinary and liturgical usages and regulations concerning obedience, food, drink, fasts and clothing were put in writing, in order to ensure their survival, to have an authentic interpretation of a fixed observance at hand and to support the centralizing and unifying tendencies present in every reform movement.[29] B. Albers published three tenth-century versions of early Cluniac usages; one of these, possibly from the time of Odo, is really an elaboration of the constitution of 817, and deals with liturgical observances and the order of the day.[30] Further

---

27. G. Schreiber, *Gemeinschaften des Mittelalters*, 129. See also E. Sackur, *op. cit.*, 1:62f. and Albert Mirgeler, *Geschichte Europas* (Freiburg: Herder, 1958), 86.

28. PL 189:1025.

29. E. Tomek, *op. cit.*, 180f.; R. Graham, *English Ecclesiastical Studies*, 1; U. Berlière, *Ascèse Bénédictine*, 24–28; idem., "L'étude des réformes monastiques," *loc. cit.*, 139; V. Hermans, *op. cit.*, 116.

30. *Consuetudines Monasticae*, 2:1–24. Cf. U. Berlière, *L'ordre monastique*, 198.

versions are extant from the years 1000 to 1030 and from the year 1043.[31] Around 1068 the monk Bernard finally undertook a compilation of the customs of Cluny which he published under the title *Consuetudines cenobii Cluniacensis*. It includes the customs of Bernard's predecessors as he had learned them, regulations of the divine office from the time of Odilo, and a more original part dealing with monastic officials, finances, organizational questions and daily life.[32]

Some ten years after Bernard finished his work, the monk Udalric (Ulric),[33] while on a mission to Germany, was asked by his

31. PL 150:1191-1300. See also B. Albers, *op. cit.*, 1:1f., 2:31-61. Cf. E. Tomek, *op. cit.*, 53; Rose Graham, "The Relation of Cluny to Some Other Movements of Monastic Reform," *Journal of Theological Studies*, 15 (1914), 181; R. Graham, *English Ecclesiastical Studies*, 4; U. Berlière, *Ascèse bénédictine*, 29f.; idem, *L'ordre monastique*, 198, and EC 3:1885.

32. M. Herrgott, *op. cit.*, 134-359; *Histoire Litteraire de la France* (Paris: H. Welter, 1865ff.), 7:596; R. Graham, "The Relation of Cluny to Some Other Movements of Monastic Reform," *loc. cit.*, 182; R. Graham, *English Ecclesiastical Studies*, 31; Kassius Hallinger, "Klunys Bräuche zur Zeit Hugos des Grossen (1049-1109). Prolegomina zur Neuherausgabe des Berhard und Udalrich von Kluny," *Zeitschrift der Savigny-Stiftung für Rechtsgeschichte*, Kanonistische Abteilung 45 (1959), 135 and 140; idem, "Woher kommen die Laienbrüder?" *Analecta Sacri Ordinis Cisterciensis*, 12 (1956), 17; H. R. Philippeau, "Pour l'histoire de la coutume de Cluny," *Revue Mabillon*, 44 (1954), 145f.

33. Udalric's life can be gathered from several extant *vitae* (MGH, SS 12: 482; ibid., 251-253, 253-267; AS Jul., 3:146-161; Joannes Mabillon, *Acta Sanctorum Ordinis S. Benedicti* (Parisiis: apud Ludovicum Billaine, 1668-1701), 2: 775-793), as was done by Ernst Hauviller in detail: *Ulrich von Cluny. Ein biographischer Beitrag zur Geschichte der Cluniacenser im 11. Jahrhundert* (Münster, i. W.: Heinrich Schöningh, 1896), 5 and 20-53. For our purposes it will suffice to note that he was born in 1029, became a monk of Cluny and held various offices until his death in 1093. Already before embracing the monastic state, Udalric gave the impression of being a dynamic person, always busy with projects of one kind or another. He had a natural inclination for sudden and unwarranted fits of anger. An idealist, he never mastered his emotions. A restless and temperamental, but really talented man he never learned to keep things in a healthy balance. The consequence was that he dissipated his energies and relied more on chance than on shrewd calculation. His knowledge of man was that gained through the eyes of a sanguine person who sets out with a great deal of optimism, only to turn to bitterness and anger when disappointed. *Ibid.*, 4.

friend William, abbot of Hirsau (1068–1091), to make a copy of the usages of Cluny. Udalric agreed and completed the project, after his return to Cluny, between the years 1082 and 1084. At first he wrote only two "books;" when William asked for additional information, he added a third one, in 1085 or, in any case, before 1087.[34]

In assembling the material for his *Consuetudines*—called, paradoxically, *antiquiores*—Udalric made use of past contributions ranging from Berno to Bernard. Some authorities even contend that he simply abridged and rearranged the customs of Bernard.[35] Udalric himself told William, "Here are the customs of our monastery, as I have found them collected and to the extent I was able to know and remember them."[36] Since Udalric entered Cluny in 1061, it was easy for him to acquaint himself with the then prevalent customs and the usages of the immediate past. E. Tomek feels therefore justified in concluding, "We may rightly see in the customs written down by Udalric the usages practiced during the entire eleventh century."[37] Contentwise, the first book of the *Consuetudines* deals with the divine office and the liturgical life of the monks, the second with the formation of the young, and the third with details of the monastic administration.[38] K. Hallinger, interested in a critical edition of the usages, pointed out some "neglect and oversight" on Udalric's part.[39]

Since the Rule of St Benedict stresses, for the most part, only general principles and leaves a great many details unsettled, it is

---

34. E. Hauviller, *op. cit.*, 5f., 67f.; *Histoire Litteraire de la France*, 7:596.

35. PL 149:635–778. E. Tomek would not call them *consuetudines*, but executive ordinances, aimed at putting into practice the spirit of the Rule. *Op. cit.*, 174. See also E. Hauviller, *op. cit.*, 69f.; R. Graham, "The Relation of Cluny to Some Other Movements of Monastic Reform," *loc. cit.*, 185; R. Graham, *English Ecclesiastical Studies*, 25–27; H. Philippeau, *op. cit.*, 141–145.

36. "Habetis enim consuetudines monasterii nostri, quas collectas utcunque notavi, quantum ego scire potui et recordari." PL 149:638.

37. E. Tomek, *op. cit.*, 184f. 38. *Ibid.*, 70.

39. "Klunys Bräuche," *loc. cit.*, 131f. According to G. de Valous (*Le monachisme clunisien*, 1:21), the customs of Cluny developed like this:

important to study the customs of a monastery, if one wants to find out how the Rule was observed in that particular place; hence the need for an analysis of Udalric's customary which is almost a comprehensive code of Cluniac monasticism. Its study will also lead to a better understanding of Cluny's reforming activity. The high points of the Cluniac usages were the divine office, the Mass, the cult of the Passion, Holy Cross and the Eucharist, the Marian devotions, the veneration of the saints and the so-called *ars moriendi*. In all these Cluny made the world of symbols considerably richer.[40]

When the Cluniac monk took his vows, he promised stability, conversion of manners and obedience, according to the Rule of St Benedict.[41] Conversion of manners included poverty, i.e., personal poverty, for the community as such could own property. This

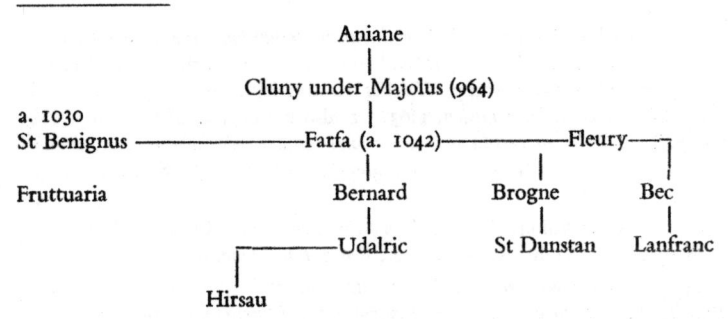

```
                         Aniane
                           |
                 Cluny under Majolus (964)
 a. 1030                   |
 St Benignus ──────────Farfa (a. 1042)──────────Fleury──┐
                           |                           |
 Fruttuaria             Bernard         Brogne        Bec
    |                      |               |           |
    ┌──────────────────Udalric         St Dunstan   Lanfranc
    |
   Hirsau
```

40. R. Graham, *English Ecclesiastical Studies*, 1; E. Tomek, op. cit., 295; Odo Casel (ed.) *Heilige Überlieferung. Ausschnitte aus der Geschichte des Mönchtums und des heiligen Kultes*. Festgabe Ildefons Herwegen (Münster, i. W.: Aschendorffsche Verlagsbuchhandlung, 1938), 263–284. Bruno Schneider who made a careful comparison of the Cluniac and early Cistercian usages found that the Cistercian *Liber Usuum* agrees with the usages of early Cluny only when this agreement involves the entire Cluniac tradition. Otherwise he noticed a greater affinity between the *Liber Usuum* and the Cluniac practices of St Benignus Abbey in Dijon. But it is also true that "Cîteaux often and unequivocally decides against the two customaries (of Bernard and Udalric)." "Cîteaux und die benediktinische Tradition," *Analecta Sacri Ordinis Cisterciensis*, 17 (1961), 98f.

41. "*Ego frater promitto stabilitatem monachi, et conversionem morum meorum, et obedientiam secundum regulam S. Benedicti, coram Deo et sanctis ejus in hoc monasterio quod est constructum in honore BB. Apost. Petri et Pauli, in praesentia domini N. Abbatis.*" PL 149:713. Cf. G. de Valous, *Le monachisme clunisien*, 1:55.

poverty was not so much an exercise in mortification as a means to assure liberty of spirit and to effect a detachment from material cares, imperative for a meaningful practice of the monastic vows.[42] It was strengthened by the vow of stability, an essential element of Benedictine discipline designed to counteract the evils of vagabondage.[43]

Since manual labor was done by lay servants, the priest monks of Cluny—unaccustomed to such labor on account of their feudal background—needed a more spiritual occupation. In this connection people still remembered the words of Paul the Deacon who said in his commentary on the Rule of St Benedict, that spiritual reading or the chanting of psalms may legitimately take the place of manual labor.[44] This is why liturgical functions took more and more of the

42. Michael v. Dmitrewski, *Die christliche freiwillige Armut vom Ursprung der Kirche bis zum 12. Jahrhundert* (Abhandlungen zur Mittleren und Neueren Geschichte, Heft 53; Leipzig: Walther Rothschield, 1913), 69f. and G. de Valous, *Le monachisme clunisien*, 1:63. Cf. also the charter of Ebbo of Déols, especially, "*sed et in vestitu nativum colorem solummodo habeant . . . et nihil omnino quod dici vel nominari potest proprium habeant.*" E. Sackur, *op. cit.*, 1:381.

43. Cf. G. de Valous, *Le monachisme clunisien*, 1:56. On the full meaning of Benedictine stability see C. Butler, *Benedictine Monachism*, 125ff.

44. "*Ille autem qui non potest legere, intelligunt multi quod fuerit intentio sancti Benedicti ut iungatur oratio. . . . Alii autem sunt qui intelligunt dicentes, non oratio illi debet iungi, sed solummodo opus. Sed superior sensus est melior; qui dicunt orare.*" Florilegium Casinense ex codice CLXXV. Commentarium Pauli Warnefridi Diaconi Casinensis in Regulam S.P.N. Benedicti, *Bibliotheca Casinensis*, Tomus quartus (Monte Cassino: Ex typographia Casinensi, 1880), 138. Ibid., 142, we are told, "*Si enim contigit ut quis habeat contemplationem tempore lectionis vel laboris; non illi fraudabit lacrimas sed ob hoc potest dimittere lectionem vel laborem et ire in oratorium causa contemplationis.*" Ibid., 96, the author declares, "*si post officium delectaveris, inspiratus divina gratia potes remorari in oratorio et ibi lacrimas tuas fundere ita tamen ut abba hoc cognoscat in te.*" Cf. also ibid., 85, on the possibility of choosing between work and reading. Elsewhere Paul the Deacon states, "*Nec enim credendum est hoc beato Patri Benedicto displicere, sed potius gratum ei esse, si quis supra id quod ille in Dei laudibus instituit, propter Dei amorem adjiciendum esse curavit. Nam et de psalmorum canendorum per singulos septimanae dies divisiones, si cui melius visum fuerit quam ipse beatus Pater instituit, ab ipso habet licentiam, ut melius aestimaverit, canere.*" Expositio Prologi Regulae Sancti Benedicti, PL 95:1595. See also G. de Valous, *Le monachisme clunisien*, 1:328.

time previously assigned to manual labor, as the Customs of Udalric, with their detailed provisions, conclusively demonstrate. Thus, whereas Matins originally consisted of twelve psalms, Cluny, besides taking over the *trina oratio* from Benedict of Aniane, increased the number to thirty. They added the seven penitential psalms and other prayers to the three psalms of Prime. Also, while St Benedict reduced the lessons read in choir during the summer, Cluny augmented them, with readings from the Old and New Testaments. Thus it took only one week in September to read the whole Book of Genesis, while six nights sufficed to read Isaiah. Fourteen prayers (versicles and *preces*) were added to Lauds, four psalms to every canonical hour from Matins to Vespers and two psalms and seventeen versicles to Compline, for the *familiares* of the monastery. Prime additionally included the Apostles' Creed, the *Confiteor* and thirty-one versicles. Psalm sixty-nine was said after every canonical hour and eventually also psalm 141, for the deceased. During Prime, psalm 141 was preceded by psalm fifty, in commemoration of the deceased abbots of Cluny. In Lent two more psalms were added to every part of the office. Then the monks went each day in procession to the chapel of the Blessed Virgin Mary, singing psalms eighty-four and eighty-six, with antiphon and collect on the way. Also recited in choir were the Matins of All Saints, with the corresponding Vespers in the evening. After the evening meal the monks recited psalm fifty while proceeding to the chapel of the Blessed Virgin where they prayed for the deceased members of the community. And since in time each day brought an anniversary, the entire Office of the Dead, with nine lessons, responsories and collects, was said daily. Lauds itself ended with an invocation of the Holy Cross and a lengthy commemoration of the saints, with antiphons, versicles and prayers—among them the holy angels, St John the Baptist, Saints Peter and Paul, all the Apostles and martyrs, St Martin of Tours, St Benedict and the Abbots of Cluny (Odo, Majolus, Odilo). This litany of the saints eventually included seventy-three names.[45] When visiting

---

45. PL 149:643-651 and 656. Udalric himself is at a loss to explain the

Cluny in 1063 Peter Damian observed that "the offices succeeded each other with such rapidity, that even in the long days of summer there remains only half an hour in which the brethren can talk in the cloister."[46] But, to continue the list, two and on occasions three conventual Masses were celebrated each day. The first of these was preceded by a short litany, where only three representatives were singled out from each class of saints. During this Mass the Introit was repeated three times in accordance with local custom, and the oration of the day was followed by six additional collects, i.e., prayers to St Peter and for kings, princes, bishops and abbots. The second Mass was to have no more than ten orations—for deceased Popes, friends, benefactors, confreres, rulers of Spain, relatives, for all those who had been buried in Cluny and, in general, for all the faithful departed—a practice which became world-wide in the contemporary *milieu* and was further strengthened by prayer associations.[47] Where monks of other monasteries had various kinds of activities, in library, scriptorium and school, the monks of Cluny went on to recite more psalms, whether in church, kitchen or garden, even while shaving, and this with a solemnity never

---

reasons for the diversity. *"Hoc autem non est mihi compertum quare ista diversitas a majoribus nostris sit inventa."* PL 149:645. Nor is he certain about the exact number of commemorations: *"Deinceps nominantur de sanctis plus minus septuaginta tres."* Ibid., 650. Cf. also E. Sackur, *op. cit.*, 1:57; E. Tomek, *op. cit.*, 187-190; J. Evans, *op. cit.*, 78 n. 2 and 81; S. Hilpisch, "Chorgebet und Frömmigkeit im Spätmittelalter," *Heilige Überlieferung*, ed. O. Casel, 2647 and J. Mahn, *L'ordre cistercien*, 23. A detailed description of the Cluniac liturgy can also be found in G. de Valous, *Le monachisme clunisien*, 1: the divine office (330-338), Mass (338-357), confession (357f.), the temporal and sanctoral (358-362), cult of the Blessed Virgin Mary (362f.), cult of the saints (363-365) and other liturgical functions (365-372).

46. PL 145:873f. The English translation is by J. Evans, *op. cit.*, 81f. n. 4. Peter Damian continues, *"Divinae quoque servitutis officia ita apud eos provide distinguuntur, atque pia ex industria protelantur, ut nec longioris diei aliquod spatium a divino vacare possit officio; . . . ita enim in ecclesiasticis atteruntur officiis ut vix claustrensi et honesta locutione, nisi signis, possit alter alteri intimare."* Loc. cit.

47. Cf. *supra*, n. 262 and PL 149:651 and 716. See also E. Sackur, *op. cit.*, 2:228f.; E. Tomek, *op. cit.*, 194f.; and S. Hilpisch, "Chorgebet und Frömmigkeit," *loc. cit.*, 268.

before seen. "Cluny saw its sole honor in being a house of God and a place of prayer."[48]

In a special chapter, Udalric gives a classification of the liturgical feasts, dividing them into six categories. Some of these were celebrated like Sundays. Others had additional adornments. This was the case when chanters vested in albs sung the Invitatory during Matins or when the main altar was incensed during the *Benedictus* canticle (Lauds). On such occasions the choir floor was usually covered with carpets. In addition two or four Gobelins were set up in the monks' choir, four or six in the sanctuary, and—on solemnities—all over the church. Five or seven candles were placed near the altar (instead of the usual three), and a great number of other lights were used all over the church, among them three huge candelabra behind the main altar and seven candles around the crucifix. The altar had three different covers which were taken off separately after certain parts of the night office. On solemnities there were more processions around the cloister, with the Gospel book, relics and torches carried along.[49] A special ritual was observed when the relics of saints were taken from Cluny for safekeeping, to protect them from robbers. This involved a senior monk, two candle bearers, a cross bearer, a thurifer, a minister of the holy water, three linen cloths, a cover, a bell and other vessels. While the church bells rang, the whole community followed the relic-bearers to the gate and then returning chanted psalm 119. The same procedure was observed when the relics were brought back to Cluny.[50] On the feast of St Majolus, the monks, joined by the oblates and, at the gate of the monastery, by the people of Cluny, went in procession—with relics, candlesticks, censer, holy water, three banners and bells—to the saint's chapel in the town of Cluny.[51]

---

48. S. Hilpisch, "Chorgebet und Frömmigkeit," *loc. cit.*, 264. See also J. Mahn, *L'ordre cistercien*, 23.

49. PL 149:654-656. See also E. Tomek, *op. cit.*, 211-213 and J. Evans, *op. cit.*, 82f.

50. PL 149:758f. Cf. E. Tomek, *op. cit.*, 230f.

51. J. Evans, *op. cit.*, 77.

A great procession was also held on Rogation Day when the monks went barefoot, carrying crosses and relics of saints.[52]

Cluny clearly accepted the view of Benedict of Aniane that nothing could be too splendid for the house and worship of God; hence its costly ornaments and its magnificent ritual. On Christmas Day, and on Easter Sunday, for instance, "493 candles burned in hanging chandeliers and five great candelabra burned around the altar; a light shone in each corner of the cloister and an extra light burned all night in the dormitory." On the feast of Candlemas, "half the church was adorned with hangings, twelve candelabra burned before the altar and five behind; on it were three golden chalices and two golden candlesticks. All the community went in procession, bearing relics, holy water, censers and candlesticks, and singing."[53] Years later, St Bernard will take exception to "the immense height, immoderate length, superfluous width, the sumptuous splendor and curious pictures" of the third church of Cluny constructed in the late eleventh century.[54]

According to E. Tomek, "Cluny's veneration of Mary surpassed by far every other example up to that time. From Cluny it found its way into the monasteries of the Cluniac observance throughout the West, especially those of the Holy Roman Empire. Through them it reached the people and developed into that cult of Our

---

52. PL 149:669f. Cf. *ibid.*, 670: "*Nudis tamen pedibus processionem ad ostium ecclesiae sunt recepturi.*" See also J. Evans, *op. cit.*, 84.

53. R. Graham, "The Relation of Cluny to Some Other Movements of Monastic Reform," *loc. cit.*, 186f., and J. Evans, *op. cit.*, 84. See also S. Hilpisch, "Chorgebet und Frömmigkeit," *loc. cit.*, 265-268.

54. "*Oratoriorum immensas altitudines, immoderatas longitudines, supervacuas latitudines, sumptuosas depolitiones, curiosas depictiones.*" PL 182:914. Peter Damian also remarked, "*Dicerem . . . quomodo ecclesia maxima et arcuata, plurimis munita altaribus, sanctorum reliquiis non modice condita, thesauro plurimo et diverso ditissima; quomodo claustrum ingens et ipsa sui pulchritudine ad inhabitandum.*" PL 145:874. The first church of Cluny was dedicated in 927. PL 133:98. The second, 140 feet long and 43 feet high, was consecrated in 981. E. Sackur, *op. cit.*, 2:372-375. The third church, begun in 1089, was consecrated in 1132. R. Graham, *English Ecclesiastical Studies*, 12, 555 feet in length, it had five naves and was the largest church of the time. One of its altars was consecrated by Urban II on October 15, 1095. RHF 14:109.

Lady which we so greatly admire in the High Middle Ages."[55] Long before Cîteaux, St Bernard and Prémontré, Cluny already championed a very special Marian devotion, particularly under Odo, Majolus, Odilo and Hugh.[56] It had a chapel dedicated to the Blessed Virgin,[57] and recited numerous offices in her honor. The *Credo* was sung during her Masses and the Marian doxology at the end of the hymns. Lauds and the other canonical hours (except Matins) ended with a special Marian commemoration, and in Advent more devotions were added. Udalric lists four great Marian feasts: the Nativity of the Blessed Virgin, the Presentation, the Purification and the Assumption.[58]

Cluny's relationship with, and indebtedness to Celtic monasticism has not yet been made the subject of extensive research. For our purposes it will suffice here to list such Celtic traits as the foundation of Cluny (and of other monasteries) by twelve monks; the jurisdiction of a particular abbot over other abbeys and the role of his monastery as the *matrix ecclesia*, i.e., headquarters of the "congrega-

---

55. *Op. cit.*, 222.

56. PL 159:887f., 890, 915. Of Odo his biographer reports, *"pater noster consuetudinem tenuit beatam Mariam matrem misericordiae vocare."* PL 133:72. Cf. Stephan Beissel, *Geschichte der Verehrung Marias in Deutschland während des Mittelalters. Ein Beitrag zur Religionswissenschaft und Kunstgeschichte* (Freiburg, i. B.: Herder'sche Verlagsbuchhandlung, 1909), 99 and 195. *Ibid.*, 310, we read that Odo introduced the custom of reciting the Little Office of the Blessed Virgin Mary on Saturdays, except during Advent, Christmas, Lent and the season from Easter to Pentecost. And Odilo, cured from paralysis through the intervention of the Blessed Virgin, *"omnibus votis dilexit, coluit atque pro viribus in omni vita sua glorificavit."* PL 142:897ff. Cf. E. Tomek, *op. cit.*, 45. Cluny's devotion to the Blessed Virgin Mary must be emphasized all the more, since Cîteaux and Prémontré have generally been considered the chief promoters of Marianism, as G. Schreiber pointed out in *Gemeinschaften des Mittelalters*, 143. See also E. Tomek, *op. cit.*, 39, 41, 45, 51, 222 and G. de Valous, *Le monachisme clunisien*, 1:362f.

57. *"Cum capella, quae est in honorem sanctae Dei gentricis Mariae et s. Petri App. principis."* Martinus Marrier, *Bibliotheca Cluniacensis* (Paris: R. Fouet, 1614), 1f. Cf. E. Tomek, *op. cit.*, 35.

58. PL 149:654–656 and 669. Cf. *ibid.*, 646f., 649f., 655, 659–661, 666f., and 683f. See also E. Tomek, *op. cit.*, 224f. and G. de Valous, *Le monachisme clunisien*, 1:362.

tion;" the cultivation of extreme poverty and austerity; the conception of the monastic life as a *militia Christiana*; the viewing of the monk as a *Christi miles* and, last but not least, the use of prayers for the dead and to the dead. Worthy of note is also the fact that Cluny had an altar dedicated to St Columban. G. Schreiber is therefore justified in saying,

> the ideals of the *desertum* and of *solitudo* were in evidence at least in the early days of Cluny. There is a definite line between Columba, Gall, and Eigil's *Vita Sturmii* and the foundation of Berno of Baume.[59]

Somewhat more is known about the influence of the Eastern Church on Cluny since it has been stated that, at least in its early history, Cluny revived certain forms and practices of the Eastern Church. It is certainly no accident that Christodulos, the great renewer of Greek monasticism and founder of the monastery of Patmos (died in 1101), when he came to Rome (1043) found the Cluniac reform quite attractive. Cluny had its contact with the East through Rome, which welcomed pilgrims from the East even after the separation of 1054, and through the Greek monks in southern Italy who lived near Monte Cassino.[60] If one can detect Byzantine influences on Cluniac architecture, sculpture and painting, it probably reached Burgundy *via* Monte Cassino. E. Werner even asserts that the papacy was quite pleased with these contacts, hoping for an eventual reunion through Cluny's cultivation of

---

59. *Gemeinschaften des Mittelalters,* 67, 90 and 129. The subject is briefly touched in Louis Gougaud, *Les saints irlandais hors d'Irlande* (Louvain: Bibliothèque de la Revue d'Histoire Ecclésiastique, 1936), 54. See also John Duke, *The Columban Church* (Edinburgh: Oliver and Boyd, 1957), 119, 121, 122f., 127 and Diana Leatham, *Celtic Sunrise. An Outline of Celtic Christianity* (London: Hodder and Stoughton, 1951), 187f. and 190f.

60. *Gemeinschaften des Mittelalters,* 129 and 414. See also E. Tomek, *op. cit.,* 210 and 214–216. Deno Geanakoplos adds in this connection, "during the twelfth century, the interior of the great French monastery church of Cluny was decorated by frescoes in so Byzantine a style that they may even have been done by a native Greek." *Byzantine East and Latin West: Two Worlds of Christendom in the Middle Ages and Renaissance* (Oxford: Basil Blackwell, 1966), 48. See also *ibid.*, 46.

eastern forms.[61] Whatever the case may be, it is a fact that ancient and medieval liturgical forms "carry essentially Byzantine characteristics."[62] Unlike their Celtic forerunners, the monks of Cluny did not engage in direct pastoral work. This caused G. Schreiber to remark, "The Eastern Church gained, once more, the upper hand in the ascetic life of the western world. Accordingly, the number of psalms was increased in the office as compared with the *pensum* of the Merovingian and the Frankish period, and the liturgy received its particular and far-reaching cultivation."[63] Yet, if "the soul of Cluny was liturgical prayer,"[64] and even constant prayer, this was not a Cluniac invention, but very similar to the anchoritic practices mentioned by John Cassian. Also, the great devotion to the Blessed Sacrament, long thought to have been of Cluniac origin, could already be found in Pachomius and others.[65] Likewise, Cluny's reintroduction of an ardent cult of Mary can clearly be traced to Byzantium which at the time was the Marian city *par excellence*.[66] Moreover, while E. Tomek still felt that the preparation

61. Ernst Werner, *Die gesellschaftlichen Grundlagen der Klosterreform im 11. Jahrhundert* (Berlin: Deutscher Verlag der Wissenschaften, 1953), 60 and 67. See also "Eastern influences on Cluniac architecture, sculpture and painting," ibid., 54–60.
62. Georg Schreiber, "Religiöse Verbände in mittelalterlicher Wertung. Lateinischer Westen und griechischer Osten," *Historisches Jahrbuch*, 62–69 (1949), 294. A. Baumstark, H. Eberding, A. Jungmann and T. Klauser produced new results in the field. *Ibid.*, nn., 35–37.
63. G. Schreiber, *Gemeinschaften des Mittelalters*, 346. *Ibid.*, 182, Schreiber writes, "The French monks of the eleventh century abstained from the exercise of pastoral functions in their proprietary churches. Every possible worth must be put in this statement . . . Cluniac monasticism stood in rigid opposition to pastoral activities by its members. For this Burgundian reform center which raised the liturgy to such splendor, saw in the conventual above all a man of common prayer. This monk was to render to God the tribute of solemn worship made possible through the fact that he turned away from the world and at the same time was denied the distraction of pastoral activities." For this reason the churches in question were staffed by secular priests. *Ibid.*, 185. Cf. also E. Werner, *Die gesellschaftlichen Grundlagen*, 19.
64. U. Berlière, *L'ordre monastique*, 195.
65. PL 149:757f. Cf. also G. Schreiber, *Gemeinschaften des Mittelalters*, 148f. and E. Tomek, *op. cit.*, 205.
66. G. Schreiber, *Gemeinschaften des Mittelalters*, 410f.

of hosts as described by Udalric was an original Cluniac practice, G. Schreiber was able to point to similar Pachomian practices, observed also by the Nestorians and Armenians.[67] E. Werner, who investigated the Eastern influences in Cluniac architecture, sculpture and painting, called attention to previously unknown or forgotten Eastern elements in the liturgy of Cluny. These include the cults of the Holy Cross and of the Blessed Virgin, the multiplication of Masses in intercession for the deceased, the preparation of hosts, the lighting of a candle on Maundy Thursday in adoration of the Blessed Sacrament, the manner of receiving Holy Communion, and on feasts, the granting of the *mixtum,* i.e., one fourth of a pound of bread and a little wine in mid-morning, and of the *pigmentum,* i.e., wine mixed with honey and spices. To this may be added the minutely detailed regulation of the monk's life and the emphasis on the representative, the splendid, the sacral element, with a corresponding de-emphasis of physical factors and engagements. Some eastern elements were, of course, known before 909; but they were given a special meaning by the great Burgundian abbey, as in the case of the *trishagion* on Good Friday, the distribution of unconsecrated hosts on Holy Thursday, and the institution of oblates and laybrothers.[68]

All this helped Cluny to produce its own *affective* spirituality which gained as much prominence in the Middle Ages as did speculative spirituality. Rejecting high-flung theories, subtle demonstrations and impractical abstractions and unaffected by the intellectualism of nascent scholasticism, it looked in its search for God for what appeals to the heart. Ascetical and mystical exercises had but one aim for the Cluniac: to produce God-loving acts without speculat-

67. *Ibid.,* 148f. Cf. also E. Tomek, *op. cit.,* 199f.

68. *Die gesellschaftlichen Grundlagen,* 36–53 and nn. 164–273. See also E. Tomek, *op. cit.,* 233 and St Basil's provisions about oblates. PG 31:955. For a comparison of Byzantine and Benedictine monasticism see Bernard Bligny, *L'Église et les ordres réligieux dans le royaume de Bourgogne aux XIe et XIIe siècles* (Grenoble: Imprimérie Allier, 1960), 249f. and *idem,* "Un aspect de la vie réligieuse," *loc. cit.,* 280f. Most useful, if not indispensable, is also Clément Lialine, "Monachisme oriental et monachisme occidental," *Irénikon,* 33 (1960), 435–459.

ing on the nature of this love. His piety found strength and nourishment in the celebration of the divine office; and because it issued from the liturgy, it remained eminently practical. It moved the monk to meditate on the mysteries of the earthly life of Christ and thus gave rise, long before Cîteaux, to the cultivation of the humanity of Christ in a characteristically Benedictine and eminently Cluniac manner.[69] Thus, according to S. Hilpisch, "not *decor*, but *affectus*, inner piety, became the watchword of the new piety" which received its stirrings from the liturgy; for behind all the grandiose pageantry there was really "simple adoration."[70]

The first abbots of Cluny "preferred a more advanced form of asceticism to the extreme and at times repugnant austerities then in vogue." While they demanded rigorous "control of the body," the customs they introduced were discreet and proved workable.[71]

---

69. G. de Valous, *Le monachisme clunisien*, 1:329. See also E. Tomek, *op. cit.*, 286.

70. "Chorgebet und Frömmigkeit", *loc. cit.*, 269. A. Mirgeler appropriately observes in this connection: "In addition to the extension of the traditional liturgical services Cluny also adopted the personal devotion of the ascetical movement. In the second church dedicated by Abbot Majolus in 981, the main choir was flanked by a cluster of side choirs which reached to the middle aisle in alcoves now called crypts. All these served for private devotion. That subterranean crypts of the dead became ground-level sites of ascetical practices shows as much a change in the saints' role as the litany of all saints before the conventual Mass. From miraculous protectors they became associates and models in the daily spiritual life." *Op. cit.*, 86f. And K. Hallinger adds: "To speak of an exclusively objective liturgical piety is simply out of the question. For the ritualism of early Cluny allows very 'unliturgical' practices. The individually personal, the subjectively warm momentum clearly raised its rival claims. Odo certainly approved the highest possible dedication in liturgical services, but—and this is important—his heart obviously belonged to solitary prayer. . . . Surprising is also Odo's criticism of the numerical multiplication of Masses, a common practice up to his time. . . . Even more surprising sounds his decided disapproval of liturgical splendor. He is against a *pomposa vox*. Personally he prefers a chalice made of glass. Also, in Odo's devotion to Christ the accent is not . . . on the solemn traditional liturgical king-representation, but on the guest of the heart. . . . Long before Bernard (of Clairvaux) Odo emphatically calls for a subjective spirituality." "Zur geistigen Welt der Anfange Klunys," *loc. cit.*, 433f.

71. Guy de Valous, "Le domaine de l'abbaye de Cluny aux Xe et XIe siècles," *Annales de l'Académie de Mâcon*, série III, 20 (1920-1921), 310.

In matters of food, the usages did not disregard the provisions of the Benedictine Rule; yet numerous exceptions were made, and in time these became the rule. The Cluniac monk's daily menu consisted of dried beans and vegetables from the garden. At noon, he ate his *mixtum*, a quarter pound of bread with some wine, and on weekdays he either had a *pitancia*, a dish of eggs and cheese, or a *generale*, i.e., eggs cooked with pepper, and pastry. On Sundays and Thursdays the usual dish was fish; fowl could be eaten only by the sick. Better dishes were served on special feasts; then onions and little cakes took the place of beans. On Sundays, Thursdays in Lent and on "double" festivals little hot cakes were given to everyone, and on the five greatest feasts, a little plum cake. On Good Friday the monks ate only dry bread and uncooked vegetables. Ordinarily the vegetables were cooked with fat, except on Ember Days and during Lent, and seasoned with salt (and pepper, if the beans were still green and tasteless). As a rule, the Cluniac monk received one pound of bread for the day, but if he ate it at dinner, he was given another half pound at supper. From Easter to Whitsunday the monks had dinner at midday and ate their second meal at sunset. This evening meal was meager; it consisted only of bread and wine, but after Quinquagesima Sunday a *generale* was served. From September 14, feast of the Exaltation of the Holy Cross, until Lent dinner was after None. In these seasons a second meal was served only on Sundays and feast days which included the octaves of Christmas, the feast of St Martin of Tours, and Epiphany. In Lent there was only one meal, taken at sunset. On workdays, understandably, a more substantial *pitancia* and *pigmentum* (spiced wine) was served at breakfast.[72]

Thus, while St Benedict allowed meat only to sick monks and granted wine reluctantly and limited food to two or three meals a day, Cluny—with its *pitancia*, *generale* and *pigmentum*—made a number of changes in the original regulations. In time these excep-

---

72. "De coquis," PL 149:726–728 and "De utensilibus coquinae," *ibid.*, 729f. Cf. also *ibid.*, 659, 696, 711f., 758, 760–763 and 786. See also E. Tomek, *op. cit.*, 200, n. 1, 253–258; R. Graham, *English Ecclesiastical Studies*, 35; J. Evans, *op. cit.*, 72, 89f., 91 and G. de Valous, *Le monachisme clunisien*, 1:310.

tions became the general rule. Apart from the diminished number of ferial days, only a very few fast days remained. This could happen because a *generale* was granted on every twelve lesson feast and on a number of other days the more simple *pitancia* was converted into a *generale*. Of course, the strenuous schedule of the monks and the rigor of the climate called for special considerations—and these were foreseen by St Benedict himself. Still, the practices of Cluny meant a further adaptation of the already modified usages of Benedict of Aniane.[73]

The same can be said in connection with St Benedict's original legislation on clothing. The wardrobe of the Cluniac monk made up an impressive and extensive list: two tunics, two cowls; two shirts; two pairs of drawers; two pairs of day shoes with straps; one pair of night boots of felt for the winter, another without felt for the summer; two pairs of gaiters; three pelisses, or—in place of one of them—a sort of short fur coat or cape; a hood made of skins; five pairs of stockings; a linen belt; a leather strap, with knife and sheath; and a case with needle and cotton. At Christmas each monk received a new cowl and a cape, on Maundy Thursday, new shoes and on the feast of St Martin, new socks; robes and drawers were distributed as needed.[74]

This change in the monk's wardrobe was, in great measure, due to such external causes as geographical differences, a rising civilization and changing times. Based on actual evolution, it took into account the prevailing realities and thus remained, according to E. Tomek, within the spirit of the Rule.[75]

Since material wealth and the availability of lay workers dispensed the "feudal" monk from field labor as a means of procuring his daily existence, manual labor as such remained only a symbolic remedy against the vice of idleness. Already centuries before,

73. E. Tomek, *op. cit.*, 257f. and J. Mahn, *L'ordre cistercien*, 23. *Ibid.*, 25, Mahn compares the Rule of St Benedict with the provisions of Aachen (817) and the customs of Cluny.

74. PL 149:707f. and 760–762. See also E. Tomek, *op. cit.*, 249–251; R. Graham, *English Ecclesiastical Studies*, 33; J. Evans, *op. cit.*, 78f. and J. Mahn, *L'ordre cistercien*, 25.

75. E. Tomek, *op. cit.*, 252f.

Cassian considered manual labor a distraction from contemplation, and Paul the Deacon expressed his belief that reading and the chanting of psalms could validly take the place of manual labor. In Cluny, which rigidly opposed the care of souls, this was done, above all, by extra offices in choir, by pageantry in the liturgy and, to a lesser degree, by such intellectual activities as the study of the liberal arts and reading. The common reading—this was after supper, when two meals were eaten, and after Vespers when there was only one meal—was usually taken from the *Conferences* of Cassian, a popular work about the early monks of the Egyptian desert. Not only the copying of manuscripts and the training of the young, but also the necessary house work was allowed to count as manual labor. This included such activities as the mending and washing of clothes, the cleaning of shoes and sandals, the baking of bread, cooking of food, service in the kitchen and cutting each other's hair. The Rule's prescriptions on manual labor were considered fulfilled if the community occasionally went outside the cloister to strip beans of their leaves and to pull out weeds; but even then the whole undertaking was reduced to a mere ritualistic exercise. The congregation started out in procession, singing psalms. Prayers continued in the garden. After working on beans and weeds, the group returned again in procession. The same performance was repeated in the afternoon. In the garden all first sat down and listened to the superior's homily. Then followed the weeding and chanting of psalms, which continued also during the return trip.[76] Psalms were

---

76. "De opere manuum," PL 149:675–677. Udalric remarks "*ego saepius vidi, non est aliud quam fabas novas et nondum bene maturas de folliculis suis egerere, vel in horto malas herbas et inutiles, et quae bonas herbas suffocabant, eruere et aliquando panes formare in pistrino.*" Ibid., 675f. Ibid., 677 Udalric records, "*quando fient in sequenti nocte duodecim lectiones, minime bis operantur.*" Cf. also ibid., 707f. and 729f. See, in addition, E. Tomek, *op. cit.*, 243f.; Henri Leclercq, *L'Ordre Bénédictine* (Paris: Les Editions Rieder, 1930), 43f.; R. Graham, "The Relation of Cluny to Some Other Movements of Monastic Reform," *loc. cit.*, 182; idem, *English Ecclesiastical Studies*, 167; U. Berlière, *Ascèse bénédictine*, 51–54; J. Evans, *op. cit.*, 85, 87 and 90; J. Mahn, *L'ordre cistercien*, 24; François Coucherat, *Cluny au onzième siècle. Son influence réligieuse, intéllectuelle et politique* (Mâcon: Académie de Mâcon, 1951), 36–39 and 77–87; G. de Valous, "Le domain de l'abbaye de Cluny," *loc. cit.*, 310; idem, *Le monachisme*

also recited during house work and related activities, and even while the monks were shaving.[77]

To counter unfavorable impressions gained from such practices, G. de Valous felt a strong need to stress that "contrarily to what has been repeated—and the fact itself merits to be noted—manual labor did have its place from the beginnings of Cluny; it has never been completely disregarded by at least some of the monks and in certain situations. But it has been considered solely as a secondary means of sanctification, and not an essential task."[78] U. Berlière even saw positive results in the gradual abandonment of agricultural labors, such as advances made in the arts, in the cultivation of letters, teaching, the copying of manuscripts and in literary productivity. But at the same time he perceived also danger signals.[79]

The community of Cluny consisted of priests, lay monks (the so-called *nutriti*, from the ranks of the *oblati*), laybrothers (in later times) and, finally, *affiliati, addicti* and *servi*.[80] As could be

---

clunisien, 1:309; H. DeWarren, "Le monachisme à l'apparition de saint Bernard," *loc. cit.*, 52 and EC 3:1887. On Paul the Deacon, see *above* n. 44.

77. PL 149:760. See also E. Tomek, *op. cit.*, 271, and G. de Valous, "Le domaine de l'abbaye de Cluny," *loc. cit.*, 310. The usages of Farfa, compiled around 1042–1043, give further details on the subject: if the brethren proceeded to work after Prime, they chanted litanies; if they went only after the chapter, then they started the *psalmi familiares* and continued them until they reached their destination. Everyone had to participate in this recitation, even the cellarer. Upon arrival the oblates went to the front, and all made a bow. Then the prior intoned the *Deus in adjutorium meum intende* three times, and continued with the *Gloria Patri*, the *Kyrie eleison*, the Lord's Prayer and *Adjutorium nostrum*. After this the brethren started their work and also resumed the psalms where they had left them off. The hebdomadary said the collects. Also during work the prior explained the reading. After work the monks returned to the monastery, again chanting psalms. When they arrived at the cloister, the abbot intoned the *Beatus vir* and the prior the *Adjutorium nostrum* and *Benedicite*. Then all returned to their customary duties, until the sacristan gave a sign with the little bell. *Consuetudines Farfenses*, B. Albers, *op. cit.*, 1: 144f.

78. *Le monachisme clunisien*, 1:311.

79. *L'ordre monastique*, 285. Cf. H. DeWarren, "Le monachisme à l'apparition de saint Bernard," *loc. cit.*, 52.

80. EC 3:1885.

expected, the traditional list of officials was increased and included in Udalric's enumeration: the abbot, the grand prior, the deans, the claustral prior, the *circatores*, the masters of the boys, the *precentor*, the *armarius*, the chamberlain, the *apocrisiarius*, the cellarer, the keeper of the wine, the gardener, the keeper of the refectory, the guest master, the constable, the almoner and the infirmarian.[81]

Following Greek practices, St Benedict had admitted oblates into his monastery, as the Rule indicates. By the time of Udalric, however, the practice had led to abuses in many places. This prompted the author of the *Consuetudines* to applaud its suppression at Hirsau which, in his words to Abbot William, brought so many one-handed, deaf, blind, hunch-backed and leprous infants into religious communities, that it caused the ruin of a great number of monasteries in France as well as in Germany.[82] Cluny, however, retained the institution and Udalric described the offering, vesting, reception, supervision, choir and chapter obligations, education, discipline, monastic investiture and profession of these oblates in great detail.[83] In fact, the institution reached its high point at Cluny. The boys took part in every monastic exercise, causing Udalric to exclaim with satisfaction: "When I saw with what zeal the boys were guarded day and night, I said in my heart, it would be difficult for a king's son to be trained with greater diligence in a palace than even the smallest boy at Cluny."[84]

81. PL 149:731-769. See also R. Graham, *English Ecclesiastical Studies*, 31-39 and J. Evans, *op. cit.*, 66f., 70-72 and 75.
82. "*Homines saeculares non magnopere curantes de alio, quam de hac sola temporali vita, postquam domum habuerint, ut dicam, plenam filiorum et filiarum, aut si quis eorumdem claudus erit aut mancus, surdaster aut caecus, bibosus aut leprosus, vel aliud hujusmodi quod eum aliquo modo saeculo facit minus acceptum, hunc quidem impensissimo voto ut monachus fiat offerunt Deo, quamquam plane non propter Deum.*" PL 149:635. "*Monasterii tui legem promulgasti, ut opus sit praefatis saecularibus alium sibi nidum providere ubi reponant pullos suos abortivos, velut exhaereditatos.... Ego autem certus sum illam te radicem funditus exstirpasse, ex qua sola praecipue omnia sunt monasteria destructa quae destructa sunt vel in Teutonica vel in Romana lingua.*" Ibid., 637. See also E. Tomek, *op. cit.*, 233 and G. de Valous, *Le monachisme clunisien*, 1:40-44.
83. PL 149:741-748. Cf. E. Tomek, *op. cit.*, 232-240.
84. "*Saepenumero videns quo studio die noctuque custodiuntur, dixi in corde meo difficile fieri posse ut ullus regis filius majore diligentia nutriatur in palatio quam puer*

St Benedict, it is believed, had no laybrothers in his monastery; in fact the institution seems hardly anterior to the eighth century. By the tenth century, however, distinctions were already made between *monachi litterati* on the one hand, and *monachi illitterati, idiotae, barbati* on the other hand. Udalric mentions *nutriti*, i.e., those who belonged to Cluny from childhood; *conversi*, i.e., persons who entered the monastery at a later age; and servants. The *conversi* were in a sense monks: they had their obligations in choir, took vows, received the habit and the *cuculla* (cowl) of the monks, could advance in the hierarchy of offices, become priests and even be elected abbots.[85] G. de Valous calls them, somewhat vaguely, "semi-monks."[86] More specific is K. Hallinger's observation:

> The *conversi* of the Cluny of the 'eighties (1080) were actually monks. They should not be confused in any way with the laybrothers, also called *conversi*, who could be found everywhere later in the century. These were not monks . . . . It must be remembered that the laybrothers are of a later origin; they are not the successors of the brothers of Udalric's time. The *conversi* mentioned by Udalric in the 'eighties of the eleventh century belong to a different, an older and specifically monastic category. With today's laybrothers they have nothing in common except the same Latin name.[87]

Around 1146 Peter the Venerable (1122-1156) listed *conversi*/*barbati* who belonged to the monastery, but were not monks. These are the laybrothers, as we understand them today. Their origin lies, then, between the times of Udalric, who knew nothing of them, and Peter the Venerable, who provided for them in his *Statutum*. An analysis of the privileges of Urban II and Paschal II enabled

---

quilibet minimus in Cluniaco." PL 149:747. See also R. Graham, *English Ecclesiastical Studies*, 153f. According to J. Evans, "Cluny was definitely not educational in its aim. Under Hugh the number of such oblates was reduced to six." *Op. cit.*, 47.

85. K. Hallinger, "Woher kommen die Laienbrüder?," *loc. cit.*, 15. Cf. idem, Gorze-Kluny (Studia Anselmiana, 22-25; Roma: Herder, 1950-1951), 1:522-524.

86. *Le monachisme clunisien*, 1:44 and 47.

87. K. Hallinger, "Woher kommen die Laienbrüder?," *loc. cit.*, 15.

K. Hallinger to conclude with reasonable certainty that a privilege of Pope Paschal, from the year 1100, offers the key to the question. It was there that, among "those who were accepted by Cluny and allowed to live in the abbey, *laici* are mentioned for the first time". At this time Cluny was given the right to have *conversi*. Accordingly, K. Hallinger concludes, "The codification of a right hitherto never claimed by Cluny points, therefore, to an entirely new legal situation with regard to the famous abbey. Cluny must have adopted . . . the practice of having laybrothers during the last decade of the eleventh century."[88]

Cluny's determination in 909 to follow the Rule in the tradition of Benedict of Aniane made the monastery a center of renewal from the very beginning. This vocation—and not mere greed or immense donations—prompted Cluny to found or take over other monasteries. Thus, with its own offspring and other monasteries submitting to it in order to be reformed by it, Cluny was destined to develop into an order. But the question is asked whether the early ties between Cluny and its followers were already indicative of a Cluniac congregation. According to Mabillon, the idea of a congregation as conceived by Benedict of Aniane was very much in Berno's mind. "Following his footsteps, Berno already headed a number of monasteries. In these he sought to have uniform observances, and during his lifetime none of these [abbeys and cells] escaped his attention."[89] This view is corroborated by Berno's will which ended with the words, "If there be, which God forbid, a stubborn deviation from any of them [i.e., regulations on the psalmody, silence, food, clothing and personal property] we order by the authority of the Holy Rule that the priors (superiors) of both places should assist one another and correct the error."[90] But while Mabillon saw no trace of any centralization in Berno's will, B. Albers, the erudite modern student of ancient monastic usages, came to different conclusions:

88. *Ibid.*, 17ff.
89. J. Mabillon, *Acta Sanctorum Ordinis S. Benedicti*, 7:67.
90. PL 133:857. See also J. Evans, *op. cit.*, 78.

I cannot adhere to his [Mabillon's] view. To me, the sentence "that the priors of both places should assist one another" means precisely to establish a central authority (*Zentralinstanz*), empowered to summon even abbots before this *forum* if they, in their stubbornness, permitted themselves to become guilty of errors. Centralization . . . is therefore envisioned and attempted by Berno. Everything was to be uniform in clothing, food and drink, in the psalmody, and other areas.[91]

Also U. Berlière saw in the unity of spirit and observance and in the bonds of charity and mutual assistance, if not the postulates of a hierarchical grouping, then the "embryo of a congregation."[92]

In 929, under Odo, the monastery of Romainmoutier was attached to Cluny so that it might form a single community with the latter. The event marked a new phase in monastic history: the establishment of intermonastic ties of a legal nature, i.e., the exchange of traditional monastic autonomy for the idea of a congregation of monasteries owing allegiance to a single head, the abbot of Cluny.[93] As J. Evans remarked, "Like his predecessors, Odo reformed many monasteries, but unlike them he tended to make these monasteries subject to Cluny. It was with him that the idea of a Cluniac *order* may be said to begin."[94] Majolus and Odilo then perfected it and laid its legal foundations. This order was based on the *traditio* principle of the feudal world and the idea of Benedict of Aniane which envisioned the union of all monasteries, in this case of the abbey of Cluny, and its affiliated houses and dependencies. With Pope John XI the papacy added its support to the movement, as can be seen from his privilege of 931. The trend continued so that by the time of Hugh, Cluny headed some two hundred monasteries, many of them dependent priories.[95] This evolution undoubtedly had its merits. An order was obviously more powerful than a single monastery or abbey, no matter how strong,

---

91. *Untersuchungen*, 22. See also *ibid.*, 21 and J. Evans, *op. cit.*, 44.
92. *L'ordre monastique*, 193.
93. K. Hallinger, *Gorze-Kluny*, 2:742, 744, 753 and 766. Cf. also G. Tellenbach, *op. cit.*, 117.
94. *Op. cit.*, 18.
95. R. Graham, *English Ecclesiastical Studies*, 7. Cf. E. Tomek, *op. cit.*, 38.

and could offer a more effective protection to the smaller houses exposed to the vicissitudes of the feudal world. Moreover it promoted unity and made collective action a reality in an age when the foundations of feudal integration were laid. With the progress of civilization the whole social fabric of the West came to be organized gradually on a larger scale. Kingdoms were built out of duchies, and great estates formed out of lesser holdings. Thus, as more and more monasteries came under Cluniac influence, Cluny and centralization became practically interchangeable.[96] The Cluniac system was, understandably, more primitive than later monastic organizations, for its edifice rested on such dissimilar pillars as royal monasteries, episcopal and papal *Eigenklöster*, dependent abbeys and priories, and mere cells. It was a rather complex unit.[97] The bonds which linked the Cluniac houses were, briefly, the visits of the abbots of Cluny, the codification of Cluniac usages, the suppression of abbatial titles in the dependent houses and, in later times, the convocation of general chapters. The priors of the various houses were all nominees of the abbot of Cluny, and with all their monks they were subjects of the same abbot. Every monk took vows of obedience to him and with his sanction. Also, abbeys restored or reformed by Cluny were quickly reduced to a dependent and subordinate status.[98]

96. U. Berlière, *L'ordre monastique*, 216; J. Evans, *op. cit.*, 18, 44; K. Hallinger, *Gorze-Kluny*, 2:736f. According to G. de Valous: "They believed in the necessity of collective action; this new conception of the monastic vocation displays itself very distinctly in the external organization of Cluny." "Le domaine de l'abbaye de Cluny," *loc. cit.*, 310. See also EC 3:1886.

97. K. Hallinger, *Gorze-Kluny*, 736f. In time the congregation of Cluny came to include (1) directly and (2) indirectly subordinated priories; (3) incorporated abbeys; (4) unincorporated abbeys under Cluniac supervision; and, finally, (5) temporarily attached abbeys to be reformed by Cluny. EC 3:1886.

98. F. Coucherat, *op. cit.*, 17–28; U. Berlière, *L'ordre monastique*, 215. J. Evans (*op. cit.*, 25f.) quotes from a papal confirmation of Hugh the Great's powers, to illustrate the point in question: "*Ut priores, monachi ejusdem ordinis ubilibet commorantes ac loca eorum . . . subjecta sint abbati Cluniacensi in spiritualibus et temporalibus pleno jure, promittantque ipsi, abbati, quoties novus instituitur, obedientiam; manualem et benedictionem recipiant ab eodem et reddant ad mandatum ipsius abbatis de singulis quae ad administrationem spiritualem et temporalem pertinent.*" Cf. *Revue Mabillon*, 1 (1905), 6.

The establishment of a genuine order under a monarchical head—soon to be imitated by Grandmont, the Carthusians and Cîteaux—necessitated, in the early eleventh century, the substitution of the traditional *decanatus* system with the so-called Cluniac priory system, in a clear departure from the Rule which had placed a dean (*decanus*) over every ten brethren. The modification became necessary because of the manors. The *decanus* became an official of the manorial administration under the Grand Prior, while the dependent priory remained the characteristic component of the congregation under the central authority of Cluny.[99] The system of concatenated monasteries both within and without Burgundy made Cluny one of the most powerful monasteries in the West and actively furthered what Schreiber called "the European idea."[100] The congregation of Cluny, as recognized by the decree of November 5, 1073, was thus based on the priory system, on stable contractual laws (*traditio, ordinatio*) defining the relationship between the abbot of Cluny and individual monasteries—for instance, the abbot's right to visit his dependencies—and on the acceptance of the (Cluniac) *Consuetudines* by the member monasteries. In the words of B. Albers, "the trend toward centralization moves like a red thread through the history of Cluny."[101] To prove his point, he cited the conclusion of Aymard's speech which designated Majolus as his successor and basically reiterated the words of Berno:

> We entrust the administration of the monastery of Cluny . . . with all abbeys, places and cells acquired in their [Berno's and Odo's] time or ours, to the just mentioned brother Majolus that regular life be observed according to St Benedict and the institutions of our Fathers and that things be administered with all integrity. . . .[102]

99. PL 149:738-740. Cf. J. Evans, *op. cit.*, 68; G. Tellenbach, *op. cit.*, 118; E. Werner, *Die gesellschaftlichen Grundlagen*, 12; and EC 3:1885. In this field the early Cistercians, though anxious to restore the original practices of the Rule, followed the example of Cluny. See K. Hallinger, *Gorze-Kluny*, 2:847.

100. G. Schreiber, *Gemeinschaften des Mittelalters*, 415. Cf. LTK 2:1240.

101. *Untersuchungen*, 22. See also EC 3:1888.

102. "*Et sicut Cluniacense monasterium . . . praedicto fratri ordinandum tradimus,*

Cluny took on added responsibilities when, urged on by his brother, Geoffrey II of Sémur, Abbot Hugh agreed to found a convent at Marcigny, in the year 1056.[103] Regular life began there in 1061, with Ermengarde, Hugh's and Geoffrey's sister, as prioress. Some nuns lived in common, others stayed in cells. To ensure complete separation from the world, a priory of monks, with twelve and eventually thirty members, was erected nearby, to look after the spiritual and temporal needs of the nuns, since the latter were determined to live in complete seclusion. In the words of a contemporary:

> The world being dead to them, they were dead to the world, and becoming unseen by all, after their profession they laid over their eyes and faces a thick veil, like a shroud. . . . Enclosed in this cloister of salvation, or rather buried alive in this sepulchre, they waited to change a temporary prison for the freedom of eternity and to change their burial for resurrection.[104]

Their love of seclusion is evident also from the nuns' refusal to leave their enclosure when the buildings caught fire, even though Hugh of Lyons, the papal legate, had urged them to seek safety on

---

atque tam ad ordinem servandum secundum beatum Benedictum et instituta patrum nostrorum, quam ad res disponendas sub omni integritate propitia divinitate vinculis obedientiae adstringimus." J. Mabillon, *Acta Sanctorum*, 7:771. According to G. Schreiber, "The purpose of this practice is to safeguard the reform under any circumstances." *Gemeinschaften des Mittelalters*, 92. See also *ibid.*, 143.

103. *"Non solum de salute sollicitus virorum, mulieres etiam de naufragio huius magni maris et spatiosi ad salutis portum educere curavit, eis viam vitae et doctrinis insinuans, et sumptibus sternens. In suo namque patrimonio, quod Marciniacus dicitur, quoddam monasterium et idoneas religioni construxit officinas ubi feminae . . . Christi complexibus astringi mererentur . . . Has profecto sub regulis hujusmodi vivere constituit, ut earum nulla vel rei necessitate familiaris, vel quolibet negotio conspectibus virorum offerentur . . . Procuratores earum, procuratores religiosi atque prudentes, sub quorum custodia nec possessio distractionem, nec honestas dispendium formidabat."* PL 159:868. Cf. *ibid.*, 949. See also GChr 4:486f.; J. Evans, *op. cit.*, 29, and R. Graham, *English Ecclesiastical Studies*, 18 and 21.

104. Translated by J. Evans, *op. cit.*, 29. Cf. *ibid.*, 30 n. 2, and F. Coucherat, *op. cit.*, 66–75.

the outside. In the name of her fellow sisters, Gisla told the archbishop:

> My father, the fear of God and the command of our abbot keep us enclosed within these limits until we die. Under no pretext, in no circumstances, can we pass the bounds assigned to our penitence, unless he who enclosed us in the name of the Lord should himself permit it. Therefore order us not to do that which is forbidden; but rather command the fire to draw back in the name of the Lord Jesus Christ.

Whereupon, as Peter the Venerable reports, the fire subsided.[105]

From the beginnings, Cluny had been the recipient of donations, i.e., of lands, churches and other gifts, in expectation of spiritual favors from the monastery. Beyond that, to promote Church reform, the abbey even solicited such donations. Accordingly, 270 donations were made under Berno and Odo, 219 under Aymard, 760 under Majolus, and 809 under Odilo, so that by the second half of the eleventh century the abbey had extensive holdings practically all over France.[106] The donors all felt that the monks' prayers would move the Lord. Their motives were numerous: some simply wished to join a prayer association; others solicited prayers or asked for burial in the monastery, inclusion in the canon of the Mass and enrolment in the list of the monastery's benefactors. Still others wished to express their gratitude for being accepted into the monastery or asked for the monks' prayers before going on a pilgrimage to a distant land. Prayers were also requested for enlightenment before an important decision, for the prosperity of a country, for victory and peace. Women liked to donate churches, hoping thus to ensure their own and their children's salvation. Donations were also made by the lower classes, to seek protection against feudal arbitrariness and to safeguard a certain minimal independence. Other motives of these donors were the fear of hell,

---

105. Petrus Venerabilis, *De miraculis*, I, 22; PL 189:890f. Cf. J. Evans, *op. cit.*, 30.

106. E. Sackur, *op. cit.*, 2:407 n. 1. Cf. Augustine Fliche, *Le règne de Philippe Ier, Roi de France (1060-1108)* (Paris: Société Française d'Imprimérie et de Libraire, 1912), 458 and EC 3:1885.

the wish to benefit from the monks' prayers, concern for the souls of the deceased and burial at Cluny. Donations were also made to have Cluny raise a son until he was old enough to join the community, to make provisions for relief in times of natural catastrophes (bad harvest, famine and similar disasters) and to obtain a *quid pro quo*, entrusting valuables to the monastery before pilgrimages to the Holy Land. Bishops, as a rule, were favorably disposed toward the transfer of possessions to Cluny and its dependencies, for the practice proved to be an effective measure against the *Eigenkirche* system, i.e., against the control of the lower church by the laity. Cluny, with its attachment to Rome as a counterweight to episcopal and lay feudalism, in fact, fought for more than two centuries to wrest private churches from the laity in order to return them to Church control. This endeavor met with particular success in France where a reform-minded episcopate actively supported the Gregorian program of freeing the Church from unlawful lay control. The success of Cluny lay in the fact that it was able to influence the laity with the soft voice of sentiment and symbol, by promoting the cult of the dead, forming prayer associations and granting burial to its benefactors. Cluny was taking over the spiritual direction of the secular lords! This had its effect. The nobility now hastened to give up churches, offerings, tithes and similar incomes, and donate them to the monastery. Out of this came the de-laicization of the lower churches (*Niederkirche*), a strengthening of the diocesan bonds, the abandonment of a bothersome co-ownership, in a word, a parish wholly under Church auspices with a definite improvement of the lower clergy's lot.[107]

107. E. Sackur, *op. cit.*, 2:228, 231 and 456. See also G. Schreiber, *Gemeinschaften des Mittelalters*, 99–125. According to Schreiber, this recovery of proprietary churches also had its dark sides: it changed the *Eigenkirche* into a new domain and made Cluny an economic and financial power strong enough to compete with the royal fist. *Ibid.*, 135. Yet, it must also be said that "He who sees the total impact of Cluny on Capetian France, he who appreciates its European outlook, will call this possession of churches a strict necessity. He will also find the zeal to acquire these proprietary churches understandable. For at stake was not just the recovery of these churches from lay control. They had not only an economic value but, beyond that, also an organizational importance. Only thus, i.e., by relying on its proprietary churches was Cluny

But it must be emphatically stressed that the program also meant an incorporation of the feudal world into the very life stream of the monastery, and this is something that the future Cistercians will categorically reject.

According to the authors of the *Gallia Christiana*, Cluny was "from its beginning free from all domination, except that of the Apostolic See."[108] As the charter of foundation stated, "the monks were to have the protection of those same Apostles Peter and Paul and the defense of the Roman Pontiff." This means, as William of Aquitaine further elaborated:

> From this day, those same monks there congregated shall be subject neither to our yoke, nor to that of our relatives, nor to the sway of the royal might, nor to that of any earthly power. And, through God and all his saints, and by the awful day of judgment, I warn and admonish that no one of the secular princes, no count, no bishop, not even the pontiff of the aforesaid Roman See, shall invade the property of these servants of God, or alienate it, or diminish it, or exchange it, or give it as a benefice to anyone, or set up any prelate over them against their will.[109]

---

able to exercise the full impact of its reform." *Ibid.*, 354. See also Paulus Volk, "Georg Schreiber Gemeinschaften des Mittelalters, Recht und Verfassung, Kult und Frömmigkeit," *Zeitschrift der Savigny-Stiftung für Rechtsgeschichte, Kanonistische Abteilung*, 35 (1948), 421 and 423. E. Werner, *Die gesellschaftlichen Grundlagen*, 6f., 12, 21-26; EC 3:1887; A. Mirgeler, *op. cit.*, 87 and Gerd Tellenbach, *Church, State and Christian Society at the Time of the Investiture Contest*, trans. R. F. Bennett (Oxford: Basil Blackwell, 1966), 79.

108. "*Fuit Cluniacum ... a sua fundatione liberum ab omni postestate praeterquam apostolica.*" *Loc. cit.*, 4: 1119. On exemption before the tenth century see Gaston Letonnellier, *L'abbaye exempte de Cluny et le Saint-Siège. Étude sur le développement de l'exemption clunisienne dès origines jusqu'à la fin du XIIIe siècle* (Archives de la France Monastique, vol. 22; Ligugé: Abbaye Saint-Martin, 1923), 13-22.

109. "*Placuit etiam huic testamento inseri, ut ab hac die nec nostro nec parentum nostrorum, nec fascibus regiae magnitudinis, nec cujuslibet terrenae potestatis jugo subjiciantur iidem monachi ibidem congregati. Neque aliquis principum saecularium, non comes quisquam, nec episcopus quilibet, non pontifex supradictae sedis Romanae; per Deum, et in Deum omnesque sanctos ejus, et tremendi judicii diem contestor, deprecor, ne invadat res ipsorum Dei servorum. Non distrahat, non minuat, non procamiet, non beneficiet aliquam personam, non aliquem praelatum super eos contra eorum voluntatem constituat.*" PL 133:851.

According to an inscription in a fourteenth-century copy of the charter, called *The Will of William the Pious:* "From this will it is evident that the Cluniacs were exempt from the time of their foundation."[110] But William could not grant exemption; only the Pope could. However, in March, 931, John XI confirmed the provisions of the charter[111] and subsequent pontiffs did likewise. In 952 Agapitus II stressed "that the said monastery pertains to the Apostolic See, for its protection and advancement."[112] Gregory V (996–999) went one step further to decree that monks "of that place [Cluny], wherever they may be, are not affected by the bond of anathema or excommunication of any bishop."[113] In 1016, Benedict VIII ruled "that it [Cluny] shall be free from all subjection to any person, whether king, bishop or count, so that its obligations are only to God, to Saint Peter and to the Supreme Pontiff of the Apostolic See. This freedom was strengthened and confirmed by all our predecessors ... for Cluny itself as well as for all its monasteries, cells, cultivated and uncultivated lands."[114] Later in the century Cluny jealously fought for the preservation of these papal privileges and found great supporters in Alexander II, Gregory VII and Urban II. The latter, in fact, bestowed more favors on Cluny than any of his predecessors. He confirmed the privileges of the monastery, granted the *pontificalia* to its abbots and, in a bull of 1095, decreed that no one should sue Cluny for altars, churches and tithes acquired before Gregory VII's legislation or obtained with proper episcopal authorization.[115]

110. "*Testamentum Guillelmi Pii—Et per illud testamentum apparet quod Cluniacenses sunt exempti a fundatione.*" Cf. M. Marrier, *Bibliotheca Cluniacensis*, 1f., and W. Williams, *Monastic Studies*, 30.

111. PL 132:1056.

112. M. Marrier, *Bibliotheca Cluniacensis*, 274. Cf. G. Tellenbach, *op. cit.*, 231.

113. W. Williams, *Monastic Studies*, 31.

114. *Ibid.* Cf. also *ibid.*, 28f.; R. Graham, *English Ecclesiastical Studies*, 41; G. Tellenbach, *op. cit.*, 97. See also PL 132:1055ff., 1068f., 1074f., 1082 and PL 141:1137.

115. PL 145:865–867; PL 148:661–666; PL 151:291 and 410; PL 163:51. Cf. also RHF 14:716; JL 5372; M. Marrier, *Bibliotheca Cluniacensis*, 514; A. Fliche, *Le règne de Philippe Ier*, 458–460 and L. Smith, *op. cit.*, 94.

To U. Berlière, "The Cluniac program is liberty *vis-à-vis* the secular power, for such freedom is the safeguard of independence and discipline."[116] K. Hallinger in turn insists that, from its inception, Cluny sponsored a strongly anti-feudal program—not its own creation, but the culmination of efforts undertaken by Benedict Biscop, Bede, Boniface and Benedict of Aniane—as can be deduced from its two-hundred-year struggle to bring the so-called proprietary churches (*Eigenkirche*) once more under Church control.[117] According to P. Schmitz, Cluny's success lay in the fact that it was able to transpose the ideals of feudal society from the social to the religious level.[118] A more recent authority on Cluny, G. de Valous, however, saw things in a different light: "Whether it wished it or not, Cluny was influenced by the society that surrounded it. It was affected, perhaps more than any other order, because its members were feudal, and it owed a great many features of its organization to the feudal system. In those centuries, when all power was based on the ownership of land, it was absolutely necessary for a monastery to secure a vast estate of landed property."[119] And understandably, for in the Middle Ages all power and economic existence rested on land; without it no monastery could possibly subsist or make any progress.[120] Moreover, as E. Werner put it, it enabled the monastery to offer economic, political and ideological benefits to every class of feudal society. Only by embracing and supporting the sociological interests of the tenth and eleventh century world, did Cluny become the capital of a vast empire; only thus could the Cluniac program hope for success.

A life of contemplation within the monastery did not isolate the

---

116. *L'ordre monastique*, 216.

117. K. Hallinger, *Gorze-Kluny*, 1:555; G. Tellenbach, *op. cit.*, 214; LTK 2:1239 and P. Volk, "Georg Schreiber," *loc. cit.*, 422.

118. *Op. cit.*, 1:146.

119. *Le monachisme clunisien*, 1:65. Cf. *Monastic Studies*, 3 (1965), 122 n. 3.

120. *Monastic Studies*, 3 (1965), 122 n. 3.

coenobium from the world, but permitted a better penetration into it. For it was the well-regulated life of the community which made it possible for the abbot to participate in contemporary politics and to fight for urgent social reforms.[121]

In H. Mager's analysis of Cluniac documents, the Cluniac priory system did not constitute a frontal attack on feudalism, even though the monks fought for freedom, as is evident from their immunities. G. Tellenbach similarly felt that Cluny was satisfied to carry out its reform within the existing order set up by the state's ecclesiastical legislation (*Staatskirchenrecht*) without any thought of transforming the latter. Thus, while it rejected feudal involvement for the individual monk, while it kept the ordinary monk within the monastery, it did not hesitate to seek an accommodation with the then prevalent feudal world in non-monastic spheres. In a number of instances it left the lords (of proprietary churches) and the advocates (*advocati*) in their places—though Cluny itself never had such advocates—accepted conditions as they were, and was satisfied with the acceptance of donations. In this view, Cluny's immunity cannot therefore be used to imply a struggle against feudalism. Far from opposing the traditional order prevailing between the Church and the contemporary world, Cluny retained a conservative stand by recognizing the legitimacy of existing conditions. In fact, Cluny could not be interested in a radical abolition of the *Eigenkirche* system, but actually had to defend it. The more possessions it acquired, the greater was the need for an accommodation between the monastery and the feudal laws governing proprietary churches (*Eigenkirchenrecht*). This is why Cluny sought papal confirmation of its possessions. Indeed the emergence of the congregation of Cluny is itself a product of the *Eigenkirchenrecht*, for Cluny had its own "proprietary churches" which it kept in a state of complete dependence. It could not champion anti-feudal programs, for how else could it have William of Aquitaine for its founder whose obvious aim was to secure a point of departure

---

121. *Die gesellschaftlichen Grundlagen*, 28.

Cluny (909–1100)

based, realistically, on existing historico-political conditions?[122] The impact of pre-Cistercian Cluny was therefore socio-religious rather than political or cultural. It must be stressed, however, that the great Burgundian abbey did not enter the stage of world history with a definite reform program or with specific demands it sought to enforce. It did not advocate the intensification of a given monastic principle or formulate a definite ascetical or ecclesiastical policy but was, one might say, by its very existence an antidote to the spirit of secularization in both monastery and Church.[123]

> The prevailing simony, the clerical concubinage, the rough and war-like ways of bishops and abbots were all corruptions standing in the way of any monastic or ecclesiastical improvement. . . . Cluny opposed them, in moderation however, and with considerable acquiescence in the apparently necessary conditions of the time.[124]

Its great and unfanatical spirit grafted the ideals of discipline into a harsh and war-like age and brought into the open the question of moral reform by directly castigating simoniac and nicolaitic practices within the regular church. Moreover, the abbots of Cluny,

---

122. G. Tellenbach, *op. cit.*, 214–216. Cf. *ibid.*, 118 and 211. On p. 119 a case is cited where the monks of St Martin de Tulle (Corrèze), together with their abbot, asked for a *pastor laicus* or *defensor*, in spite of bad experiences had in the past. "*Cernentes autem monachi privatos se esse pastore laico qui honorem illorum defensaret, consilio inito complacuit omnibus ut filium notum Ademari supradicti vicecomitis* (the founder of Tulle), *nomine Donarellum, exciperent ut eos protegeret; quod et fecerunt. Cumque quadam die eum honorifice Mulcedonum duxissent ut ibi staret, in ipsa quidem nocte aufugit ab eis velut stultus, quamvis esset. Qui cum mane illucescente eum perquirerent, non invenerunt, quia reversus ad suum stultum mercimonium fuerat. Tunc exosum eum omnes habentes dimiserunt in suam stultitiem perdurantem. Et post eum expetierunt sibi Bernardum vice-comitem Torenae ad sui defensionem et tradiderunt ei castrum suum Mulcedonum cum caslania. . . . et ipsam cessionem non fecerunt stabilem, sed tantum in vita sua, post mortem quoque ejus Sancto Martino remaneret.*" See also J. Evans, *op. cit.*, 15.

123. H. Leclercq, *L'ordre bénédictine*, 43. Cf. E. Sackur, *op. cit.*, 2:449.

124. Henry O. Taylor, *The Medieval Mind. A History of the Development of Thought and Emotion in the Middle Ages*, 2 vols., 4th ed. (Cambridge, Mass.: Harvard University Press, 1951), 2:375f.

frequent travelers in western and southern Europe to attend synods or other business, had first-rate opportunities to acquaint themselves with the actual situation. In this connection, it may not be out of place to think that, to counter neo-Manichaean inroads, they purposely began to draw from the heritage of the Eastern Church. This would help to explain the introduction of the feast of the Exaltation of the Holy Cross, the spread of Marian devotions and the promotion of various Eucharistic services. By exchanging men's earthly love of women for the supernatural love of Mary and by expanding and solemnizing the liturgy, Cluny was able to counteract the spiritualistic, anti-sacral and anti-feudal currents present in most contemporary heresies. The liturgical life of Cluny had thus its influence on the outside world. It enabled the monks to reach and influence also the lower strata of the population, to become the *confidants* of the poorer classes who always tended to see in them the representatives of a genuine Christianity.[125]

A study of the first five abbots' administration shows some connection between Cluny and the reform named after Gregory VII, at least in the earlier stages of this reform. This can be seen from the fact that to a turbulent and confused contemporary world in which the secular arm dominated the spiritual realm of the Church, it proclaimed that the jurisdiction of the Church outranks all claims of the laity. Hence it felt that the Church was justified in using ecclesiastical censures against unruly kings and secular lords. Moreover, like the Gregorians, Cluny also fought against priestly marriages, simony and other evils. Yet, its main concern was not the secular Church; its influence—though stronger than ever before —was therefore an indirect one. "An international power, by looking beyond the bishop to the Pope as head, it had enormously

125. A. Fliche, *La réforme grégorienne*, 1:60. See also G. Schreiber, *Gemeinschaften des Mittelalters*, 140 and E. Werner, *Die gesellschaftlichen Grundlagen*, 82–85. According to Werner, the liturgical usages stressed by Cluny, with their eastern ingredients, are a reaction to the heresy of the eleventh century and can be understood only from a sociological point of view. *Ibid.*, 85. On Cluny's hospitality, see PL 149:753, "*Illi qui pauperes recensuerunt testati sunt septemdecim millia fuisse, quibus et in Christi nomine ducenti quinquaginta baccones divisi sunt.*" See also R. Graham, *English Ecclesiastical Studies*, 36 and 39.

strengthened the prestige and power of Rome" (L. Smith).[126] Still, Cluny's role in the Gregorian reform must not be exaggerated, even if, in a Roman synod of 1077, Gregory VII acknowledged that

> ... among all the abbeys beyond the Alps there shines first and foremost that of Cluny, under the protection of the Holy See. Under its saintly abbots it has reached so high a stage of honor and religion that, because of the zeal wherewith God is there served, without doubt it surpasses all other monasteries, even the most ancient.[127]

It is a fact that the reform movements of the late eleventh century, which all stressed strict and even extreme poverty, were not directly influenced by Cluny. Some historians even see in the reform movements in southern France a reaction against the great Burgundian metropolis with its Carolingian traditions, at least as far as monastic matters are concerned.[128] This would confirm A. Fliche's conclusion that Cluny's role in the Gregorian Reform was not as great as historians generally thought for quite some time.[129] All one can say is that Cluny appreciated the ideals of Gregory VII, but, retaining an attitude of non-political reserve, left the struggle to the Curia. However, its administrative and fiscal organization served as a model for the popes of the period. Cluny always sought to retain its independence, even *vis-à-vis* the papacy, as can be seen from its clash with Gregory VII over taxation in Spain and the contacts it maintained with the emperor, Henry IV, during the height of the investiture struggle.[130]

At the end of the eleventh century Cluny remained the most

126. *Op. cit.*, xxvi. Cf. G. Schreiber, *Gemeinschaften des Mittelalters*, 140.
127. Translated by J. Evans, *op. cit.*, 34.
128. Charles Dereine, "Vie commune, règle de saint Augustin et les chanoines réguliers aux XIe siècle," *Revue d'Histoire Ecclésiastique*, 41 (1946), 389 n. 6.
129. *La réforme grégorienne*, 1:41f.
130. G. Tellenbach, *op. cit.*, 217 and G. Schreiber, *Gemeinschaften des Mittelalters*, 135. According to Schreiber the view that identifies the Gregorian Reform with the reform of Cluny is in need of an "unavoidable revision." See also A. Fliche, *La réforme grégorienne*, 1:60.

regulated monastery in France. From its beginning it had been blessed with extraordinary abbots. Doubly exempt—from lay and local ecclesiastical control—and with its direct allegiance to Rome, it maintained a central position in the Christian West. Noted for its wise economic policies, for its well-defined statutes and its brilliant organization, it was able to spread its reform through prayer associations (intercession for the dead; *suffragia*) and through the annexation and subsequent reformation of numerous monasteries. From a material point of view, the abbey was stronger than ever.[131] Were there any signs of a let-up? When Peter Damian, a man of almost superhuman asceticism and a convinced champion of eremitic life, visited Cluny in 1063, he could not hide his admiration for what he saw. Even though the monks did not lead a solitary life, he had reasons to praise their good spirit, the strict observance of silence, the cheap clothing, the never ending round of church services, the care of the sick, the support of the poor and an admirably non-discriminating hospitality.[132]

Cluny's influence was actually felt in all countries of western Europe. It is sufficient to recall the close ties of friendship between Majolus and the Ottonian house and Odilo's associations with the German rulers and with King Robert of France. To this must be added Cluny's social consciousness, its promotion of the Truce of God idea, its relief of the poor, its support given to travelers and pilgrims, its early participation in the Spanish *Reconquista* and its mediation in political conflicts. From the time of Leo IX the Cluniacs had a hand in almost every papal action, and Hugh the

---

131. Cf. Ursmer Berlière, "Les origines de l'ordre de Cîteaux et l'ordre bénédictine aux XIIe siècle," *Revue d'Histoire Ecclésiastique*, 2 (1901), 266; A. Fliche, *Le règne de Philippe Ier*, 465 and EC 3:1888 and 1890.

132. "*Etsi solitudinis habitationem non incolunt,*" there is "*cor unum et anima una,*" "*taciturnitas,*" "*vestium vilitas,*" "*ciborum vestium aequalitas.*" PL 145:873f. Peter Damian greatly admired the prayer life of Cluny which was so akin to that of the solitaries of Cassian. In line with the eremitic tradition, field labor had given way to the recitation of psalms, constant prayer and the struggle against passions. Cf. A. Louf, *op. cit.*, 195. In a way Cluny may be said to have influenced Romuald and Peter Damian. *Ibid.* See also PL 144: 374–378 and 873f; and R. Graham, *English Ecclesiastical Studies*, 42.

Great maintained contacts with more European bishops than any of the non-Cluniac French monasteries. O. Ducourneau even speaks of a "universal influence."[133]

The "essence" of Cluny is variously explained in terms of its liturgical splendor, its openness to or aversion from the world, its feudal greatness, or its exclusively monastic outlook. Accordingly its contribution to monastic development and its claim to greatness are seen in the restoration or, perhaps, updating of the Benedictine Rule to contemporary needs, in the implementation of Benedict of Aniane's legacy (ritualism; monastic reform; centralization), its *libertas* ideal, its piety and liturgy, or, last but not least, in the codification of monastic discipline by Bernard and Udalric in the eleventh century. This *consuetudo monastica* was the fundament on which the reform movement of the eleventh century rested. The *raison d'être* of this updating and adaptation—some somewhat unhistorically like to call it mitigation—is in line with the legitimate tradition of interpreting points of the Rule, which had made allowances for differences in time, place, and climate. It did not, as Pope Gelasius II stated, imply a weakening of the monastic vows.[134] Thus, even though Cluny went considerably beyond the ideals of Benedict of Aniane—it further expanded the liturgy, sharply reduced manual labor and made notable changes in matters of food and clothing—"it cannot be said that the Cluniac observance was a mitigated one, representing a broader and more humane tendency in the practice of the Rule."[135] The liturgy, the various

---

133. *Op. cit.*, 17. See also PL 149:736–740 (on travel); E. Tomek, *op. cit.*, 259; G. Tellenbach, *op. cit.*, 223ff. and H. Workman, *op. cit.*, 228.

134. "*Sicut in beati quoque Benedicti regula quaedam de hujusmodi observantiis scripta sunt quae nostris temporibus per monasteria longe aliter fiunt, neque tamen enim propter hoc monachorum professio creditur infirmari.*" PL 163:496. Cf. U. Berlière, "Les origines de l'ordre de Cîteaux," *loc. cit.*, 273; E. Tomek, *op. cit.*, 285 and *ibid.*, 180; G. Schreiber, *Gemeinschaften des Mittelalters*, 142; LTK 2:1239; Louis Bouyer, *The Cistercian Heritage*, trans. Elizabeth Livingstone (Westminster, Md.: The Newman Press, 1958), 7; and K. Hallinger, "Zur geistigen Welt der Anfänge Klunys," *loc. cit.*, 418–420.

135. Cf. *Monastic Studies*, 3 (1965), 125. See also U. Berlière, "Les origines de l'ordre de Cîteaux," *loc. cit.*, 275f. O. Ducourneau, *op. cit.*, 17ff. and J. Mahn, *op. cit.*, 23ff.

offices, and the two or three daily community Masses required active participation of the monks during the greater part of the day, silence was rigorously observed and common life, with its demand for unreserved obedience, its constant submission to minute regulations and its severe penalties for transgressions and violations, was a constant and permanent reality.[136] One may also add that, from the middle of September until Easter, fasting was not a rarity and that abstinence from flesh meat was absolutely enforced.

All this would not have been possible without the consistent leadership and the personal greatness of the first abbots of Cluny or without the close ties that linked Cluny to Rome as a papal *Eigenkloster* which safeguarded its independence and guaranteed papal support and protection. Moreover, Cluny had a hierarchical organization which effectively linked a multitude of dependent houses to the mother abbey. This was Cluny's own creation and proved most helpful in its role as a peace-maker and in its care of the poor and pilgrims. Cluny left a lasting imprint on Christian piety in the West, proved to be a powerful mediator between East and West and displayed politically a truly universal—European—outlook.[137]

While Cluny attained such heights, it also nurtured the seeds of its own decline; and this for a number of reasons. First of all, the rule of Cluny breathed more the time-bound spirit of 817 than the authentic, ageless thought of St Benedict. Its reform was not inspired directly by the old Rule, but by a broad-mindedness which allowed a free interpretation, with additions and ramifications suggested by experience.[138] Cluny went so far in the process

---

136. PL 149:705, 708f., 734. Cf. E. Tomek, *op. cit.*, 266–270; J. Evans, *op. cit.*, 86f.; G. de Valous, *Le monachisme clunisien*, 1:219-225; O. Ducourneau, *op. cit.*, 31.

137. B. Albers, *Untersuchungen*, 1f.; Alice M. Cooke, "A Study in Twelfth Century Religious Revival and Reform," *Bulletin of the John Rylands Library*, 9 (1925), 144; U. Berlière, "L'étude des réformes monastiques," *loc. cit.*, 149; G. Schreiber, *Gemeinschaften des Mittelalters*, 81; E. Werner, *Die gesellschaftlichen Grundlagen*, 27; LTK 2:1239f.

138. G. Schreiber, *Gemeinschaften des Mittelalters*, 142f. See also S. Hilpisch, *Benedictinism*, 49.

that it did not observe important provisions of the Rule at all: it practically had no field labor, it mitigated the rules of fasting, demanded little reading, increased the number of monastic officials, discontinued the novitiate as a year of formation and applied very inadequate methods in the selection of candidates—to mention only a few examples. The disappearance of agricultural labor and the overemphasis on liturgical prayer could not but upset the traditional balance of prayer, work and spiritual reading (study) on which Benedictine monastic life rested. Also the practice whereby the abbot of Cluny appointed—at least until Hugh's time—his successor, even if it was done for the purpose of safeguarding the monastery's independence, for the sake of continuity and for the elimination of discord, brought further modifications in the observance of the Rule. Some of these were unequivocal mitigations. For instance, while the Rule foresaw only infrequent recreations, Cluny had them—theoretically at least—twice a day (excepting Sundays and feasts), i.e., one after the chapter and the other after Sext. Greater allowances were also made in clothing, food and drink so that a comparison of Bernard and Udalric clearly reveals a Cluny becoming ever more relaxed. The monastic habit was no longer similar to what the poor of the country wore. The influx of donations made it, understandably, more difficult to maintain a life of religious simplicity in the monastery and, on the other hand, brought never-ending secular and feudal responsibilities which proved detrimental to an effective reform program.[139]

Cluny saw the monk's vocation in the solemn execution of liturgical prayer. But since the divine office did not require every hour of the monk's day and since the discontinuation of field labor

139. PL 149:666, 675–685, 726, 731–733, 741, 745, 759, 763. Cf. PL 137: 777–780 and PL 182:914f. See also E. Sackur, *op. cit.*, 2:26; E. Tomek, *op. cit.*, 47, 235, 381, 387; U. Berlière, *L'ordre monastique*, 195f.; S. Hilpisch, *Benedictinism*, 49; O. Ducourneau, *op. cit.*, 30f.; G. Schreiber, *Gemeinschaften des Mittelalters*, 143; Roger Grand, *L'agriculture au moyen age de la fin de l'empire romain au XVIe siècle* (Paris: E. de Boccard, 1950), 148; H. DeWarren, "Le monachisme à l'apparition de saint Bernard," *loc. cit.*, 50f.; H. Philippeau, "Pour l'histoire de la coutume de Cluny," *loc. cit.*, 148f.; LTK 2:1240 and EC 3:1885.

left additional "free" hours that had to be filled with some occupations, Cluny proceeded to multiply prayers and offices, with involved and complicated ceremonies, elaborate chants and a great deal of pageantry. All this—in G. de Valous' estimation, the divine office alone occupied from four to eight hours of the monk's day— left the Cluniac "pretty well breathless" at the end of the day so that many a time he actually preferred signs to the spoken word.[140] One may ask at this point whether the Cluniac solution meant any real advances in the liturgy. To S. Hilpisch the Cluniac formula was a mere accumulation of prayers and devotions.[141] C. Butler judged it "a transformation of the life designed by St Benedict."[142] According to U. Berlière, a tradition was created that the celebration of the office was not just the most important factor of monastic life as intended by St Benedict but practically the *only* occupation of the monks. This upset the equilibrium so wisely established by the Holy Legislator and led the order into catastrophe.[143]

Responsible for this development—and in no small degree—was the abandonment of manual and field labor. In this Cluny simply continued a trend begun under Charlemagne which saw only members of the feudal aristocracy admitted into the various monasteries, while St Benedict had made no such distinctions between free Romans, slaves and Germans (Goths). In the monastery these lords retained their servants who, of course, were not bound

---

140. *Le monachisme clunisien*, 1:322. *Ibid.*, 328 de Valous writes, "The divine office which in the mind of St Benedict is the most important factor within the framework of monastic life became with Benedict of Aniane and Cluny so-to-speak the only occupation of the monk." Cf. J. Mahn, *op. cit.*, 22f. According to U. Berlière: "Odo and his successors attached an extreme importance to liturgical prayer; they heightened its celebration by a great variety of ceremonies; they increased its splendor by a perfect execution of the chant, the splendor of vestments and beauty of edifices. The spirit of Cluny was really liturgical prayer." *L'ordre monastique*, 195. Cf. A. Cooke, "A Study in Twelfth Century Religious Revival," *loc. cit.*, 144; E. Bishop, *op. cit.*, 228; S. Hilpisch, *Benedictinism*, 49; R. Graham, *English Ecclesiastical Studies*, 42; H. Leclercq, *L'ordre bénédictine*, 43; R. Grand, *L'agriculture au moyen age*, 148; EC 3:1887. See also PL 149:668, 703–705 and PL 145:873f.

141. "Chorgebet und Frömmigkeit," *loc. cit.*, 268.

142. *Benedictine Monachism*, 359.   143. *L'ordre monastique*, 115.

by any monastic vow. Thus, and as a result of generous donations, the monasteries became great land owners, with numerous vassals and manorial subjects. To the monks, most of whom had by the end of the eleventh century become priests, servile work and household duties seemed therefore nothing short of degrading. Since in the absence of intellectual and related interests, study, reading, scholarship or public teaching could not be introduced as a substitute for everyone, the only remaining alternative was the already mentioned extension of the monks' prayer life.[144] In this connection some historians felt that it is no backward step to adopt a solution of this kind if physical work is considered degrading and there is a lack of sufficient talent for intellectual work, but rather it is actually the expression of a spirituality which is more affective than speculative.[145] Others, however, saw dangers in such a development. "The additions and supplements . . . made life at Cluny, if one observed it faithfully, not only laborious, but extremely tiresome."[146] The result was fatigue, tepidity, boredom, formalism and routine.[147]

Then there was the monarchical—and, one should say, un-Benedictine—system of grouping houses which enhanced Cluny's power and effectiveness, but on the other hand also had its liabilities. In the words of Butler: "Such a system cut at the root of the old family ideal and resulted in a kind of feudal hierarchy consisting of one great central monastery and a number of dependencies spread over many lands."[148] Some of the latter numbered no more than

---

144. PL 149:675-685. See also A. Cooke, "A Study in Twelfth Century Religious Revival," *loc. cit.,* 144; U. Berlière, *L'ordre monastique,* 196 and J. Mahn, *L'ordre cistercien,* 23.

145. J. Mahn, *L'ordre cistercien,* 23.

146. Alexis Presse, *La réforme de Cîteaux* (Dijon: Imprimérie Bernigaud et Privat, 1932), 5.

147. *L'ordre monastique,* 286. Cf. H. Leclercq, *op. cit.,* 43f.

148. *Benedictine Monachism,* 238. Cf. EC 3:188; A. Cooke, "A Study in Twelfth Century Religious Revival," *loc. cit.,* 143f.; H. DeWarren, "Le monachisme à l'apparition de saint Bernard," *loc. cit.,* 57.

four monks, and their priors were but shadows of the abbot of Cluny with no claim to their confreres' loyalty.[149] Given this excessive governmental rigidity and the absence of intermediate organs, not even the greater monasteries had any meaningful conventual life or, one could say, any inherent principle of life. The independence of individual monasteries was destroyed, in order to keep them bonded together under one man who escaped all control and, moreover, was frequently away from the nerve center. If this supreme authority fell into incapable or unworthy hands—as it was bound to happen sooner or later—the whole structure had to feel the consequences. And there was no remedy for such an emergency. In virtue of his greatness, the abbot of Cluny—whose legislative, juridical and administrative powers reached a new height by the time of Hugh—stood above the discipline of the *Consuetudines*. For a long time he was strong enough to appoint his own successor and to act like the Jesuit general[150] of later centuries. For instance, wherever Odilo went, he was followed, according to his biographer, by such a multitude of monks that, instead of seeing in him a leader and a prince, one would think to behold an archangel of monks.[151] In his *Carmen ad Rotbertum regem*, Adalbero of Laon (d. 1030), however, voiced different views about "king Odeylo, of Cluny," the commander of legions of monks, whose every order—even the most outlandish—must at once be obeyed.[152] In it the bishop of Laon sharply attacked the Cluniac practice of incorporating

149. G. Schreiber, *Gemeinschaften des Mittelalters*, 87–92.

150. U. Berlière, "Les origines de l'ordre de Cîteaux," *loc. cit.*, 457. Cf. also 453. *Ibid.*, 266 the author states, one might ask "whether the Cluniac system was a legitimate application, a justified interpretation of the mind of St Benedict." See also E. Tomek, *op. cit.*, 287; J. Evans, *op. cit.*, 25 and 35; G. Schreiber, *Gemeinschaften des Mittelalters*, 91f.; H. DeWarren, "Le monachisme à l'apparition de saint Bernard," *loc. cit.*, 48 and E. Werner, *Die gesellschaftlichen Grundlagen*, 12.

151. "*Quocunque exibat, quocunque praecedebat, tanta sequebatur eum frequentia fratrum, ut iam non ducem ac principem, sed revera putares eum esse archangelum monachorum.*" PL 142:9. Cf. E. Sackur, *op. cit.*, 2:98.

152. See *below*, n. 153.

monasteries with undue haste, ridiculed Cluny's claim to a *lex antiquissima* when, in reality, it cared more for novelties, and—in a fit of early Gallicanism—condemned the monastery's "ultramontanism." He also criticized the monks' worldliness, their provocative behavior and progressive ways and expressed his conviction that promoting them to various offices and social status would bring ruin to the Church. For if a quiet monk were sent to Cluny, he would return after a few days in a great cap of bear's fur, a long robe drawn up to his knees and split in front, an embroidered baldric with a bow and arrows, a hammer and tongs, a sword, flint, steel and tinder, and with spurred shoes and curled-up toes. Adalbero saw only one remedy: to call on King Robert to put an end to the monks' influence.[153]

Another critic was, at the turn of the century, St Bernard of Tiro who strongly objected to the idea of having an archabbot at Cluny. Finding no such institution in Sacred Scripture or in the Rule of St Benedict, he branded it a form of pride and tyranny, even, if the account is true, in the presence of Pope Paschal II. The incident may not be wholly authentic; still it indicates the existence of some pronounced anti-Cluniac feelings at the beginning of the twelfth century.[154]

Cluny championed an ideal which differed from that of St Benedict; hence it could not be lasting. Cluny's preponderance lasted for some two centuries; then the crisis came. It was brought

---

153. PL 141:771–786. Cf. E. Sackur, *op. cit.*, 2:94–100; J. Evans, *op. cit.*, 127; M. Mourre, *op. cit.*, 317 n. 4. A French translation, procured by E. Pognon, can be found in *L'An mille* (Paris: Gallimard, 1947), 221ff.

154. "*Cluniacensis abbas, juxta Isaiae vaticinium, ad uxorem meam hinnire non desinit et mihi qualicunque abbati tamen veluti archiabbas superba tyrannide dominari appetit; et quod nostra ecclesia ut ancilla sibi famuletur, sua regnet et imperet, efficere satagit . . . . Quod genus ambitionis novum et inauditum . . . hoc sane detestabile malum . . . . In litteris etenim collectis archiepiscopos, archipresbyteros, archdiaconos legimus; archiabbatem vero nomine, in illis necdum invenimus. S. Benedicti Regula (cujus ego professor, qui impetor, et ille est qui me impetit, ut abbas solummodo jus disponendi omnia in suo monasterio habeat, constituit; de archiabbate vero penitus tacuit.*" PL 172:1401f. See also D. Knowles, *The Monastic Order in England*, 201.

on by difficulties of an economic nature and, even more, by an exaggerated spirituality, a ritualistic relaxation of monastic fervor, a gradual alienation from Rome, structural weaknesses, a tendency to incorporate monasteries under false pretexts or through coercive methods, an attempt to monopolize the monastic order, a feudalization of the monastic offices and an increasing involvement—at times not entirely unselfishly, as when promoting the Truce of God in order to shield its possessions against feudal wars—in feudal and political affairs. Cluniac monasteries thus became, more and more, refuges for the feudal nobility where eating, drinking and a work-free existence soon took precedence over the spiritual ideals of monasticism. Too closely tied to the feudal world, Cluny was finally unable to satisfy the great number of generous souls who emerged in great numbers at the end of the eleventh century looking for a life of seclusion, poverty and asceticism. Nor was it able to attract, much less to absorb, the great *pauperes Christi* movement which was gaining momentum at the close of the eleventh century.[155] Cluny, as G. Schreiber concluded, had fulfilled its mission:

> The new foundations of Cîteaux and Prémontré could only emerge after Cluny had completed its work on the *Eigenkirche*. The whole atmosphere which surrounded these new foundations —the *Exordium Parvum* rejects cities—called, *a priori*, for that minimal measure of delaicization and purification (*Verkirchlichung*) which Cluny had brought to the lower Church. Only

---

155. LTK 2:1240. See also E. Tomek, *op. cit.*, 287; R. Grand, *L'agriculture au moyen age*, 148; H. DeWarren, "Le monachisme à l'apparition de saint Bernard," *loc. cit.*, 48; E. Werner, *Die gesellschaftlichen Grundlagen*, 27 and 103f.; Augustin Fliche, *Histoire de l'Eglise depuis les origines jusqu'à nos jours*. Vol. VIII: *La Réforme grégorienne et la reconquête chrétienne (1057–1123)* (Paris: Bloud & Gay, 1950), 466 and G. Tellenbach, *Church, State and Christian Society*, 82. According to K. Hallinger, such factors as the acceptance of *conversi*, the establishment of large communities, the appointment of the abbot of Cluny by his predecessor, the exclusion of non-monks from elections, centralization and the amovability of the local priors, clearly show that Cluny did not adopt secular feudalism *in toto*: "Zur geistigen Welt der Anfänge Klunys," *loc. cit.*, 439. This may be so, but it must not be forgotten that Cluny set up a feudal system of its own.

Cluny (909–1100)

now was the road free for these new foundations in France. With the exception of inconsequential individual cases, Cîteaux and Prémontré no longer needed to busy themselves with the transfer of lay churches. Cluny and its priories had done their invaluable spadework for Alberic and Stephen Harding.[156]

Thus, Cluny really paved the way for Cîteaux.

---

156. *Gemeinschaften des Mittelalters*, 136. See also *ibid.*, 355f.: "At the close of the eleventh century Cluny emerges as a powerful economic empire. And this, basically, because one had to see in it the proprietor of a great many churches. The Cistercian ideal on the other hand brings a restoration and intensification of the poverty ideal. The turn to the *vita apostolica* is stressed. Cîteaux wants the primitiveness, the simplicity and plainness of this *vita apostolica* . . . and stresses that the monk should live from his own work." See also E. Werner, *Die gesellschaftlichen Grundlagen*, 112.

THE CRISIS OF CENOBITISM

TRADITIONAL MONACHISM experienced a serious crisis in the eleventh century, a crisis which began around 1050 AD and lasted, roughly, for one hundred years. Germain Morin called it a "crisis of cenobitism."[1] According to Jean Leclercq it was basically a crisis brought on by material wealth.[2] This is undoubtedly true, but not exclusively so, for there were other factors contributing to the difficulties. It would therefore be better to say that the crux of the problem was the insufficiency of the Benedictine and Cluniac formula to satisfy generous souls already on the lookout for new solutions. One of the latter was Cîteaux; a consideration of the "crisis" will therefore furnish both background and perspective for the events of 1098.

In the long history of monasticism, religious houses made their appearance both in the vicinity of cities (urban monachism) and in the countryside, i.e. far from human settlements (eremitic monachism). Both forms had their advantages and their legitimation in tradition. In the eleventh century, however, the trend moved toward setting up monasteries in the immediate vicinity of cities or within the periphery of fortified places. One reason for this development was undoubtedly the need for shelter; another was the hazardous situation in the face of intermittent Norse and

---

1. Germain Morin, "Rainaud l'Ermite et Ives de Chartres: un épisode de la crise du cénobitisme au XIe-XIIe siècle," *Revue Bénédictine*, 40 (1928), 99–115.

2. Jean Leclercq, "La crise du monachisme aux XIe et XIIe siècles," *Bolletino dell'Istituto Storico Italiano per il Medio Evo e Archivio Muratoriano*, 70 (1959), 24.

Hungarian raids and, later, the perils brought on by constant feudal skirmishes. Moreover, in some instances monks were put in charge of cathedral churches. Then too, abbeys—always practicing hospitality—began to attract a steady populace and thus became population centers. One has only to think of the markets held on monastic grounds, of the flow of donations and the monks' eagerness to round out their possessions through the acquisition of adjacent lands. This in turn brought tenants and rentiers and then artisans, merchants and other small holders to the immediate vicinity of monasteries, a situation advantageous to and welcomed by both sides. It enabled the monks—whether this was good or not—to give up field labor and, to a lesser extent, even household work. The new population for its part could expect help from the monks in times of distress and, being under the abbot's jurisdiction, enjoy legal protection from the whims of lay lords. This, of course, had its impact on monastic life. It resulted, as contemporary critics hastened to point out, in a new mentality and a different outlook on liturgy and manual labor.[3]

One of these critics was Raynald of the Melinais. A canon regular, he became an itinerant preacher and eventually retired into the solitude of Craon where he died in 1103.[4] His experiences caused him to compose a satire on claustral life as observed in urban surroundings. Convinced that it is extremely difficult to keep the evangelical counsels and follow the example of the apostles in such an atmosphere, Raynald strongly condemned the idea of having monasteries in, or too close to cities where one can hear the noisy dancing and chattering of women from the monks' dormitory. These allurements will inevitably arouse human curiosity and the con-

---

3. J. Leclercq, "La crise du monachisme," *loc. cit.*, 19f. See also E. Sackur, *op. cit.*, 2:215, 416f., 431 and 433f.; H. DeWarren, "Le monachisme à l'apparition de saint Bernard," *loc. cit.*, 51 and E. Werner, *Die gesellschaftlichen Grundlagen*, 26. According to E. Sackur, there was regular international commerce in the abbeys of William of Dijon where one could find Frenchmen, Englishmen, Germans and even Italians and Greeks; *op. cit.*, 2:212.

4. G. Morin, "Rainaud l'Ermite," *loc. cit.*, 113f.

sequence will be that monks will seek the opportunity to speak with women.[5]

As Paul Giseke writes on the subject:

The peaceful quiet of monastic seclusion has disappeared long ago. This, because the monks lived in the center of a busy world: near highways and populous settlements. And there was no traveller on the road who did not pay a visit to hospitable monasteries. Excepting noon, both gate and hostel were open all day without any discrimination so that a colorful medley of all kinds of people—priests and knights, peasants and vassals, entertainers and, especially, all sorts of hirelings and servants—could enter and leave, either because of the attention received in the hostel, or drawn by curiosity or else because of business, so that the monastery looked like an open street. Nor were women excluded from the hospitality of the guest-house: the wives of manorial officials, in particular, had the right to visit there.[6]

In this situation, the popular view of a monastery was that of a constantly occupied community busy with elaborate and lengthy church services. People did not look for contemplative ascetics within the confines of those impressive and much-decorated monastic buildings which had come to house the monks. They also took note of the changes made in the monks' food, clothing and discipline—changes which solved some problems but also created a host of new difficulties.

It has already been described how Cluny enriched the monk's wardrobe. It also provided more comfortable sleeping quarters than

---

5. "*Quid dicemus de his, qui in urbibus commorantes saepius audiunt ab ipso dormitorio ipsas mulierum cantilenas, et earum strepitus, et choreas, et inquirunt principum et vulgi rumores, et aliquando videntur, et locuntur cum mulieribus, et habitant inter fumantes coquinas?*" G. Morin, "Rainaud l'Ermite," *loc. cit.*, 109. Cf. also *ibid.*, 105. Raynald's conclusion is, "*Nosti quia evangelicis apostolicisque sanctionibus obedire necessarium est; hoc autem vix aut numquam in coenobiis urbe vel oppido constitutis fieri potest.*" *Ibid.*, 103.

6. Paul Giseke, "Ueber den Gegensatz der Cluniazenser und Cistercienser," *Jahrbuch des Pädagogiums zum Kloster Unser Lieben Frauen in Magdeburg*, 50 1886), 17.

envisioned by the Rule and allowed the monks to sleep in shirt and pelisse, whereas St Benedict expressly wished that the monks sleep fully dressed. Similarly, while the Rule mentions no morning sleep, Cluny advanced Lauds and deferred Prime so that the monks could return to bed after Lauds. In the refectory, Cluny abstained from blessing the dishes not specified by the Rule in the belief that in such case they would not count as additional dishes. As for drinks, the Rule of St Benedict was interpreted in such a way that every monk received his full measure of wine at each meal, even if during Lent one meal was omitted. After the office of None the monks went to the refectory for a drink, whether they were thirsty or not, and before the evening reading (*collatio*) there was another *bibitio*. These practices had their inevitable effects on fasting so that only fragments of the old Benedictine observances remained. These original rules also prescribed that the monks should keep silence at all times and speak only when answering questions. Cluny developed sign language into an art and, moreover, permitted talking in the cloister after chapter. But a monk could only talk after he took a book in his hand and sat down; this in order to keep at least the letter of the Rule stating that all should sit while one of the monks will read from a book which edifies the audience. The life of the monk was now spent in prayer and, to a lesser degree, in reading. The former —with all the additions to the Benedictine *pensum* and its highly elaborate ceremonial—occupied most of the monk's time. Priests in church wore costly vestments, and on great feasts the entire community, monks and brothers, went to the services in albs and maniples. The effect of singing was heightened by the use of the falsetto; to gain ease in the latter, the monks drank a special juice obtained from sweet wood. Also, while the Rule wished that a novice take his vows after completing a full year's novitiate, the Cluniacs allowed the novice to make profession at any given time within the year of probation, oftentimes only after a month or even a single day, in order to make sure that he would not relapse into his former ways. Further Cluniac departures from the Rule were the readmission of fugitive monks, the discontinuation of the solemn welcoming of guests by the abbot, who also stayed in the refectory instead of eating with the guests and the shortening of the siesta during the summer fast days in order to have None and thus the community meal at an earlier hour.[7]

Monastic life was in a far worse predicament in other French monasteries. Many of them were simply victims of isolation and individualization, and this in an age when Christian society was getting organized, when feudal power was made to yield before the rising influence of the crown, and new congregations of canons, combining the monastic vocation with the duties of the secular priests, became the centers of influence and initiative. In such a state of affairs the multiplication of priories and cells could only hasten the break-up of conventual life. It was the abbots' duty to visit them regularly, but this, in the given situation, meant that they had to spend much of their time away from home, obviously to the detriment of their monks and their monastery. The system also afforded abbots the welcome opportunity to send troublesome and uncomfortable monks to distant dependencies, hardly an ideal solution. The temptation was great in these distant places to set up a life of comfort and ease, an existence of limited objectives, at the obvious expense of the religious spirit. The system became so ingrained that not even the leading reformers of the time, Robert of Chaise-Dieu, Albert of Marmoutier, Gerard of Sauve-Majeur and Robert of Molesme—to mention only the outstanding —felt strong enough to make changes, and bishops simply tended to acquiesce in the situation.[8]

There were also monasteries which had a long local tradition—a case in point would be Lérins—where Benedictinism was but one element of time-honored customs and traditions. Other monasteries had but one *raison d'être*, the preservation of their material and institutional *status quo*. In this they may have succeeded, but not infrequently at the expense of losing all contacts with the new intellectual and religious currents in contemporary society. Given

---

7. *Ibid.*, 3–14.
8. U. Berlière, "Les origines de l'Ordre de Cîteaux," *loc. cit.*, 457. See also H. DeWarren, "Le monachisme à l'apparition de saint Bernard," *loc. cit.*, 46 and 49.

these aims and in the absence of adequate activities, these monasteries were literally forced to limit the number of their inmates by admitting only as many recruits as were needed to fill the various offices, and as could be cared for by the monastery's revenues.[9]

On the other end of the line there was Cluny, with its highly centralized administration. The system had its drawbacks; with its inadequate constitution and other anomalies, it offered no satisfactory answers to the problems of the period in question.[10]

Abbots added their share to the difficulties. For one thing, some of them were simply unworthy of their office. The count of Arles, for instance, found the abbot of Montmajeur "a man of flagitious life" who squandered the goods of his monastery.[11] Then, as could be expected, simoniac abbots were by no means a rarity—as, for instance, the abbots of St Nicholas, St Medard and St Peter. Not least cause in this was King Philip I who found simoniac practices attractive enough as a means to increase his revenues. (This in spite of Abbo of Fleury's contention that the king is the *defensor natus* of the monastic order, who must protect it from unruly lords and ill-willed bishops.)[12] Ivo of Chartres even had to reprimand an abbot whose harshness gave way to physical violence against his monks.[13]

An even more outspoken critic was St Peter Damian. In his *De fuga dignitatum ecclesiasticarum*, St Peter Damian deplored the fact

9. U. Berlière, "Les origines de l'Ordre de Cîteaux," *loc. cit.*, 467. On Lérins see H. DeWarren, "Le monachisme à l'apparition de saint Bernard," *loc. cit.*, 51.

10. U. Berlière, "Les origines de l'Ordre de Cîteaux," *loc. cit.*, 265.

11. George G. Coulton, *Five Centuries of Religion*. Vol. I: *St. Bernard. His Predecessors and Successors. 1000–1200 A.D.*, 2nd ed. (Cambridge: University Press, 1929), 255.

12. RHF 14:540 and 670; JL 4548 and 4608; Gregory VII, *Reg.* IV, *Ep.* 20, PL 148:474; A. Fliche, *Le règne de Philippe Ier*, 474f. and 493; *idem, La réforme grégorienne*, 1:58. Cf. E. Sackur, *op. cit.*, 1:290. On Abbo of Fleury see *Collectio canonum*, PL 139:477–479.

13. "*Quidam frater monasterii tui (Vindocinensis) nomine Daniel ad nos veniens graviter conquestus est a tua fraternitate se inordinate et miserabiliter multoties tractatum tam contumeliis verborum quam injuriis verberum, et qualem te in se expertus est, talem te existere in omnes, aut pene omnes pronuntiat.*" *Ep.* 82, PL 162:103.

that abbots who should be dead to the world were constantly involved in secular affairs. They have so many cares and worldly concerns that they are always busy with litigations and judicial contestations. This they do not for spiritual reasons, but to extend the boundaries of their monastery, to hoard money and to secure whatever may still be worth attaining. This is also why they are seen among the spectators of feudal tournaments, this is the reason why they are regular visitors in courts, episcopal *curiae* and palaces. They do not even hesitate to take their quarrels to the king. Small wonder therefore that the monastery is but a hospice to them, while their real "home" is the back of the horse, and their garments are the well-kept rider's outfit rather than the priestly vestments which they allow to be eaten up by moths. So much in the world, they are better informed about matters in court than the courts themselves; hence if one wishes to learn about happenings in the world, all one has to do is to ask an abbot. A man like this who is speaking all day and counseling during the night, will find it difficult to take part in community exercises, to speak of the things of heaven and to enforce the rule of silence on his subjects. Equally detestable are the faults of many recently ordained abbots. Never perfect monks, once they are abbots they act as *born* abbots, with a ruler-like bearing, a domineering disposition and a suddenly acquired ability to administer severe looks, display an imperious voice, use a sharp word of reprimand and to be quick in judging. They develop ruling into a fine art, by giving arbitrary orders, issuing categorical prohibitions, and by binding and dispensing, moving and removing. Unable to obey while monks, these new abbots are now all of a sudden convinced that they know everything better than others, and have no reason or need to consult their fellow religious. They act more like officers in a prefecture than administrators of an ecclesiastical office. Like the former, they shower their favors on their admirers but are vindictive toward those who have their reservations about their conduct. They claim to be entitled to better food than that which is given to the rest of the community; they need private rooms and, though young and vigorous, a staff to hold in their hand. Hence Peter Damian's exclamation: woe to all abbots who forget the words of St Benedict: "Let the abbot who was entrusted with the care of souls be constantly mindful that he will be called upon to render an account." To him it was almost better not to be an abbot at all.[14]

Even saintly abbots gave occasions to criticism. St Majolus and Hugh the Great, for instance, though great reformers and organizers, were also noted for building imposing edifices, basilicas, cloisters, etc., in proportions and dimensions few lay lords could afford to imitate.[15] Peter Damian reports in this connection, how a man saw Richard, abbot of Saint-Vannes, spend his eternity in hell, setting up scaffoldings, as if fortifying castles. "For in his lifetime the abbot was the victim of this weakness: he spent almost all his energies on vain building projects, squandering, on a large scale, the Church's money on frivolous walls."[16]

According to John of Fécamp (d. 1078), abbots "had become richer than bishops.... There is no more difference between the great ones of this world and abbots cultivating their friendship."[17] Robert of Torigny (d. 1186) similarly deplored the behavior of contemporary abbots. Abandoning the spirit of simplicity, they have become the victims of luxury. And because of their—not always necessary— dealings with outsiders in markets and episcopal *curiae* or even as pilgrims to the Holy Land, they act more like castellans than abbots or monks. Unable or unwilling to fulfill their obligations in the monastery, they are responsible for the diminution of the religious spirit in their houses; for riches and

14. PL 145:457-460.
15. J. Leclercq, "La crise du monachisme," *loc. cit.*, 20.
16. "*Vidit Richardum Verdunensem abbatem, velut excelsas machinas erigentem, et anxium atque sollicitum tanquam munita castrorum propugnacula construentem. Hoc enim morbo laboraverat abbas ille, dum viveret, ut in exstruendis inaniter aedificiis omnes fere diligentiae suae curas expenderet, et plurimas facultates Ecclesiae in frivolis hujusmodi moeniis profligaret.*" PL 144:465. Cf. J. Leclercq, "La crise du monachisme," *loc. cit.*, 23.
17. Jean Leclercq and Jean-P. Bonnes, *Un maître de la vie spirituelle au XIe siècle. Jean de Fécamp* (Paris: J. Vrin, 1946), 201-203. See also Jean Leclercq et al., *La spiritualité du moyen age* (Histoire de la spiritualité chrétienne, 2; Paris: Aubier, 1961), 163.

power bring nothing but decadence for monks.[18] This is also why Raul Glaber remarked: "Whenever the religious fervor of abbots relapses, monastic discipline declines at once, and seeing this example, the rest of the faithful will similarly transgress the laws of God."[19]

But abbots were not the only ones to blame; contemporary monks had their own share in bringing on the crisis. Also there was the wholesale clericalization of monks, i.e. the change from the lay to the clerical state. According to C. Butler, this change was the most important of all the changes which affected Benedictine history.[20] There were problems of adjustment in the eleventh century and far-reaching consequences in subsequent developments.

At first Benedictine monks—like their eastern counterparts—were not priests. Things began to change when Pope Gregory I brought the Benedictines to Rome. This move into the city made agricultural work obviously impossible; hence the change to a sedentary life with indoor activities, the administration of cathedrals and the execution of public liturgical prayer after the manner of canons. Then came the employment of the Benedictines as bishops and missionaries in the conversion of Europe. This of course called for more priests and for more years of preparation for the ministry.[21] The trend so continued that "by the year one thousand, it became the established rule that monks should receive ordina-

---

18. "*Videntes itaque abbates nominatissimorum monasteriorum quae reges Francorum et alii consulares et potentes in praediis suis aedificaverant, sed propter abundantiam divitiarum nimium dissoluta erant.*" *De immutatione ordinis monachorum*, 7; PL 202:1313. Cf. E. Sackur, *op. cit.*, 2:233 and 469; U. Berlière, "Les origines de l'Ordre de Cîteaux," *loc. cit.*, 265f., and J. Leclercq, "La crise du monachisme," *loc. cit.*, 24.

19. "*Quandocunque defuit religiositas pontificum, ac marcessit districtio regularis abbatum, simulque monasterialis disciplinae vigor tepescit, ac per illorum exempla caetera plebs mandatorum Dei praevaricatrix existit.*" *Radulphi Glabri Historiarum libri quinque*, PL 142:637.

20. C. Butler, *Benedictine Monachism*, 294.

21. V. Hermans, *op. cit.*, 113f. Cf. PL 170:537 and PL 189:142. See also J. Leclercq, *The Love of Learning*, 233. On the medieval concept of the monastic priesthood see *idem*, "On Monastic Priesthood According to the Ancient Medieval Tradition," *Studia Monastica*, 3 (1961), 152–154.

tion"[22] and in 1078 the priesthood was in effect made a *conditio sine qua non* for a monk's eligibility to the office of abbot.[23] This clericalization was directly responsible for the final abandonment of manual labor and the emergence of increasing numbers of servants even in the kitchen and the monastery garden.[24]

There were other less attractive features in the eleventh-century monk's portrait. Contemporary authors generally deplore the monks' great interest in material things to the detriment of their spiritual ideals. They bewail the relaxation of discipline, the disappearance of simplicity and the prevalence of gross immorality. Udalric of Cluny complained (and wrote his *Consuetudines*, in part, for the purpose of combating the practice) that parents like to rid themselves of unwanted or handicapped and bothersome children by giving them to monasteries.[25] On other occasions, bishops compelled wayward subjects to take the monastic habit.[26] With such inmates—Udalric lists both physical and moral deficiencies—decadence could hardly be staved off. Even at Cluny, the penal code had provisions for and sanctions against drunkenness, anger, swearing, quarreling, calumny, pride, envy, covetousness, the

---

22. C. Butler, *Benedictine Monachism*, 294. See also "The Priesthood For Monks," *Monastic Studies*, 3 (1965), 59. Cf. PL 170:537.

23. See below, p. 123, n. 37. Cf. Paul M. Viollet, *Droi publique. Histoire des institutions politiques et administratives de la France* (Paris: L. Larose et Forcel, 1890–1903), 1:365.

24. C. Butler, *Benedictine Monachism*, 294f. See also U. Berlière, "Les origines de l'Ordre de Cîteaux," *loc. cit.*, 449.

25. "*Aliud sibi nidum providere ubi reponant pullos suos abortivos, velut exhaereditatos . . . eis scilicet Deo dicatis, quidem tamquam ancillis suis et nutricibus abutentes.*" PL 149:637. Cf. E. Hauviller, *op. cit.*, 69, and 80 n. 6, and *above*, p. 66, n. 82. See also the account of Guibert of Nogent, in PL 156:850f.: "*Nostris monasteria vetustissima numero extenuata temporibus, rerum antiquitus datarum exuberante copia, parvis erant contenta conventibus, in quibus perpauci reperire poterant, qui peccati fastidio saeculum respuissent, sed ab illis potissimum detinebantur ecclesiae, qui in eisdem parentum devotione contraditi, ab ineunte nutriebantur aetate. Qui quantum minorem super suis, quae nulla sibi videbantur egisse, malis metum habebant, tanto intra coenobiorum septa remissiore studio victicabant.*"

26. Ch. Dereine, "Vie commune, règle de saint Augustin et les chanoines réguliers aux XIe siècle," *loc. cit.*, 387.

possession of private property, perjury, absence without leave, malingering, conversations with women, and others.[27] In many a monastery one could see monks wandering around aimlessly, dragging themselves with their canes to the infirmary, in a life hardly different from that of pensioners.[28] Hence Peter Damian's outcry: "Shame has perished, honesty has vanished, religion lies prostrate and all virtues have assembled, as it were, and taken flight in a group. For all seek only their own interests and, scorning the desire of heaven, strive insatiably after earthly things."[29]

In his *Liber Gomorrhanus* Peter Damian draws a picture of monastic morals, too sad to be reviewed here.[30] Elsewhere he catalogues at great length the many abuses.[31]

But, to continue the list, already Odo of Cluny is said to have complained that if there is meanness among men, its source is found in monasteries.[32] Ivo of Chartres chided the monks for their extravagant habit.[33] Firmatus described how monks disgruntled with religious life sought all kinds of subterfuges and escapes; the most common of these was the securing of an office which furnished the excuse to live habitually outside the cloister. Thus some monks became chaplains of secular lords and lived in quarters often as spacious as the lord's own residence.[34] Then, in the words of an anonymous satirist, there were "sacrilegious monks who were

---

27. J. Evans, *op. cit.*, 86.   28. H. Leclercq, *op. cit.*, 50.

29. "*Periit pudor, honestas evanuit, religio cecidit et velut facta omnium sanctorum virtutum turba procul abscessit. Omnes enim quae sua sunt quaerunt, et contempto coelesti desiderio, terram insatiabiliter concupiscunt.*" *Opusculum XII. Apologeticum de contemptu saeculi;* PL 145:252f.

30. PL 145:159–190.   31. PL 145:457–460.

32. "*Sed, ut pater Odilo saepius plangere solitus est, ita contigit: Heu! pro dolor! inquiens, quoniam invidentiae, licet in caeteris grassetur hominibus, tamen in finibus aliquorum monachaliter vivere professis cubile sibi locavit.*" PL 142:689. Cf. E. Sackur, *op. cit.*, 2:93.

33. C. Spahr, *De fontibus constitutivis*, 62.

34. Germain Morin, "Une traité de S. Guillaume Firmat sur l'amour du cloître et les saintes lectures" (*Exhortatio Firmati monachi in amorem claustri et desiderium lectionis divinae*), *Revue Bénédictine*, 31 (1914), 249. Cf. J. Leclercq, "La crise du monachisme," *loc. cit.*, 23.

(literally) buying churches."[35] Finally, in his *Invectio in militem qui causa paupertatis saeculum relinquens in monachatu divitias adeptus est*, Serlo of Bayeux pointed to the root of so many contemporary evils: "*Fit monachus miles, sed fit de paupere dives*," should a knight join the monks, his poverty is gone at once.[36]

Mabillon lists a number of additional shortcomings, such as simony, wanderlust, familiarity with guests and seculars, vanity, cupidity, love of riches, disregard for silence, lack of faith, laziness, ambition, sloth and lack of simplicity.[37] According to the already mentioned John of Fécamp "clergy and laity, priest and monk differ but little in acts and manners."[38] Thus in numerous instances, monks, disregarding canonical legislation, engaged in direct pastoral activities: they attended Church councils, baptized, imposed penances, acted as confessors and public speakers, accepted prebends, became grammarians, rhetoricians and even sophists (philosophers), took oaths (when their vows should suffice) and wore arms.[39] According to Raynald the hermit, corruption reached such dimensions that it was difficult to find traces of evangelical perfection. Monks rarely spoke or meditated on the salvation of their soul; their conversation centered more on food, drink, bed and clothes. They were wont to sharpen their tongue against the abbot's greed

---

35. *Sacrilegis monachis emtoribus Ecclesiarum*
    Composui satyram, carmen saeculare clarum.
    Quam quia vir magnus corroborat Hugo Diensis
    Noster amicus eam legat Hugo Suessionensis.
    Cf. Wilhelm Lühe, *Hugo von Die und Lyon, Legat von Gallien* (Breslau: F. W. Jungfer, 1898), 131 n. 1.

36. Cf. A. Boutémy, "Deux poèmes inconnus de Serlon de Bayeux et une copie nouvelle de son poème contre les moines de Caen," *Le Moyen Age*, 51 1938), 254-260 and J. Leclercq, "La crise du monachisme," *loc. cit.*, 22.

37. Joannes Mabillon, *Annales Ordinis S. Benedicti occidentalium monachorum patriarchae* (Lucae: L. Venturini, 1739-1740), 5:88, 143, 204, 230, 429, 448, 471, 494, 499, and 577.

38. "*Clerus et populus, sacerdos et monachus, nil in actibus nil in moribus differunt.*" Cf. J. Leclercq, *Un maître*, 201ff. and *idem*," La crise du monachisme,'' *loc. cit.*, 24.

39. J. Mabillon, *Annales ordinis S. Benedicti*, 5:7, 108, 119, 167, 169, 208, 261, 282, 361, 389, 431, 447, 506 and 520.

and they liked to criticize officials in order to get them removed and be appointed in their place. They wandered outside the monastery, with their tongues if not with their feet, and they were more interested in the litigation of kings and dukes than in the recitation of psalms. Their ears were more attuned to secular rumors than to divine inspiration.[40] Hence, Raynald has nothing but scorn for these "fat and rubicund cenobites, with their protruding bellies and their bony cheeks, follicating in greatly varied clothing, who say, in a manner to be insulting, that to live canonically or in solitude one must not do penance .... thus imitating the worthless deception of the Pharisees."[41] Reason suggests that "these persons should be held as ungodly traitors of Christ. And authority supports reason."[42]

Specific examples should further illustrate the point just made. Abbo of Fleury, a relentless foe of immoral monks and nuns, was murdered by those whom he sought to reform.[43] At St Benignus in Dijon, before Jarento became abbot, "religion was languishing, the abbey oppressed with debt, the church stripped of its ornaments and the buildings half ruined."[44] Around 1070, Anno, archbishop of Cologne, looked in vain for worthy monks who could settle the monastery of Siegberg.[45] St Aigulfus, abbot of Lérins, was murdered

---

40. "*Multi ... ignorantes quanta in coenobiis dominetur corruptela, adeo ut in ipsis nulla vel minima evangelicae perfectionis inveniebantur vestigia ... raro de salute animarum meditantur aut loquuntur ... sermo quippe eorum praecipuus de cibis et de potibus, de pitantiis et generalibus, de stratis et vestimentis, et vestimentorum mutatoribus.*" G. Morin, "Rainaud l'Ermite," *loc. cit.*, 104–106.

41. "*Haec quidem sunt contra pingues coenobitas et rubicundos, tumentes inflato ventre, et vernantes rosea facie, et veste multiplici follicantes; qui insultantes dicunt, canonice vivere vel solitarie non esse paenitentiam agere, sed inutilem simulationem, pharisaeum imitantes.*" G. Morin, "Rainaud l'Ermite," *loc. cit.*, 108.

42. "*Ratio enim mihi suadet, non aliter sentiendum esse de talibus, quam de impiis Christum negantibus. Et rationi auctoritas consentit.*" *Ibid.*, 107.

43. G. Coulton, *op. cit.*, 1:257. Cf. Henry C. Lea, *History of Sacerdotal Celibacy in the Christian Church*, 3rd ed. (New York: The Macmillan Co., 1907), 1:176; A. Fliche, *La réforme grégorienne*, 1:50. See also Abbo's *Collectio canonum*, PL 139:489 and his *epp.* 5, 8, 9 and 11; *ibid.*, 423, 429, 432 and 436. For Abbo's violent death, see *ibid.*, 384f.

44. G. Coulton, *op. cit.*, 1:254.

45. PL 143:1532 and MGH, SS 11:476. Cf. also O. Ducourneau, *op. cit.*, 10

by his rebellious subjects.[46] Pope Gregory VII was amazed that the monk Robert, a man of unspeakable ambition and a perjurer, could usurp the episcopal see of Chartres.[47] The monks of St Vincent, Laon, had a greater interest in material goods than a desire for heavenly blessings.[48] Discipline was greatly relaxed at the abbey of Clusa.[49] Ivo of Chartres deplored the anarchy and licence which prevailed in the monasteries of Saint Maur-des-Fossés and Saint Pierre de Lagny.[50] Licence gained the upper hand in other places as well.[51] Maurilius, abbot of Fécamp and subsequently of a monastery in Florence, found poison in his drink.[52] William, bishop of Limoges, a former prior of Saint Martial, died of poison, murdered by those who resented his reforms.[53] In 1093 Philip I gave the abbey of Saint Magloire in Paris to Bernard of Saint Venant, abbot of Marmoutier, for its worldly inmates were in great need of reform.[54] In the abbey of Saint Bertin, Thérouanne, each monk had his *peculium* around the year 1095; this enabled him to give and receive gifts without permission and to lead a life of dissoluteness and negligence.[55] In 1097 Archbishop Hugh of Lyons intervened to restore peace between the abbot of St Giles and his monks.[56]

46. J. Mabillon, *Acta sanctorum Ordinis S. Benedicti*, 2:659f. See also G. Coulton, *op. cit.*, 1:257.

47. PL 148:468. Cf. A. Fliche, *La réforme grégorienne*, 2:249 n. 1.

48. *Vita S. Geraldi*, AS, Apr. 1:417. Cf. A. Fliche, *Le règne de Philippe Ier*, 470f.

49. MGH, SS 12:199. Cf. A. Fliche, *Le règne de Philippe Ier*, 470f.

50. "*Audivi enim a fratre tuo Raimberto monasterii nostri monacho, quod exteriorum tribulationum crebra infestatione vexatus et propter indisciplinatam monasterii tibi commissi conversationem quodam taedio labefactus.*" *Ep.* 26, PL 162:38. See also *ep.* 65: "[*Latiniacensis abbas et monachi ejus*] *qui nescio qua nova libertate suos excessus tuentur . . . qui libertate in occasionem carnis abutuntur;*" *ibid.*, 82.

51. Some examples are listed in A. Fliche, *La réforme grégorienne*, 1:33.

52. PL 188:405. See also G. Coulton, *op. cit.*, 1:257.

53. J. Mabillon, *Annales ordinis S. Benedicti*, 5:338. Cf. *ibid.*, 348, 373, 385, 399 and 404.

54. *Ibid.*, 310. See also O. Ducourneau, *op. cit.*, 10.

55. For the documentation see O. Ducourneau, *op. cit.*, 10.

56. W. Lühe, *op. cit.*, 92. Cf. also JL 5720–5721.

Gilbert, abbot of Saint Germain in Auxerre, elected in 1083, was deposed in 1098, for failing to counteract the spirit of laxity in his monastery.[57] And Hugh, abbot of Saint Martin, who had survived a blow on the head made with an axe, was another victim of poisoning, in 1098.[58] Hugh of Cluny attributed his difficulties with Bishop Norigaud of Autun "to the calumny of his own monks, a plague which is said to have so infected all contemporary monasteries that they scarcely had a monk who merited his father's blessing."[59]

Immorality was also found in convents, as seen from the example of Saint Eloi in Paris and the scandalous behavior of the nuns of Saint Fare.[60]

In spite of this overwhelming evidence it must be stressed, however, that corruption was by no means universal, for there were monasteries that had withstood the inroads of decadence. Cluny, Marmoutier, St Benignus under Abbot Jarento (died in 1112), La Chaise Dieu, Bèze, Bec,—to mention only the most prominent—retained or restored a model observance and were led by truly outstanding personages.[61] Bernold's chronicle lists similar instances.[62] This will answer C. Butler who remarked: "While not

57. GChr 12:361. Cf. O. Ducourneau, *op. cit.*, 11.

58. G. Coulton, *op. cit.*, 1:257.

59. "*Hugonis abbatis discordia cum episcopo Aeduensi. Ceterum totam hanc persecutionem tribuit calumniae monachorum suorum, quae pestis ita generali tale omnia illius temporis monasteria corrupisse dicitur, ut jam paene nullus sit in eis filius qui patris benedictionem mereatur.*" J. Mabillon, *Annales ordinis S. Benedicti*, 5: 396. Cf. L. Smith, *op. cit.*, 200 n. 1 and G. Coulton, *op. cit.*, 1:265.

60. Maurice Prou, *Recueil des actes de Philippe Ier, roi de France (1059–1108)* (Paris: Imprimérie Nationale, 1908), 470f. See also Ivo of Chartres, *ep.* 70: "*Audivi turpissimam famam de monasterio Sanctae Farae, quod jam non locus sanctimonialium, sed mulierum daemonialium prostibulum dicendum est, corpora sua ad turpes usus omni generi humani prostituendum.*" PL 162:90.

61. H. Leclercq, *op. cit.*, 49. Cf. O. Ducourneau, *op. cit.*, 11. See also GChr 2:330; PL 150:719; PL 158:70–80; PL 162:848f. and 941.

62. "*His temporibus in regno Teutonicorum communis vita multis in locis floruit, non solum in clericis et monachis religiosissime commanentibus, verum etiam in laicis, se et sua ad eandem communem vitam devotissime offerentibus, qui etsi habitu nec clerici nec monachi viderentur, nequaquam tamen eis dispares in meritis fuisse creduntur.*" Bernoldi Chronicon, MGH, SS 5: 452f.

for a moment questioning the reality and value of all the numerous revivals and reforms that are so striking a feature of Benedictine history, we must bear in mind that it is a natural trick of the panegyrists of reforms and reformers to depict in colors much too black the general state of things when the hero appeared on the scene."[63]

The abandonment of manual labor brought equally fateful consequences to contemporary monachism. Once a basic element of the monastic *horarium*, it had now fallen into disuse, as has already been seen from the example of Cluny. Beside the reasons previously listed, several additional factors account for this development. Given the strong class differentiation of the feudal world, a lord or a free man joining a monastery could easily continue to consider manual labor incompatible with his dignity, in the belief that he must go on living like the noble and free in the outside world. Then there was the flow of donations—lands, churches, altars, tithes—which freed the monk from the need to procure his livelihood by means of field labor. Also important is the fact that a majority of the churches recovered from laymen during the earlier stages of the Gregorian Reform were given to monasteries rather than to parishes administered by the secular clergy. Nor should the influence of eastern monasticism with its disregard for manual labor be left unmentioned. In any case, the increase of donations and the presence of fixed revenues (gold *denarii*) brought considerable wealth to monasteries, freed them from material worries and gave them the security needed for the quiet pursuit of labor-free activities. Manual labor was supplanted by the celebration of the Mass with great frequency, the extension of the liturgical services and the multiplication of claustral and administrative offices.[64] Whatever manual labor remained became a mere religious ceremony.[65]

63. *Benedictine Monachism*, 359. Cf. G. Coulton, *op. cit.*, 1:256 n. 3.

64. U. Berlière, "Les origines de l'Ordre de Cîteaux," *loc. cit.*, 449 and 446f. See also Alberich Gerards, "Die ersten Cistercienser und die Handarbeit," *Cistercienser-Chronik*, 59 (1952), 1f.; R. Grand, *op. cit.*, 148 and J. Leclercq, *The Love of Learning*, 233.

65. PL 149:675–677.

The liturgy, on the other hand, tended to grow richer between the ninth and twelfth centuries and reached a point where, in certain instances, it accounted for almost all of the monk's daily activities. From the middle of the tenth century, it became a general custom all over France, Germany, England and Italy to say the fifteen gradual psalms—in some places thirty psalms during the winter season—before Matins and to recite, daily, the seven penitential psalms, the litany of all saints, the Office of the Dead (with Vespers, Matins and Lauds), the Office of All Saints (Vespers and Lauds) and, after each canonical hour, the so-called *psalmi familiares*. The monk thus became a man of public prayer, performing—in return for donations and favors received—duty-bound services for the well-being of the founders and benefactors of his monastery and for society in general. The result was that the divine office became, contrary to St Benedict, the only essential, if not the only occupation, of the monk since each monastery had its fixed revenues, and its members, many of them priests now, could live from the fruits of the altar as did the canons. In this matter there was little difference between monks on the one hand, and clerics and canons on the other.[66]

Yet, even if the monks of the eleventh century had not had so many dealings with the contemporary world, they could not have stopped the "world" from entering their monasteries. For princes and lords, as a rule, had few scruples about the sanctity of the monastic retreats. Always on the move, they—in virtue of their feudal prerogatives—liked to hold their court in monasteries, with little concern about the preservation of the monastic atmosphere. Moreover, gratitude toward donors and benefactors often obliged monasteries to accept *praebendarii* and *familiares* to whom, on account of their age and previous position in the world, all kinds of allowances had to be made. Special considerations like these could only be detrimental to monastic discipline. According to P. Giseke,

---

66. E. Bishop, *op. cit.*, 224. See also U. Berlière, "Les origines de l'Ordre de Cîteaux," *loc. cit.*, 467f.; Ch. Dereine, "Odon de Tournai," *loc. cit.*, 149 and J. Leclercq, "La crise du monachisme," *loc. cit.*, 25.

the so-called *familiares* . . . were a real pest for the quiet and discipline (of monasteries); their disgraceful life was directly responsible for the decline of some abbeys. Neither praying nor working, they lived in the monastery which clothed and fed them; they were good for nothing but gossiping, detraction and stealing. Since they were always with the monks and lived with them, they sought to find out their secrets in order to relate them to the outside world, and whatever they could carry away they took to their wives and children who lived in a nearby city.[67]

Secular interference was further heightened by the so-called advocates or defensors, i.e. lay protectors of monasteries. This practice of having lay protectors derived its justification from the Pauline passage: "No one serving as God's soldier entangles himself in worldly affairs" (2 Timothy 2:4). Accordingly such protectors (*advocatus*, avoué, Vogt) came to be charged with the execution of administrative duties in churches and monasteries and with the representation of the latter before the courts. The system was highly effective and beneficial in the time of Charlemagne. By the middle of the ninth century, however, royal power could no longer offer effective protection, whereupon churches and monasteries began to turn to the most powerful lords—counts, viscounts, and other nobles—for the purpose. Pope Leo IX put the seal of approval on the system.[68] These protectors obviously expected a *quid pro quo*,

---

67. P. Giseke, *op. cit.*, 17f. Cf. also B. Bligny, "Un aspect de la vie religieuse," *loc. cit.*, 285; U. Berlière, "Les origines de l'Ordre de Cîteaux," *loc. cit.*, 468 and M. Prou, *op. cit.*, 474.

68. "*Equum et salutare visum fuit nobis ut praedictam ecclesiam [sanctorum Bertarii et Ataleni] a Raynardo comite suisque progenitoribus conditam apostolicae auctoritatis scuto muniremus . . . Constituimus . . . congregationem sanctimonialium venerabiliter stabilire et . . . confirmari eo tenore, ut quicumque de ejus corporis posteritate Fonteniacum castellum justa haereditate possiderit, advocatiam ipsius loci habeat solide.*" Ep. 49, PL 143: 661. See also diploma 3: "*Advocatiam autem praedicti loci Walterius sibi et uxori suae Adilae retinuit et post eos uni suorum haeredum, qui major natu fuerit. Constituit etiam, ut ulli suorum haeredum hanc advocatiam tenenti cuiquam in beneficium eam dare liceat, sed ipse eam in suo domino* (really, *dominio*) *possideat. Quae post eum ad filium suum Odelricum deveniat, et post eum quicumque propinquior haeres castrum Daguliacum jure possederit, eandem advocatiam teneat.*" Ibid., 589. See also Adolf Waas, *Vogtei*

i.e. special favors, for their services. The office could be held for life and inherited like other feudal offices. Somewhat later the protection of an episcopal church was entrusted to the *vice-dominus*, while the *advocatus* kept his function in the monasteries. The system, wide-spread as it was, had firm roots in Burgundy.[69]

The *advocatia* had both good and bad sides. It united reform-minded monasteries and helped the monks in their reforming activities. This enabled the monks to improve the morals of the lower clergy and show their concern for the common people. On the other hand, there was nothing but trouble if the advocates—as was frequently the case—placed their selfish interests before the welfare of their *protégés*. In this case the protectors turned into oppressors and this created a situation which gave rise to endless complaints. In the words of a contemporary, "the earthly *advocatia* was in most cases nothing but oppression." Elsewhere one hears the complaint that "those whom we believe to be the appointed defenders of the Church are not defenders at all, but actually the worst oppressors, the most unbearable violators of its goods."[70] But even in these cases, monks simply could not afford to give up their advocates, for they needed their protection against a multitude of other nobles who were often more unscrupulous and more greedy than their own defensors. Papal protection, as in the case of Cluny, was no practical answer to the problem of harassment, for Rome was far away and had its own difficulties, while the advocate was, at all times, near at hand.

---

und Bede in der deutschen Kaiserzeit (Arbeiten zur deutschen Rechts- und Verfassungsgeschichte, Heft 1; Berlin: Weidmannsche Buchhandlung, 1919–1923), 34 n. 4.

69. R. Holtzmann, *op. cit.*, 151 and 153. See also P. Viollet, *op. cit.*, 1: 372–374.

70. "*Plerumque terrena advocatia ecclesiarum magna fuit oppressio.*" Jacques Flach, *Les origines de l'ancienne France* (Paris: Libraire de la Société de Recueil Sirey, 1896–1917), 1:439. *Ibid.*, we read also of another complaint, "*Tales quos hodie cernimus deputatos ecclesiae tutores non solummodo non sunt, verum etiam sunt pessimi insecutores et rerum ejus intolerabilissimi pervasores.*" See also Jean Richard, *Les ducs de Bourgogne et la formation du duché du XIe au XIVe siècle* (Paris: Société Les Belles-Lettres, 1954), 68.

The Crisis of Cenobitism

The Cluniacs had rendered great services in the suppression of the *Eigenkirchenrecht*, the so-called proprietary church law, but strengthened the *advocatia* system in the process. The next step was that the great lords soon perceived in it unique possibilities for the furtherance of their overriding ambition: the establishment of a territorial state. Hence the nobility's eagerness to obtain the office. In this sense the *advocatia* is but a continuation of the *Eigenkirche* system.[71]

According to G. Coulton, "the monastic system of (agricultural) economy necessarily led to the breakdown of the Rule."[72] Neither Cluny nor other reforms undertaken between the ninth and the eleventh centuries were able to remedy this situation. Monasteries were part of an economic and social system which made a breakaway extremely difficult if not altogether impossible. In the words of U. Berlière:

> Benedictine abbeys, still linked to a system of exploitation which was outdated by three centuries, found themselves on the verge of imminent ruin, and more than one of them sustained a financial crisis. This situation will only end on the day when the administration will be brought in line with the needs of the time and the new methods of exploitation, adopted by the orders born in the twelfth century, will be introduced.[73]

In this connection it must be recalled that Benedictine monachism actually grew up with feudalism which in turn was the product of political necessities resulting from the disintegration of the Roman and the Carolingian empires. Feudalism was an adequate and beneficial solution of contemporary realities and needs. Since power and security rested on landed property and abbeys had acquired great estates, monasticism was able to exercise a considerable influence on contemporary society, penetrate its entire organism and render great services to everyone. This embeddedness into

---

71. E. Werner, *Die gesellschaftlichen Grundlagen*, 15-18.
72. G. Coulton, *op. cit.*, 1:269f.
73. U. Berlière, *L'ordre monastique*, 290.

feudalism, however, contained the seeds of insurmountable problems so that the predominance of feudalism could not but affect monasticism. It increased the need for going into the world and brought the world into the monastery, a situation that could be harmonized neither with the letter nor with the spirit of the Benedictine Rule. The loser in this collision of ideas was regular life. It became the victim of increasing prosperity, of human weakness and sociological handicaps.[74]

Measures aimed at a reform were not lacking during this period. One of them was the establishment of ties and controls between monasteries.

In other instances flourishing monasteries took over decadent houses in order to restore religious discipline, and worthy bishops and lay lords made worldly clerics take the monastic habit, appointing zealous monks in their place. But these endeavors offered no adequate help to traditional Benedictine monachism, which had become a part of the feudal world. Hence it was impossible to introduce effective changes and remedies without turning over the whole contemporary social order and thus hastening the ruin of existing monasteries.[75]

The victory of the monk—so obvious during the golden age of Cluny and in the earlier phases of the Gregorian Reform—was followed by a slackening in the second half of the eleventh century. Traditional monachism began to show signs of having exhausted its resources. The result was fatigue. The Christianization of feudal society and the great exertions it involved had inescapably sapped its strength. New solutions were needed to satisfy ardent souls and, as will be seen, the century provided them in full measure.

74. E. Sackur, *op. cit.*, 2:30–32; U. Berlière, "Les origines de l'Ordre de Cîteaux," *loc. cit.*, 268f. and 457 and E. Werner, *Die gesellschaftlichen Grundlagen*, 26.

75. U. Berlière, "Les origines de l'Ordre de Cîteaux," *loc. cit.*, 466; H. Leclercq, *op. cit.*, 49; Ch. Dereine, "Vie commune," *loc. cit.*, 387; B. Bligny, "Un aspect de la vie réligieuse," *loc. cit.*, 285 and A. Gerards, "Die ersten Cistercienser," *loc. cit.*, 2.

MONASTIC REFORM: CONCILIAR LEGISLATION IN ELEVENTH-CENTURY FRANCE

IN HIS ARTICLE ON THE OBSERVANCE of the Benedictine Rule by the early Cistercians, K. Spahr voiced the belief that local synodal enactments in eleventh-century France undoubtedly influenced the thinking of the Cistercian pioneers.[1] He did not, however, elaborate; hence the need for a detailed consideration of the subject. This will also supplement the chapter on the crisis of cenobitism.

The practice of holding diocesan or provincial synods in Gaul dates, contrary to some experts' opinion,[2] from pre-Merovingian times. At least twenty-three councils are recorded between the years 314 and 506.[3] Clovis held a council, at Orleans, in 511; between that year and A.D. 695 fifty-six more such gatherings took place.[4] They dealt mostly with local diocesan matters, as proposed by the

---

1. Kolumban Spahr, "Die Anfänge von Cîteaux," *Bernhard von Clairvaux Mönch und Mystiker*. Internationaler Bernhardkongress, Mainz, 1953, ed. Joseph Lortz (Wiesbaden: Franz Steiner Verlag, 1955), 220f.

2. Paul Hinschius, *Das Kirchenrecht der Katholiken und Protestanten in Deutschland. System des katholischen Kirchenrechts mit besonderer Rücksicht auf Deutschland* (Graz: Akademische Druck- und Verlagsanstalt, 1959), 3:539ff. and Robert Holtzmann, *Französische Verfassungsgeschichte von der Mitte des neunten Jahrhunderts bis zur Revolution* (Berlin: R. Oldenbourg, 1910), 159.

3. C. Munier (ed.) *Concilia Galliae A. 314–A. 506.* (CCSL, vol. 148; Turnholti: Typographia Brépols Editores Pontificii, 1963), 3–228.

4. Carolus de Clercq (ed.), *Concilia Galliae A. 551–A. 695.* (CCSL, vol. 148A; Turnholti: Typographia Brépols Editores Pontificii, 1963), 3–326. On the council of Orleans see Mansi 8:350.

bishop. According to R. Holtzmann, they attained "no great importance" and the attempt to organize them on a yearly basis failed.[5] Be this as it may, one must nevertheless point to the fact that several councils—it will suffice to mention Angers (453), Vannes (between 461–491) and Agde (506)—considered the problems affecting the monk's life, especially various aspects of vagrancy.[6] The councils of the sixth and seventh centuries also considered fidelity to monastic vows, the observance of the Benedictine Rule and the elimination of worldly ways in the monastery.[7] Canon fifteen of the council of Autun (663–680) stated in particular:

> On the subject of abbots and monks this was decided: Whatever canonical legislation or the Rule of Saint Benedict teaches, they must fulfill and observe in every detail. . . . Monks must practice total obedience; let them be shining examples of frugality; let them be fervent in the divine office, steadfast in prayer and persevering in charity. . . . Let them be of one heart and one mind. Let no one make claims to ownership; let them have all things in common, let them work in common and practice hospitality at all times.[8]

The great council of Aachen (817) with its impact on contemporary monasticism and that of subsequent centuries has been considered in the first chapter of this work[9] and need not be reviewed here. It will suffice to recall that it did not establish an effective precedent, for after the disintegration of the Carolingian empire church councils became a rarity. They met only at great and irregular intervals, and during the tenth century, with its weak monarchs on the Frankish throne, no national synod was held at all before the year 991. There were, however, local synods during the tenth century and in the first half of the eleventh century, with litigations and problems of discipline, administration and protection against attacks and oppression prominently figuring on their

5. *Op. cit.*, 159.   6. CCSL, vol. 148:138, 153, 205ff.
7. Cf. CCSL, vol. 148A:348.   8. *Ibid.*, 319.
9. See above, pp. 9ff.

agenda.[10] The councils of the early eleventh century—especially those of Poitiers (1000), Verdun-sur-les-Doubs (1016), Elne (1027), Bourges (1031), Limoges (1031), Elne (1050) and Narbonne (1054)—sought, above all, to promote the cause of peace.[11] Somewhat later, i.e. from the middle of the eleventh century, the synodal movement gained full strength as a result of its furtherance by the revitalized papacy. Whereas the German monarchy felt strong enough to take an active interest in church and monastic reform through the instrumentality of church councils, the Frankish kings saw councils summoned and held in their realm without their being consulted on the matter. With the success of the Gregorian reform among the French clergy, the papacy was able to seize the initiative in France. It was the Pope and his legates, and not the king, who summoned and conducted provincial or local councils in eleventh-century France.[12]

That there was a need to deal with monastic problems in the early tenth century is seen from the council of Trosly (909)[13] which drafted a lengthy canon in an attempt to rectify monastic ills. It deplored the sad state of monasteries ruined by Norse raids and internal difficulties.[14] Among the latter it singled out the evils caused by the so-called *commenda* system whereby laymen were rewarded with and given charge of monasteries contrary to monastic traditions and Church law. It meant the installation of lay abbots (*abbates laici*) who, more often than not, brought women,

---

10. P. Hinschius, *op. cit.*, 3:483f. and 569–572. See also Henri Maisonneuve, *La morale chrétienne d'après les conciles des Xe et XIe siècles* (Analecta Mediaevalia Namurcensia, 15; Louvain: Éditions Nauwelaerts, 1962), 1f.

11. P. Hinschius, *op. cit.*, 3:484. Cf. also H. Maisonneuve, *op. cit.*, 25.

12. P. Hinschius, *op. cit.*, 3:485 and 571.

13. Mansi 18a:263–308. See also Charles-Joseph Hefele and Henri Leclercq, *Histoire des conciles d'après les documents originaux* (Paris: Letouzey et Ané, 1911), 4(2):722ff.; E. Sackur, *op. cit.*, 1:33; A. Fliche, *La réforme grégorienne*, 1:31 and H. Maisonneuve, *op. cit.*, 9f.

14. "*Monasteriorum . . . quaedam a Paganis succensa vel destructa, quaedam rebus spoliata & ad nihilum prope redacta.*" Mansi 18a:270.

children, soldiers and dogs with them into the monastery.[15] Unable to read and ignorant of both Scripture and the Rule of St Benedict, these abbots were unable to fulfill their obligations, i.e. explain the Rule, instruct their charges and enforce the legislation aimed at improving religious life.[16] Such a disregard for the Benedictine ideals could not but impair the monks' religious fervor. Thus monks developed a dislike for humility and simplicity and became intent on travel and even on vanities which good laymen abhor as indecent or unbecoming. Dissatisfied with community life, they began to promote their own interests for the sake of shameful gains.[17] To remedy this anomalous situation, the council prescribed that abbots be chosen only from the monastic order and that they should be men well-versed in religious discipline. They should be guides and models to their subjects and show them the way which leads by degrees, but steadily, to perfection. To combat the evils of vagrancy they should provide their subjects with all the necessaries in food and clothing as ordained by the Rule of St Benedict. This will help them to lead a life of moderation and simplicity, to avoid contacts with the world and to fight vanity. For the monk's life must always be in harmony with the etymology of his name.[18]

15. *"Nunc autem in monasteriis Deo dicatis . . . abbates laici, cum suis uxoribus, filiis & filiabus, cum militibus morantur et canibus"* Mansi 18a:271. Their behavior left much to be desired: *"Terrenis negotiis vacant . . . moribus vivunt incompositis;"* (ibid., 270). The system was a clear violation of Church law, for neither could religious have a lay superior nor could laymen interfere in the internal affairs of a monastery. *"Contra omnem ecclesiae auctoritatem praelatis utuntur extraneis . . . Prohibent quippe sacri canones ne aliquis laicus de religione praesumat"* (ibid.). See also *"commenda,"* EC 4:50 and *"commende,"* DDC 3:1029.

16. Mansi 18a:270.

17. *"Auditur enim, quod spreta humilitate & abjectione monastica, ornamentis & his etiam quae bonis laicis indecentia & turpia sunt, operam impendent; & nequaquam contenti communibus, rebus propriis & lucris turpibus inserviant."* Mansi 18a:272.

18. *"Monastica vita sine regularis abbatis providentia ad pristinum et optimum vivendi nequit reformari ordinem."* Mansi 18a:270. *"Censemus igitur, ut status monasteriorum inviolatus, juxta antiquam regulae traditionem & canonum constituta, servetur: & ut abbates sint religiosae personae & quae regularem noverint disciplinam . . . Sane ne ulla monachis evagandi vel de talibus praesumendi quippiam detur occasio, provideant abbates, vel praepositi monasteriorum, ut . . . omnia illis in*

Monastic Reform: Conciliar Legislation in Eleventh-Century France 117

In the absence of serious monastic initiatives, local bishops came to consider it their duty to concern themselves with the monasteries in distress, just as they were charged, in virtue of their office, with the reformation of their own clergy. A case in point of such episcopal concern is the council of Koblenz which met in 922. While acknowledging the monks' right to elect their abbot from among themselves, as ordained by the Rule of St Benedict, it still felt that monks engaged in the ministry of souls should be placed under the local bishop's jurisdiction.[19] The synod of Augsburg (962) went even further and would have liked to place all monks under the bishop's jurisdiction.[20] In this light must also be seen the dispute between Cluny and the bishop of Mâcon which was brought before the council of Anse (1025). The latter reaffirmed canon 4 of the council of Chalcedon which placed abbots and monks under the local ordinary, even though Cluny could claim papal exemption.[21]

---

victualibus et vestibus necessaria, sicut regula praecipit, opportune ministrentur . . . Monachi vero . . . juxta suam professionem, sobrie & pie ac simpliciter vivant . . . non saecularibus curis vel negotiis occupentur, non pompas mundiales requirant, non ecclesiastica jura inquietent, sed juxta proprietatem sui vocabuli quiete otium amplectantur;" ibid., 272. This idea will also animate the early Cistercians: *"monachus . . . nominis sui ethimologiam hec* [i.e. *seculares actus*] *fugiendo sectari debet."* J. Van Damme, *op. cit.*, 13.

19. Can. 6: *"Hoc quoque statutum est, quatenus ecclesiae quorumcumque monachorum in singulis parochiis sitae, episcoporum, ut decet, divinitus subdentur regimini . . . Ipsi proculdubio monachi episcopis suis in omnibus obediant."* Mansi 18a:438. See also H. Maisonneuve, *op. cit.*, 9 and Giles Constable, *Monastic Tithes from their Origins to the Twelfth Century* (Cambridge: At the University Press, 1964), 57ff.

20. *"Oportet etiam episcopum, in cujus dioecesi coenobium situm est, monachorum providentiam gerere: & si aliquid correctione dignum reperit, corrigere festinat."* Mansi 18a:438. Cf. also H. Maisonneuve, *op. cit.*, 9f.

21. *"Relegentes ergo sancti Chalcedonensis & plurimorum authenticorum conciliorum sententias, quibus praecipitur, qualiter per unamquamque regionem abbates & monachi proprio subesse debent episcopo."* Mansi 18a:423f. Cf. A. Fliche, *La réforme grégorienne*, 1:15. One could also refer to the so-called constitutions of Odo, archbishop of Canterbury, promulgated after the council of London (a. 944) which urged the monks *"ut in omni humilitate et obedientia die noctuque hoc adimplere studeant, permanentes in timore Dei in ecclesiis ubi se voto constrixerunt. Non sint vagabundi, neque gyrovagi, qui nomen monachi desiderant, officium*

118   *The Eleventh-Century Background of Cîteaux*

The church councils between the years A.D. 1000 and 1150 made numerous references to serious monastic shortcomings in contemporary Frankish houses. Most frequently mentioned are apostasy, simony and, in general, a widespread disregard for the ideals of St Benedict. To remedy the situation, the synods published a great number of canons, demanding, above all—in strong terms and under pain of adequate sanctions—an end to lay mastery over churches. According to G. Schreiber, their "tone was extremely harsh and, at the same time, revolutionary to the ear of the layman."[22] The same author published a list of eleventh-century Frankish synods which dealt with monastic reform just as A. Fliche, G. Coulton, P. Hinschius and C. Richard had done before him in a somewhat different manner.[23]

The conciliar enactments themselves accurately portray the contemporary situation. The synod of Bourges (1031) for instance stressed the importance of clerical celibacy in the face of widespread abuses and promised effective measures against all delinquents. It further objected to the practice in which lay lords kept priests in a dependent status on benefices[24] and condemned monks guilty of unauthorized travel and vagrancy. It discouraged the latter from transferring from one monastery to another in a quest of honors and

---

autem ejus contemnunt: sed secundum exempla apostolorum, per habitum humilitatis, laboribus manuum, & lectione sacra, & continuis orationibus se exercentes, parati . . . patremfamilias expectent." Mansi 18a:396.—The Cistercians did not seek exemption in the early years of their history. According to J. Mahn, "A most perfect uniformity prevailed between the Cistercian monasteries, and, in conformity with canon four of the council of Chalcedon, the Cistercians never established themselves in a diocese without the authorization of the bishop. This precaution was even formally prescribed by the Charter of Charity." *Op. cit.*, 131ff. Cf. J. Van Damme, *op. cit.*, 15.

22. *Gemeinschaften des Mittelalters*, 338. See also G. Coulton, *op. cit.*, 1:260.

23. G. Schreiber, *Gemeinschaften des Mittelalters*, 301; A. Fliche, *La réforme grégorienne*, 1: 397, 2:440f. and 3:347; idem, *Le règne de Philippe Ier*, 364f.; G. Coulton, *op. cit.*, 1:260; P. Hinschius, *op. cit.*, 3:534 n. 4; Carolus Richard, *Analysis Conciliorum Generalium et Particularium* (Venetiis: Typographia Balleonia, 1776–1780), vol. 2.

24. Can. 21; Mansi 19:506. See also Hefele-Leclercq 4(2):953 and H. Lea, *op. cit.*, 1:207.

offices. It excepted only the case where the changeover was a necessity or beneficial to the soul in the sense that the new place offered greater possibilities for an observant life. But one always needed the abbot's or the bishop's permission for the undertaking. Otherwise, if a monk who took the monastic habit of his own accord and vowed to lead a life according to the Rule of St Benedict in complete freedom left his monastery without authorization, he was liable to excommunication until making the required amends. If after such satisfaction, the abbot of the monastery or other monks of the same place should deny him readmission, he was to join the clerics attached to the (parish) church or stay in the guest house, but wear the monastic habit, practice the spirit of reverence and observe the law of abstinence.[25]

The council of Limoges which met in the same year, spoke out against the shortening of the monastic office. Twelve lessons were to be read during the Nocturns and not nine, as in the case of the canons who followed the Roman *cursus*.[26]

According to Ordericus Vitalis, Pope Leo IX held a council in the city of Reims while visiting France in 1049. This council condemned clerical incontinence, the carrying of arms by churchmen and the evils connected with proprietary churches and altars. It also censured simony (e.g. the use of money or similar goods to

---

25. Can. 24: "*Ut illi qui voluntarii, & secundum regulam S Benedicti habitum monachi susceperunt, & postea voluntarii dereliquerunt, communione fidelium priventur usque ad emendationem dignam. Et si abbates, vel alii monachi nolunt eos suscipere: maneant cum clericis in monasteriis, vel apud ecclesias, in habitu monastico, & reverentia, atque abstinentia.*" Mansi 19:506. Cf. also can. 25: "*Ut ... monachi de monasteriis suis, ubi prius titulati sunt, nisi causa rationabilis necessitatis vel aedificationis animae, vel ordinem melius observandi, ad alium monasterium non transeant propter adipiscendum aliquod ministerium vel honorem, vel occupationem terrenam, absque consensu episcopi sui vel abbatis.*" Ibid. On the question of excommunication see Gratian, *Decreti Pars Secunda*, XI, iii, 1ff.; PL 187:838ff.; DDC 5:615–628 and Heinrich Fries (ed.), *Handbuch Theologischer Grundbegriffe* (München: Kösel Verlag, 1962–1963), 1; 375ff., esp. 379.

26. "*Numquid canonici monachos pro duodecim lectionibus vel monachi canonicos pro novem numero reprehendere possunt? ... Duodecim comprobavit ille vir spiritu omnium justorum plenus sanctusque papa Gregorius.*" Mansi 19:534. See also Hefele-Leclercq 4(2):957.

secure one's election as abbot) and apostate monks unfaithful to their vocation.[27]

The council of Toulouse (1056) set the lowest age limit for abbots at thirty years. It further decreed the ineligibility of a cleric to the office of abbot if he had become a monk for the sole purpose of obtaining this dignity and stated that such a person must remain in the abbey as a simple monk or else face excommunication. Abbots were told to fulfill their obligations toward their monasteries and provide their subjects with all the necessaries in food and clothing, as called for by the Rule of St Benedict. On no account must they tolerate monks retaining personal possessions. Should an abbot or a monk fail on this account, then the local bishop will have the authority to step in and take the necessary corrective measures.[28]

In 1059, Pope Nicholas II threatened with excommunication all vagrant monks, unless they returned to their monastery and observed regular discipline.[29] The Pontiff also reminded abbots and monks that they are not allowed to appropriate things for personal use and warned that simoniac practices will result in the loss of

27. Ordericus Vitalis, *Historia Ecclesiastica*, PL 188:416. See also Mansi 19:742; Hefele-Leclercq 4(2):1011ff.; C. Richard, *op. cit.*, 2:9. H. Lea, *op. cit.*, 1:221 n. 3 and A. Fliche, *La réforme grégorienne*, 1:137. Important for our purposes is can. 8 which states *"Ne quis monachus . . . a suo gradu apostataret."* Mansi 19:742. Philippe Labbé published additional, though defective, texts in *Sacrosancta Concilia* (Lutetiae Parisiorum: Impensis Societatis Typographicae, 1671), 9:1048.

28. See especially can. 2: *"Item placuit confirmare . . . ut abbas . . . ante triginta annos non ordinetur;"* can. 5: *"Statuit idem sancta synodus, ut si quis clericorum adipiscendae abbatiae causa monachus effectus fuerit, in abbatia quidem monachus permaneat, sed ad ipsum honorem, ad quem adspirabat, nullatenus accedat. Quod si praesumpserit, excommunicetur;"* and can. 6: *"Item decrevit, ut abbates curam monachorum & monasteriorum exerceant, & eis victum & vestitum secundum regulam sancti Benedicti praebeant: & hoc agentes proprium eos habere nullatenus permittant. Ipsi vero monachi absque voluntate abbatis praeposituram aliquam non teneant. Abbas autem vel monachus has institutiones corrigentes, a propriis corrigantur episcopis."* Mansi 19:847. See also Hefele-Leclercq 4(2):1122ff. and C. Richard, *op. cit.*, 2:10.

29. *Ad episcopos Galliae*, 2: *"De monachis vero propositum non servantibus decrevimus ut quousque ad propositum redeant et in monasterio regulariter consistant, communione privati permaneant."* Mansi 19:873. See also Hefele-Leclercq 4(2):1168f. and *above*, n. 24.

that office or privilege obtained in such a manner. Finally he decreed abbots who disposed of community goods or objects pertaining to the divine service without the consent of the community would incur excommunication.[30]

In the same year, the council of Rouen condemned the practice of taking the monastic habit because of promises made or hopes entertained of being raised to the abbatial office.[31]

To combat simony, the council of Vienne (1060) felt the need to reaffirm the provisions of the council of Chalcedon prohibiting the acquisition of an ecclesiastical office or dignity, including that of an abbot, through purchase or agreements of a similar nature. Hence its decision that in case of infringement the giver of such favors will lose his rank and dignity, and the receiver will forfeit his ill-acquired office or benefice, with no prospect of ever recovering it.[32]

This enactment was repeated, almost verbatim, by the council of Tours, also of the same year. A further ordinance decreed that no one may accept a church, either small or large, from a layman without the consent of the bishop of the diocese. Nor should churches be accepted by anyone if donated by a cleric or a monk, for this would amount to venality, in which case both the giver and the receiver will lose the church in question. Turning its

30. *Decreta Nicolai II. Papae:* "14. *Ut nullus Abbas obedientias suas vendat, neque nullus monachus emat obedientias. Quod si praesumpserint, utrique ordine officioque careant, quia simoniace agunt. Et monachi proprium omnino non habeant.* 15. *Abbatibus . . . quid de rebus ecclesiasticis vel sacro ministerio alienare vel obligare absque permissu & subscriptione conventus sui nihil liceat. Quod si praesumpserit, degradetur, communione concessa; & quod temere praesumptum est & alienatum ordinatione sui episcopi revocetur.*" Mansi 19:875f.

31. "*Ut nullus habitum monachi suscipiat, spem aut promissionem habens ut abbas fiat*" Mansi 19:898. See also Hefele-Leclercq 42:1168.

32. "*Sancti Spiritus auctoritate, ut Chalcedonensi synodo sententia de simoniacis prolata, ab omnibus observetur, quatenus quicumque deinceps pecunia, aut aliqua interveniente conventione saeculari, aut quolibet modo, contra canonicam censuram, episcopatum, abbatiam, aut archidiaconatum seu archipresbyteratum, aut aliquam dignitatem ecclesiasticam, seu aliquem gradum, vel ministerium, vel beneficium, quod nonnisi clericis habere sanctorum Patrum sancivit auctoritas, dare vel accipere quolibet modo canonibus contrario tentaverit: & dans a proprio decidat gradu et dignitate: & accipiens ministerium seu beneficium male usurpatum numquam recuperaturus admittat.*" Mansi 19:925f. See also Hefele-Leclercq 4(2):1202.

attention to the problem of vagrancy the council also decreed that a monk who deserts his abbey will be excommunicated and considered an apostate until he makes adequate reparations. If after such a penance the abbot refused to reinstate him, he (the abbot) will be suspended from community life after three warnings, until he changes his mind about the readmission of the repentant culprit.[33]

The council of Caen (1061) advised abbots sojourning in the countryside to stay in the vicinity of monasteries, so as not to give public offense as vagrants.[34]

A few years later, the synod of Toulouse (1068) urged monks "to live religiously according to the Rule of St Benedict."[35]

The question of vagrant monks who either left their monastery on their own initiative or were expelled because of a misdeed, figured also on the agenda of the council of Rouen (1072). The decision was that every effort should be made to effect the return of these fugitives to their monastery, even if it meant the use of force. If the abbot denied them readmission, they were to be supplied with alms and given permission to support themselves through their own handiwork, as long as they kept mending their ways.[36]

33. Can. 4: *"Nullus ecclesiam magnam vel parvam, deinceps sine consensu episcopi, in cujus parochia est, a laicis praesumat accipere quolibet modo: sed neque a clerico, vel monacho, seu laico, sub pretii alicujus venalitate. Quod si fecerit: & vendens, & emens, ea careat."* Mansi 19:927. See also can. 10: *"Quicumque monasticae religionis desertor inventus fuerit: a regno Dei & a consortio Christianorum, sicut apostata, excludatur, & alienus existat, donec resipiscens digne paeniteat. Similiter qui ejusmodi digne paenitentes tertio recipere noluerit, tertio admonitus, si non adquieverit, a communione fratrum suspendatur, sive sit abbas, sive abbatissa, donec acquiescant."* Ibid., 928. See also Hefele-Leclercq 4(2):1202f.

34. *"Ut abbates, aliique Praelati ruri commorantes in urbes monasteriis vicinas se conferrent, ne cum publica offensione huc illucque vagari viderentur."* Mansi 19:937.

35. This council met on the occasion of the restoration of the diocese of Lectour and decided, under the presidency of Hugh of Silva Candida, *inter alia*, *"Judicatum est igitur a fratribus omnibus illius sancti conventus . . . monachos . . . religiose & secundum regulam sancti Benedicti vivere."* Mansi 19:1066.

36. Can. 12: *"Item monachi et sanctimoniales, qui relictis suis ecclesiis per orbem vagantur, alii pro nequitiis suis a monasteriis expulsis: quos pastorali auctoritate oportet compellere, ut ad monasteria sua redeant. Et si expulsos abbates recipere noluerint, victum eleemosynae eis tribuant, quae etiam manuum labore acquirant, quousque si vitam suam emendaverint viderentur."* Mansi 20:38. See also Hefele-Leclercq 4(2):1282, and C. Richard, *op. cit.*, 2:12.

Another council of Rouen, which met in 1074, prescribed that only those may be blessed as abbots who in their previous life proved themselves in regular discipline. A monk guilty of a public crime was therefore ineligible; nor could he be appointed to an office that would take him outside the monastery. The council further insisted that monks should not take up new customs, but adhere to the traditional practices of their order. They should observe the Rule of St Benedict in its integrity, and make no departures from it in such areas as silence, vigils, fasts, clothing and the taking of oaths.[37]

The canons of the council of Poitiers (1078) censured abbots who accepted abbeys, churches or benefices from the king, a count or any other lay person, for in the council's mind such favors could only be conferred by the local ordinary. It also condemned the accumulation of benefices—bishoprics, abbeys, archdeaconries, cathedrals, prebends, etc.—in accordance with the rule: "One prelate, one church." Then it decreed stiff penalties against those guilty of simony. Whoever procures a favor or an office through simony, will be deposed and the cause of the scandal removed. Similarly abbots who sought to remain in the order of deacons for obvious reasons of comfort were directed to have themselves ordained to the priesthood or else lose their office. Abbots and monks were also told to abstain from the practice of imposing penance, unless commissioned by the ordinary, and to abstain from seeking the possession or control of churches which did not belong to them previously.[38]

---

37. Can. 2: "*Quod nullus ordinetur abbas, nisi prius diuturna conversatione monasticae vitae disciplinam assecutus fuerit.*" Mansi 20:398. In this connection can. 6 prescribes, "*Nullus monachus corporali crimine publice lapsus abbas ordinetur vel in aliquo exteriori officio praeficiatur.*" Ibid., 399. On the observance of the Rule see can. 7 which ordains "*Ut regula B. Benedicti in utroque sexu incommutabiliter observetur, ut neque in vigiliis, neque in jejuniis, sive indumentis ab ejus institutionibus dissideant; nec . . . si alia lege vivere voluerint, quam ordo exigit, permittantur. Juramenta quae contra regularem observantiam faciunt, omnino omittant & silentium quod penitus omiserint, teneant.*" Ibid. See also Hefele-Leclercq 5(1):112f. and C. Richard, *op. cit.*, 2:14.

38. Can. 1: "*Ut nullus episcopus, abbas, presbyter, vel quaelibet persona de clero*

The council of Lillebonne (1080) legislated that, whenever a church was donated to monks, the priest or chaplain of the church in question was to retain the rights he had before the donation. In case he died or became incapacitated, then the abbot was to look for another priest and present the new chaplain, either in person or through a representative, to the bishop for confirmation. If the priest decided to become a monk, he was to make sure that the church where he was installed by the bishop was well provided for, especially with regard to vestments and liturgical books, but only as far as the means at hand allowed it. If the priest preferred to live by himself, the abbot was to give him from the church's income as much as he needed for his livelihood and the proper fulfillment of his duties. If the abbot failed on this account, then the local bishop was to intervene and ensure the execution of these provisions.[39]

In 1082, the council of Meaux decreed that abbeys with less than ten monks or not sufficiently endowed to support such a number should be reduced to simple cells and subjected to Cluny or

---

accipiat de manu regis vel comitis, vel cujuslibet laicae personae donum episcopatus, vel abbatiae, vel ecclesiae, vel aliquarum ecclesiaticarum rerum. Sed episcopus a suo metropolitano, abbas, presbyter & ceterae inferiores personae a proprio episcopo." Can. 2: *"Ut nemo . . . abbatiam . . . in duabus ecclesiis . . . exerceat nisi in una tantum: & neutram horum quisquam per pecuniam acquirat. Et quicumque tali modo jam adquisisse comprobatur, omni remota occasione deponatur."* Can. 5: *"Ut nullus abbas, monachus vel quilibet alius poenitentias injungat, nisi quibus proprius episcopus hanc curam dederit."* Can. 6: *"Ut abbates, monachi . . . ecclesias quas numquam habuerunt non emant, nec alio modo sibi vindicant."* Can. 7: *"Ut abbates diaconi, qui presbyteri non sunt, presbyteri fiant aut praelationes amittant."* Mansi 20:498. See also Hefele-Leclercq 5(1):229ff.

39. Can. 12: *"Si donatur monachis ecclesia, presbyter qui tenet ecclesiam honorifice teneat quicquid de eadem ecclesia haberet antequam monachi eam haberent: & tanto melius, quanto sanctioribus associatur hominibus: eo autem mortuo, vel aliquatenus deficiente, abbas idoneum quaerat presbyterum & episcopo eum per se vel per nuntium suum ostendat. Quem si recipiendus est, episcopus recipiat. Si vero presbyter cum monachis religiose vivere voluerit, videat ut ecclesia, quem episcopali licentia intravit, honeste tractetur, tam in vestimentis, quam in libris & ceteris ecclesiae serviendae necessariis secundum ejusdem ecclesiae facultatem. Quod si presbyter cum monachis vivere noluerint, tantum ei det abbas de bonis ecclesiae, unde & bene vivere & ecclesiae servitium convenienter valeat adimplere. Quod si abbas facere noluerit, ab episcopo cogatur ut faciat."* Mansi 20:557.

Marmoutiers. Too much opposition, however, brought the resolution to nought.[40]

The council of Melfi (1089), though not held on French soil, had nevertheless its impact also on France, especially with its prohibition that laymen grant tithes, churches or similar favors to monasteries without the consent of the local ordinary or the permission of the Roman Pontiff. It also told abbots to abstain from soliciting gifts for someone's reception into the monastery and asked the bishops to put an end to monastic vagrancy.[41]

The question whether monks could legitimately engage in parish work and participate in curial functions was discussed by the council of Autun (1094) under the presidency of Archbishop Hugh of Lyons. It answered in the negative, seeing in the monks' claim to such ministrations a usurpation of the rights of the diocesan clergy. Similar sentiments inspired the injunction which called on monks to abstain from making propaganda among canons in order to win them for the monastery.[42]

40. "*Ego Robertus in Meldensi concilio a Romano legato nomine Hugone Meldensis ecclesiae consecratus episcopus notum facio . . . quod in episcopatu nostro quaedam erat ecclesia . . . quae abbatiae nomen habebat, sed per incuriam habitantium dignitatem hujus nominis amiserat. Ordinavit igitur supradictum concilium, ut hujusmodi abbatiae cellae fierent & cellae nominarentur, religiosisque monachis traderentur.*" Mansi 20:587. See also G. Tellenbach, *op. cit.*, 273; J. Evans, *op. cit.*, 26f.; W. Lühe, *op. cit.*, 92 n. 1; Antonio de Yepez, *Crónica de la Orden de San Benito Patriarca de religiósos* (Irache: por Matias Mares, 1609–1621) 4:331; Joannes Mabillon, *Annales Ordinis S. Benedicti occidentalium monachorum patriarchae*, 6 vols. (Lucae: Typis Leonardi Venturini, 1739–1745), 5: Appendix 19; RHF 14:38.

41. Can. 5: "*Nullus laicus decimas suas aut ecclesiam, aut quidquid ecclesiastici juris est, sine consensu episcopi, vel Romani pontificis, monasteriis aut canonicis offerre praesumat.*" Can. 6: "*Nullus abbas, nullus ecclesiarum praepositus, quae juris sunt ecclesiastici accipere sine episcopi concessione praesumat.*" Can. 7: "*Nullus abbas pretium exigere ab eis qui ad conversionem veniunt aliqua placiti occasione praesumat.*" Can. 10: "*Constituimus, ne quis episcopus qua primas monachum quemlibet vagantem in sua diocesi provinciave retineat, nisi abbatis proprii fuerit literis regulariter commendatus.*" Mansi 20:723. See also Hefele-Leclercq 5(1):344 and C. Richard, *op. cit.*, 2:16.

42. "*Monachis interdicitur, ne . . . parroechialium sacerdotum officia in parrochiis usurpent.*" Bernold of Constance, *Chronicon*, P.L. 154; 351f. Mansi 20:799. Hefele-Leclercq 5(1):387; W. Lühe, *op. cit.*, 15 and 96; "Tables chronologi-

The great assembly of Clermont, summoned and attended by Pope Urban II in 1095, strictly prohibited the retention and ownership of tithes, altars or churches by laymen, and that clerics accept spiritual favors from seculars. It also ruled that in churches belonging to monks the faithful should not be ministered to by monks but have a chaplain installed by the bishop at the monks' recommendation; his appointment, transfer and daily needs remained the bishop's responsibility.[43] This legislation may have had its precedent in the Roman synod of 1083 which stated that no monk could rightfully assume the functions of a parish priest, except in case of necessity, i.e. when baptism needed to be administered or absolution to be granted; but even then only if no diocesan priest was at hand.[44]

In seeming contrast, the council of Nîmes (1096) defended the monks' right to direct pastoral ministrations. It decreed that monks who renounced the world have on account of their vocation a strong desire to pray for sinful men and are, consequently, better qualified to forgive sins than the secular clergy. Moreover, since the monks are imitators of the apostles who, as we read in the Acts of the Apostles, "were of one heart and one soul, and . . . had all things in common" (4:32), they are valid administrators of the

---

ques," *Bernard de Clairvaux*, 568. In some instances monks undertook the *cura animarum* as a result of stipulations made by donors; cf. M. Prou, *op. cit.*, 264, citing the case of Bec. In this connection the councils of Poitiers (1078), Clermont (1095) and Rome (1096) emphatically stressed the rights of the local ordinary. Cf. A. Fliche, *Le règne de Philippe Ier*, 477. For the decision on the canons, see Mansi 20:801f.: "*Nullus abbas vel monachus canonicos regulares a proposito professionis canonicae revocare atque monasticum habitum suscipere audeat ut monachi fiant, quamdiu ordinis sui ecclesiam invenire queant in qua canonice vivendo Deo servire & animam salvare possint. Quod si temerario ausu id agere temptaverint, anathematis vinculo obligentur.*" See also below, n. 50.

43. Can. 15: "*Ut nullus ecclesiasticorum aliquem honorem a manu laicorum accipiat. Ut clericus nullum ecclesiae honorem a laicali manu accipiat.*" Can. 20: "*Unde et interdictum est omnibus laicis, ne amplius altaria vel ecclesias sibi retineant.*" Mansi 20:818. See also can. 33: "*In ecclesiis ubi monachi habitant, populus per monachum non regatur, sed capellanus, qui populum regat, ab episcopo per consilium monachorum instituatur; ita tamen, ut ex solius episcopi arbitrio tam ordinatio quam depositio et totius vitae pendeat arbitrio.*" Ibid., 820. See also below, n. 50.

44. Can. 6; Hefele-Leclercq 5(1):308. See also *ibid.*, 403 n. 4 and G. Schreiber, *Gemeinschaften des Mittelalters*, 299.

sacrament of penance.[45] But the council was also aware of monastic shortcomings. It branded the monks who had accepted benefices from laymen "thieves and robbers" and strongly condemned the retention of such possessions. Likewise, it directed monks never to invite persons under excommunication or interdict to take part in the divine office or to grant them burial on monastic grounds.[46]

The last council to be considered here, that of Poitiers (1100), decreed: since it is the local bishop's exclusive right to tonsure his clerics, abbots should restrict such functions to members of the Order of St Benedict. In addition, they were directed not to use the pontifical insignia—gloves, sandals and ring—without the prior permission of the Holy See, and monks were warned not to wear

---

45. Can. 2: "*Sunt nonnulli stulti dogmatis . . . asserentes monachos qui mundo mortui sunt et Deo vivunt sacerdotali officio indignos, neque poenitentiam, aut Christianitatem, seu absolutionem largiri posse per sacerdotalis officii injunctam gratiam: sed omnino falluntur . . . B. Gregorius monachico habitu pollens . . . Augustinus . . . Anglorum praedicator egregius & Pannoniensis Martinus, aliique quam plurimi viri sanctissimi, pretioso monachorum habitu fulgentes, nequaquam annulo pontificali subarrharentur. Neque enim Benedictus monachorum praeceptor sanctissimus, hujus rei aliquo modo interdictor fuit: sed eos saecularium negotiorum dixit expertes esse debere. . . . Credimus igitur, a sacerdotalibus monachis ligandi solvendique potestatem digne administrari: si tamen digne contigerit eos hoc ministerio sublimari. Quod evidenter affirmat, quisquis statum monachorum & habitum considerat.*" Can. 3: "*Oportet eos qui saeculum reliquerunt majorem sollicitudinem habere pro peccatis hominum & plus valere eorum peccata solvere, quam presbyteri saeculares. Quia hi secundum regulam apostolicam vivunt & eorum sequentes vestigia, communem vitam ducunt, juxta id quod in actibus eorum scriptum est: 'Erat illis cor unum et anima una, & erant illis omnia communia'.*" Mansi 20:934f. See also Hefele-Leclercq 5(1):447f., and Ernest Lavisse (ed.), *Histoire de France illustrée depuis les origines jusqu'à la Révolution*. Tome II, Deuxième partie: *Les premiers Capétiens (987–1137)* (Paris: Libraire Hachette, 1911), 218. On monasticism and pastoral ministry, see Philipp Hofmeister, "Mönchtum und Seelsorge bis zum 13. Jahrhundert," *Studien und Mitteilungen*, 65 (1955), 209–273; J. Leclercq, "On Monastic Priesthood," *loc. cit.*, 152ff.; Hefele-Leclercq 5(1):448 n. 1; DACL 3:229 n. 1 and G. Schreiber, *Gemeinschaften des Mittelalters*, esp. 293ff.

46. Can. 8: "*Clericus vel monachus qui ecclesiasticum de manu laici susceperit beneficium, quia non intravit per ostium, sed ascendit aliunde sicut fur et latro, ab eodem separetur officio.*" Mansi 20:936. Can. 16: "*Monachi nullo modo recipiant ad sepulturam, aut quodlibet divinum officium, excommunicatos, aut raptores, aut interdictos.*" Ibid., 937. See also Hefele-Leclercq 5(1):449.

the maniple before the reception of the subdiaconate. They were once more forbidden to accept tithes and altars from laymen and to engage in direct pastoral activities, i.e. to baptize, preach and administer the sacrament of penance.[47]

A topical arrangement of the synodal decrees just described reveals at once the major problems faced by contemporary monachism. The decrees stressed, first of all, the importance of the Benedictine Rule and the need to observe it without modifications. Accordingly, abbots were bidden to be mindful, as St Benedict desired, of their obligations toward their monks and their monastery and monks were encouraged to be equally faithful to the Benedictine ideals. To assure this, the councils prescribed a number of remedies for existing contemporary ills.

Thus from now on only priests experienced and tried in monastic discipline were to become abbots. Persons guilty of a public crime or of simony, and clerics entering the monastery for the sole purpose of making a career as abbots were no longer eligible to the highest office in the monastery. The holders of this office were directed not to use the *pontificalia* without authorization, engage in excessive

---

47. Can. 1: *"Ut nullus praeter episcopum clericis coronas benedicere praesumat, exceptis abbatibus, qui illis tantummodo coronas faciant, quos sub regula beati Benedicti militaturos susceperit."* Can. 5: *"Ut nemo monachorum deinceps manipulis utatur, nisi fuerit subdiaconus ordinatus."* Can. 6: *"Ut nullus abbatum utatur chirothecis, sandalis, annulo: nisi quibus fuerit per privilegium a Romana ecclesia concessum."* Can. 9: *"Ut neque clerici vel monachi per pecuniam altaria vel decimas a laicis vel quibuslibet personis sibi adquirant, similiter sub excommunicatione interdicimus."* Mansi 20:1123. Can. 10: *"Ut clericis regularibus jussu episcopi sui baptizare, praedicare, poenitentiam dare, mortuos sepelire liceat."* Ibid., 1132f.— The use of the maniple, at first a papal prerogative, was subsequently granted to the deacons of Rome and later to all clerics in major orders. Eventually also acolytes, laybrothers and, in general, all who participated in the office of the choir were allowed to wear a maniple in certain churches. As Lanfranc wrote to John of Reims, *"Plerique autumant manipulum esse commune ornamentum omnium . . . nam et in coenobiis monachorum etiam laici . . . solent ferre manipulum."* Ep. 13; PL 150:520. According to Rupert of Deutz, *"A senibus usque ad infantes manipulos portamus."* De divinis officiis, II, 23; PL 170:54. Carthusian nuns are given a maniple at their consecration even today. The council of Poitiers shows that such practices did not meet with universal approval. Cf. Valentin Thalhofer and Ludwig Eisenhofer, *Handbuch der Katholischen Liturgik* (Freiburg i. B.: Herder, 1912), 1:550ff. and 2:402f.

travelling or seek additional honors, benefices and churches. They were to tonsure only their own subjects and to abstain from imposing ecclesiastical censures on outsiders and laymen in general.

The provisions dealing with ordinary monks stress that the latter should lead a life worthy of a religious; this is best done by observing the Rule of St Benedict with the utmost fidelity. Accordingly, monks should not engage in direct pastoral work—baptize, preach, or hear confession—unless requested by the bishop of the diocese, but leave this type of the apostolate to chaplains taken from the diocesan clergy. Nor should they leave their monastery and transfer to another, except in case of necessity, i.e. when such a change would be to the advantage of their soul. Unauthorized leaves, such as vagrancy, desertion and apostasy, called for censures, including the penalty of excommunication, which was to be lifted only after the culprit's return to his monastery.[48] Finally, as laymen were forbidden to interfere in church matters by making decisions about altars, churches and benefices, so were abbots and monks ordered to refuse such favors offered by laymen or to grant special spiritual benefits to persons under excommunication or interdict.

Early Cîteaux was not only aware of these synodal enactments, but actually anxious to implement them. This is why it came into being, why it sought a life based on the original ideals of St Benedict, free from all heterogeneous additions made by subsequent centuries. This is also why it rose against traditional monachism and rejected tithes[49] and proprietary churches—and, with the latter, pastoral

---

48. On the problem of the *transitus*, also faced by the Cistercian pioneers when leaving Molesme for Cîteaux, see the canons of the councils of Rouen (1072), London (1075), Gerone (1078), and Beneventum (1090); Mansi 20:398, 451, 520 and 937. See also Charles Dereine, "La fondation de Cîteaux d'après l'Exordium Cistercii et l'Exordium Parvum," *Cîteaux*, 10 (1959), 127; Joseph Turk, "Cistercii Statuta Antiquissima," *Analecta Sacri Ordinis Cisterciensis*, 4 (1948), 41ff.; J. Mabillon, *Annales ordinis S. Benedicti*, 4:118, 340f.; Mansi 19:537f.; PL 140:796; and *below*, pp. 263ff., nn. 118–125.

49. If the information of Ordericus Vitalis is correct, Abbot Robert urged the monks to return their tithes and oblations to the diocesan clergy and to live by the labor of their hands instead. The assembly of the monks however rejected the proposal. Robert and a number of like-minded monks thereupon seceded from Molesme and established Cîteaux. PL 188:638. The pioneers of

care[50]—why it opted for economic self-sufficiency (autarky), for a genuine restoration of manual labor and for the admission of non-aristocratic laybrothers. The impact and implications of these measures should become clear later in this investigation; for the moment it will suffice to conclude that there were definite shortcomings in eleventh-century monasticism, that the Church took note of them and proceeded to rectify them. The desire for a wholesale renewal became thus evident and soon took increasingly effective forms.

Cîteaux then enforced the hitherto more or less theoretical prohibition of monastic tithes. "*Ecclesias, altaria, sepulturas, decimas alieni laboris, vel nutrimenti, villas, villanos, terrarum census, furnorum vel molendinorum redditus et cetera his similia monastice puritati adversantia, nostri et nominis et ordinis excludit institutio.*" J. Van Damme, *op. cit.*, 28. See also *ibid.*, 13 and G. Constable, *op. cit.*, 137ff.

50. According to G. Schreiber, in a world where monasteries had amassed both lands and proprietary churches, Cîteaux rises in protest and mounts a frontal attack against such feudal practices. In a new perspective, it advocates a return to the Rule and, accordingly, calls for autarky and manual labor. It renounces pastoral care which it finds onerous and obstructive to its inward-turned asceticism and rejects oblations, tithes, the burial of outsiders and other favors to laymen. It left all this, and with it pastoral care, to the diocesan clergy and to the parish in general. Thus "the ideals of the eastern Church made a victorious comeback." *Gemeinschaften des Mittelalters*, 292. See also *ibid.*, 211, 354 and 367.

THE ELEVENTH CENTURY: RENEWAL IN EARNEST

THE ELEVENTH CENTURY, with all its indications of monastic decline, was nevertheless destined to become a century of renovation *par excellence*.[1] The advance of the Gregorian Reform, reform attempts from within the monastic order and new ways of thinking providing the climate for a number of new institutions were largely responsible for this development which, at the end of the century, saw the emergence of Cîteaux.

As a mixture of such components as Cluny, Farfa, Aniane, Vivarium and the Lateran monastery, traditional monachism took on forms in the eleventh century that could no longer satisfy ascetics filled with higher aspirations. According to G. Coulton: "All our evidence tends to show that there were very few houses in which the Rule (of St Benedict) was kept in anything like its original strictness."[2]

Attempts at a monastic reform from within were not lacking during the tenth and the eleventh centuries, which could claim a number of religious reformers. In Lorraine John of Vandière (d. 976), reformer of the monastery of Gorze in 933, demanded a strict observance of the Rule and introduced ascetical practices

---

1. H. DeWarren, "Le monachisme à l'apparition de saint Bernard," *loc. cit.*, 45.

2. *Loc. cit.*, 1: 273. See also H. DeWarren, "Le monachisme à l'apparition de saint Bernard," *loc. cit.* 52, and J. Leclercq, "La crise du monachisme," *loc. it.*, 21.

exceeding by far the demands of the Cassinese code.³ Richard, abbot of St Vanne in Verdun (d. 1046), was another reformer who tirelessly sought to restore a life consonant with the Benedictine ideals.⁴ In what is today Belgium, Gerard of Brogne (d. 959) set up an observance similar to that of Benedict of Aniane which stressed disciplinary and ascetical practices and became the model of all monasteries in the neighborhood.⁵ Around 940, Guibert (d. 942) founded the monastery of St Peter at Gembloux in the diocese of Liége whose monks were recruited from the abbey of Gorze.⁶ Poppo, abbot of Stavelot (d. 1048), successfully promoted his monastic reform, first in conjunction with Richard of St Vanne, then, as a sort of general abbot to a whole group of monasteries in Lorraine.⁷ In England, St Dunstan (d. 988) labored for fifteen years to reform the abbey of Glastonbury, in an endeavor to restore regular Benedictine life.⁸ Not surprisingly, Burgundy had one of the greatest reformers of the period, William, abbot of Saint Benignus in Dijon (d. 1031), whose influence reached as far as Italy, Germany and Fécamp in Normandy.⁹ According to Raoul Glaber,

3. MGH, SS 4:337-377; AS, Feb. 3:686-725. Cf. P. Schmitz, *op. cit.* 1:161f. U. Berlière, *L'ascèse bénédictine*, 74 and A. Hauck, *op. cit.*, 3:352ff.

4. MGH, SS 11:281ff. Cf. also U. Berlière, *L'ascèse bénédictine*, 74; idem, "L'étude des réformes monastiques," *loc. cit.*, 145; B. Albers, *Consuetudines Monasticae*, 5:113-133 (on the rule and book of customs) and A. Hauck, *op. cit.*, 3:476ff.

5. MGH, SS 15(2):654-673. U. Berlière, "L'étude des réformes monastiques," *loc. cit.*, 141; idem, *L'ascèse bénédictine*, 74 and A. Hauck, *op. cit.*, 3:346ff.

6. AS, Maj. 5; U. Berlière, "L'étude des réformes monastiques," *loc. cit.*, 142f.; P. Schmitz, *op. cit.*, 1:162; *Revue Mabillon*, 4 (1887), 303-307; A. Hauck, *op. cit.*, 3:370ff.

7. MGH, SS 11:291-316; U. Berlière, *L'ascèse bénédictine*, 74; P. Schmitz, *op. cit.*, 1:165; A. Hauck, *op. cit.*, 3:499ff.

8. Dunstan had also been on the continent where he spent some time at Gand which had close ties to Fleury. Cf. U. Berlière, "L'étude des réformes monastiques," *loc. cit.*, 139. The author aptly remarks: "As one sees, all these reform movements are not only parallel, but concentrical." Ibid. See also PL 139:1423ff.; idem, 137:413ff., and D. Knowles, *The Monastic Order*, 31ff.

9. *Vita S. Guillelmi abbatis Divionensis*, PL 142: 698-720. Cf. W. Williams, *Monastic Studies*, 99ff., especially 110, and A. Hauck, *op. cit.*, 3:461ff.

William's reform, patterned after the *Consuetudines* of Fructuaria, a Piedmontese abbey William founded between 1001 and 1003, embraced some forty monasteries and included the monastery of Saint Michael in Tonnerre, a station in the life of St Robert of Molesme.[10] The customs of Fructuaria, drawn up for the most part by William himself, were based on the Rule of St Benedict and the Cluniac usages then in vogue.[11] In the words of the chronicler of St Benignus: "He [William] restored . . . the discipline of regular life as established by St Benedict, which had almost perished through the negligence of preceding generations, to its pristine state."[12] His doctrine was "that, according to the precepts of St Benedict's Rule, they [the monks] should always display humility, in word, in action and in the quality of clothing."[13] In Auvergne, St Robert (d. 1067) founded and organized along Benedictine principles the monastery of Chaise-Dieu in the vicinity of Brioude from disciples who had gathered around his hermitage.[14] And a few years later, St Gerard (d. 1095) laid the foundations of the abbey of Sauve-Majeure (1079) on a tract of forest donated by the Count of Poitou and restored manual labor—in the form of clearing the land—for his monks.[15]

10. "*Erant namque tam monasteria atque cellulae monachorum circiter quadraginta.*" PL 142: 715. Cf. GCh 4:676 and A. Hauck, *op. cit.*, 3:464 n. 3. On Tonnerre, in connection with Robert of Molesme, see *below*, ch. VII, n. 3.

11. B. Albers, *Consuetudines Monasticae*, vol. 4.

12. "*Regularis vitae disciplinam, quae jam pene desiderat per veterum negligentiam, prout beatus Benedictus eam composuit in pristinum statum corrigendo restauravit, ac per diversas mundi partes per plura monasteria a regulari tramite devia, tam per se quam per suos, quos abbates ordinaverat, monastico ordini subdidit.*" Chronicon S. Benigni Divionensis, PL 162:823.

13. "*Ejus doctrina fuit ut juxta quod praecipit sancti Benedicti Regula in verbo, in omni actione, in vestitus qualitate, humilitatem videntibus se semper ostenderent.*" Ibid., PL 162:837.

14. PL 171:1505–1532 (*Vita*). Cf. AS, Apr. 3, and *L'eremitismo in occidente nei secoli XI e XII. Atti della seconda Settimana Internazionale di Studio, Mendola, 30 agosto—6 settembre 1962* (Miscellanea del Centro di Studi Medioevali, IV; Milano: Società Editrice Vita è Pensiero, 1965), 201. Hereafter cited, *L'eremitismo in occidente.*

15. AS, Apr. 1:412–421. J. Mabillon, *Annales*, 4:469; 5:100f., 151ff. Cirot de la Ville, *Histoire de la Grande-Sauve* (Paris: Mequignon, 1844f.), vol. 1.

All these foundations indicated the existence of reform centres outside the radius of Cluny. Working in specific regions and supported by powerful patrons, they won over one French monastery after the other for the reform. They represent independent endeavors, with such common traits as fleeing the world and leading a life based on the broad foundations of the Benedictine Rule. But since their effectiveness rested on the prestige of one man—the founder—their success was, unfortunately, not lasting.[16]

Of a like, if not greater importance was the abbey of Fleury on the Loire, reformed by Odo of Cluny, and in time a flourishing reform center with its own usages[17] and a great devotion to St Benedict of Nursia. The roots of the latter go back to the years 672–673, when Aigulf, a monk of Fleury, visited Monte Cassino, took the relics of St Benedict from the ruins of the monastery and brought them to Fleury where they were fittingly enshrined and always given due honors.[18] In one of his sermons at Fleury, Odo of Cluny likened St Benedict to Moses of the Old Testament.[19] This veneration reached even greater proportions during the eleventh century when Fleury, by now a center of intensive literary activities, produced an impressive literary output in glorification of the great Benedict, a fact mostly overlooked by students of the period.[20]

A further sign of renewal may be seen in the foundation of the

16. E. Sackur, *op. cit.*, 2:438. Cf. H. DeWarren, "Le monachisme à l'apparition de saint Bernard," *loc. cit.*, 57. In this connection U. Berlière remarks, "Hence let us well beware that when studying the various reform movements of this period we isolate the one from the other. The ancient monks were not isolated in their solitudes to such an extent that they took no interest to acquaint themselves with the various manifestations of contemporary religious life. The pilgrimages of a Cassian in Egypt, of a St Benedict of Aniane and of a John de Vandière (Gorze) in Italy had but one aim, to put to profit the knowledge they were able to receive in the contracts made with the masters of the spiritual life and with monastic observances." "L'étude des réformes monastiques," *loc. cit.*, 144.

17. B. Albers, *Consuetudines Monasticae*, 5:134–151.

18. *Historia translationis Sancti Benedicti in Galliam*, AS, Mart. 3:301. Cf. E. Sackur, *op. cit.*, 1:89 and 2:357 and 402; M. Mourre, *op. cit.*, 249f.; "Mont-Cassin," DACL, 11:2460.

19. E. Sackur, *op. cit.*, 2:334f.   20. *Ibid.*, 2:348–351.

convent of Marcigny by Hugh of Cluny, shortly after the middle of the century. This was done, in part, with a view to reducing the dangers of clerical incontinence in Burgundy, by providing an opportunity for converts of both sexes to take the religious habit and submit to monastic discipline.[21]

While this went on, eastern monachism continued to influence its western counterpart. At the close of the tenth century, St Gerard, bishop of Toul (d. 994), had, for instance, gathered a great number of Greek monks in his residence where they celebrated the daily divine praises "as it was done in their native land."[22] A few years later, Richard of St Vanne made the acquaintance of the hermit Simeon while on a pilgrimage to Jerusalem and brought him back to Lorraine where at the *Porta Nigra* of Trier he lived as a recluse until his death in 1035.[23] At the council of Limoges (1031) a cleric of Angoulême told the assembled fathers that a few years before several hermit-monks from Mount Sinai had settled in their region and that he had consulted two of them, Simeon and Cosmas, on the question of whether St Martial should be accorded the honors given to an apostle.[24] In 1037, "the Greek abbot Bartholomew" is listed in Benedict IX's entourage.[25] Greek pilgrimages "to the tombs of the apostles" went on, even after the break of 1054. From Rome and from southern Italy eastern monachism, with its stress on solitude, contemplative peace and aversion to secular learning,[26]

21. E. Petit, *Histoire op. cit.,* 1:197. Cf. also *above,* pp. 72f, nn. 103–105.

22. MGH, SS 4:501. Cf. Louis Gougaud, "L'oeuvre des *Scotti* dans l'Europe occidentale (Fin VIe—Fin XIe siècles)," RHE, 9 (1908), 274 n. 2.

23. *L'eremitismo in occidente,* 165 and *ibid.,* 62 n. 94. Cf. N. Huyghebaert, "Moines et clerc italiens en Lotharingie (VIIIe—XIIe siècle), *Fédération archéologique et historique de Belgique,* 33e congrès (Tournai, 1949), 95–111.

24. *"Ego autem quemdam Graecum peritum interrogans. . . Ante hos plures annos quidam ex fratribus de monte Sinai in hanc partem advenerunt occiduam Dei disponente nutu, moribus graves, doctrina catholica fidei profluentes, vita per omnia honesti, utriusque linguae periti: qui cum diu nobiscum Engolismae fuissent expectantes principem civitatis, et literis Graecis & Latinis eos videremus ad unguem imbutos, super hac re interrogare curavimus eos."* Mansi 19:517.

25. "*Bartholomaeus abbas Graecus;*" *ibid.,* 19:587.

26. *L'eremitismo in occidente,* 355 n. 2. *Ibid.,* 374 is a good outline of Greek monastic ideals and practices. See also G. Grützmacher, *op. cit.,* 40–42.

continued to reach the West. This is seen from the case of the "poor Beneventan (hermit) named Ursus," who arrived in Lorraine between the years 1060 and 1070.[27] In 1088, Bari in southern Italy solemnly welcomed the remains of St Nicholas, bishop of Myra.[28]

Nor did Celtic monks give up their missionary efforts, their *peregrinatio pro Christo*, on the continent, even though the austere rule of St Columban (d. 615) had to yield, gradually, to the more discreet Rule of St Benedict in the West—a development the great abbeys of Luxeuil, Bobbio, Honau, Remiremont and St Gall were unable to stem.[29] From the middle of the ninth century, Celtic monasteries and hospices sprang up in increasing numbers on the continent.[30] St Kaddroe (d. 975) who arrived with his twelve companions on the continent shortly before the middle of the tenth century, found in the forest of Thierache "a place destined for them ... from centuries where they could serve the Lord, living by the labor of their hands."[31] Kaddroe, for a while a member of the abbey of Fleury, eventually became abbot of Waulsort and was subsequently called upon to take charge of the monastery of St Clement at Metz which had lost its religious fervor. In 975 the monastery of St Martin of Cologne was given to Celts "in perpetuity."[32] The already mentioned Gerard of Toul sheltered not only Greek but also Celtic monks—*Scotti*, the only term used to designate "Irish" in contemporary texts—in his episcopal residence.[33] Before the turn of the century, the Irishman Fingen became abbot of St Clement's

---

27. "*Pauper Ursus, natione Beneventanus;*" *L'eremitismo in occidente*, 58 and 62 n. 94.

28. Ordericus Vitalis, *Historia Ecclesiastica*, PL 188:534. Cf. A. Mirgeler, *op. cit.*, 82ff.

29. G. Schreiber, *Gemeinschaften des Mittelalters*, 399 and 414. See also H. Taylor, *op. cit.*, 1:374.

30. L. Gougaud, "L'oeuvre des *Scotti*," *loc. cit.*, 272.

31. "*Locum a seculo eis paratum, ubi labore manuum suarum viventes Domino possent servire.*" *L'eremitismo in occidente*, 50 n. 28. See also AS, Mart. 1:474; E. Sackur, *op. cit.*, 1:181–186; U. Berlière, "L'étude des réformes monastiques," *loc. cit.*, 143; L. Gougaud, "L'oeuvre des *Scotti*," *loc. cit.*, 267 n. 5 and 273.

32. L. Gougaud, "L'oeuvre des *Scotti*," *loc. cit.*, 274. See also PL 147:780.

33. See *above*, n. 21.

The Eleventh Century: Renewal in Earnest 137

at Metz; he ended his reforming career in the abbey at St Vanne in Verdun.[34] In 1042 the monastery of St Pantaleon, Cologne, was handed over to Celtic monks.[35] Before the middle of the century the *Scottus* Animchad (d. 1043) had lived as a recluse on the outskirts of Fulda. Paternus, another *Scottus*, died in a fire in 1058, after spending many years as a solitary near Paderborn. Marianus Scottus was at St Martin's in Cologne from 1056 to 1058 and then went as a recluse to the already mentioned region of Fulda from 1059 to 1069. Mucheratus lived as a hermit near Ratisbon, around the year 1075. A second Marianus Scottus settled St Peter's in Ratisbon,[36] while other Celts made similar foundations in the cities of Würzburg, Nuremberg, Erfurt and Vienna.[37]

Turning back to traditional monachism, it should be recalled that since the Rule of St Benedict was a rule for beginners which stressed discretion, it purposely left certain questions (e.g. active versus contemplative life) unsettled, and made allowances to geography, climate, local conditions and human factors. Regular observance in the various individual monasteries showed great variety in questions of discipline (food, clothing, silence and work) and liturgical celebrations. Community life, already punctuated by frequent feast days and various liturgical seasons, had for the same reason, even more variations. This called for regulation, a fixation of the manifold activities and services of the monk. As a result of

34. L. Gougaud, "L'oeuvre des *Scotti*," *loc. cit.*, 273f.
35. *Ibid.*, 275.
36. *Ibid.*, 276, with documentation on Animchad, Paternus, Marianus Scottus and Mucheratus.
37. Wilhelm Levison, "Die Iren und die Fränkische Kirche," *Historische Zeitschrift*, 109 (1912), 21. See also Bernhard Bischoff, "Il monachesimo irlandese nei suoi rapporti col continente," *Il monachesimo nell'alto medioevo e la formazione della civiltà occidentale* (Settimane di Studio del Centro Italiano di Studi sull'alto medioevo, IV; Spoleto: Presso la Sede del Centro, 1957), 121–163, esp. 123, 130–134. Cf. *above*, p. 58, n. 59. G. Schreiber notes in this connection, "At the outset, Cluny, Camaldoli, Cîteaux and Prémontré moved in the direction of solitude; they sought forestal regions and the inaccessibility and seclusion of the Celtic settlers. They established a zone of silence around themselves, and this was to suffer no disturbance from the outside." *Gemeinschaften des Mittelalters*, 38.

this, articulated and minutely detailed usages (*consuetudines, usus*) were drawn up in a great many monasteries in France, Burgundy, Lorraine and England during the tenth and eleventh centuries. Disciplinary and liturgical usages were put in writing, so as to ensure the survival and the legitimate interpretation of a particular observance and to facilitate its adoption by neighboring or related monasteries.[38]

These usages, circulating informally from house to house and spreading a definite standard of life, established certain spiritual bonds between individual monasteries. The adoption of common usages promoted the idea of unity which is the basis of every monastic reform movement. Thus in England, the plan was conceived to have a single constitution for all monasteries.[39] As U. Berlière remarked, "The search for unity in monastic observances manifested itself perhaps never in a livelier and more complete fashion than during the tenth and eleventh centuries."[40] For in all great monastic reforms there is a tendency to mark the common family origin by a more or less complete adherence to a uniform observance.[41] As for the eleventh century, in spite of divergences in detail and local particularities, a closer look at the usages then in force— e.g. Gorze; Fulda; St Emmeram, Ratisbon; St Maximilian, Trier; Fleury; Marmoutier; Cluny; St Benignus, Dijon; Hirsau; Farfa, etc.—reveals remarkably similar traits. This can be seen from the number of prayers added to the divine office; the regulations on food and drink; the reception of postulants; the education of oblates; the title, number and jurisdiction of the monastic officials

---

38. Ursmer Berlière, "Les coutumiers monastiques," *Revue Bénédictine*, 23 (1906), 261f. Cf. *idem*, "Les origines de l'Ordre de Cîteaux," *loc. cit.*, 453; *idem*, "L'étude des réformes monastiques," *loc. cit.*, 139; J. Evans, *op. cit.*, 78 n. 3 and H. DeWarren, "Le monachisme à l'apparition de saint Bernard," *loc. cit.*, 52f. and 56.

39. *Regularis Concordia. The Monastic Agreement*, trans. Thomas Symons (London: Nelson & Sons, 1953). See also U. Berlière, "L'étude des réformes monastiques," *loc. cit.*, 139.

40. "Les coutumiers monastiques," *Revue Bénédictine*, 23 (1906), 262.

41. *Ibid.*, 261f.

The Eleventh Century: Renewal in Earnest

and other features.[42] As B. Albers has demonstrated, the surviving *usus* texts are all Cluniac in nature, going back, in direct line, to Benedict of Aniane. The ideas and ideals which animated the reformers of the tenth and the eleventh centuries are unmistakably taken from Ardo's biography of Benedict, from the latter's *Concordia regularum* and from the *Capitulare monasticum* of 817.[43] But in none of these usages is there any question of a subordination, as devised by Benedict of Aniane; one can speak, at the most, of spiritual bonds resulting from the adoption of common usages, bonds that served as models to later reforms in the eleventh century.[44]

These developments were, in a way, the result of a more intensive study of the Church Fathers, among them Augustine, Jerome, Ambrose, Hilary, Boethius, Cassiodorus, Isidore and, to a lesser degree, Leo the Great. The works of more recent authors were also popular. Bede was read in all monasteries and many also read in Hrabanus Maurus, Alcuin, Paschasius Radbertus, Florus, Hincmar and Haymo. Added to this list in time were Peter Damian, Ivo of Chartres and Anselm of Canterbury.[45] Of the greatest importance was the fact that "everybody at this time read Cassian."[46] And deGellinck further explained:

> It is above all Cassian who merits our attention, for the unfavorable verdict of pseudo-Gelasius notwithstanding, he found his way into every library after the ninth and tenth centuries. . . . This diffusion reveals the extensive and deep influence he had on ascetical training during the entire Middle Ages.[47]

---

42. U. Berlière, "Les origines de l'Ordre de Cîteaux," *loc. cit.*, 453; *idem*, "L'étude des réformes monastiques," *loc. cit.*, 139; O. Ducourneau, *op. cit.*, 15; B. Bligny, "L'Eglise et les ordres réligieux," *loc. cit.*, 249f.

43. U. Berlière, "Les coutumiers monastiques," *loc. cit.*, 262 and 266. See also J. Evans, *op. cit.*, 78 n. 3.

44. U. Berliére, "Les origines de l'Ordre de Cîteaux," *loc. cit.*, 453.

45. *Idem*, *L'ascèse bénédictine*, 109f.

46. E. Delaruelle, *L'eremitismo in occidente*, 187. On contemporary Cassian manuscripts, see CSEL 17:xiiiiff.

47. See *above*, n. 44.

Cassian's Conferences certainly had their influence on the eremitic revival in the eleventh century, a subject to be discussed later in this chapter.[48] Finally, mention must also be made of the popularity of Origen. After the ninth century the Origen texts became more numerous, and from the eleventh century a great number of evangeliaries, Latin apocryphal sermons and other texts attributed to Origen are still extant. Origen, it seems, was read not only privately, but also in public worship—also by the Cistercians—as part of the official liturgical services.[49]

But the spiritual writers of the eleventh century did not engage in a mere copying of the Fathers; they also set out to systematize traditional teachings. They began by looking at Christian piety from a subjective point of view, in which *ratio* claimed its rights from *auctoritas,* where the emphasis was on personal experience as a prerequisite of religious certitude. Already St Augustine characterized the struggle for sanctity as a personal affair between the soul and God and thus, so to speak, "interiorized" God. But he did not give a greater role to the person of Christ whose humanity remained somehow in the background. The great innovation of the eleventh century—and to some extent of Cluny—was that it developed a new attitude in the individual toward Christ. The aim was now to imitate Christ, especially the human Christ, subject to the Father, doing the will of the Father, humble and compassionate toward his brethren to the extent of accepting suffering and even death on the cross. Piety now became affective rather than speculative, which, it was felt, tended to take over all the activities of the soul, and, after reaching a certain degree, increasingly used up the

---

48. U. Berlière, "L'étude des réformes monastiques," *loc. cit.,* 154. See also G. Morin, "Rainaud l'Ermite," *loc. cit.,* 103 n. 8. Worthy of note is also an incident in the *vita* of Benedict II, abbot of Chiusa. *"Sub eodem tempore cum operam daret . . . ad intelligendas Regulae quasdam sententias quarum scrupulo movebatur . . . sanctus Benedictus monachorum legislator et signifer in somnis illi apparuit....Deinde dicebat illi: 'Si vis, inquit, charissime, de quibus ambiguis plenius informari, et monasticae ordinis perfectionem desideras adipisci, quaere tibi librum Joannis Cassiani, qui Patrum Instituta ac Collationes stylo prosequitur latiori'."* PL 150:1478.

49. Jean Leclercq, "Origène au XIIe siècle," *Irénikon,* 24 (1951), 425 and 427f.

The Eleventh Century: Renewal in Earnest 141

heart. These "affectives" had understandably, little love for abstract ideas so dear to speculative minds. The motto was now, "make present the image of God,"[50] i.e. imitate Christ by an unconditional obedience to God, by a love for all men and a life of penance, poverty and austerity.

In this connection must be mentioned the frequent reference to *theoria* in medieval hagiographical texts, a term familiar to Cassian[51] which is best translated as "contemplation of heavenly things."[52] It implies the greatest possible abstinence from engagements demanding practical, pragmatic and laborious activities. This life was to be a life of constant mortification. It calls for a great amount of labor and much struggling in order to repress the instincts of the body and purify both conscience and soul through mortification. Contemplation, on the other hand, reaches the pure heights of the soul: it is a life filled with the love of God, a life of all delight, because uninterrupted by death, it enriches the individual with untainted goodness and leads to *theoria*, the abandonment of the soul to God. The outside world is in this sense nothing but a place of distractions; it has nothing to offer to the contemplative soul. This is why "theoretical" life must be cultivated and strengthened.[53] In Cassian's

50. "*Christum portemus in ore, Christum portemus in corde, Christum portemus in manibus. . . . Sic* (enim) *monet sanctus apostolus Paulus . . . Glorificate et portate Deum in corpore vestro. Quid est Deum portare? Imaginem Dei representare, Christum imitari. Hanc imaginem portat innocentia, portat justitia, hanc portat veritas, hanc portat castitas, hanc portat sobrietas, et omnis honestas.*" Ivo of Chartres, *Sermo XI*, PL 162:576. See also Robert Folz, "Le problème des origines de Cîteaux," *Mélanges Saint Bernard*, XXIVe Congrès de l'Association Bourguignonne des Sociétés Savantes, VIIIe Centenaire de la mort de S. Bernard (Dijon: Association des Amis de Saint Bernard, 1954), 285 and Pierre Pourrat, *La spiritualité chrétienne. II: Le Moyen Age* (Paris: Librairie Lecoffre, 1951), 19ff.

51. "*Videtis ergo principale bonum in theoria sola, id est in contemplatione divina dominum posuisse.*" *Conlationes*, 1:8. CSEL 13:15.

52. Louis Gougaud, *Érémites et réclus. Études sur d'anciennes formes de vie réligieuse* (Moines et monastère, 5; Ligugé: Abbaye Saint-Martin, 1928), 34 n. 2. See also idem, "La Theoria dans la spiritualité médiévale," *Revue d'Ascétique et de Mystique*, 3 (1922), 381–391 and Jean Leclercq, *Étude sur le vocabulaire monastique du moyen age* (Studia Anselmiana, 48; Roma: Herder, 1961), 80ff.

53. René Niderst, *Robert d'Arbrissel et les origines de l'Ordre de Fontévrault* (Rodez: Imprimérie G. Subervie, 1952), 28 and 114 n. 15. In Celtic monachism

thought it is more important to cure one's own ills than to be concerned with the troubles of others.[54]

The awareness that these ideals could not be realized in the world, inspired a vast *fuga mundi* literature during the Middle Ages with calls, as early as the eleventh century, for a contempt of the world. John of Fécamp (d. 1078),[55] for instance, referred to man's earthly existence as "this worst life" and "this most unhappy life."[56] He was against the enjoyment of transitory and constantly changing things, for the love of this world implies a hostility to God and the all-good other life. His pessimistic and negative view about temporal things—worthless to him because transitory—caused him to reject all earthly goods and profane realities and opt for a purely contemplative life based on a deep and fervent love of God.[57]

Similar sentiments animated the invalid monk, Herman of Reichenau (d. 1054),[58] as can be gathered from his poem *De contemptu mundi* which he addressed to nuns. His words, "I have such a contempt for this world and all its treasures and for this mortal life . . . that all transitory things seem completely nil and empty. . . . I am disgusted to live,"[59] reveal a very somber view of man's earthly

---

we find this definition of *theoria*: "*Tertium genus est anachoretarum qui jam coenobiali conversatione perfecti semetipsos includunt in cellulis procul a conspectu hominum remotis, nemini ad se praebentes accessum sed in sola contemplatione theorica viventes perseverant.*" Ibid., 120 n. 71.

54. "*Multis modis praeclarior virtus sublimiorque profectus est animae propriae curare languores quam corporis alieni.*" *Conlationes* 15:8. CSEL. 13:434.

55. A brief account of John of Fécamp's life is found in Robert Bultot, *La doctrine du mépris du monde. IV: Le XIe siècle 2. Jean Fécamp, Hermann Contract, Roger de Caen, Anselm de Canterbury* (Christianisme et valeurs humaines; Louvain: Éditions Nauwelaerts, 1964), 11.

56. "*Haec pessima vita*," "*ista infelicissima vita.*" Ibid., 22.

57. Ibid., 12 and 22. On John of Fécamp see also Gerard Sitwell, *Spiritual Writers of the Middle Ages* (Twentieth Century Encyclopedia of Catholicism, 40; New York: Hawthorn Books, 1961), 25–32.

58. R. Bultot, *op. cit.*, 4(2):24f.

59. "*Tanto mihi hic praesens mundus cum suis omnibus et ipsa haec vita mortalis contemptui et tedio est, et e contrario tam ineffabili desiderio et dilectione futurus ille non transiturus mundus, et aeterna illa et inmortalis vita, ut quasi nichili et inane cuncta transitoria haec omnino reputentur et flocci pendantur a me. Tedet quidem me vivere.*" Ibid., 48 n. 52. Cf. Berthold of Reichenau, *Annales*, MGH, SS 5:268.

life. This life, which is nothing but suffering, sadness, unfulfillment and an animal-like existence is nothing but sadness, boredom, illness, fear, pain, with a desire for the worthless and a longing for putrid and fetid carnal pleasures—the worst of all pleasures. A world of such vanity and misery does not deserve to be loved. It must be completely given up for the life which leads to heaven or, rather, is already on earth, the beginning of heaven.[60]

Roger of Caen (d. about 1095), who spent most of his life in the monastery of Bec,[61] is the author of another *Carmen de contemptu mundi*.[62] In his view, the qualities of a true monk are a humble mind, contempt of the world, a chaste life and a holy sobriety. This contempt of the world is imperative, for earthly goods, being temporal, are worthless; the desire of earthly satisfactions is the source of constant suffering; it can rob man of eternal life. Hence the author's exhortation not to become a subject of the realm of sin but to rise above the things of the earth and walk on the narrow and steep road leading to heaven.[63]

This list would not be complete without the names St Peter Damian (whose views will be discussed in the following chapter) and St Anselm of Canterbury (d. 1109),[64] who had equally strong ideas on the subject of world-weariness. According to Anselm, God possesses, in an eminent way, all the goods that can be desired; hence it is vanity to seek earthly goods which are, more often than not, simply occasions of sin and leading to the loss of God. Man's present condition is really an exile, and the life of the layman a river of mud. One must therefore give up the idolatrous desire, worship

---

60. *Ibid.*, 28, 33, 45f.   61. *Ibid.*, 50.

62. PL 158:689. Cf. R. Bultot, *op. cit.*, 4(2):50.

63. "*Mens humilis, mundi contemptus, vita pudica, Sanctaque sobrietas, haec faciunt monachum.*" PL 158:689. "*Gaudia perpetuos pariunt mundana dolores, Tollit et aeternum vivere vita brevis.*" *Ibid.*, 691. "*Noli te regno peccati subdere, noli, Quae citius fugiunt, ista caduca sequi. Sed satagas humiles transcendere terras, Arctumque ad caelos arripe fortis iter.*" *Ibid.*, 703. Cf. R. Bultot, *op. cit.*, 4(2): 54, 68, 70f.

64. R. Bultot, *op. cit.*, 4(2):73 n. 3.

and possession of earthly goods and embrace the monastic life instead. Anselm seems to equate Christian life with the monastic vocation, which takes precedence over all other forms of serving God, because it involves total dedication.[65]

What had brought on such sentiments, the "crisis of cenobitism" in the eleventh century, was to a great extent a crisis of prosperity. This gave rise to satirical writings on the subject and sounded the battle-cry for the restoration of a genuine and effective poverty.[66]

Voluntary poverty embraced as part of an ascetical program has a long history.[67] The ideal of pre-Christian reformers, it had its champions from the time of the early Church to the present. It is hardly surprising, therefore, that by the middle of the eleventh century spiritual writers, discerning people, and even the broad masses began to detect a difference between the Christian ideal of poverty and the example given by worldly priests and monks. As a result of donations or the wise administration of abbots, monasteries and their inmates had become rich. This bred a certain neopaganism in monasteries: it led to a relaxation of discipline, and to extravagance in constructions and equipment. Abbots spent much of their time litigating in courts, to recover possessions lost during the tenth century, or engaged in banking practices, often, because of miscalculations, with disastrous results. In the view of their contemporaries, it was this lack of poverty which accounted for the monks' cupidity, their indifference—if not aversion—to things spiritual, for the venality in the administration of the sacraments, and the abuses stemming from secular involvements. In the face of such a deterioration, a large segment of the

---

65. *Ibid.,* 139f. On Peter Damian see Robert Bultot, *La doctrine du mépris du monde. IV: Le XIe siècle 1. Pierre Damian* (Christianisme et valeurs humaines; Louvain: Éditions Nauwelaerts, 1963).

66. More on this has been said in the preceding chapter. See also J. Leclercq, "La crise du monachisme," *loc. cit.,* 24f.; J. Leclercq and J. Bonnes, *Un maître de la vie spirituelle,* 184–197 and 218–220.

67. A good survey is found in Bernard Bligny, "Les premiers Chartreux et la pauvreté," *Le Moyen Age,* 22 (1951), 28–35.

population rose to denounce ecclesiastical and monastic wealth, and the monks' interference in the affairs of the world. Recalling that the Church is really a community of saints, it produced, from its own midst, heroic souls who set out to cultivate the ideal of poverty by a return to the sources: the simplicity of the patriarchs, the tradition of the Gospels (with regard to the poor Christ) and the practices of the primitive Church.[68] As Raynald the Hermit put it: "The path of the primitive Church is simply the life of the apostles and disciples of Christ inspired by the evangelical counsels."[69]

This individualism which made salvation a strictly personal affair and the growing perception of the evils caused by prosperity led to a great revival of eremitic monasticism in the second half of the eleventh century. It grew out of the realization that monasteries no longer provided the atmosphere for contemplation and peace. They had become rich. Then there was their ritualism, the rigidity for the sake of unity, and the interminable *laus perennis*, i.e. endless round of offices. In addition, more and more monks had become priests with the result that they began to incorporate parishes, to admit laymen to monastic services and to accept nominations to episcopal sees. Last but not least, the status of many a monastery had changed from that of immunity into an aristocratic seigneurie, anchored in public law and with certain public functions and responsibilities. This led to the widespread belief that the developments just listed were inspired by the devil, that the Benedictine monk did not really leave the world, that a person was therefore justified in making his salvation a strictly personal affair by fleeing the world and human society and retiring to a solitary place where one could fight the devil *solus cum solo* and surrender himself to undisturbed con-

---

68. Jean Leclercq, et al., *La spiritualité du Moyen Age* (Histoire de la spiritualité chrétienne, 2; Paris: Aubier, 1961), 161; idem, "La crise du monachisme," *loc. cit.*, 24f.; M. Dmitrewski, *op. cit.*, 75f.; G. Schreiber, *Gemeinschaften des Mittelalters*, 211; B. Bligny, "Les premiers Chartreux," *loc. cit.*, 27-31 and 35; E. Werner, *Die gesellschaftlichen Grundlagen*, 79 n. 412.

69. "*Primitivae ecclesiae formam nihil aliud esse quam apostolorum discipulorumque Christi vitam evangelicis praeceptionibus plene informatam;*" G. Morin, "Rainaud l'Ermite," *loc. cit.*, 101.

templation. Such a life alone offered effective safeguards against avarice and the love of earthly goods.[70]

The desert had always attracted men wounded by the world and its riches, and by persons longing for a closer union with God. In the Christian era, eremitic monachism was, from the beginning, a legitimate form of asceticism. All one has to do is to recall men like Rufinus, Palladius, Cassian, Theodoretus, the authors of the *Verba Seniorum* and the *Apophtegmata Patrum*, Gregory of Tours and Gregory the Great, to prove the point. Important for our purposes is to note here that with its Byzantine contacts, Italy had always been a land of hermits, housing Basilian monks and anchorites in Calabria as early as the fifth and sixth centuries. Though it did not become a part of the Benedictine world, eremitism stayed alive even after the victory of the Cassinese code. It grew especially strong during the tenth century when, in view of the social and clerical decadence of northern Italy, preachers of penance and solitary life—men like Nilus, Romuald, Simeon, Dominic of Foligno, Venerius, and others—began to appear in public. They recalled the spiritual legacy of the East and urged their audience to embrace a solitary penitential life. From Italy, the movement spread all over western Europe, undoubtedly because conditions had been favorable for its reception—it will be sufficient to recall the revival of commerce and the changes which had occurred in the social structure of society,—because eremitism had a universal appeal, and because contacts with Italy (pilgrimages, etc.) continued undisturbed. The result of all this was that the West turned once more to the works of the fourth-century Fathers, especially to Cassian and the *Vitae Patrum*, studied the life of Moses, Elijah and John the Baptist with renewed interest, and restored the cult of the ancient hermits, particularly that of St Anthony of the Desert. This

---

70. B. Bligny, "L'Église et les ordres réligieux," *loc. cit.*, 239, 246–251; G. Morin, "Rainaud l'Ermite," *loc. cit.*, 101; idem, "Un traité inédit de S. Guillaume Firmat," *loc. cit.*, 249; G. Schreiber, *Gemeinschaften des Mittelalters*, 211; J. Leclercq and J. Bonnes, *op. cit.*, 22f.; J. Leclercq, "La crise du monachisme," *loc. cit.*, 25f.; idem, *La spiritualité du Moyen Age*, 161; *L'eremitismo in occidente*, 239 and 241. Cf. also Louis Gougaud, "Essai de bibliographie érémitique," *Revue Bénédictine*, 45 (1933) 281–291.

was not done for the purpose of intellectually enriching the soul; it was the outcome of the then prevalent conviction that since contact with the world was dangerous and the "secure" existence provided by monasteries wholly unsatisfactory for one's salvation, both must be definitely avoided.[71]

The movement also reached France and grew especially strong in its western forestal regions during the last decade of the eleventh century. Here clerics and laymen, men and women, rich and poor, soldiers and peasants, lettered and unlettered, embraced in great numbers a life of poverty and solitude. They acted out of religious motives, driven by a certain restlessness which was then "in the air" and by a genuine desire for perfection, since most of the leaders were intelligent and learned men, well versed in the Bible and acquainted with such authorities as Cassian, Celtic monachism and Gregory the Great. Then there was the attractiveness of the idea of solitude, the fame and example of a leader, mystical considerations, reflection, natural or acquired dispositions, the longing for a life of poverty, prayer and penance, and the discovery of a model in hagiography.[72] A final reason may be seen in the collective inter-

---

71. B. Bligny, "L'Église et les ordres réligieux," *loc. cit.*, 251f.; *idem*, "Les premiers Chartreux," *loc. cit.*, 35; R. Bultot, *op. cit.*, 4(1):65 n. 166, 121, 132; 4(2):22ff., 46, 50, 106f., 113 n. 126, 140; C. Butler, *Benedictine Monachism*, 18f.; C. Dereine, "Odon de Tournai," *loc. cit.*, 150 n. 48; Anselm Dimier, "Encore les emplacements malsains," *Revue du Moyen Age Latin*, 4 (1948), 60ff.; *L'eremitismo in occidente*, 29f. and 41; A. Fliche, *op. cit.*, 8:446; Walter Franke, *Romuald von Camaldoli und seine Reformtätigkeit zur Zeit Ottos III* (Historische Studien, Heft 107; Berlin: Emil Ebering, 1913), 111ff.; Louis Gougaud, *Érémites et réclus. Études sur d'anciennes formes de vie réligieuse* (Moines et monastères, 5; Ligugé: Abbaye Saint-Martin, 1928), 10 n. 2; Heinrich Guenter, *Legenden-Studien* (Köln: J. P. Bachem, 1906), 127; K. Hallinger, "Woher kommen die Laienbrüder?," *loc. cit.*, 92–94; "Hermits," CE 7:280; D. Knowles, *The Monastic Order*, 192; Jean Leclercq, "Un congrès sur l'érémitisme," *Studia Monastica*, 4 (1962), 404; *idem*, *Un maître*, 21, 23 and 25; Mansi 7:954; 8:331; 10:769; and 11:963; E. Sackur, *op. cit.*, 1:323-325; P. Salmon, "L'ascèse monastique," *loc. cit.*, 271 n. 2 and 275 n. 2; and Ernst Werner, "Neue Texte und Forschungen zur Charta Caritatis," *Forschungen und Fortschritte*, 29 (1955), 25 n. 2; *idem*, *Die gesellschaftlichen Grundlagen*, 105 n. 535; *idem*, *Pauperes Christi*, 27ff.; 78.

72. J. Leclercq, "La crise du monachisme," *loc. cit.*, 29; *idem*, *La spiritualité du Moyen Age*, 163ff. and R. Niderst, *op. cit.*, 23.

action of political, economic and social factors, i.e. the public disorder, the economic revival and the population growth of the period. In view of these, the movement to break away from feudal ties, to get away from abbeys so closely linked to feudalism, and to go to the desert where one could find a freedom not offered by the contemporary feudal world gained increasing momentum.[73] It must be stressed, however, that in spite of the latter factors, the trend toward eremitism was neither an exclusively lay movement, nor simply a movement of the poor. It had no social program as such and was not revolutionary in nature.[74]

The hermits established themselves in deserted villages, ruins of chapels, huts, caves or in forests in primitive, makeshift constructions of branches and leaves. Here they led a life of more solitude, more asceticism and more prayer. They worked with their own hands, denied themselves necessary food and clothing, chastised their body with scourgings and hair shirts and spent long hours in prayer, constantly praying the psalms. They also liked to read the Bible, especially the Exodus, and were greatly devoted to John the Baptist, John the Evangelist, St James, St Michael, and St Mary Magdala. They procured their modest needs from their garden, their strip of land, forest or apiary, or from the products of such manual skills as the weaving of baskets. Their diet was meager: it consisted of bread, cereals, vegetables, milk and eggs. Their activities involved field labor and artisanry (including the copying of manuscripts) and hospitality to visitors and pilgrims, an indication that they did not break off every human contact. This is also seen from the fact that they instructed their confreres, went to the funerals of deceased hermits, practiced charity and hospitality, and formed friendships with other hermits and were friendly to animals.[75] Eventually they also began an apostolate of itinerant preaching (usually on the

---

73. *L'eremitismo in occidente,* 53–65, 186 and 188f. See also R. Niderst, *op. cit.,* 28f., and "De religiosis Calabriae, et vita et conversatione eorum," PL 204: 1013ff.

74. *L'eremitismo in occidente,* 65 and 69.

75. *Ibid.,* 37–39, 65, 188, 190–197 and 232–235. The nature of the hermits' work was in part inspired by Acts 18:3.

request of a zealous bishop), chastising clerical abuses, attending church councils and collecting alms.[76]

In spite of great individual differences, the hermits nevertheless had a number of common characteristics. They shared an instinctive horror of money and riches, and a corresponding desire to imitate Christ in his poverty. They sought an effective poverty, seclusion, rigorous fasts, prolonged prayer and manual labor. They wore "native colors," kept their hair unshorn, lived in unhealthy places and went on "pilgrimages for Christ,"—i.e. into voluntary exile, often for life—an idea so dear to Celtic monachism. Since they lived "alone," i.e. outside the protection offered by the feudal order, theirs was a humble existence; it was poor, even in the liturgy; it was by no means secure—really a life of penance.[77]

As for organization, some hermits established themselves in the vicinity of cenobitic monasteries and remained under the abbot's jurisdiction. Others were independent solitaries, whether they stayed in one place or went on a *peregrinatio*. There were also *laurae*, i.e. congregations of hermits, organized on the broad foundations of the so-called Augustinian Rule or the Rule of St Benedict. Still other groups remained unorganized and simply sought to lead a life based on the Gospels.[78]

In some cases individual hermits drifted toward heresy—usually the result of ignorance, an excessive asceticism, or simply hypocrisy.[79] Most of them, however, retained their fervor and moved either toward cenobitism or were absorbed by the new eremitico-

---

76. See *below*, n. 81.

77. *L'eremitismo in occidente*, 223f., 226f., 230; J. Leclercq, "La crise du monachisme," *loc. cit.*, 29.

78. *Ibid.*, 32–34.

79. G. Morin, "Rainaud l'Ermite," *loc. cit.*, 99, 102 and 115. Cf. Ivo of Chartres, *ep.* 256, PL 162: 261; J. Leclercq, "La crise du monachisme," *loc. cit.*, 29f.; Ernst Werner, *Pauperes Christi. Studien zu sozial-religiösen Bewegungen im Zeitalter des Reformpapsttums* (Leipzig: Koehler & Amelang, 1956), 78; *L'eremitismo in occidente*, 198f., 239 and 241; Herbert Grundmann, *Religiöse Bewegungen im Mittelalter* (Hildesheim: Georg Olms Verlagsbuchhandlung, 1961), 13ff. and 40ff.

monastic foundations which made their appearance later in the century.[80]

Closely connected with the rebirth of eremitism, the will to return to the sources and to be witnesses of authentic Christianity, was the emergence during the second half of the eleventh century of itinerant preachers, mostly from the ranks of the hermits. While there had been *pauperes Christi* from the monastic order since the ninth century—often as a counterweight to the Cluniac idea of poverty—now this "apostolic" ideal found followers also among the clergy and the laity. Moved by the example of Christ, these aspirants to evangelical perfection gave up all material goods and embraced a life of austerity and seclusion in forestal hermitages. Their model was Christ, the apostles and the Fathers, all of whom had led a life of poverty and preaching (cf. Luke 9:1-6). Coming from different social environments, they did not adopt the counsels of the Fathers to the letter but followed them instead according to their own personal interpretations. When people came to them to hear their exhortations and to receive their counsel, they began a more systematic apostolate. Moving from place to place, they engaged in preaching and cared for the sick, the poor and the needy. Considered intercessors with God and thought to be endowed with miraculous powers, they were extremely popular with the masses, and became their confessors, consolers and counselors, attracting both clerics and laymen, at times entire families and women.[81]

Thus, in a reversal of existing social norms, they suddenly found themselves surrounded by spontaneously formed heterogeneous communities, anxious to become imitators of Christ and the apostles in public life. On occasions this phenomenon certainly had also non-religious motives, for in a number of cases the movement led to anti-ecclesiastical and anti-feudal tendencies, and to neo-Manichaean excesses. On the whole, however, saints and new

---

80. *L'eremitismo in occidente*, 66. See also *below*, ch. VI.

81. B. Bligny, "L'Église et les ordres réligieux," *loc. cit.*, 252, 254; M. Dmitrewski, *op. cit.*, 75; E. Werner, *Die gesellschaftlichen Grundlagen*, 80, 82; idem, *Pauperes Christi*, 281 and Charles Dereine, "Les origines de Prémontré," RHE, 42 (1947), 364.

The Eleventh Century: Renewal in Earnest 151

religious foundations at the end of the eleventh century were able to channel the movement, as can be seen from the lives of such saints as Robert of Arbrissel, Vitalis of Savigny and Bernard of Tiron.[82]

Meanwhile the *pauperes Christi* movement, ably championed by Humbert of Silva Candida, made steady advances in spite of the violent disapproval of worldly bishops. It did not take long before Rome perceived the great possibilities offered by the movement. The result was that the papacy enlisted it as its direct ally before the century was over. The guiding spirit of this new poverty movement, Hildebrand, called for a return to the ideals of the primitive Church at the Roman synod of 1059.[83] As Pope he liked to use such expressions as the "poor Christ," "poor Redeemer," "poor in Christ," or "poor of Christ."[84] This was in line with the spirit of the time, not an attempt at demagoguery as E. Werner would want his readers to believe when stating: "There can be no doubt that the Pope took up this slogan with demagogic intentions, in order to win the lower strata of the populace for his program of overcoming clerical incontinence and breaking the power of the feudal episcopate."[85]

Church renewal in the eleventh century bears the name of Gregory VII (Gregorian Reform),[86] even though it began before him and reached its culmination after his pontificate. Its aim, *libertas Ecclesiae*, i.e. the liberation of the Church from external and internal enemies, was first enunciated in Burgundy and Lorraine—

---

82. R. Folz, "Le problème des origines de Cîteaux," *loc. cit.*, 285; J. Leclercq, "La crise du monachisme," *loc. cit.*, 31. On Bernard of Tiron see PL 172:1432, 1435 and 1438.

83. J. Mabillon, *Annales*, 4:686.

84. "*Sed cum pauper Jesu ille pius consolator . . .* " *Reg.* V, 21, PL 148: 506; "*pauper et pius noster Redemptor;*" *Reg.* VI, 17, *ibid.*, 526; "*Quid autem mirum si principes mundi et potentes saeculi nos pauperes Christi, pravitatibus illorum obviantes odiunt;*" *Reg.* IX, 21, *ibid.*, 622.

85. *Die gesellschaftlichen Grundlagen*, 79. Ibid. 80 Werner however admits that the papacy sought the help of Robert of Arbrissel and Bernard of Tiron in the reform of the clergy.

86. Augustin Fliche, *La réforme grégorienne* (Paris: E. Champion, 1924-1937), 3 vols.

more specifically, in the region of Liége—by men like Ratherius, bishop of Verona and Liége (d. 974), Wazo, bishop of Liége and a leading theologian and theoretician of the Gregorian Reform (d. 1048), Frederick of Lorraine, the future Pope Stephen IX (d. 1058), Gerard of Cambrai (d. 1051), and Cardinal Humbert of Silva Candida, a former monk of Moyenmoutier (d. 1061). In his works Humbert condemned the *Eigenkirche* system and advocated a separation of temporal and spiritual jurisdiction. With his *Adversus simoniacos* (1058)[87] he sounded the battle-cry against simony and priestly marriage and systematized the new *libertas* ideas. The success of the reform was promoted by the rapid growth in the western world of greater differentiation and reflection. Additional factors were the new canon law collections, the advance of scholasticism, state initiatives toward sovereignty, the emergence of the bourgeoisie and knighthood, the foundation of new religious orders, the shift to the subjective and personal element in Christian piety, the cult of the humanity of Christ, the impact of the newly emerging heresies, and, finally, the fact that by the eleventh century the western world had become totally christianized. The Gregorian Reform brought therefore not only a relentless struggle against simony, clerical marriage and lay investiture, but also strove to establish a united hierarchy under a papacy very conscious of its primacy. It involved the drawing of a clear line between the priestly and the lay element in the Church and sought to make of the clergy a sort of supranational corporation strongly attached to Rome. Since this clergy was to disengage itself from the affairs of the world—in order to be holier and more spiritual—there was the additional need of redefining the relationship between Church and state.[88]

Gregory VII, who had the opportunity to get acquainted with the reform movement in Lorraine during his stay in Cologne, was keenly aware of its aspirations and worked for its success with untiring zeal, until his death in Salerno. Anxious to free the Church

87. PL 143:1007ff.

88. U. Berlière, "L'étude des réformes monastiques," *loc. cit.*, 137f. Cf. LTK 4:1196–1199.

from lay tutelage, from secular evils and clerical vices, he set out to put an end to the *Eigenkirche* system, to "de-laicize" the hierarchy, to repress unjustified lay interference in Church matters, to reform the clergy and to organize the laity into a truly Christian community. In this objective he was strongly influenced by Augustine's *De Civitate Dei*, as can be seen from the frequent use of such Augustinian terms as *pax, justitia* and *obedientia*, employed to characterize the kingdom of the *Rex Justus* in his letters, just as there are also the references to *discordia, superbia* and *inobedientia*, applied to the enemies of this kingdom.[89] To do justice to Gregory, one must see in his alliance with the Pataria in his support of monastic "agitators" in Suabia and Francia, and in his call on the laity to assist him in the eradication of clerical vices, drive to go beyond the Cluniac program of freeing the Church from lay control, by working for the primacy of the spiritual order over the temporal.[90] Such objectives were clearly a postulate of the contemporary state of affairs, presenting the Popes of the century—between 1073 and 1119 all were monks—with the problem of harmonizing the medieval social order with the non-feudal tenets of Christianity. They had to come to terms with a society where the militaristic element retained a dominant role and where the governmental system was based on the principle of the *seigneurie* and the fief. This explains the papal efforts to make the feudal system serve Christian ideals and thereby also serve the Apostolic See.[91] In this they had powerful allies: old and new monastic congregations, an increasingly cooperative episcopate and truly remarkable papal legates in several countries.[92]

89. James P. Whitney, *Hildebrandine Essays* (Cambridge: University Press, 1932), 76.
90. This must be said against E. Werner, *Pauperes Christi*, 200f. Cf. also LTK 4:1200.
91. B. Bligny, "L'Église et les ordres réligieux," *loc. cit.*, 465.
92. To this may be added that the century was blessed with many very gifted churchmen, such as Ivo of Chartres (d.1115), Anselm of Laon (d.1117), Roscelin (d. a. 1120), Baudry of Borgeuil (d. 1130), Lanfranc (d. 1089), Anselm of Canterbury (d. 1109), Abelard (d. 1142), William of Champeaux (d. 1122), Hildebert of Lavardin (d. 1134), Geoffrey of Vendôme (d. 1132), etc. Cf. R. Niderst, *op. cit.*, 8.

A case in point was France, which had its outstanding champion of Gregorianism, Hugh of Lyons. Possibly related to the ducal family of Burgundy, Hugh was born before 1043. He became subsequently a monk of Romans, chamberlain of the archbishop of Lyons, and—with the assistance of Gregory VII—bishop of Die in 1073, then finally archbishop of Lyons around 1082, an office he held until his death in 1106.[93] Gregory VII appointed him legate for most of France and Burgundy, an office Hugh administered— with some interruptions—during the following pontificates.[94] An uncompromising reformer, more Gregorian than Gregory himself, he worked indefatigably with unselfish dedication on Church reform,[95] by deposing and excommunicating simoniac, unchaste, insubordinate and uncanonically elected bishops and abbots, installing worthy replacements, summoning a great many local councils, repressing the power of the metropolitans, condemning the king's shameful conduct, fighting lay investiture, attacking lay rule of the lower churches, visiting dioceses, issuing reform decrees, proceeding against married clerics, depriving ecclesiastics of the exercise of their priestly faculties, referring—if necessary—cases to Rome, attending Roman synods, settling controversies, and other such activities.[96]

93. A definitive biography of Hugh still needs to be written. Such an undertaking will have to consider, *inter alia,* Hugh's own writings in PL 157:507ff.; Pope Gregory VII's letters to Hugh in PL 148, *passim;* Hugh of Flavigny's *Chronicon,* PL 154: *passim;* J. Mabillon, *Annales,* 5: *passim;* the partial bibliographies in A. Fliche, *La réforme grégorienne,* 2:218 n. 1 and *idem, Le règne de Philippe Ier,* 358 n. 10; GCh 4:100ff.; Theodor Schieffer, *Die päpstlichen Legaten in Frankreich vom Vertrage von Mersen* (870) *bis zum Schisma von 1130* (Berlin: Verlag Emil Ebering, 1935), *passim;* W. Lühe, *op. cit., passim* and the works of Hefele-Leclercq, A. Rony, A. Fliche, G. Tellenbach, J. Whitney and W. Schwartz.

94. PL 148:539.

95. On Hugh's personality see especially W. Lühe, *op. cit.,* 89, 119–129, and Fliche, *La réforme grégorienne,* 1:65, 223ff., 232, 423 and 2:196, 205ff.

96. Cf. PL 148:343f., 476ff., 505f., 508, 563, 603f., 634, 790; PL 154:278; RHF 14:767, 778ff.; MGH, SS 5:438; J. Mabillon, *Annales,* 5:30, 87, 96, 101, 108f., 118, 136, 138, 140, 142, 146, 148, 162, 164, 166, 172ff., 239, 281, 311f., 359; T. Schieffer, *op. cit.,* 88f., 106; W. Lühe, *op. cit.,* 11, 39ff., 53, 55, 60, 62f.,

The Eleventh Century: Renewal in Earnest 155

Hugh, the former monk who had such monastic friends as Anselm of Canterbury, Anselm of Lucca, Ivo of Chartres, Hugh of Cluny, Hugh of Grenoble, Richard of St Victor's in Marseille, Jarento of Dijon, Godfrey of Vendôme, Robert of Molesme and Bruno, the founder of the Carthusians, turned with equal dedication to the reform of the monastic order. In his predilection for monks, he was at all times an enthusiast of monastic order and discipline and saw in monastic life the highest ideal the secular clergy should emulate. Always helpful and generous toward monasteries, he encouraged the laity to do likewise by making donations. He settled disputes between feuding monasteries or monasteries and laymen, raised monastic standards by fighting contemporary evils, favored the appointment of bishops from the monastic order, appointed monks to important offices in the Church and supported the new monastic reform movements—among them Cîteaux—with a special benevolence.[97]

Monastic reform figured also in another sphere of the Gregorian Reform: in the writings of contemporary canonists. Burchard of Worms (d. 1025), for instance, stressed that monks owe obedience to the local ordinary, for monasteries are under the bishop's jurisdiction. The latter's permission is needed for the creation of new monastic settlements, or for the transfer of an existing monastery to a more suitable place. The bishop must also see to the correction of possible abuses through regular yearly visits. With his permission an abbot may resign his office; but the latter may not arrange things in such a way that one of his relatives or friends takes over as his successor; the right of election belongs to the community. An abbot cannot be the superior of more than one monastery. If he is

---

78ff., 129, 136; A. Fliche, *La réforme grégorienne*, 2:179, 186, 210f., 216, 218ff., 226f., 252, 265ff.; 3:19, 195, 350; *idem, Le règne de Philippe Ier,* 355ff., 359ff., 363ff.; A. Fliche, V. Martin, *op. cit.*, 8:91ff., 261; Hefele-Leclercq, *op. cit.*, 5(1): 217; G. Schreiber, *Gemeinschaften des Mittelalters,* 303; A. Rony, *op. cit.*, 5ff.; R. Holtzmann, *op. cit.*, 141.

97. PL 157:515 and 525; GCh 4:106, 108f.; *ibid.* 13:1191, and 14: *Instr.* 12; RHF 13:630; J. Mabillon, *Annales,* 5:119, 359, 367f., 428; T. Schieffer, *op. cit.*, 162; W. Lühe, *op. cit.*, 12f., 15, 94, 130; A. Fliche, *Le règne de Philippe Ier,* 363, 376ff.

lacking in prudence, humility, chastity, moderation, clemency, or discretion, or negligent in the observance of the laws of God, he is to be relieved of his office by an assembly of the local bishop and the neighboring abbots, even if the community should wish to retain him. Abbots were also enjoined to let no woman enter the monastery and to tolerate no earthy conversation with them. They should help the poor and needy and do everything for God's honor. Monks, on the other hand, are told to abstain from such priestly functions as preaching and the hearing of confessions and from taking oaths and accepting sponsorships. They are warned against disobedience, unchastity, conspiratorial tendencies, thievery, unauthorized leaves and vagrancy, and such worldly pursuits and activities as secular pleasures, litigations, cheating, gluttony and drunkenness.[98]

The author of another *Collectio canonum*, Anselm of Lucca (d. 1086), a former monk and stalwart of the Gregorian Reform, also made references to monastic life. As he saw the law, monasteries could be founded only with the bishop's permission, and since they are sacred places, they cannot be transferred to other places or become secular hostels. Once they are established, no one can raise

---

98. *Burchardi Wormaciensis Ecclesiae episcopi Decretorum Libri Viginti*; PL 140:649, 651, 676f., 724, 793f., 796f., 804–812, 854, 871, 925–927, 1010. It may be of interest to quote VIII, 90 in full: *"Ministri autem altaris Domini, vel monachi, nobis placuit, ut a negotiis saecularibus omnino abstineant. Multa sunt ergo negotia saecularia, de his tamen pauca perstringamus, ad quae pertinet omnis libido, non solum immunditia carnis sed etiam omnis carnalis concupiscentia. Quidquid plus justo appetit homo, turpe lucrum est; munera injusta accipere vel etiam dare pro aliquo saeculari conquaestu, pretio aliquem conducere, contentiones, et lites, et rixas amare, in placitis saecularibus disputare, excepta defensione orphanorum et viduarum, conductores aut procuratores esse saecularium rerum, turpis verbi vel facti jocularem esse, vel jocum saecularem diligere, aleas amare, ornamentum inconveniens proposito suo quaerere, in deliciis vivere velle, gulam et ebrietatem sequi, pondera injusta vel mensuras habere, negotium injustum exercere. Nec tamen justum negotium est contradicendum propter necessitates diversas, quia legimus sanctos apostolos negotiasse, et in regula S. Benedicti praecipitur praevidere per quorum manus negotium monasterii transeat. Canes et aves sequi ad venandum, et in omnibus quibuslibet causis superfluum esse. Ecce talia et his similia ministris altaris Domini necnon et monachis omnino contradicimus. De quibus dicit apostolus: Nemo militans Deo implicat se negotiis saecularibus."*

claims contrary to the wishes of their founders. Aspirants to the monastic life, whether presented by their parents or seeking admission of their own accord, must be carefully tested for a considerable length of time before they are received into the community. In general, a person becomes a monk as a result of parental offering or by taking the vows of his own accord. Clerics, though they are of a higher status than monks, cannot be monastic superiors unless they become monks. Only those should be elected abbot who show themselves worthy by their actions and example. Monks must avoid all contentions. They must also be prevented from arbitrarily expelling their abbot and electing a new one in his stead. They should not administer the sacrament of baptism in their monastery but may offer Masses for deceased laymen and grant them burial on monastic grounds.[99]

The outstanding canonist of the period, Ivo of Chartres (d.1115), also repeats the principle: monasteries are under the bishop's jurisdiction; hence monks owe due respect to their ordinary who has the duty to visit them regularly and make sure that their houses are not infected by the spirit of worldliness. Other provisions state that children under age cannot be compelled to become monks against their will and that all who wish to join the community must be tested before admission. Monks, though theirs is a special vocation given only to a few, must not become proud on this account. They must not have possessions, nor be guilty of avarice and rapine, vagrancy, desertion and apostasy. Instead, they should work regularly and stay away from all worldly business, including the practice of law and medicine. Though they may be ordained to the priesthood if they are worthy, they should not be sponsors, administer baptism in their churches, celebrate Mass for the public or hear the confession of laymen. In line with Alexander II's reminder to the clergy and people of Florence, monks, no matter how religious they

---

99. The critical edition of Anselm's collection was produced by Friedrich Thaner, *Anselmi episcopi Lucensis collectio canonum una cum collatione minore. Iussu Institutis Savigniaci, Fasc. I* (Innsbruck: Wagner, 1906). Cf. RHE, 9 (1908), 563–566. See also *Sancti Anselmi episcopi Lucensis Collectio Canonica in libros XIII distributa;* PL 149:499, 502–504, 516–518.

are, must stay within their cloister as prescribed by St Benedict and completely abstain from public preaching. Monasteries, as has been said, may not be converted to other purposes; individuals may leave them for another house only if they are in search of a stricter life.[100]

The Gregorian Reform was also instrumental in the emergence of the so-called "canons regular" during the second half of the eleventh century. Canons were originally priests who followed a certain rule in imitation of the early Christians (Acts 2:44f.) or engaged in a specific service (cathedral school, etc.) under the direction of a bishop, such as Eusebius of Vercelli, Ambrose of Milan, Augustine of Hippo and Martin of Tours. St Chrodegang of Metz (d. 766) composed his *Regula vitae communis* for canons in 763. This rule, basically an adaptation of the Benedictine Rule with greatly relaxed provisions on poverty, was subsequently expanded by the councils of Aachen (789), Mainz (813) and, again, Aachen (816), the last of which drew up a rule of 147 articles. In spite of this, Chrodegang's rule was short-lived, mostly on account of the laxity, avarice and covetousness prevalent in canons' houses between the ninth and the eleventh centuries. Thus efforts to impose canonical rule on the clergy of the cathedral and collegiate churches failed.[101] The remedy came with the Lateran council of 1059, during which Hildebrand made an impassionate plea to priests willing to fight the existing decadence. He urged them to have a share in Church renewal by returning to the traditions of the early Church. The result was the council's decision that priests should live like monks, i.e. beside keeping chastity, they should also lead a common life,

---

100. *Ivonis Carnotensis episcopi Decretum;* PL 161:81, 91, 202–205, 262, 456, 491, 519, 543–545, 548–556, 564, 567f., 571f., 581f., 653f., and 892. Cf. also *idem, Panormia, ibid.,* 1341f.

101. Charles Dereine, "Vie commune, règle de St. Augustin et les chanoines au XIe siècle," *loc. cit.,* 365–406; *idem,* "L'élaboration du Statut canonique des Chanoines réguliers spécialement sous Urbain II," *ibid.,* 46 (1951), 534–565; *idem,* "Chanoines," DHE, 12:287–298; John C. Dickinson, *The Origin of the Austin Canons and Their Introduction into England* (London: S.P.C.K., 1950), *passim;* U. Berlière, "Les origins de l'Ordre de Cîteaux," *loc. cit.,* 466; J. Leclercq, "La crise du monachisme," *loc. cit.,* 25; *L'eremitismo in occidente,* 166; H. Grundmann, *op. cit.,* 489 n. 4.

with a common refectory and common sleeping quarters. The council's decree may be considered the birth certificate of what was to become the new order of canons. The result of it was that in Rome and in regions dependent on it clerics disaffected with contemporary worldliness set out to lead a common life based on the "apostolic life" of the first Christian community.[102] Four years later, in 1063, another council under Nicholas II reaffirmed the provisions of 1059 and once more approved the introduction of common life in the residences of canons.[103]

It seems that only a few houses of canons had adopted full common life before 1063. These were, as has been said, in Rome and certain adjoining regions. From there the reform spread—often in conjunction with the restoration of ancient monasteries or the establishment of hospitals and eremitic foundations—to Spain and eastern France. Meeting with favorable social conditions, they spread particularly in France or, more specifically, in the extreme south of Provence, in Gascony, in Lower Lorraine and in the northwest.[104]

Toward the end of the eleventh century it became a standard practice to group canons' houses into congregations, even though one could not speak of a full-grown order of canons as yet. It was

---

102. *"Praecipientes statuimus, ut hi praedictorum ordinum (i.e. sacerdotum, diaconorum, subdiaconorum) qui eidem praedecessori nostro obedientes castitatem servaverunt, juxta ecclesias quibus ordinati sunt, sicut oportet religiosos clericos, simul manducent et dormiant, & quidquid eis ab ecclesiis competit, communiter habeant. Et rogantes monemus ut ad apostolicam, scilicet communem vitam summopere pervenire studeant, quatenus perfectionem consecuti cum his qui centesimo ditantur, in coelesti patria mereantur adscribi."* Mansi 19:908. Cf. Charles Dereine, "La vita apostolica dans l'ordre canonical du IXe au XIe siècle," *Revue Mabillon*, 51 (1961), 47–53; J. Mabillon, *Annales* 4:686f.; J. Dickinson, *op. cit.*, 26, 29, 36, 40f., 58; M. D. Chenu, "Moines, clercs, laics au correfour de la vie évangélique (XIIe siècle)," RHE, 49 (1954), 63; J. Leclercq, *La spiritualité du Moyen Age*, 173; Placid Lefèvre, "Prémontré, ses origines, sa primitive liturgie, les relations de son code législatif avec Cîteaux et les chanoines du Saint-Sépulcre de Jerusalem," *Analecta Praemonstratensia*, 25 (1949), 97.

103. Mansi 19:1025. Cf. J. Dickinson, *op. cit.*, 33 and 43.

104. J. Dickinson, *op. cit.*, 42f., 46ff., 58; Ch. Dereine, "Vie commune," *loc. cit.*, 393, 402; G. Schreiber, *Gemeinschaften des Mittelalters*, 304.

at this time, too, that the canons became institutionalized, through rules and regulations of their own. They adopted the newly discovered *Regula S. Augustini* attributed to the Doctor of Hippo, who had led a "canonical life" with some of his priests. This rule, which abolished private property, is first recorded in 1067, in a charter of Saint Denis in Reims; from then on it is frequently mentioned in contemporary documents and liturgical texts. Championed by Gervasius of Reims, Ivo of Chartres and William of Champeaux, it was eventually approved "by the regularizing Pope Urban II," and, around 1115, declared the authentic rule which was to be applied "literally."[105]

These canons led a regulated, ascetical and virtuous life, spent partly in the celebration of the divine office and partly in pastoral care, the so-called *cura animarum*, which was considered to be alien to the monastic vocation. And with this a fully observed *vita communis* which they professed to be synonymous with the *vita apostolica*, i.e. with a life based on the authority of apostolic precedent and the lives of the Fathers. This, of course, meant the replacement of the mitigations of Aachen and a greater approximation to the Benedictine ideals. In many ways the canon led a life similar to the monastic life. His basic rule was "that he must live in concord" and "that he neither claim nor have anything as his own."[106] He renounced the world, lived in a community, in a regular house, where one could find all the elements of a genuine asceticism: poverty in dwelling, vestment and food, modesty in manner, brotherly support, manual labor, etc. However, great moderation prevailed in these practices, particularly in the area of fasts and penances. But the canon differed from the monk of

105. Ch. Dereine, "Vie commune," *loc. cit.*, 392, 401, 405; J. Dickinson, *op. cit.*, 49, 57f.; J. Leclercq, "La crise du monachisme," *loc. cit.*, 25; *idem*, *La spiritualité du Moyen Age*, 173; G. Schreiber, *Gemeinschaften des Mittelalters*, 304; *idem*, "Studien über Anselm von Havelberg zur Geistesgeschichte des Hochmittelalters," *Analecta Praemonstratensia*, 18 (1942), 70; P. Lefèvre, "Prémontré," *loc. cit.*, 97.

106. "*Primum ut concorditer vivat . . . Non dicat nec habeat proprium.*" Jean Leclercq, "Documents pour l'histoire des chanoines réguliers," RHE, 44 (1949), 567.

his time, for he actively and purposively engaged in the *cura animarum* which involved preaching and other pastoral activities.[107]

Some canons, undoubtedly under the influence of Peter Damian, opted for a more heroic way of life. Following the example of the Desert Fathers, they withdrew to solitary places, gave up all feudal and ecclesiastical property, and led a life of great austerity, in order to arm themselves against the dangers connected with material wealth and to live solely from manual labor. They were renowned for their cultivation of learning and for their great charity toward the poor pilgrims. Hermit-canons like these appeared in the dioceses of Limoges, Clermont and Rodez before the middle of the eleventh century; after 1070 they could be found practically everywhere.[108]

In a world of clerical decadence the rise of the canons regular brought not only an improvement in priestly standards and a strengthening of the diocese as such; it also affected the monastic order. The ideals of the *vita communis* could not but inspire zealous monks to emulate the life of the canons, in order to recover the primacy of the more perfect life inherent in their vocation. They joined the canons' counteroffensive against secularism and the evils of the *Eigenkirche* system, and wholeheartedly worked for the victory of the *vita communis*. In some instances their endeavor actually led to the establishment of new religious communities.[109]

Strange as it may sound, the forces of renewal were also strengthened by the emergence of various heresies during the eleventh century. Some of these had survived from antiquity; others were brought to the West by traders from the East. Thus, at the end of the tenth century, Gnostic and Manichaean doctrines made their reappearance in the West, via Dalmatia and the Greek

---

107. J. Leclercq, *La spiritualité du Moyen Age*, 174f.; *idem*, "La crise du monachisme," *loc. cit.*, 25f.; C. Dereine, "Vie commune," *loc. cit.*, 401; J. Dickinson, *op. cit.*, 26, 49, 52f., 58; G. Schreiber, *Gemeinschaften des Mittelalters*, 304; M. Chenu, "Moines, clercs, laics," *loc. cit.*, 63.

108. J. Dickinson, *op. cit.*, 39; C. Dereine, "Les origines de Prémontré," *loc. cit.*, 361f.; *L'eremitismo in occidente*, 215.

109. U. Berlière, "Les origines de l'Ordre de Cîteaux," *loc. cit.*, 466; G. Schreiber, *Gemeinschaften des Mittelalters*, 304, 400; J. Dickinson, *op. cit.*, 26–29; H. Grundmann, *op. cit.*, 492.

East. The result was that by the early eleventh century there were traces of neo-Manichaeaism in Italy, which then spread to Spain, northern France and Germany, and had a strong appeal in the newly emerging cities and among the people living near markets. They did not appear as a well-rounded doctrinal system nor were they mere theological speculations. According to Ilarino da Milano, their origin must be sought in purely religious inspiration.[110] Yet, the fact that clerics, teachers and nobles were among their recruits admits the plausibility of other conclusions. Be this as it may, in view of the widespread evils of simony, Nicolaitism, worldliness and all the feudal encroachments, the adherents of the new doctrines, with their stress on piety, poverty and abnegation, and their strict views about marriage, made a strong case for themselves. They made headway because they found an ally in the rising reform movement which called for more spirituality and a greater religiosity.[111]

The new ideas took concrete forms in the West when in the year 1000 a peasant named Leuthard began to spread heterodox doctrines,[112] and when somewhat later a number of persons in southern France denied the importance of baptism, rejected the crucifix, marriage and almsgiving and called for strict ascetical practices.[113] In 1022 advocates of Manichaeism in the city of Orleans denied that God was triune, rejected the possibility of miracles, and proposed unconventional ideas on the origin of heaven and earth.[114] Next we hear of the Cathari stirring up trouble at Monteforte near

---

110. Ilarino da Milano, "Le eresie popolari del secolo XI nell' Europa occidentale," *Studi Gregoriani*, 2 (1947), 88.

111. B. Bligny, "Les premiers Chartreux," *loc. cit.*, 31; H. Grundmann, *op. cit.*, 476, 482; Ilarino da Milano, "Le eresie popolari," *loc. cit.*, 79f., 88; E. Werner, *Die gesellschaftlichen Grundlagen*, 71, 76f., 88.

112. Rodulfus Glaber, *Hist.* II, 11; PL 142:643: "*Exurgens (Leutardus) venit domum . . . dimittensque uxorem . . . fecit divortium . . . crucem et Salvatoris imaginem contrivit . . . decimas dare dicebat esse omnimodis superfluum et inane . . . dicebat prophetas ex parte narrasse utilia, ex parte non credenda.*" Cf. also H. Grundmann, *op. cit.*, 477.

113. E. Werner, *Die gesellschaftlichen Grundlagen*, 73.

114. "*Dicebant ergo deliramenta esse, quidquid in veteri ac novo canone certis signis ac prodigiis veterisbusque testatoribus de trina unaque Deitate beata confirmat*

The Eleventh Century: Renewal in Earnest   163

Turin, especially with their condemnation of private property.[115] Burgundy had its difficulties in 1030, when the sectarians incited the people to refuse payments to the bishop, denied the supernatural graces of the priesthood, condemned the veneration of the crucifix and images and rejected the sacraments of baptism, the Eucharist and penance, saying that in their view sacraments had no power to obtain supernatural graces.[116]

At about the same time the disciples of Gandolf started to cause difficulties at Arras. They stressed the need of absolute poverty and admitted in a council before bishop Gerard:

> Our law and discipline is this: to leave the world, to keep the body from the desires of the flesh, to make one's livelihood from the labor of his hands, to seek no one's injury, to show kindness to all of similar beliefs.[117]

They also stressed that salvation can be worked out personally, i.e. independently of other aids, and sought to convey the idea that their

---

auctoritas. Coelum pariter ac terram, ut conspiciuntur, absque auctore initii semper extitisse asserebant . . . Epicureis erant hereticis similes, quoniam voluptatum flagitiis credebant, non recompensari ultionis vindictam. Omne Christianorum opus, pietatis duntaxat et justitiae, quod aestimatur pretium remunerationis aeternae, laborem superfluum judicabant esse." R. Glaber, *Hist.,* III, 8; PL 142:660. Cf. Mansi 19:373ff.; RHF 10:212, 224, 498, 607; Hefele-Leclercq, 4(2):929 n. 2; H. Grundmann, *op. cit.,* 477; E. Werner, *Die gesellschaftlichen Grundlagen,* 77. |

115. R. Glaber, *Hist.,* IV, 2; PL 142:672f. Cf. H. Grundmann, *op. cit.,* 478 and M. Dmitrewski, *op. cit.,* 85.

116. *"[Leutherius archiepiscopus] si ad praesens dignum fuisset perfrui saeculum, nequaquam pullulasset nova haeresis Burgondionum, qui ut mihi innotuistis asserunt se rebelli mente nil debere suis episcopis."* Odoranni opuscula, X; PL 142:819. Cf. ibid., 823, and E. Werner, *Die gesellschaftlichen Grundlagen,* 74f.

117. *"Lex et disciplina nostra quam a Magistro accepimus, nec evangelicis decretis nec apostolicis sanctionibus contraire videbitur, si quis eam diligenter velit intueri. Haec namque hujusmodi est, mundum relinquere, carnem a concupiscentiis fraenare, de laboribus manuum suarum victum parare, nulli laesionem quaerere, charitatem cunctis quos zelus hujus nostri propositi teneat, exhibere. Servata igitur hac justitia, nullum opus esse baptismi."* Mansi 19:425. Cf. *Gerardi I Cameracensis episcopi Acta synodi Atrebatensis;* PL 142:1272.

doctrine was really a return to the religiosity of the early Christians. In their zeal they rejected the contemporary practices concerning churches and altars, turned against the recitation of psalms and condemned the use of incense and bells.[118] Next, i.e. around 1040, the bishop of Châlons spoke out against "a certain rustic" who spread similar doctrines in his diocese, rejecting marriage, the veneration of the crucifix and images, the authority of the Church, the traditional interpretation of the Old Testament and the payment of ecclesiastical dues.[119] After 1050 the whole movement came to a sudden halt, even though the council of Toulouse (1056) still felt the need to issue a decree prohibiting contacts with heretics.[120] But it was only a temporary standstill, as the Pataria in Milan, with its protest against clerical richness and its demand for clerical rights, indicates.[121] This was also the time when Berengar of Tours (d. 1088) disseminated his teachings on the Eucharist, seeing in the consecrated bread and wine no more than a sacrament *representing* the Body and Blood of Christ. He was condemned by the councils of Paris and Rome and, in later years, by the papal legate, Hugh of Die.[122] Heterodox ideas began once more to

118. PL 142:1271-1312. Cf. Ilarino da Milano, "Le eresie popolari," *loc. cit.*, 61ff.; Mansi 19:423-460; Hefele-Leclercq, 4(2):940ff.; M. Dmitrewski, *op. cit.*, 85; E. Werner, *Die gesellschaftlichen Grundlagen*, 78f.

119. "[Catalaunensium episcopus] aiebat in quadam parte diocesis suae quosdam rusticos esse, qui perversum Manichaeorum dogma sectantes, furtiva sibi frequentarent conventicula." *Vasonis Leodiensis episcopi Vita*, XXIV; PL 142:750. See also H. Grundmann, *op. cit.*, 478, and E. Werner, *Die gesellschaftlichen Grundlagen*, 72 and 75.

120. "*Cum haereticis & cum excommunicatis ullam participationem vel societatem habentem praecipue excommunicamus: nisi correctionis vel admonitionis causa, ut ad fidem redeant catholicam. Si autem adjuvantes eos defendere conati fuerint: vinculo simul excommunicationis cum eis subditi permaneant.*" Mansi 19:849. Cf. PL 140:714. See also H. Grundmann, *op. cit.*, 483.

121. B. Bligny, "Les premiers Chartreux," *loc. cit.*, 34; *L'eremitismo in occidente*, 245. Cf. Mansi 19:865f. and Hefele-Leclercq, 4(2):1126ff., 1191ff., and 1253f.

122. A. Fliche, *Le règne du Philippe Ier*, 517-526; Hefele-Leclercq, 4(2): 1040ff., 1056, 1061, 1063, 1118, 1169; Willi Schwartz, "Der Investiturstreit in Frankreich," *Zeitschrift für Kirchengeschichte*, 42 (1923), 303.

thrive toward the end of the century, often as a by-product of the popularity of apostolic poverty and itinerant preaching.[123]

Though varied in many ways, the new doctrines still reveal a number of common ascetico-moral traits. They demanded complete abstinence from meat and downgraded the sacrament of marriage. They condemned the adoration of the cross and the veneration of relics and images, rejected the sacraments of baptism, the Eucharist and penance, the latter on account of their belief that the penitential code was too lax to obtain salvation. The neo-Manichaeans—whether in Armenia or Aquitaine—all demanded a perfect poverty and stressed the importance of manual labor. They believed that the Catholic Church had lost her *raison d'être*, because she had become wealthy. Thus their anti-ecclesiastical doctrines and tendencies had a decidedly anti-feudal streak, a pronounced dislike for the feudal establishment.[124] E. Werner even believes that the new ascetical ideals had a certain influence on St Bernard of Clairvaux and other orthodox ascetics of later centuries.[125]

Concluding this chapter it will be sufficient to indicate that by the second half of the eleventh century the world outside the monastery was showing signs of improvement. In the political sphere, disorder gradually subsided and gave way to a strengthening of national dynasties. This fact, as well as the new municipalities, laws, precedents and administrations offered a growing measure of order, protection and security, and enabled the monarchs to free themselves from the "indiscriminate anarchy of feudalism."[126]

Side by side with this development went the purification of the

---

123. H. Grundmann, *op. cit.*, 483; B. Bligny, "Les premiers Chartreux," *loc. cit.*, 33f.; A. Fliche, *Le règne de Philippe Ier*, 522–526; M. Dmitrewski, *op. cit.*, 85. See also Charles Molinier, "L'Église et les sociétés cathares," *Revue Historique*, 94 (1907), 233ff. and PL 182:676.

124. H. Grundmann, *op. cit.*, 479, 483; E. Werner, *Die gesellschaftlichen Grundlagen*, 78, 82; *idem, Pauperes Christi*, 203f.; B. Bligny, "Les premiers Chartreux," *loc. cit.*, 34; M. Dmitrewski, *op. cit.*, 85; C. Molinier, "L'Église et les sociétés cathares," *loc. cit.*, 233f.

125. *Pauperes Christi*, 201.

126. H. Taylor, *op. cit.*, 1:306. Cf. J. Whitney, *op. cit.*, 98.

Church from such contemporary evils as simony and Nicolaitism and her disengagement from feudal entanglements. The program began, logically, with the reform endeavors of the monks, first undertaken by Cluny, then by others—both individuals and groups. The battle-cry of these latter was: Away from the (feudal) world, from the authoritarianism of archabbots, and back to the Rule and the traditions of the apostolic Church. They saw the remedy for existing abuses in a more ascetical, more simple and more spiritual life and a withdrawal into solitary regions. This traditional monachism was no longer able to offer to ardent souls. Then came the reform of the secular clergy along monastic lines, as can be seen from the emergence of the canons regular, whose apostolate combined the ideals of the monastic and the diocesan life.[127]

The eleventh century is thus truly a landmark in the history of monasticism, as the topics and events discussed in this chapter should sufficiently prove. But more still was to be done. For this, new forces, new approaches were needed and—as will appear in the next chapters—these were not slow in coming.

---

127. H. Taylor, *op. cit.*, 1:306; G. Coulton, *op. cit.*, 1:273f.; E. Werner, *Pauperes Christi*, 199f.; G. Morin, "Un traité inédit de S. Guillaume Firmat," *loc. cit.*, 249.

THE ELEVENTH CENTURY: NEW RELIGIOUS ORDERS

MONASTIC REVIVAL in the eleventh century brought not only reform attempts within traditional monachism but also gave rise to new monastic foundations both in Italy and north of the Alps. In line with contemporary thinking, these foundations advocated a return to apostolic—rather than sixth-century—traditions and stressed the need for poverty, simplicity and a complete detachment from the world—but in ways different from the then accepted monastic standards. In the process, the one great body of traditional monachism was divided into a number of new institutions like Camaldoli, Fonte Avellana, Vallombrosa, Grandmont and the Grande Chartreuse, all indebted to Benedictinism, but also introducing new constitutional frameworks in which the Rule of St Benedict served more as a point of departure.

The renewal in Italy began around the year 1000. With the influx of Eastern refugees, the presence of Greek monks in Calabria and a greater interest in the Desert Fathers, it tended to move away from the traditional cenobitic way of life toward eremitic monachism.[1] Its greatest champions, St Romuald of Ravenna, the founder of Camaldoli, and St Peter Damian, the reformer of Fonte Avellana, will always be prominent in monastic history for their role in this monastic revival.

1. David Knowles, *From Pachomius to Ignatius. A Study in the Constitutional History of the Religious Orders* (Oxford: Clarendon Press, 1966), 16ff.

Romuald,[2] born around 952, joined the abbey of San Apollinare in Classe in his native city of Ravenna, to atone for a murder committed by his father Sergius. Unable to satisfy his inborn love of solitude and self-discipline in the abbey, he joined a hermit named Marinus; with him he led the life of a wandering hermit in central and northern Italy for some four years. The desire to learn more about eremitic monachism took him next to the abbey of St Michael of Cuxa in the Pyrenees whose abbot, Guarinus, a man of wisdom and experience, was well-acquainted with eastern monachism. Here Romuald built a hermitage for himself near the monastery, followed a life of ascetical rigor which included fasts, manual labor and agriculture and devoted himself to the study of ancient monastic authors, especially Cassian. Thus he acquired an even greater love of eremitism.[3] Recalled, ten years later, to Italy to prevent his father from leaving the monastery, he began the career of a monastic reformer, fighting abuses in existing monasteries and establishing dozens of new hermitages and monasteries. The most famous of these, the Sacro Eremo of Camaldoli, was founded in 1012 after a vision in which Romuald saw white-robed monks living in separate cells around an oratory built in honor of

2. Romuald's biography, by Peter Damian, is found in PL 144:955ff. See also Paul Kehr, *Italia Pontificia* (Berlin: Weidmann, 1908), 3:171ff.; L. E. D. Brockhoff, *Die Kloster-Orden der katholischen Kirche* (Frankfurt: Gustav Bender, 1875), 164ff.; Max Heimbucher, *Die Orden und Kongregationen der katholischen Kirche* (Paderborn: Max Schöningh, 1907), 1:410ff.; DOR 1:577ff.; P. Schmitz, *op. cit.*, 3:15f.; *The Book of Saints. A Dictionary of Servants of God Canonized by the Catholic Church: Extracted from the Roman and Other Martyrologies.* Compiled by the Benedictine Monks of St Augustine's Abbey, Ramsgate (New York: The Macmillan Co., 1947), 516; W. Franke, *op. cit*.

3. "*Marinus et Romualdus, non longe a monasterio degentes ad singularem vitam cui assueti fuerant revertuntur. . . . Tribus vero annis ipse et Joannes Grandenius sarculis terram frangentes et triticum seminantes ex manuum suarum labore vixerunt. . . . Librum de vita Patrum legens quod quidam fratres per continuam hebdomadam singulariter jejunantes Sabbatorum die pariter convenirent.*" PL 144:961f. Reference is made to Palladius, Anthony and Athanasius. *Ibid.*, n. 200. See also Bruno of Querfurt, *Vita Quinque Fratrum*, MGH, SS 15:716ff.: "*Hic . . . Romualdus primus nostrorum temporum non propria praesumtione sed secundum Collationes patrum hereminarum per pulchra sublimi humilitate magna vivit et quae est recta via nos instruxit.*" Cf. W. Franke, *op. cit.*, 108.

the Savior. This became the center of his reform. Romuald appointed the first prior of Camaldoli and then continued his reforming activities until his death at Val di Castro near Camerino on June 19, 1027.

Romuald left no rule of his own; he gave his followers the Rule of St Benedict as he had reinterpreted it, i.e. with additions and restrictions and with no allowances for geographic and climatic differences. His own example served as a commentary.[4] He purposely sought to displease men,[5] always wore one or more hair shirts, never washed his clothes, but was content if they were soaked by rain. While others took meager meals, he often fasted all day or returned tastier food. During Lent he contented himself with flour and herbs.[6] "When traveling on horseback with the brethren, he followed far behind them, always singing psalms, as if he were in his cell, and never ceasing to shed tears."[7] To his disciples he gave the advice:

> Sit in your cell, as in Paradise; leave all memory of the world behind you; watch your thoughts, as a good fisherman watches the fish. Salvation consists in the chanting of psalms; do not abandon it. Remain always, in fear and trembling, in the presence of God, like one who stands before an emperor. Gain self-mastery, and be like a child, content with the grace of God.[8]

Wherever he went, "his first concern was to construct an oratory in a cell and then enclosing himself, seal its door."[9] As a rule, he spent the Lenten seasons in his cell, unless called to the outside by an emergency.[10] At Sytria he stayed in his cell for seven years,

---

4. M. Heimbucher, *op. cit.*, 1:402; P. Schmitz, *op. cit.*, 3:15; CE 3:208.

5. "*Romualdus . . . hoc mirabile in suis moribus habuit, quod displicere hominibus per studium querebat, tunc se magnum existimans.*" Bruno of Querfurt, *op. cit.*, 717.

6. PL 144:996f. Cf. *ibid.*, 964. See also S. Hilpisch, *op. cit.*, 159f.

7. PL 144:986. Cf. H. Taylor, *op. cit.*, 1:393.

8. Bruno of Querfurt, *op. cit.*, 738. Cf. S. Hilpisch, *Geschichte des benediktinischen Mönchtums*, 159.

9. PL 144:983. Cf. *ibid.*, 970, 972, 976, 982 and 986.

10. "*Quadragesimali vero tempore, nisi necessitate inevitabili cogeretur, in cellula jugiter morabatur.*" PL 144:1004.

keeping unbroken silence.[11] He liked swamps as refuges. As Peter Damian reports:

> the venerable man dwelt for a while in a swamp (near Ferrara). At length the poisonous air and the stench of the marsh drove him out; and he emerged hairless, with his flesh puffed and swollen, no longer looking quite human for he was as green as a newt.[12]

To his immediate successors Romuald's legacy survived in the form of extremely severe oral traditions. Around 1080 Blessed Rudolph, the fourth prior of Camaldoli, codified the existing practices by putting them in writing. In view of individual differences he lessened Romuald's original severity and made additions and changes in matters like food, wine and silence, while retaining the five-day fast as practiced before.[13]

Romuald founded Camaldoli with a handful of companions who lived in a cluster of separate cells around their chapel built on a steep mountain at an altitude of some 1,200 meters. To be true followers of the Desert Fathers, they observed the Rule of St Benedict in its stricter interpretation and went, in some instances, even beyond its prescriptions. Thus they lived in primitive cells,

---

11. *"In Sytria denique vir venerabilis per septem fere annos inclusus mansit et silentium continuum inviolabiliter tenuit."* PL 144:996.

12. *"Inclusus est etiam quodam tempore vir venerabilis in palude Commiaclensi (Commacchio), quae dicitur Origarum: unde postmodum prae nimio palustris coeni foetore et corrupto aere ita totus tumefactus et depilatus exiit, ut neququam eadem quae inclusa fuerat species videretur. Nam et caro ejus tota eatenus erat viridis, ut vix stellioni discolor appareret."* PL 144:972. Cf. H. Taylor, *op. cit.*, 1:391.

13. In the lenten seasons they fasted five days a week, on bread, salt and water. A pittance was granted on Thursdays. Fish could also be eaten, and wine was served on the feasts of St Andrew, St Benedict, the Annunciation, Palm Sunday and Holy Thursday. During the rest of the year there were only three weekly fast days, but wine was given even on these. On feasts of twelve lessons the community ate in common. Cf. Joannes E. Mittarelli and Anselmus Costadoni, *Annales Camaldulenses ordinis sancti Benedicti quibus plura interseruntur tum ceteras Italico-monasticas res, tum historiam ecclesiasticam remque diplomaticam illustrantia* (Venetiis: Aere Monasterii S. Michaelis de Muriano, 1755–1773), 3:542ff.; DOR 1:589; M. Heimbucher, *op. cit.*, 1:403; P. Schmitz, *op. cit.*, 3:15; CE 3:204 and 208.

observed constant silence and led a life of absolute poverty. They deprived themselves of material necessities, went barefoot, neglected their outward appearance, shaved their heads but kept long beards and wore cheap, hair-shirt-like tunics. Their diet consisted of bread and water; it was only on Sundays and Thursdays that they also took fruits and vegetables. In Advent and during Lent they fasted on bread and water, except on Sundays; some even volunteered for a third lenten season. In these seasons the majority remained in the cells; only those who lived next to the chapel went there to say the divine office in common. In addition to the latter, their prayer life called for a great many extra exercises, among them litanies, readings and two extra psalteries each day. Work usually meant the weaving of baskets and tent-making—not for the sake of material gains, but to avoid idleness—and, in summer, some field labor. They felt no need for scholarly studies. On Sundays they attended Mass and afterwards had their chapter of faults.[14]

Peter Damian described the hermit's life at Sytria near Avellino where Romuald had spent seven years after the foundation of Camaldoli:

> Such was the mode of life at Sytria that not only in name but in fact it was another Nytria. The brethren went barefoot; unkempt and haggard; they were content with the barest necessaries. Some were shut in with doomed doors, seemingly as dead to the world as if in a tomb. Wine was unknown, even in extreme illness. Even the attendants of the monks and those who kept the cattle fasted and preserved silence. They made regulations among themselves and laid penances for speaking.[15]

---

14. PL 144:993 and 963. See also J. Mittarelli and A. Costadoni, *op. cit.*, 1:80 and 3:512ff.; Lucas Holstenius and Marianus Brockie, *Codex regularum quas sancti patres monachis et virginibus sanctimonialibus servandas praescripsere* (Graz: Akademische Druck und Verlagsanstalt, 1957–1958), 2:193ff.; DOR 1:585f.; L. Brockhoff, *op. cit.*, 164ff.; M. Heimbucher, *op. cit.*, 1:402f.; P. Schmitz, *op. cit.*, 3:15f.; S. Hilpisch, *Geschichte des benediktinischen Mönchtums*, 162; CE 3:208; and M. Dmitrewski, *op. cit.*, 71 nn. 2–4.

15. "*Taliter autem in Sytria vivebatur ac si ex similitudine non solum nominis sed etiam operis altera denuo Nitria videretur, omnes siquidem nudis pedibus incedentes, omnes inculti, pallidi et nimia omnium rerum extremitate contenti. Nonulli vero*

Pope Alexander II's approval of the nine existing settlements in 1072 may be considered the legitimation of Camaldoli as an order,[16] with a highly centralized government. Gregory VII took the new order under papal protection and decreed:

> In order to retain forever its original fervor and stability, the said oratory and its cells must always remain on the path of eremitism and the lofty heights of contemplative life. No one may give an abbot to the place or convert it into a coenobium, for it must be dedicated to solitary life.[17]

In 1113, Pope Paschal II confirmed Camaldoli as the motherhouse of the new order and thus formally separated it from the Black Benedictines.[18]

As has been seen, Romuald's monastic ideal was a life devoted exclusively to God: a life of prayer, solitude and eremitic asceticism. Such a life demanded a complete separation from human society, an opposition to everything of the world, a rejection of all political (feudal) involvements and a hostility to culture and learning. For such a life Romuald preferred hermitages to monasteries. St Benedict had admitted that his (cenobitic) Rule was only a directive for beginners—though he may have known that the majority of his monks were not likely to go beyond it. Romuald, however, sought a further goal for all, not just for a few chosen souls, in eremitic life. Monasteries, he felt, were for the weak, for those

---

damnatis januis clausi, ita mortui videbantur mundo, velut in sepulchro jam positi. Vinum ibi nemo noverat, nec si etiam gravissimam quisquis aegritudinem pateretur. Sed cur ego de monachis loquor, cum et ipse monachorum famuli, ipsi quoque custodes pecorum jejunarent, silentium tenerent, disciplinas inter se invicem facerent, et de quibuslibet verbis poenitentiam flagitarent." PL 144:1002. Cf. H. Taylor, *op. cit.*, 1:395.

16. PL 146:1373f. Cf. M. Heimbucher, *op. cit.*, 1:403 and CE 3:204.

17. PL 148:645ff. Cf. D. Knowles, *The Monastic Order in England*, 194.

18. P. Kehr, *op. cit.*, 3:176f. Cf. P. Schmitz, *op. cit.*, 3:115. According to H. Hélyot, before Romuald established Camaldoli he was simply a reformer of the Black Monks. But since the latter did not appreciate his proposals, rejected his leadership and even threatened his life, he saw it necessary to found a new order. DOR 1:585.

who were still in the process of learning: they were means toward the end, i.e. training places for future hermits.[19]

This thinking clearly shows Eastern monastic influences. Already at Ravenna, the New Byzantium of the century, Romuald had an admiration for the Desert Fathers. At Cuxa he studied the writings of Cassian and Cyril of Scythopolis. Through his disciples he later came into contact with Greek monachism in Italy. These experiences convinced him of the need to gather and organize the scattered Western anchorites into colonies in the vicinity of cenobitic monasteries. This would put an end to existing irregularities caused, more often than not, by the uncurbed self-will of lone and isolated hermits. For his organizational framework he took the Rule of St Benedict (which calls for community living under a rule and a superior) and blended in the ideals of Cassian.[20] In some instances, as in the adoption of Greek confessional practices[21] and the employment of lay associates who took vows but did not become monks and remained ineligible for higher offices, he even went beyond the practices of Marseilles.[22] Moreover he retained, alone among other reformers, the institution of the recluse, which enabled a hermit to retire—after a long preparation in the *laura,* and with the permission of the superior—to a cell in order to devote himself to more demanding spiritual and ascetical

19. W. Franke, *op. cit.,* 150; S. Hilpisch, *Geschichte des benediktinischen Mönchtums,* 161f.; P. Schmitz, *op. cit.,* 3:15; J. Leclercq, "La crise du monachisme aux XIe et XIIe siècles," *loc. cit.,* 27f. As in Romuald's life, this eremitic training was to lead to a charismatic apostolate. Cf. A. Louf, *op. cit.,* 192f.

20. W. Franke, *op. cit.,* 113, 121ff., 157, 159f., 164f., 175; E. Sackur, *op. cit.,* 1:324 n. 2; P. Schmitz, *op. cit.,* 3:14f.; G. Schreiber, *Gemeinschaften des Mittelalters,* 420; D. Knowles, *The Monastic Order in England,* 193; A. Louf, *op. cit.,* 193. Cf. A. Louf, 195, on the influences of Cyril of Scythopolis which "explains the typical Palestinian character of the Romualdian foundations."

21. For details see W. Franke, *op. cit.,* 165. Cf. also DTC 3:872ff.

22. "*Et ipsi monachorum famuli, ipsi quoque custodes pecorum jejunarent, silentium tenerent,*" PL 144:1002. Cf. W. Franke, *op. cit.,* 165 and 176. *Ibid.,* 176ff. Franke offers proofs for the existence of *conversi* prior to their appearance in the reform of John Gualbert, who is traditionally credited with their introduction. See also E. Werner, *Pauperes Christi,* 107.

exercises. The recluse left his cell only on rare occasions, e.g. during the last three days of Holy Week, and spoke to no one except the superior and the lay brother who brought him his meager supplies.[23]

At Camaldoli, Romuald had also set up a hostel, Fontebuono, at the foot of the mountain, with one monk and three *conversi* in charge. In 1102 Fontebuono was transformed into a cenobitic establishment which followed the Rule of St Benedict in its original strictness. It had no abbot, possibly because Romuald was also influenced by the Cluniac priory system. Its *raison d'être* was to provide for the material needs of the hermits and to serve as a place where the latter could retire in case of illness or old age. The cenobitic element however never obtained any significant weight at Camaldoli.[24]

Romuald became, as no one before him, the great organizer of anchoretic life in the West. He would have liked to convert the whole world into one single hermitage.[25] In line with this thinking, he reformed a great number of Benedictine monasteries and, in most cases, established hermitages around them, usually in swamps and forests. Prior to the foundation of Camaldoli this amounted to nearly one hundred monasteries and hermitages. The monks and hermits of these places had certain common bonds. They were under the same superior, the abbot, who lived in a hermitage

23. DOR 1:585 and 589f.; L. Brockhoff, *op. cit.*, 166; P. Schmitz, *op. cit.*, 3:15f. and A. Louf, *op. cit.*, 53.

24. DOR 1:589 and 592. Cf. L. Brockhoff, *op. cit.*, 166; M. Heimbucher, *op. cit.*, 1:403f.; P. Schmitz, *op. cit.*, 3:16f.; W. Franke, *op. cit.*, 150. According to A. Louf, Fonte Buono never became a monastery of the common life; *op. cit.*, 193. To this may be added the foundation of St Prisca di Luca, near Mugello in Tuscany, for cenobitic Camaldolese nuns, by Blessed Rudolph, in 1086.

25. "Putaretur totum mundum in eremum velle convertere et monachico ordini omnem populi multitudinem sociare." PL 144:938. In this connection H. Taylor remarked, since in Romuald's view perfection is best achieved through withdrawal from the world, "the only consistent social function left to such a man is that of turning the steps of his fellows to his own recluse path of perfection." *Op. cit.*, 1:396. Cf. also E. Sackur, *op. cit.*, 1:328 n. 7; D. benediktinischen Mönchtums, 159.

but visited the cenobites on Sundays. It was the monastery's duty to care for the material needs of the hermits who spent little time outside their cells.[26]

Monastic reform was not, however, Romuald's only concern. Favored by emperors and princes,[27] he also fought abuses in the Church.[28] On one occasion he was almost strangled by a simoniac abbot.[29] He also took an active interest in the christianization of eastern Europe—possibly to win the crown of martyrdom. He sent his missionaries to Poland and Russia. Illness alone prevented him from going to Hungary in person.[30]

The revival and consolidation of eremitic monasticism in the contemporary Western world is Romuald's lasting achievement. With elements borrowed from cenobitic monasticism, he had been able to devise a regular—if rudimentary—framework for the

26. *"Dum moraretur autem Romualdus adhuc in Pereo, imperator Otto monasterium ibi ad honorem S. Adalberti eo suggerente construxit. . . . Abbate ergo illic ex Romualdi discipulis constituto et fratribus aggregatis coepit eos Romualdus sub magna tenere custodia, et docebat eos sub regulari vivere disciplina. Praecepit etiam abbati ut in eremum secedens per totam hebdomadam in cella consisteret, diebus vero Dominicis fratres ad monasterium veniens visitaret."* PL 144:981f. Cf. W. Franke, *op. cit.,* 127ff.; P. Schmitz, *op. cit.,* 3:15; CE 3:204. During his career as a wandering reformer, Romuald stayed in numerous places, among them Classe, Pont-de-Pierre, Bagno, Pereum, Bifolco, Parenzo, Val di Castro, Camaldoli, the region of Orvieto, Sytria, etc. DOR 1:581ff. Bruno of Querfurt deplored the idea of building monasteries in swamps. "Who is not sick—he wrote—from the oldest to the youngest? What can he do in a cell whose feet are so weak that he is unable to go to church on Sunday to receive communion? What does a man benefit from reading, what kind of a prayer is that, when one cannot lift his members from his bed?" Hence, in his view, it would be better to go to Poland instead of perishing in the swamp of Pereum. *Op. cit.,* 720; S. Hilpisch, *op. cit.,* 158.

27. PL 144:973, 975, 981, 1003. Romuald was also a contemporary of St Nilus and a close friend of William of Dijon. Cf. W. Franke, *op. cit.,* 158.

28. *"Inter caeteros autem praecipue saeculares clericos qui per pecuniam ordinati fuerant durissima severitate corripiebat et eos nisi ordinem sponte desererent, animo damnabiles et haereticos asserebat."* PL 144:986. See also S. Hilpisch, *Geschichte des benediktinischen Mönchtums,* 159 and J. Mahn, *op. cit.,* 28.

29. PL 144:991. Cf. also *ibid.,* 992; H. Taylor, *op. cit.,* 1:383f.; and S. Hilpisch, *Geschichte des benediktinischen Mönchtums,* 158f.

30. PL 144:977ff. and 989.

hitherto unorganized forms of Western anchoretism, and this without doing violence to eremitic ideals. In the process he effected a symbiosis of *coenobium* and hermitage, a project which will be imitated by subsequent reformers.[31]

The great reformer of Fonte Avellana, Peter Damian,[32] also a native of Ravenna, was born in 1007. After a childhood filled with great hardships he attended schools of higher learning, first in his native city, then at Parma. Later, as a teacher, he was renowned for his learning and severe ascetical practices. Never happy in the world, he became a monk, eventually joining the community of Fonte Avellana, an abbey founded by a group of independent hermits following the Rule of St Benedict.[33] After his entrance he developed an even greater love for bodily mortifications seeking to acquire an exclusive taste for the things of the spirit. In time he became procurator, and in 1043 superior of the community. He always refused the title of abbot, calling himself *peccator monachus* instead.[34] In 1057 Pope Stephen IX named him cardinal archbishop of Ostia. As such he undertook a number of legations for the papacy, without changing his favorite ascetical practices. In 1067 Alexander II reluctantly granted him permission to retire to Fonte Avellana. Peter died of a fever on his return from a legation to Ravenna on February 22, 1072.

31. W. Franke, *op. cit.*, 127ff. and 150. Cf. *ibid.*, 120; "Romuald's reform of contemporary anchoretism, in the final analysis, lies in the transfer of cenobitic organizational forms" to the former. See also S. Hilpisch, *Geschichte des benediktinischen Mönchtums*, 161; H. Taylor, *op. cit.*, 1:395. W. Franke also pointed out that Romuald knew canon law and made his ordinances in accordance with it. *Op. cit.*, 118f. Cf. PL 144:986f. and 991. See also D. Knowles, *From Pachomius to Ignatius*, 18 and *idem*, *The Monastic Order in England*, 194.

32. For Peter Damian's life, see PL 144:113ff; Reginald Biron, *St Pierre Damian (1007-1072)* (Paris: Victor Lecoffre, 1930), especially VIf.; Fridolin Dressler, *Petrus Damiani Leben und Werk* (Studia Anselmiana, fasciculus xxxiv; Roma: Herder, 1954); D. Knowles, *The Monastic Order in England*, 194 n. 1; J. Whitney, *op. cit.*, 95 f.; A. Fliche, *La réforme grégorienne*, 1:176ff.; S. Hilpisch, *Geschichte des benediktinischen Mönchtums*, 163; *The Book of Saints*, 471; DOR 2:298; A. Louf, *op. cit.*, 191.

33. R. Biron, *op. cit.*, 11.

34. PL 143:1336. Cf. J. Leclercq, "La crise du monachisme," *loc. cit.*, 23.

Peter Damian always knew the meaning of bodily mortifications. Even in his childhood he was accustomed to humble circumstances and lowly work. He went barefoot and poorly clad, tended swine and suffered many beatings from the members of his family. Later, as a well-known professor, he wore a hair shirt under his clothes, in addition to his numerous fasts, vigils and prolonged prayers. To fight temptations he once plunged into an icy river. At Fonte Avellana he perfected his asceticism. He observed the rule in all its strictness, showed an utter neglect for his body, rejected everything that savored of softness and sought out the most arduous tasks avoided by others. He never drank wine, fasted on bread and water four times a week and was satisfied with vegetables on the remaining days. He liked to chastise his body by walking barefoot and by using light robes even in winter. He kept long vigils and spent many nights in prayer. Shocked by his imperfections, he frequently disciplined himself, even as a cardinal.[35]

This emulator of St Romuald was also a man of many literary talents and a great teacher. Plagued by painful headaches at Fonte Avellana—the result of his rigorous self-discipline—he sought alleviation in the study of Sacred Scripture and was soon asked to give conferences to his own and to neighboring communities.[36] Eventually he turned to writing and left a literary output of some 50 sermons; 60 smaller works; 8 "books" of correspondence; hagiographies; poems and prayers. While on a conference tour, he wrote the life of St Romuald.[37] His writings reveal such sources as Sacred Scripture, Palladius, Sulpicius Severus, the *Collationes Patrum*, the *Instituta Patrum* and the lives of Saints Anthony, Paul

---

35. "*Bonae indolis Christi miles tantis illico jejuniorum, vigiliarum caeterumque afflictionum laboribus se coepit atterere, ut ii qui diuturnis jam studiis exercitati fuerant, illius mores et vitam intuentes, sua cogerentur acta contemnere.*" PL 144:122. Cf. *ibid.*, 137ff. See also A. Fliche, *La réforme grégorienne*, 1:177f. and 186; R. Biron, *op. cit.*, 12f.; F. Dressler, *op. cit.*, 58; S. Hilpisch, *Geschichte des benediktinischen Mönchtums*, 164.

36. PL 144:123f.

37. PL vols. 144 and 145. For the works' authenticity, see Giovanni Lucchesi, *Clavis S. Petri Damiani* (Faënza: Seminario Vescovile, 1961).

and Hilarion.[38] Since more than half of his treatises are addressed to priests and monks, it is possible to ascertain Peter's ideas on the monastic life with a definite measure of certainty.[39]

Peter Damian always felt that monastic life was superior to life in the world. The latter was nothing but gluttony, avarice and pleasure-seeking to him. Its goods—fame, riches, beauty, and the like—are only apparent goods, for they are obstacles to one who is seeking God.[40] This judgment applied also to contemporary cenobitism in which worldliness, in all its forms, was very much the order of the day.[41] Hence Peter's conviction that a true monk must admit his guilt, reject the biblical "old man," leave the world and seek a haven among the anchorites of the desert. For only a life of contemplation in the desert can establish a lasting union with God.

38. PL 144:351, 395, 706, 711 and PL 145:351, 377, 513f. and 619. In this connection it is of interest to list the works found in the library of Fonte Avellana, as recorded by Peter Damian: The Old Testament, The New Testament, the Acts of the Martyrs, homilies of the Fathers and commentaries of Gregory, Ambrose, Augustine, Jerome, Prosper of Aquitaine, Bede, Remigius, Amalarius, Haymo and Paschasius. PL 145:334.

39. E.g., the following *opuscula*, 7, 10, 12, 13, 14, 15, 16, 24, 25, 29, 43, 45, 46, 47, 48, 49, 50, 51, 52, 56, and 58. PL 145:159, 221, 251, 291, 328, 335, 366, 480, 491, 518, 679, 696, 703, 710, 715, 721, 731, 748, 763, 807 and 831. Cf. F. Dressler, *op. cit.*, 62; Mansueto Della Santa, *Ricerche sull'idea monastica di San Pier Damiano* (Studi e Testi Camaldulesi, No. 11; Camaldoli: Edizioni Camaldoli, 1961); A. Fliche, *La réforme grégorienne*, 1:193 and V. Hermans, *op. cit.*, 121.

40. PL 145:251ff. Cf. F. Dressler, *op. cit.*, 57ff. and A. Fliche, *La réforme grégorienne*, 1:193.

41. Peter Damian especially deplored that the cenobites of his day reverted to the life they promised to give up (PL 145:253), that their piety had sunk very low and that they were quite negligent in the observance of their rules (PL 145:291ff.). He found regular monasteries so corrupt that novices leaving them had more vices than when they entered (PL 145:362). Then there were such additional abuses as the love of money (PL 145:253ff), unnecessary travel (PL 145:260f), special treatment in the monastery (PL 145:507), the combination of the active and contemplative life, leading to the loss of both (PL 145:277), the love of good clothes (PL 145:267), excessive care of the body in the form of medication and extravagant food (PL 145:726), vain conversation with laymen (PL 144:422) and the love of secular learning (PL 145:695). Cf. also PL 145:455 and John J. Wang, *Saint Peter Damian the Monk* (New York: Fordham University Thesis, 1957), 146ff.

The Eleventh Century: New Religious Orders 179

In his view, "to the aspirant of perfection the monastery is neither a permanent mansion nor a temporary habitat; it is not the attainment of the intended goal, but the resting place of the journey."[42] The monastery is only a novitiate. It provides the milk which precedes the more solid food of the hermit.[43] If someone wants to stay in it permanently, this should be tolerated;[44] but he who goes to the desert deserves to be applauded for preferring "the strictness of eremitic life to monastic laxity."[45] Accordingly Peter reproached a monk who left the desert in order to become the abbot of a cenobitic monastery[46] and urged another to return to the hermitage, in these words:

> Return, dearest son, with all haste to the desert, lest, while the monastery's broad road delights your adolescence, the restrictions of the desert become odious to you through oblivion caused by non-practice.[47]

Similarly, when an abbot protested that one of his monks had gone to the desert in violation of the Benedictine Rule, Peter

---

42. "*Ad perfectionis igitur summam tendenti monasterium dicitur esse non mansio, non habitatio, sed hospitium; non finis intentionis, sed quaedam quies itineris.*" PL 144:393. Cf. PL 145:246 and 339; F. Dressler, *op. cit.*, 60; H. Taylor *op. cit.*, 1:385; A. Fliche, *La réforme grégorienne*, 1:205; idem, *op. cit.*, 8:446 and P. Schmitz, *op. cit.*, 2:405.

43. "*Velut in convalle primae conversationis incipiat; deinde jam spiritualibus exercitiis roboratus, tanquam a lacte ad solidum cibum transiens, verticem perfectionis ascendat.*" PL 144:394.

44. "*B. Benedictus . . . tolerabilius tamen ducit nos infirmos ac debiles in monasterii portu vel ignobiliter vivere quam in tempestuosa naufragi mundi voragine deperire. Fratres igitur in monasterio immobiliter permanentes tolerandi sunt; ad eremum vero fervido spiritu transmigrantes plausibus ac praeconiis efferendi.*" PL 144:395. Cf. E. Dressler, *op. cit.*, 43.

45. "*Non itaque ad monasterialem laxitudinem ab eremitica [via] vos libeat districtione descendere.*" PL 144:334.

46. PL 144:387ff.

47. "*Ad eremum ergo, charissime fili, sub omni celeritate revertere, ne dum monasterialem adolescentiam tuam latitudo delectat, eremi districtio per oblivionem desuetudinis quandoque, quod absit, et in odium veniat.*" PL 144:405.

Damian disagreed. He pointed to the first chapter of the Rule which acknowledges the existence of hermits and to St Benedict's admission that his Rule was but a rule for beginners, i.e. a preparatory school for eremitic life.[48]

Separation from the world also called for an end to vagrancy. Peter strongly condemned the wanderlust of contemporary monks which had greatly contributed to the crisis of cenobitism in his days. To him every itinerant monk was suspicious. Hence his advice to his followers:

> Whoever wishes to reach the summit of perfection should keep within the cloister of his seclusion, cherish spiritual leisure and shudder at traversing the world, as if he were about to plunge into a sea of blood. For the world is so filthy with vices that any holy mind is befouled even by thinking about it.[49]

Or, to put it more succinctly: "Sit in your cell, control your tongue and your stomach, and you will be safe." For this cell is a jail only to vagrants; to those who stay, it is a sweet cubicle.[50]

Unlike Romuald, Peter Damian recorded the specifics of his reform. This he did in *De ordine eremitarum et facultatibus eremi Fontis Avellani*[51] and, in a later work, *De suae congregationis institutis*.[52] As a general principle he states: "Whatever is found in the Rule of St Benedict or in the Institutes or Collations of the Fathers, is part of

---

48. PL 144:392ff. Cf. A. Fliche, *La réforme grégorienne*, 1:241.

49. "*Quisquis ergo monachus perfectionis culmen festinat attingere, intra remotioris suae se claustra cohibeat, spirituale otium deligat; discurrere vero per saeculum, velut mersare se in lacum sanguinis perhorrescat. Tot enim criminum magis ac magis in dies mundus contaminatione polluitur, ut quaelibet sancta mens sola ejus consideratione foedetur.*" PL 144:287.

50. "*Sede in cella tua, et retine linguam tuam, et ventrem, et salvus eris*" (PL 145:339). "*Vagantibus cella carcer est, permanentibus suave cubiculum*" (PL 145:278). And what is more: "*Tantopere quippe vagatio est vitanda, ut nec per ipsam cellulam spatiari inaniter liceat*" (PL 145:350). See also A. Fliche, *La réforme grégorienne*, 1:196f. This stability was not demanded in early eremitic history. Cf. F. Dressler, *op. cit.*, 49.

51. PL 145:327ff.   52. PL 145:335ff.

this discipline."[53] This means that, whereas Romuald set out to regulate the life of scattered anchorites, Peter Damian legislated for an already established community of hermits. He headed his monastery as its prior who was first among equals, the so-called *seniores*. The community itself included hermit monks who spent most of their time in their cells "in contemplation, silence and fasting," *conversi* who took care of the more menial tasks and had less rigorous prayer obligations, and, finally, novices. Detailed rules regulated the acceptance of the latter and, as could be expected, the novices were not immediately admitted to full eremitic life.[54]

Withdrawal into the desert implied that the tyro wished to engage in a direct fight with the devil on the battlefield of the spirit and was determined to be victorious. The hermit's life is therefore the life of a soldier of Christ. Fully trained, he has the strength to stand his ground alone, even in the very first battle line. Faithful to his oath to the flag, he keeps his spiritual armor in readiness to fight the devil, who is lurking in the dark to surprise the careless and the untrained. Constant vigilance in this struggle will eventually lead to peace, and labor will give way to rest and repose. The hermit must therefore be an enemy of the world, poor and naked, subdued by fasts and chastisements and filled with a holy ignorance.[55] This is why the religious of Fonte Avellana liked to call themselves "penitents." To them, monastic life was a life of penance which impelled the monk to seek out all that was arduous and difficult. In this view, a true monk goes barefoot, with unwashed hands and feet, and unkempt hair, and constantly chastises his body, through such means as repeated genuflections, long prayers with outstretched arms, and the use of the discipline. He spontaneously accepts destitution and the idea of spending a lifetime in an

---

53. "Quidquid enim in B. Benedicti Regula, quidquid in institutis sive in collationibus Patrum est dictum, huic competere disciplinae perpendimus." PL 145:351.

54. "Solitariae vitae proposito tria sunt praecipue exteriora, videlicet congrua speciali prae ceteris observatione tenenda: quies scilicet, silentium atque jejunium." PL 145:339. Cf. F. Dressler, *op. cit.*, 45 and 62.

55. PL 144:554 and 919. PL 145:338. Cf. also F. Dressler, *op. cit.*, 49f.; A. Fliche, *La réforme grégorienne*, 1:193 and 204f.

austere cell, keeping perpetual silence, total obedience and long prayer vigils.[56] To mortify their spirit, the hermits of Fonte Avellana rejected all intellectual work, excepting only the study of the psalms and spiritual reading, and adamantly opposed the cultivation of the new science of dialectics. Manual labor, though not specifically mentioned among the observances of Fonte Avellana, was a regular feature in the monks' life. Peter Damian alluded to it when stating that he took up writing as a substitute for it, because of ill health.[57] Strict silence—a precaution against distraction and sin—prevailed in all regular places; it was only broken for confession or in case of an emergency. Even novices, just beginning their training, could talk only once or twice a week, usually after Vespers.[58] As for monastic poverty, the reformer of Fonte Avellana boldly turned the Benedictine *sufficientia* into *extremitas* and *penuria,* in the conviction that world-rejection can only be achieved through total poverty. For this reason he accepted only a minimum of possessions, i.e. only as much as was needed for the support of the community. He insisted that personal poverty must be absolute, with no exceptions, for a small infection would eventually corrupt the whole organism. This is why the hermit took nothing with himself when he moved from one cell to another. This is also why his clothing was light, poor and undyed, even when he had to appear outside the hermitage, for good clothes are simply an occasion for scandal. His shoes and stockings had to last

---

56. "*Taceo de vilitate spontanea et asperitate vestium, de duritia, de austeritate cubilium, et de districta censura silentii, de amore perpetuae inclusionis.*" PL 144:332. Cf. also PL 145:330, 338, 344, 353; R. Biron, *op. cit.,* 17, 19, 23; A. Fliche, *La réforme grégorienne,* 1:205; P. Schmitz, *op. cit.,* 2:405 and S. Hilpisch, *Geschichte des benediktinischen Mönchtums,* 164.

57. R. Biron, *op. cit.,* 26; A. Fliche, *La réforme grégorienne,* 1:204; P. Schmitz, *op. cit.,* 2:403. Cf. PL 145:306 on the study of dialectics. Peter Damian prescribed manual occupations insofar as they did not conflict with stability and prayer, for prayer was the principal "labor" of the hermit. Hence his admiration for Cluny's ideal of perpetual prayer even though it meant the exclusion of manual labor. Cf. PL 145:874 and A. Louf, *op. cit.,* 195.

58. "*Eremitae officium est in jejunio silentioque quiescere.*" PL 145:339. Cf. ibid., 332: "*In cellulis continuum tenetur . . . silentium.*" See also PL 145:344, 350 and PL 144:444; F. Dressler, *op. cit.,* 50, 52 and R. Biron, *op. cit.,* 18 and 23.

for a whole year. He slept on a hard bed, kept bodily hygiene to a minimum to avoid giving a pleasant appearance, and had his head shaven each month, except during Advent and Lent; in these seasons he was even forbidden to wash his head. As in the time of St Benedict, baths were allowed only to the sick.[59]

Similar principles guided the regulations on food. The hermit's diet consisted of meatless solid food, cooked dishes, various kinds of fruits and vegetables, and, on occasion, of fish and wine. His bread ration was the same as in cenobitic monasteries. According to the season of the year, the hermit fasted four or five days a week; on such occasions he took only bread, salt and water. He kept this fast also when away from the monastery. From Easter to mid-September he had two meals on Sundays and Thursdays, and also on Tuesdays during the summer months. He cooked his meals in his cell, always one dish for each meal. He never ate meat and even gave up fish during Advent and Lent, except on the feasts of Saints Martin, Andrew, Benedict, and on Holy Thursday and Palm Sunday. Wine, at first prohibited even to visiting laymen, was eventually served on Sundays, Thursdays, great feasts, and on the days of Advent and Lent when fish could be eaten, to invigorate the hermits' bodies weakened by constant mortifications. But to lessen the number of these exceptions, the hermits transferred lesser feasts to non-fasting days, i.e. to Tuesdays and Thursdays, also fasted on most octaves, and ate only one meal on twelve-lesson feasts between mid-September and Easter. On account of their work, the *conversi*, though following the hermits in every other respect, fasted only four times a week during Advent and Lent, and three times a week during the rest of the year. Further allowances were made on Sundays and great feasts, when the procurator could

---

59. "*Juxta id quod exiguitati loci humilis competebat, studuimus eotenus possessiones acquirere: ut praedictum fratrum numerum possis, nisi exercendi cura defuerit, sustentare.*" PL 145:334. Cf. ibid., 330: "*In hoc nempe loco, qui fons Avellani dicitur, plerumque viginti plus minus monachi per cellulas, sive in assignata cuique obedientia degimus; ut omnes simul cum conversis et famulis tricenarium quinarum numerum aut vix, aut breviter, excedamus.*" See also PL 145:344, 351, 353, 517ff. R. Biron, *op. cit.*, 23f. 26; F. Dressler, *op. cit.*, 48, 51f. and A. Fliche, *La réforme grégorienne*, 1:193, 198, 201ff.

serve a third dish; it was not uncommon, however, to reject such favors and better dishes in general, and some religious even fasted on the Sundays of Advent and Lent.[60]

The spirit of penance pervaded also the hermits' prayer life. They said the canonical hours in common, as in cenobitic monasteries, but did not return to their beds after the night office; instead they recited psalms until the beginning of Lauds. In addition to the regular office, they prayed two more psalters each day—one for the living, another for the dead—whenever there were two hermits in a cell. To the first psalter they added the prayers of St Romuald, i.e. special doxologies after every fifth psalm, three *Our Fathers*, the canticles of the entire week, the hymn *Te Deum*, the canticle *Nunc dimittis*, the Creed, the *Glory to God in the Highest*, and finally litanies and orations. The second psalter had nine lessons, i.e. three readings after every fiftieth psalm. If a hermit was alone in his cell, he recited the psalter for the living and, according to his strength, the entire or a half psalter for the deceased. All hermits attended Mass on Sundays.[61]

Among the penitential exercises propagated by Peter Damian was the discipline. In this he followed the example of such contemporaries or near-contemporaries as Regino of Prüm, Guy of Pomposa and Poppo of Stavelot. He justified the practice from the example of Christ and the apostles, from the life of countless martyrs who had undertaken similar chastisements and from the inadequacy of existing penitential tariff books. He prescribed the discipline for every Friday. The result was that Fonte Avellana soon had its own penitential system. Three thousand strokes, for instance, were taken to be the equivalent of what the Church would consider one year's penance. Beating oneself for the duration of ten psalms equalled one thousand strokes; for the duration of the 150 psalms, five years' penance; and for the duration of twenty psalters, one hundred years' penance. When a hermit died, his confreres

60. PL 145:330ff., 340ff., 346ff., 352f., 857ff.; R. Biron, *op. cit.*, 17f.; F. Dressler, *op. cit.*, 50f.; A. Fliche, *La réforme grégorienne*, 1:200 and 262. See also R. Bultot, *op. cit.*, 4(1):112 n. 282 and 132 n. 330.

61. PL 145:226f., 332, 343f., 350 and 564. See also R. Biron, *op. cit.*, 24f.; F. Dressler, *op. cit.*, 52f. and A. Louf, *op. cit.*, 197.

fasted for seven days and offered seven scourgings of one thousand strokes for his soul. Bodily mortification became thus the chief attribute of the hermits' ascetical life where the spiritual was subordinated to the physical, as can be seen from the practice of chastising the body even during prayer and meditation.[62] Peter Damian even defended a monk who disobeyed his abbot in order to go beyond the ascetical demands of the Rule. He felt that even if the practices in question were not prescribed for cenobites, the fact that they were intended for hermits shows that they were in no way against the Rule of St Benedict which made several allusions to eremitic life.[63]

This asceticism produced examples of heroic mortification at Fonte Avellana. Peter's favorite disciple, Dominicus Loricatus, "the Mailed," was a man of such incredible penances. He wore for years an iron coat of mail which he took off only when scourging himself with two scourges instead of the usual one. Of great endurance, he often did one hundred years' penance in six days. Once during Lent he set out to do a thousand years' penance, i.e. scourge himself through two hundred psalters, and was able to carry out his resolve before the season was over. At night he often scourged himself through nine consecutive psalters and felt disappointed at not being able to add one more psalter. Once, however, he succeeded in scourging himself through twelve consecutive psalters and thirty-one additional psalms.[64]

62. PL 144:331, 347ff., 414ff., 422ff. and PL 145:333 and 343. Cf. R. Biron, *op. cit.*, 19f.; A. Fliche, *La réforme grégorienne*, 1:201ff., 243; P. Schmitz, *op. cit.*, 2:405; S. Hilpisch, *Geschichte des benediktinischen Mönchtums*, 165.

63. A. Fliche, *La réforme grégorienne*, 1:262. It may be useful to recall here A. Mirgeler's observation: "The life of the early desert fathers became the starting point of the monastic reform, for martyrdom as the goal of Christian perfection was out of the question in a Europe rapidly turning Christian even in the perimeters.... But the northern attempts to imitate the fathers of the desert soon had to come to the realization that the northern climate did not permit the total abstemiousness in food and clothing they desired. As a substitute, new forms of asceticism came into practice which remained throughout the Middle Ages, above all the scourging of oneself." *Op. cit.*, 84.

64. PL 144:1015ff. Cf. H. Taylor, *op. cit.*, 1:397f.; R. Biron, *op. cit.*, 22f.; S. Hilpisch, *Geschichte des benediktinischen Mönchtums*, 165f. and P. Schmitz, *op. cit.*, 3:16.

Others performed similar penances. One hermit, for instance, ate only twice a week for a year and a half. Another ate crumbs instead of bread. A third used to recite two consecutive psalters with outstretched arms. A fourth knew only fifty psalms by heart; these he prayed seven times a day. He also stayed in his cell for fifteen years without ever leaving it or cutting his hair and shaving his beard. He lived on bread and drank stale water to which he added tasteless vegetables on Sundays.[65]

In spite of this extreme rigor, Peter Damian also knew what moderation and discretion meant for the rest of the community. Thus he abolished fasting during the octaves of Christmas, Easter and Pentecost, except for those who were capable of greater hardships and occasionally allowed better meals on feasts of twelve lessons—which, however, were a rarity. He also granted meat to the sick. In consideration of individual needs, he permitted a *siesta* during the summer months. To forestall abuses and to keep the hermits fit for the regular exercises, he also insisted that extraordinary mortifications should be undertaken only on a voluntary basis. This is why he limited scourging to forty psalms on ordinary days and to sixty during Advent and Lent.[66]

Although Peter Damian did not intend to found a new religious order, Fonte Avellana soon became a center of monastic reform with its own foundations. Other monasteries also accepted its way of life. Peter Damian paid frequent visits to the latter and saw to it that they observed regular discipline. This congregation of Fonte Avellana was able to maintain its independent existence

---

65. PL 145:325 and 753ff. Cf. R. Biron, *op. cit.*, 31; and S. Hilpisch, *Geschichte des benediktinischen Mönchtums*, 166.

66. PL 144:433f. Cf. PL 145:348ff. and R. Biron, *op. cit.*, 16f., and 25. According to M. Della Santa, Peter Damian's personal evolution was marked by a "progressive maturation which enabled him to render his ascetical demands accessible to a greater number ... One can notice an ... evolution which led him from an exaltation of the eremitic at the expense of the cenobitic ideal, to a more matured enthusiasm." A. Louf, *op. cit.*, 192. Hence, "there is no indication that all the cenobites indiscriminately were called to pass eventually to the desert." A. Louf, *op. cit.*, 194.

until 1570; then it was attached to the order of Camaldoli.⁶⁷

Selfless, uncompromising and energetic, Peter Damian was a man of genius with one overriding ambition: to lead souls to God. This made him a prime mover in the Gregorian Reform. Employing his great talents, he mercilessly attacked simony, Nicolaitism and intemperance, unafraid to speak his mind to Popes, kings and princes. But his main concern were the monks of his time. Not content with combating a multitude of abuses prevailing in their houses, he passionately urged them to leave the easier path traced by the Rule of St Benedict and accept the more perfect way, the hermit's way. This may not have been basically different from Romuald's ideal; still, as has been seen, Peter Damian will always be more than the reformer of Fonte Avellana.⁶⁸

Monastic renewal in Italy moved not only in the direction of eremitism; it also produced a cenobitic revival. This was to a large extent the work of the Florentine, St John Gualbert.⁶⁹ A wayward

67. R. Biron, *op. cit.*, 14ff.; P. Schmitz, *op. cit.*, 3:16; A. Fliche, *La réforme grégorienne*, 1:205. Gregory VII took Fonte Avellana under papal protection. Cf. PL 148:669f.—Unlike Romuald's set-up, the hermitages and *coenobia* of Peter Damian never formed a single institution, but remained completely independent of each other (A. Louf, *op. cit.*, 193), united only by a *vinculum caritatis*, "the first traces of a form of congregation based on charity"—an idea borrowed later by Vallombrosa and Cîteaux; A. Louf, *op. cit.*, 194.

68. P. Schmitz, *op. cit.*, 2:403; A. Fliche, *La réforme grégorienne*, 1:188, 190ff., 205f.; D. Knowles, *The Monastic Order in England*, 194ff.; F. Dressler, *op. cit.*, 60ff. and S. Hilpisch, *Geschichte des benediktinischen Mönchtums*, 164f. For Peter Damian's contribution to medieval piety, the cultivation of Christ's passion and propagation of Marian devotions—including the little office of the Blessed Virgin Mary—see PL 145:565ff. and 920ff. Cf. also R. Biron, *op. cit.*, 26 and 28; P. Schmitz, *op. cit.*, 2:403f.; D. Knowles, *The Monastic Order in England*, 196 and D. Geanakoplos, *op. cit.*, 45.

69. For John Gualbert's life, see PL 146:671ff. (by Atto) and PL 146:765ff. (by Andreas of Sturmi); AS, Jul. 3:311ff.; MGH, SS, 30:1076ff.; Diego de Franchi, *Historia del patriarcha S. Giovan Gvalberto primo abbate di Vallombrosa* (Fiorenze: G. B. Landini, 1640); Alfonso Salvini, *S. Giovanni Gualberto fondatore di Vallombrosa* (Alba: Pia Società San Paolo, 1943); Placido Lugano, *L'Italia benedittina* (Roma: F. Ferrari, 1929), 307ff.; J. Mabillon, *Acta sanctorum ordinis S. Benedicti*, 6(2):266ff.; *The Book of Saints*, 333; L. Brockhoff, *op. cit.*, 170f.; M. Heimbucher, *op. cit.*, 1:409; DOR 3:838ff.; P. Kehr, *op. cit.*, 3:83; P. Schmitz, *op. cit.*, 3:16f.; S. Hilpisch, *Geschichte des benediktinischen Mönchtums*, 167.

youth, John changed his ways after a vision and joined the community of San Miniato Abbey in his native city. Realizing that the abbot was a simoniac and longing for a more solitary life, he left it again to look for a more suitable place. After wandering through the Romagna he visited Camaldoli, but did not stay. He wished to avoid ordination to the priesthood[70] and had come to the conclusion that his ideal was not the hermitage but the monastery. He then, i.e. around 1036, retired to *Aqua Bella,* a lonely place, between Florence and Camaldoli, subsequently named Vallombrosa. After seven years spent in solitary life he established a small monastery with newly arrived companions. He became their prior and then, against his wish, also their abbot. Life at Vallombrosa was half cenobitic, half eremitic, with a purely contemplative interpretation of the Benedictine Rule. External activities, manual labor and administrative duties were entrusted to lay brothers. The reform was approved by Pope Victor II in 1055. It spread subsequently to other parts of Italy and before the century was over also to France. John Gualbert became thus the founder of a congregation having established nine of the monasteries before his death in 1073.

The monastery of Vallombrosa was founded in the year 1038 or 1039. It consisted of separately built simple huts patterned after the layout of Camaldoli, and an additional hospice built for prospective newcomers. The founders called their place a "hermitage." In time, however, the eremitic element gave way to more cenobitic arrangements, in accordance with the founder's desire to return to the original observance of the Benedictine Rule.[71] This idea had been on his mind for a long time. After leaving San Miniato, he went about, inquiring "whether he could find a monastery where

70. "*Tunc prior ejusdem loci volens virum Dei ad sacros ordines promovere et stabilitatem loci promittere, renuit penitus, quia fervor ejus in coenobitali vita tantum erat, et secundum sancti Benedicti regulam vivere.*" PL 146:676.

71. DOR 3:840f.; M. Heimbucher, *op. cit.,* 1:408f.; CMH 5:668. According to Denis Meade, "It is difficult to say whether Abbess Itta's two references to the settlement as an *eremus* and one reference to it as a *locus* indicate a life style or merely the simplicity and remoteness of the establishment." "From Turmoil to Solidarity: The Emergence of the Vallumbrosan Monastic Congregation," *The American Benedictine Review,* 19 (1968), 329.

the Rule of . . . blessed Father Benedict was observed."[72] Hence, "he carefully examined many monasteries, but found that they did not observe the Rule properly."[73] This increased his determination "to found a monastery in a suitable solitude, so that he may be able to live according to the Rule of St Benedict."[74] Then, after he became abbot of Vallombrosa, "he began to explore, with great zeal, the correct meaning of the Rule and to devote all his energies to its full observance."[75] The outcome of these endeavors was a cenobitic life according to the Rule of St Benedict, with restrictions of a penitential nature to ensure a strictly contemplative life. In the words of C. Butler:"The Vallombrosians near Florence maintained a cenobitical life, but eliminated every element of Benedictine life that was not devoted to pure contemplation."[76]

Considering eremitic life to be the gift of a few chosen souls, John Gualbert decided in favor of the *vita communis* in his new establishment. He was grateful for the vocations sent by divine Providence, restored the original Benedictine idea of a full year's novitiate, "decided to observe the Rule of St Benedict with regard to them [i.e. the novices] in all particulars, and began to test these newcomers as called for by the Rule."[77] He subjected them

---

72. *"Beatus Johannes ivit in Romandiolam ad perquirendum si invenire posset aliquod monasterium in quo observaretur regula beati patris nostri Benedicti."* PL 146:676. Cf. Roger Duvernay, "Cîteaux, Vallombreuse et Etienne Harding," *Analecta Sacri Ordinis Cisterciensis,* 8 (1952), 386 n. 5. See also *ibid.,* 387; U. Berlière, *L'ordre monastique,* 272; P. Salmon, "L'ascèse monastique," *loc. cit.,* 277 n. 5.

73. R. Duvernay, "Cîteaux, Vallombreuse," *loc. cit.,* 387 n. 1.

74. *"Dixitque se desiderare in aliqua solitudine monasterium condere, ut secundum regulam sancti benedicti vivere posset."* R. Duvernay, "Cîteaux, Vallombreuse," *loc. cit.,* 386 n. 4.

75. *"Vir Dei, sumpto officio et abbatis nomine coepit sensum Regulae diligenter inspicere et ad ejus observationem totis viribus operam dare."* PL 146:679. Cf. *ibid.,* 775.

76. *Benedictine Monachism,* 302. Cf. M. Dmitrewski, *op. cit.,* 71; S. Hilpisch, *Geschichte des benediktinischen Mönchtums,* 167f; E. Werner, *Pauperes Christi,* 101; D. Knowles, *The Monastic Order in England,* 194.

77. *"Cernens igitur pater Johannes tot talesque viros sibi coelitus in auxilium missos, disposuit cum eisdem beati Benedicti regulam in omnibus observare, coepitque*

to severe penances and humble work and severely punished transgression, usually in the form of beatings.

The first religious of Vallombrosa lived in single cells, keeping strict silence both there and in the other regular places. Completely separated from the world, they stayed in the monastery until death. They were not allowed to go outside the monastery for the transaction of some business, to visit the sick, attend funerals or do pastoral work. Hence they rejected churches and altars—whose care, John Gualbert felt, "belonged to the canons, but not to monks"— as well as lands and denied burial to laymen in their monasteries.[78]

Another characteristic of the Vallombrosians' observance was their cultivation of extreme poverty. Often a single loaf of bread had to suffice for three persons. The monks fasted throughout the year, and even more so during Advent and Lent. Not surprisingly, a person's whole belongings could be put in a single sack.[79] As in eastern monachism, John Gualbert refused admittance to rich candidates as long as they kept a single piece of money.[80] The

---

noviter venientes ea probatione suscipere quam insinuat regula." PL 146:677. Cf. R. Duvernay, "Cîteaux, Vallombreuse," *loc. cit.*, 389, 404, 410ff. and M. Heimbucher, *op. cit.*, 1:410.

78. PL 146:679. Cf. *ibid.*, 775: *"Vir Dei nullum monachorum permittebat ad mercata vel ad loca saecularia ire, infirmos extra monasterium visitare . . . Vetuit defuncta ad monasterium deferenda; prohibuit accipere capellas . . . . Canonicorum, non monachorum, hoc esse officium dicebat."* See also R. Duvernay, "Cîteaux, Vallombreuse," *loc. cit.*, 392ff.; Andreas Januensis, *Vita sancti Joannis Gualberti* (Florence: State Archives, ms. conv. 260-223), 19r; Brunetto Quilici, "Giovanni Gualberto e la sua riforma monastica," *Archivo storico italiano*, 99 (1941), 113ff., and 100 (1942), 45ff., especially p. 66; S. Hilpisch, *Geschichte des benediktinischen Mönchtums*, 167f.; H. DeWarren, "Le monachisme à l'apparition de saint Bernard," *loc. cit.*, 54 n. 53 and 59.

79. *"Manserunt ibi multo tempore, ligneum habentes tantummodo oratorium. Indigentiam victuum tantam tunc perpessi sunt, ut plerumque tres unum per diem dividerant panes. Quaecumque erant camerulae, vestiarii, unius sacci capacitas continebat."* PL 146:667. Cf. *ibid.*, 772. As for manual labor, see PL 146:776: *"Ejus [Joannis] admonitione pariterque exemplo in tantum amorem observandae Regulae venerunt ut nec manuum opera, nec alia, quae videtur Regula praecipere, gravia omitterant."* Cf. H. DeWarren, "Le monachisme à l'apparition de saint Bernard," *loc. cit.*, 60. On the renunciation of meat, see PL 146:681.

80. *"Hoc ei donum a Jesu Christo collatum est, ut personam potentis vel divitis non libentus sumeret."* PL 146:773. Cf. *ibid.*, 678. See also M. Dmitrewski, *op. cit.*, 72.

The Eleventh Century: New Religious Orders 191

monks' habit was simple, at first ashen, as a sign of penance, then tawny colored, and finally, black. In this they also slept.[81] To cultivate poverty and simplicity, their churches were free of all ornaments.[82]

While infringements of the Rule were severely punished—usually in the form of beatings—stricter ascetical practices were left to the individual's discretion; they were counseled, but never made obligatory. This explains the rule that no one should wear a hair shirt against his wish, bathe in icy water or flog himself until bleeding.[83]

On the other hand, the divine office reflected the splendor of Cluny as B. Albers, who edited the usages of Vallombrosa, concluded:

> The oldest usages of the Vallombrosans are closely related to those of the Cluniacs and to those of some German monasteries; hence, i.e. on the basis of their oldest customs, one is not justified in seeing in the Vallombrosans a new branch of the Benedictine order; they should simply be considered as Benedictines who adopted the usages then observed by the Black Benedictines.

---

81. *"Fratres . . . ejus examplo vel admonitone frequenter instructi cum omni obedientia fideliter observabant; vilitatem et extremitatem vestium adeo diligentes ut cilicina tunc veste uterentur."* PL 146:679. See also *ibid.,* 776: *"Procuraverunt Fratres pro sustentatione vestium habere gregem ovium; quas cum providus Pater diversi coloris esse cerneret, nigredinis, et albedinis, timuit ne si seorsum faceret nigram et seorsum albam, alter aliquando pannum vellet nigrum alter album, et hac de causa inter Fratres oriretur diversitas mentium, sicut exterius esset diversitas vestium: qua de causa fieri praecepit pannum promiscuum [griseum]."* Cf. PL 146:727; R. Duvernay, "Cîteaux, Vallombreuse," *loc. cit.,* 400; B. Quilici, "Giovanni Gualberto," *loc. cit.,* 66; L. Brockhoff, *op. cit.,* 171; M. Heimbucher, *op. cit.,* 1:413; H. DeWarren, "Le monachisme à l'apparition de Bernard," *loc. cit.,* 60.

82. *"Ligneum habentes tantummodo parvum oratorium."* PL 146:677. Cf. *ibid.,* 772.

83. *"Vilitatem et extremitatem vestium adeo diligentes ut cilicina tunc veste uterentur, quam nemo ferre cogeretur invitus, nec ad ferendum volens prohiberetur."* PL 146:679. Cf. *ibid.,* 776. See also B. Quilici, "Giovanni Gualberto," *loc. cit.,* 66; S. Hilpisch, *Geschichte des benediktinischen Mönchtums,* 167f. and CE 15:263.

With the Cluniacs they shared in particular the horror of simony . . . .[84]

To ensure undisturbed contemplation to his monks and to facilitate the training of young recruits, John Gualbert admitted non-professed lay brothers into his monastery. These brothers cared for the temporal needs of the monks, practiced a special craft and settled all outside business. Their habit was shorter than that of the monks and its hood was fitted with sheepskin. Because of the nature of their work, they were required to say fewer prayers. Also, they were not obliged to silence in cases of necessity and when outside the monastery, and were allowed to wear linen clothes during the summer on account of the heat.[85]

Vallombrosa itself was formally donated to John Gualbert by Itta, abbess of San Ellero. She also supplied the new foundation with food, oil, books and other necessaries and had the power to appoint its superior. This situation came to an end however when Pope Victor II approved Vallombrosa in 1055 and granted its monks the right to elect their own superior.[86] The arrival of candidates—especially after John Gualbert somewhat lessened his original

---

84. Bruno Albers, "Die aeltesten Consuetudines von Vallumbrosa," *Revue Bénédictine*, 28 (1911), 436. Cf. U. Berlière, *Ascèse bénédictine*, 34; B. Quilici, "Giovanni Gualberto," *loc. cit.*, 67 and H. DeWarren, "Le monachisme à l'apparition de Bernard," *loc. cit.*, 60. See also A. Louf, *op. cit.*, 207.

85. "*Deus . . . misit ad eum etiam laicos viros timoratos, qui legem Domini per omnia custodire cupientes, in bonis moribus fere nihil a monachis distabant, extra vestium qualitatem et silentium quod, in exterioribus occupati, nequiebat plenius observare. Tales igitur tam probatos conversos pater ad mercaturam et omnia exteriora secure mittebat.*" PL 146:679. Cf. ibid., 776: "*A diebus quibus monachi coeperunt ad eum venire, Deus . . . misit ei fideles laicos diversi ordinis . . . Nihil omnino a monachis distabant praeter quod permittebantur uti lineis vestibus in nimio fervore aestatis et praeter silentium quod in exterioribus occupati observare nequibant.*" See also R. Duvernay, "Cîteaux, Vallombreuse," *loc. cit.*, 400, 403, 418ff.; DOR 3:842f.; B. Quilici, "Giovanni Gualberto," *loc. cit.*, 61f.; L. Brockhoff, *op. cit.*, 171f.; M. Heimbucher, *op. cit.*, 1:332; S. Hilpisch, *Geschichte des benediktinischen Mönchtums*, 167; E. Werner, *Pauperes Christi*, 107f.; H. DeWarren, "Le monachisme à l'apparition de saint Bernard," *loc. cit.*, 60.

86. PL 146:677f. Cf. *ibid.*, 772 and 774. See also R. Duvernay, "Cîteaux, Vallombreuse," *loc. cit.*, 389 (*Instrumentum*); P. Kehr, *op. cit.*, 3:87 and M. Heimbucher, *op. cit.*, 1:409f.

strictness—enabled the establishment of new foundations. Other, already existing monasteries also adopted his reforms and attached themselves to Vallombrosa. John became their chief abbot and visitor. He regularly visited his houses, appointed their superiors, urged everyone to observe strict poverty and made corrections wherever it was needed.[87] By 1073, the year of John's death, the congregation had uniform observances and its houses were bound to each other by bonds of charity. Soon thereafter, Gregory VII exhorted the Vallombrosans to imitate the ideals of their founder.[88] Under this Pontiff Vallombrosa emerged as a full-fledged order, with abbeys, priories, hospices and cells. Like Cluny, it had a centralized government, with yearly general chapters and a chief abbot whose duty it was to promote discipline, to visit houses, issue decrees, correct abuses, remove incompetent superiors, punish unworthy religious and comfort the victims of oppression. As at Cluny, all monks made their vows in relation to him.[89] In a privilege issued in 1090, Pope Urban II prescribed uniformity to all the twenty Vallombrosan monasteries. He confirmed the status of the abbot of Vallombrosa who was to be elected by all the local superiors in a general congregation.[90] It was around this time that

87. PL 146:680 and 777. Cf. ibid., 778: *"Directis itaque Fratribus et ordinatis Praepositis per singula loca, Pater ea, cum ab infirmitate sublevaretur, visitare, et qualitatem cunctorum diligenter noscere studebat. Quae vero corrigenda erant, sollicite corrigiebat et quae ordinanda, caute et provide ordinabat."* See also M. Heimbucher, *op. cit.*, 1:410 and D. Meade, "From Turmoil to Solidarity," *loc. cit.*, 323ff.

88. PL 148:644; J. Mansi 20:374; D. Knowles, *The Monastic Order in England*, 194.

89. PL 146:680 and 778. Cf. B. Quilici, "Giovanni Gualberto," *loc. cit.*, 62ff.; S. Hilpisch, *Geschichte des benediktinischen Mönchtums*, 168; R. Duvernay, "Cîteaux, Vallombreuse," *loc. cit.*, 440. See also below, n. 92.

90. PL 151:322f. *"Constituimus autem, ut eorum omnium [monasteriorum] caput, vestrum, quod in Valle Umbrosa situm est, monasterium habeatur . . . Sane cum terminus vitae pastori vestro divina dispositione contigerit, qui eius loco substituendus fuerit, quia et vobis et aliis omnibus praeesse debebit, omnium, qui ceteris praesunt monasteriis consensu et iudicio eligatur. Quod si forte ex ipsis abbatibus quilibet Domino disponente ad hoc generale regimen electus fuerit, ad vestrum principale coenobium principaliter transeat, et eius iudicio . . . caetera omnia unita vobis monasteria disponantur."* See also PL 146:725: *"Nos vestro provectui,*

the order made its first advances into France where Corneilly near Silviacum was established probably before 1090 and Malanum—later called *Casale Benedictum,* Chézal-Benoît—between 1093 and 1098, just a few years before the foundation of Cîteaux.[91]

Shortly before his death, John exhorted his followers to remain strong in fraternal charity:

> It is most beneficial to preserve brotherly unity entrusted to the care of one person. For as a river dries up if it is diverted into many outlets, so does fraternal charity decrease . . . if it is dissipated into diverse channels. Therefore, to preserve this mutual charity undiminished and for a long time to come, it is my wish that after my death your care and counsel should remain with the lord Rudolph, just as it had rested on me during my lifetime.[92]

At first the monks of Vallombrosa did not become priests. Internal considerations however and the need to combat simony in nearby Florence soon convinced John Gualbert that his monks

---

annuente Domino, provectus adjungere cupientes, coenobium vestrum pro B. Mariae semper Virginis reverentia, cui dicatum est, in Romanae Ecclesiae proprietatem et tutelam, atque protectionem apostolicae Sedis accipimus; et Apostolicae illud auctoritatis privilegio munientes ab omnium personarum jugo liberum permanere decernimus." Cf. P. Kehr, *op. cit.,* 3:88 and M. Heimbucher, *op. cit.,* 1:411. On the status of the abbot of Vallombrosa, see PL 146:807: *"Horum quippe rectores annuatim conveniant memoria retinentes bonitatem et sanctitatem nec non instituta boni et primi Patris, sibi offerunt alteri alterutrus quaecumque sub cura habent videlicet et substantias, secundum imperium Vallis Imbrosae abbatis quem super se electum habent in vice Joannis primi abbatis. Et sunt in fide una unum cor et animum habentes, potius parati mori quam ab alterutro dividi."*

91. PL 146:728f. Cf. R. Duvernay, "Cîteaux, Vallombreuse," *loc. cit.,* 455 n. 4 and 456; H. DeWarren, "Le monachisme à l'apparition de Bernard," *loc. cit.,* 60; M. Heimbucher, *op. cit.,* 1:411. According to R. Duvernay, Vallombrosa had at least 19 monasteries in 1090, 34 in 1100 and 38 in 1115. *Loc. cit.,* 454 n. 1.

92. *"Ad hanc [charitatem] vero inviolabiliter custodiendam valde utilis est unitas fraterna, quae se constringit sub unius personae curam, quoniam sicut flumen a suo alveo siccatur, si in multis rivulis dividatur: sic fraterna unitas minus valet ad singula, si fuerit sparsa per diversa. Idcirco, ut in longo ista charitas inviolabilis permaneat vobiscum, volo ut in domino Rodulfo vestra cura et consilium post meum obitum pendeat, saltem sicut in me pependit in mea vita."* PL 146:701. Cf. B. Quilici, "Giovanni Gualberto," *loc. cit.,* 62 n. 254. See also PL 146:807, *"Et sunt in fide una, unum cor et animum habentes, potius parati mori quam ab alterutro dividi."*

should be ordained to the priesthood.[93] From that time on Vallombrosa waged a relentless struggle against simony and other clerical abuses in Florence, so that in the words of Pope Alexander II, it was through the efforts of John Gualbert that simony disappeared in that region.[94] Of course, this involvement was not in line with the Vallombrosan principle of seclusion. It may have been motivated by the higher ideals of the *sentire cum Ecclesia* principle; but it does not justify E. Werner's assertion that Gualbertine monachism was wholly directed toward the city.[95] Another of John's concern was the erection of hospices and the renovation of dilapidated churches. The former were well endowed, since each abbey devoted one third of its revenues to their upkeep.[96]

John Gualbert was, perhaps, not as inventive in his reforms as Romuald or Peter Damian had been; still he secured a lasting place for himself in monastic history, through his successful application of certain eremitic features to cenobitic monachism. In his conception the monks were strictly contemplative cenobites supported by laybrothers, all of whom lived in a centralized order under an abbot general.[97] With this formula he strengthened Benedictine cenobitism in its hour of crisis. He helped it to overcome its internal difficulties and to challenge the victorious tide of eremitism.

According to D. Knowles:

Vallombrosa . . . had a twofold significance. (1) It was the first reforming monastery of the revival of the eleventh century in

---

93. *"Pater pius, more solito nimia pietate commotus, non solum illos, sed etiam quos jam in interiori cella novitiorum habebat et qui venerant induere monasticum habitum, inde abstraxit, et a Rodulfo episcopo Tudertino, sanctissimo et catholico viro, gradatim ordinari fecit."* PL 146:699. Cf. E. Werner, *Pauperes Christi*, 104f.

94. PL 146:683, 686, 690ff., 698f., 730, 777, 786, 792ff. Cf. J. Mahn, *op. cit.*, 28. John Gualbert also fought clerical incontinence; PL 146:682.

95. *Pauperes Christi*, 108.

96. *"Hospitalia quoque constructa et ecclesiae vetustae renovatae ejus auxilio cognoscuntur."* PL 146:682. Cf. B. Quilici, "Giovanni Gualberto," *loc. cit.*, 47 and L. Brockhoff, *op. cit.*, 172.

97. B. Quilici, "Giovanni Gualberto," *loc. cit.*, 60f.; M. Heimbucher, *op. cit.*, 1:410; J. Leclercq, "La crise du monachisme," *loc. cit.*, 27; S. Hilpisch, *Geschichte des benediktinischen Mönchtums*, 168. For the prayers composed by John Gualbert, see PL 146:969ff.

which the Rule of St Benedict was officially interpreted in a strict sense, thus probably exceeding the severity intended by its author.... (2) In order to free his monks from the distractions and temptations of administration ... John Gualbert added a class of non-clerical *conversi*, the class which in another form came to be known as laybrothers.[98]

In this sense Vallombrosa was clearly an anticipation, if not a forebear, of other contemporary reforms, including that of the early Cistercians.

Monastic revival north of the Alps—and, more specifically, in France—began with a great upsurge of eremitic life in the middle of the eleventh century. The development was in many ways spontaneous; in time, however, religious leaders—and their number was by no means unimpressive—succeeded in channeling the movement into more organized forms. In the process they laid the foundations of new religious institutions, two of which merit our special consideration here; the order of Grandmont and the Carthusians.[99]

The founder of the Grammontensians, Stephen of Thiers,[100] was born in the Auvergne around 1045. In his youth he accompanied his father to Bari, to visit the tomb of St Nicholas.[101] Unable to return because of illness, he was left in the care of archbishop Milo of Beneventum who also took charge of his education. While in Calabria, Stephen came into contact with Greek monasticism[102] and developed a great liking for their anchoretic practices. After

---

98. D. Knowles, *From Pachomius to Ignatius*, 18f.   99. *Ibid.*, 17 and 20.

100. For Stephen's life, see PL 204:1005ff.; AS, Feb. 2:205ff.; DOR 2:414ff.; Jean Becquet, "S. Etienne de Muret," DSAM 4:1504ff.; A. Lecler, "Histoire de l'abbaye de Grandmont," *Bulletin de la Société Archéologique et Historique du Limousin*, 57 (1907), 130; L. Brockhoff, *op. cit.*, 176f.; M. Heimbucher, *op. cit.*, 1:415; *The Book of Saints*, 550; P. Schmitz, *op. cit.*, 3:18.

101. Since the translation of St Nicholas' relics took place in 1087, the visit was probably made to St Michael on Mount Galgano. Cf. R. Graham, *English Ecclesiastical Studies*, 209.

102. "*Religiosa congregatio ... ab omni cura temporalium erat remotior. Pecudibus possessionibusque ac universis rerum mundanarum occupationibus ita penitus renuntiaverat, quod unde professores sui ad tumultum saeculi revocarentur non habeat ... nullus in ea aliquid proprium possidebat ... nullos nonnisi seipsos habebant ministros ... corporalis autem subsidii sollicitudinem solummodo in Deum projecerant, unanimiter in claustro viventes.*" PL 204:1013.

Milo's death he spent some time in Rome in pursuit of further studies. Soon, however, feeling the call to a life of seclusion and contemplation, he returned to France where around 1076 he retired to a self-built hermitage at Muret, not far from Grandmont in the diocese of Limoges, which was "a veritable desert: rugged, cold, sterile, isolated, inaccessible, frequented more by wild beasts than by humans."[103] After he spent a year in complete seclusion and strict asceticism, disciples began to arrive. This necessitated the establishment of a regular monastery patterned after such models as Calabria and Camaldoli and, possibly, also the Grande Chartreuse. Stephen headed the community as its *corrector* until his death on February 8, 1124. Soon after the establishment of this community, disputes about the territory of Muret forced it to move to the neighboring desert of Grandmont which then became the permanent center of Stephen's reform.[104] Grandmont developed into an order before 1100, with houses—eventually—all over France. It had sixty of them by 1170—some in England—and survived until the stormy days of the French Revolution.[105]

103. "*Deinde . . . ad nemorosum montem, qui non longe distat ab urbe Lemovicarum, et Muretum dicitur, Christo ducente pervenit, ubi fontes reperit et rupes terramque desertam et inviam quae novo hospiti suo potum frigidissimum et domum ventis expositam offerens, afflictionem corporis et requiem mentis manifestis indiciis promittebat. Porro tota silvestris et sterilis, ut omni fere tempore hiemalis, hominibus insueta, assueta feris, aliud non poterat polliceri.*" PL 204:1015f. Cf. A. Lecler, "Histoire de l'abbaye de Grandmont," *loc. cit.*, 138. R. Duvernay believes Milo died in 1076, and Stephen spent four years in Rome before returning to his native country. Hence "the date of this foundation is not 1076, as is generally asserted, but posterior to 1080 (probably 1081 or 1082)." "Cîteaux, Vallombreuse," *loc. cit.*, 456f. See also RHF 11:169; A. Fliche, *Le règne de Philippe Ier*, 469; Philippus Jaffé and Gulielmus Wattenbach, *Regesta Pontificum Romanorum ab condita Ecclesia ad annum post Christum natum MCXCVIII* (Lipsiae: Veit et comp., 1885), 1:606; Jean Becquet, "La règle de Grandmont," *Bulletin de la Société Archéologique et Historique de Limousin*, 87 (1958), 29; H. Workman, *op. cit.*, 250 n. 4.

104. PL 204:1028f. Cf. also Jean Hauréau, "Sur quelques écrivains de l'Ordre de Grandmont, d'après le no 17187 de la Bibliothèque Nationale," *Notices et Extraits des Manuscrits de la Bibiothéque Nationale* 24-2 (1876), 255; R. Graham, *English Ecclesiastical Studies*, 211.

105. L. Brockhoff, *op. cit.*, 177f.; M. Heimbucher, *op. cit.*, 1:416; P. Schmitz, *op. cit.*, 3:18.

Stephen of Thiers left no written rule to his disciples. As he explained:

> In my Father's house there are many mansions, and there are many ways which lead to it. These divers ways have been put in writing by various Fathers. They are called the Rules of St Basil, St Augustine, and St Benedict. These are not the source of monastic life, but only its offshoots; they are not the root but only the leaves. The Rule from which all others derive, like streams flowing from a single source, is the Holy Gospel.[106]

This rule he urged his disciples to follow.[107] Thus in an obvious departure from existing practices, Stephen adopted none of the known monastic rules, but left everything undetermined on purpose. To visiting cardinals he declared that he and his followers were neither canons—for these administer churches and dispense the sacraments; nor monks who think only of God; nor hermits who avoid all contacts with the world and stay in their cells to devote themselves to prayer, penance and silence.[108] Still, even

---

106. "*Ad domum illam Patris summi, in qua filius multas testatur esse mansiones diversae viarum optiones . . . sunt. . . . Quae viarum diversitates quamvis a diversis Patribus scripto sint commendatae, ita quod appelletur Regula beati Basilii, Regula beati Augustini, Regula beati Benedicti, tamen non origo religionis, sed propagines sunt; non radix sed frondes sunt; una est enim fidei et salutis prima ac principalis Regularum Regula, a qua omnes aliae, quasi quidam rivuli de uno fonte, derivantur, sanctum videlicet Evangelium.*" PL 204:1035f. Cf. R. Graham, *English Ecclesiastical Studies*, 212.

107. "*Evangelii praecepta, quantum ipso [Christo] donante poteritis, adimplere curate.*" PL 204:1138. This is also why shortly before his death Stephen exhorted his followers, "*in hac regula de Evangelico sumpta perseveraveritis.*" PL 204:1026.

108. "*Ecce vestibus monachorum et canonicorum . . . non utimur, ut videtis, quoniam etiam tantae sanctitatis vocabula nobis non usurpamus. Nam canonicorum institutio quae habet potestatem ligandi atque solvendi quemadmodum apostoli, supereminet potestati monachorum ideoque ut diximus usurpare vitam illorum minime audemus. . . . Nomine autem monachorum non utimur, quia nomen sanctitatis et singularitatis sortiti sunt vocabulum . . . illi specialiter monachi dicuntur qui sui amplius curam (non) agunt, nec aliud cogitant nisi tantummodo de Deo. Eremitarum vero vitam imitari minime valemus, quia in hoc specialiter est vita omnium eremitarum: devitare saeculi tumultus, et permanere in cellulis suis, quatenus vacent orationi et silentio.*" PL 204:1022f.

in Stephen's lifetime, the outlines of an organization—profession, common meals with reading and meetings in the chapter room—made their appearance.[109] The so-called *Rule of St Stephen* was actually compiled under Stephen of Lissac, the fourth prior of Grandmont. It contains the usages of the mother-house as observed some twenty or thirty years after the founder's death. It drew from a number of sources: the maxims and ascetical practices of Stephen, the Rule of St Benedict and the customs of the Carthusians. Approved by Pope Hadrian IV, it was further elaborated in the times of Innocent III and John XXII.[110]

The community of Muret consisted of clerics devoted to divine worship and contemplation, and *conversi* who took care of the material needs of the establishment. The contemplative clerics led the life of solitaries; like the anchorites of the ancient *laurae* they assembled only for the celebration of the divine office and for the community exercises in the cloister, chapter room, refectory and dormitory.[111]

The clerics' only occupation was contemplation and prayer. The latter included the divine office, the little office of the Blessed Virgin Mary, the office of the dead and of the Holy Trinity (with nine lessons), the conventual Mass, processions for the dead and—last, but not least—private devotions. Added to these were numerous genuflections and the so-called *orationes familiares*. The trend was thus clearly in the direction of an *oratio continua*, continuous prayer.[112] In this connection the founder also called for strict silence

---

109. PL 204:1016, 1018ff. Cf. K. Hallinger, "Woher kommen die Laienbrüder," *loc. cit.*, 9.

110. *Regula Sancti Stephani Confessoris*; PL 204:1135ff. *Liber sententiarum seu Rationum Sancti Stephani*; PL 204:1085ff. Cf. J. Becquet, "La règle de Grandmont," *loc. cit.*, 30; L. Brockhoff, *op. cit.*, 177f.; M. Heimbucher, *op. cit.*, 1:415.; P. Schmitz, *op. cit.*, 3:18 and CMH 5:668.

111. P. Schmitz, *op. cit.*, 3:18.

112. [*Clericis*] "*ab omni cura temporalium liberis injungimus, ut . . . divinis laudibus et contemplationi solummodo intendentes . . . spiritualia ministrent.*" PL 204:1156f. See also *ibid.*, 1154: "*In hoc enim vestra et omnium eremitarum vita maxime debet constare, ut cum continuae orationis usu et silentio tumultum saeculi declinantes, in cellis vestris quiescatis.*" Cf. also PL 204:1013, on the offices of the

and complete seclusion, to secure full alertness in the fight against the devil, in imitation of Christ's example in the desert. He admired the life of St John the Baptist and considered his establishment a community of solitaries. Hence his ordinance: "Let them always remain in the desert and in solitude, dead to and rejected by the world."[113] For the noise and tumult of the world can only be avoided by "constant prayer . . . silence and a solitary life." This is also why:

> once they have entered the solitude of the order, they never go back to this world, either on business or to visit their kinsfolk, or to make purchases at markets and fairs or to appear in courts of law, but they are as men who are dead to this world.[114]

In line with such thinking, they almost never admitted laymen to the divine office. They were equally opposed to the admission of outsiders to their Sunday services since they have their own parish churches. Nor did they go out to preach, hear sermons, visit the sick or minister to the dying, for this, they felt, was the duty of parish priests.[115]

A further safeguard of seclusion was strict poverty. In the words of his biographer, Stephen "following the footsteps of his Redeemer, loved poverty of the spirit to such a degree that he did not wish to call anything his own on the earth."[116] Dissatisfied with existing monastic rules which proscribed personal ownership but placed no

---

Blessed Virgin Mary, the dead, and the Holy Trinity—the latter with nine lessons—; as well as A. Lecler, "Histoire de l'abbaye de Grandmont," *loc. cit.*, 141; and J. Leclercq, *La spiritualité du Moyen Age*, 181.

113. "*Velut mortui et abjecti a mundo semper maneant in solitudinis eremo.*" J. Hauréau, "Sur quelques écrivains de l'Ordre de Grandmont," *loc. cit.*, 257. Cf. PL 204:1154f. and 1025 and Jean Becquet, "Les institutions de l'Ordre de Grandmont au Moyen Age," *Revue Mabillon*, 42 (1952), 34.

114. R. Graham, *English Ecclesiastical Studies*, 214. Cf. PL 204:1150ff.

115. PL 204:1141. Cf. ibid., 1142, "*Nec etiam judicia poenitentiae viris exterioribus injungere praesumatis; hujusmodi namque negotium nihil ad vestrum spectat propositum.*" See also PL 204:1022f., 1151, 1155 and R. Graham, *English Ecclesiastical Studies*, 213.

116. "*Redemptoris sui sequens vestigia, paupertatem spiritus in tantum dilexit, quod in terra nihil fere voluit possidere.*" PL 204:1008. Cf. M. Dmitrewski, *op. cit.*, 73.

The Eleventh Century: New Religious Orders 201

limits on community possessions he prohibited the acquisition of lands outside the enclosure and the possession of animals—whether they were received or raised by the brethren made no difference—for this would necessitate the acquisition of extra pastures and lands.[117] He and his followers also rejected proprietary churches, ministries, tithes, interests, leases of Church lands, Mass stipends, mills and fixed revenues.[118] In view of this policy, they felt no need to keep charters.[119] If alms were withheld from them, they sought no redress, for they had resolved never to go to court.[120] This caused R. Gratien to remark: "The order of the hermits of Grandmont imposed the strictest curbs on riches. All they possessed was a forest they cleared for their sustenance."[121] Hence it was very fitting that Stephen called his followers "poor brethren" (later changed by the faithful to "good men," *boni homines*).[122]

---

117. "*Omnes terrarum possessiones quae sunt extra metas locorum vestrorum, vobis tanquam peregrinis et hic manentem civitatem non habentibus sed futuram in coelis inquirentibus, ex toto interdicimus.*" PL 204:1140f. See also, *ibid.*, 1142f., "*Omnis generis bestias vobis interdicimus . . . nihil enim vehementius religionem dissipat quam cupiditas et multitudo divitiarum.*" Cf. R. Graham, *English Ecclesiastical Studies*, 212; P. Schmitz, *op. cit.*, 3:18; J. Becquet, "Les institutions de l'Ordre de Grandmont," *loc. cit.*, 34 and *idem*, "La règle de Grandmont," *loc. cit.*, 16ff.

118. "*Ecclesias et res ad ipsas pertinentes, praedicta ratione, scilicet qui cum caeteris mundanis eas amore divino reliquistis, vobis rehabere omnino prohibemus . . . . Si quis autem ecclesias dare vobis voluerit, nullatenus accipiatis.*" PL 204:1141f. Cf. J. Becquet, "Les institutions de l'Ordre de Grandmont," *loc. cit.*, 34 and *idem*, "La règle de Grandmont," *loc. cit.*, 16ff.

119. "*Vobis praecipimus, ut de rebus vobis datis vel dandis nunquam scriptum causa placitandi faciatis, nec etiam placitare praesumatis.*" PL 204:1149. Cf. J. Becquet, "La règle de Grandmont," *loc. cit.*, 18.

120. "*Memores consilii Jesu Christi dicentis* Qui auferat quae tua sunt ne repetas (Lc 6) *numquam cum viris exterioribus judicio contendatis.*" PL 204:1148. Cf. *ibid.*, 1149f., "*Firmissime vobis praecipimus ut numquam propter vestra vel aliena [negotia] cum aliquo placitare sive judicio contendere praesumatis, nec causas nec controversias aliorum in manu vestra recipiatis.*" See also R. Graham, *English Ecclesiastical Studies*, 213 and J. Becquet, "Les institutions de l'Ordre de Grandmont," *loc. cit.*, 34.

121. J. Becquet, "La régle de Grandmont," *loc. cit.*, 19 n. 34.

122. "*Bonus homo debet semper loqui de Deo vel cum Deo; nam in oratione sua cum Deo, cum proximo loquitur de Deo.*" PL 204:1102. Cf. A. Lecler, "Histoire de l'abbaye de Grandmont," *loc. cit.*, 144 and P. Schmitz, *op. cit.*, 3:18.

The Grammontensians mortified themselves also in their diet. Whether sick or well, they never had meat or lard, and fasted for more than seven months during the year. From mid-September to Easter they ate only one meal a day, except Sundays, the feast of All Saints and Christmas Day. From Septuagesima Sunday until Easter they even gave up eggs and cheese. They had two daily meals only from Easter to mid-September, usually after Sext and Vespers, except if there was a fast day.[123] If they had no food, they were to contact the local bishop. If no help was forthcoming and they had not eaten for two days, then two brethren could go out and beg at mills and in houses, but not from their friends.[124]

Their habit—originally a coarse tunic with a scapular and hood, first brown, then black—displayed the same penitential spirit. According to the *Mirror of Grandmont*: "They wear sack cloth next to their skins, that is clothing made of very coarse flac or hemp, and over that a brown tunic, a scapular or short cloak with a round hood, woolen gaiters and leather shoes."[125]

One of the chief innovations made by Stephen was the exclusive authority given to the *conversi* in matters of administration, manual labor and contacts with the outside world. This he did in order to guarantee absolute seclusion and unhindered contemplation to the clerics. The *praeceptors* or *conversi* were warned, however, not to resort to domination, but to fulfill the demands of fraternal charity.[126]

The reform of Stephen of Thiers is characterized by its extreme

---

123. PL 204:1158f. Cf. R. Graham, *English Ecclesiastical Studies*, 213f.

124. PL 204:1143 and 1145. Cf. R. Graham, *English Ecclesiastical Studies*, 213.

125. PL 204:1157. Cf. R. Graham, *English Ecclesiastical Studies*, 213; J. Hauréau, "Sur quelques écrivains de l'Ordre de Grandmont," *loc. cit.*, 257 and L. Brockhoff, *op. cit.*, 177.

126. "Ne colloquio saecularium aut sollicitudine exteriorum divinum officium interrumpatur et mens eorumdem satietatis internae dulcedinis obliviscatur, ob hoc agendis aliis fratribus, clericis videlicet et conversis, non dominatione sed charitate praecipiant." PL 204:1157. Cf. J. Leclercq, *La spiritualité du Moyen Age*, 180; M. Heimbucher, *op. cit.*, 1:416; K. Hallinger, "Woher kommen die Laienbrüder," *loc. cit.*, 9; R. Graham, *English Ecclesiastical Studies*, 212f.; J. Hauréau, "Sur quelques écrivains de l'Ordre de Grandmont," *loc. cit.*, 257.

The Eleventh Century: New Religious Orders 203

ascetical demands in matters of poverty and seclusion, and the unusual responsibilities given to the laybrothers in the administration of the house. Whether it ought to be classified as Benedictine must be decided by Stephen's claim that he and his followers were neither canons, nor monks nor hermits, and not by the spurious bull of Gregory VII which encouraged Stephen to found a new institution based on the ideal of St Benedict.[127] Stephen's sojourn in Calabria, the cultural and monastic crossroad between the Byzantine East and the Latin West at the time, certainly had its influence on his thinking and on the revolutionary nature of his rule, with its incipient laicistic traits so alien to western Christianity.[128] Lastly, Stephen's unqualified rejection of possessions is a further indication of the growth—from 1080 onward—of the movement which set out to fight all feudal forms in contemporary monastic life.[129]

The founder of the Carthusians, Bruno of Cologne,[130] was born

---

127. PL 204:1022f. Cf. ibid., 1014f. For Pope Gregory's letter see PL 148:653ff. According to L. Delisle, this document is a forgery. "Examen des treize chartres de l'Ordre de Grandmont," *Mémoires de la Société des Antiquaires de Normandie*, 20 (1853), 172ff. and 188. Cf. A. Lecler, "Histoire de l'abbaye de Grandmont," *loc. cit.*, 136f.; L. Brockhoff, *op. cit.*, 177 and D. Knowles, *The Monastic Order in England*, 203.

128. K. Hallinger, "Woher kommen die Laienbrüder," *loc. cit.*, 9. In this connection G. Schreiber observes, "The strangeness of the regulations set up by him were felt only too well in the Christian West." *Gemeinschaften des Mittelalters*, 406. See also A. Louf, *op. cit.*, 203f.

129. PL 204:1014ff. Cf. K. Hallinger, "Woher kommen die Laienbrüder," *loc. cit.*, 9. According to A. Louf, Stephen's doctrine "does not seem to have any literary connection with previous monastic sources. No doubt it is unique in this respect among the literature of that period, but it can be explained by the fact that Stephen was illiterate." *Op. cit.*, 203f. This view, if correct—it is contradicted by PL 204:1012ff.!—remains unsatisfactory. Cf. G. Schreiber, *Gemeinschaften des Mittelalters*, 406 and K. Hallinger, "Woher kommen die Laienbrüder," *loc. cit.*, 9.

130. *Vita antiquior*, PL 152:482ff.; *Vita altera*, PL 152:493ff.; *Vita tertia*, PL 152:526. Cf. PL 156:853; AS, Oct. 3:503ff.; Hermann Löbbel, *Der Stifter des Carthäuser-Ordens der heilige Bruno aus Köln* (Kirchengeschichtliche Studien, tom. V, fasc. 1; Münster, in W.: Verlag Heinrich Schöning, 1899); Walter Nigg, *Vom Geheimnis der Mönche* (Zürich: Artemis Verlag, 1953), 180 and 183ff.; DOR 1:848ff.; M. Heimbucher, *op. cit.*, 1:487ff. and *The Book of Saints*, 177.

P

of noble parents around 1030. He received his higher education at Reims and developed a great love for scholarship in the process. In time he became a teacher of renown and rector of the cathedral school. As such he taught future clerics and produced a number of scholarly works, mostly on biblical themes from the psalms and the epistles of St Paul. After two decades of successful teaching, Archbishop Manasses appointed him chancellor of the archdiocese. Bruno's experiences with Manasses—an unscrupulous and worldly man who caused a great deal of trouble to Pope Gregory VII and his legate, Hugh of Lyons—his disappointment over the low morals of the clergy and the conviction that a truly Christian life is only possible apart from human society, caused him to resign his office and leave the world. When bidding farewell to Reims, he told his friends:

> Let us withdraw from the middle of Babylon, let us leave Pentapolis, already aflame from fire and sulphur, and seek, with St John the Baptist, the caves of the desert, as did blessed Paul, Anthony, Arsenius, Evagrius and other saints.[131]

Then he went on to urge his listeners to embrace the solitary life of perpetual penance, to reject the riches, pleasures and honors of the world, to take up their crosses and follow the poor Christ in poverty on the narrow way which leads to eternal life. For the advantages of the desert are obvious from the lives of Christ, St John the Baptist, Paul, Anthony, Hilarion, the two Macarii, Eulalius, Arsenius, Evagrius, Basil, Benedict and many others. And it is also true that the gift of tears and fervor in the chanting of psalms, spiritual reading, prayer, meditation and contemplation can hardly be acquired outside the desert.[132]

---

131. "*Exeamus de medio Babylonis, egrediamur Pentapolim, igne et sulphure jam succensum et exemplo beati Pauli eremitae, beatorum Antonii, Arsenii, Evagrii aliorumque sanctorum cum beato Joanne Baptista antra deserti quaeramus.*" PL 152:484.

132. PL 152:484. Cf. also *ibid.*, 421, "*Quid vero solitudo eremique silentium amatoribus suis utilitatis jucunditatisque conferat, norunt hi solum, qui experti sunt;*" and *ibid.*, 499, "*Solitudo namque est via quae ducit ad vitam.*" See also PL 152:422, 485f. and 500.

Bruno and two companions—Peter and Lambert—then set out to find a "perfect solitude." They first went to Robert, abbot of Molesme. They did not join the monastery, but obtained permission to settle in a nearby forest, called Sèche-Fontaine, where they "lived eremitically" and were soon joined by men who shared their ideas.[133]

133. As the various *funebres sancti tituli* attest, Bruno, before settling in the Grande Chartreuse, spent some time as a hermit in another "desert." PL 152:559, 569, 574, 592f. Cf. *ibid.*, 250ff. and (Anon.), *Aux sources de la vie Cartusienne* (La Grande Chartreuse, 1960), 399ff. The same information is gathered from Bruno's life, "*Et sancto eos ducente Spiritu . . . longo et molesto ac duro itinere ad beatissimum Hugonem, episcopum Gratianopolitanum se conferunt. In ipso autem itinere ad quemdam magnae religionis eremitam divertunt, ut ab eo, tamquam experto, discant de vita solitaria.*" PL 152:532. According to J. Mabillon, this hermit leader was Robert, abbot of Molesme: "*Quibusdam monumentis adducor, ut credam, illum magni nominis eremitam non alium esse quam Robertum abbatem Molismensem. Extat in illius monasterii tabulario Rainardi de Barro et Joannis de Laniaco charta, qua 'terram apud Siccam-Fontanam, labore hominum partim jam complanatam' laudante Valentino comite Brenensi et Barrensi, cujus 'hoc casamentum' erat, ecclesiae Molismensi conferunt. Cum vero ecclesia loci illius quam aedificaverant Petrus et Lambertus discipuli magistri Brunonis, qui cum eo in territorio illo erant, et eremitice vixerant, a domno Roberto Lingonensi episcopo in honore beatae semper virginis Mariae dedicaretur, atriumque benediceretur, praedictus comes et idem Raynardus et Acelinus cum multis aliis praesentes fuerant.*" PL 152:251. This occurred around 1081. Cf. PL 152:251; J. Mabillon, *Annales Ordinis S. Benedicti*, 5:205; and *Aux soucres de la vie Cartusienne*, 116 and 139. In the eighteenth century, the Theatine Tracy questioned the validity of Mabillon's conclusions on eremitic life at Sèche-Fontaine, insisting that the documentary evidence does not justify them. Cf. *Aux sources de la vie Cartusienne*, 120. Modern research however vindicated the great Maurist. Cf. *Aux sources de la vie Cartusienne*, 126ff.; Jacques Laurent, *Cartulaires de Molesme* (Paris: Alphons Picard & Fils, 1907–1911), 1:24, 75f. and 2:134. Moreover, some historians interpreted several of the funeral rolls written after Bruno's death in the sense that Bruno was for a time a monk of Molesme. Cf. PL 152:251 nn. 47, 68, 139, 143. See also *ibid.*, 559, 569, 574, 592.; H. Löbbel, *op. cit.*, 100 and *Aux sources de la vie Cartusienne*, 117f. and 139f. This view, too, is untenable, as convincingly demonstrated in *Aux sources de la vie Cartusienne*, 125 and 133f. The present state of the question can therefore be summarized, as follows: (1) Bruno, Peter and Lambert settled down, as a group, at Sèche-Fontaine and lived eremitically; (2) their ways parted after some time, i.e., when Bruno left for the Grande Chartreuse; (3) Peter and Lambert opted for cenobitic life, stayed at Sèche-Fontaine and constructed a chapel with the consent of Molesme; (4) the edifice was solemnly donated to Molesme on the day of its dedication, in 1086, by Robert, bishop of Langres; (5) a sojourn of Bruno at Molesme prior to his retirement to Sèche-Fontaine seems improb-

When the place turned out to be inadequate for their purposes, Bruno and five of his companions left Sèche-Fontaine and once more began to look for "a place suitable for eremitic life."[134] Urged on by Seguin, abbot of La Chaise Dieu, and with the permission of Hugh, bishop of Grenoble, a former student at Reims, Bruno then retired to a relatively spacious and uninhabited wilderness in the rugged mountains of the Dauphiné, some six leagues from Grenoble. From the name of the place the settlers were called Carthusians. They started regular life on June 24—the feast of St John the Baptist—1084,[135] and had hardly mastered their first difficulties when an unexpected blow struck them. In 1090, Pope Urban II, another of Bruno's former pupils, summoned his old teacher to Rome, to assist him with his counsels. Bruno obediently obliged, even though this meant the temporary end of his foundation, since some of his disciples dispersed in all directions, while others followed him to Rome. Bruno, far from happy to see them in the Eternal City, prevailed on them to return to their charterhouse which had meanwhile been taken over by Seguin, but was restored to its former owners on the Pope's order. Bruno's request to be permitted to return to his foundation was always refused; but he was given permission to retire to a solitude in Italy and still be at hand when needed by the Pope. This and the generosity of local lords enabled Bruno to make his second foundation, La Torre, in Calabria. From there he wrote to his followers in France: "I live here in a desert, far removed from human dwellings, with holy associates—some of them learned men. . . ." He exhorted his distant

---

able. Cf. *Aux sources de la vie Cartusienne*, 112. For possible reasons why Bruno left Sèche-Fontaine, see H. Löbbel, *op. cit.*, 101; J. Laurent, *op. cit.*, 1:125; and *Aux sources de la vie Cartusienne*, 140, 142, 145 and G. Schreiber, *Gemeinschaften des Mittelalters*, 199.

134. "*Quaerebant vero locum eremiticae vitae congruum, necdumque repererant.*" PL 152:533. Cf. ibid., 255 and PL 153:769.

135. "*Ascenderunt in montem et intraverunt ac inhabitare coeperunt dictam eremum Carthusiae circa solemnitatem nativitatis sancti Joannis Baptistae, anno salutis nostrae supra millesimum octogesimo quarto.*" PL 152:508. Cf. J. Laurent, *op. cit.*, 1:126.

spiritual sons to observe the rigors of the rule, to practice humility, patience and true charity in all things, and to flee, like a pest, the ill-boding company of laymen.[136] His desire of seeing his old foundation once more was never fulfilled, not even after the death of Urban II, for by then old age and infirmities had taken their toll. These caused his death, at the age of seventy, on October 6, 1101. The death notice sent out by La Torre went to Molesme and also to the newly established Cîteaux in Burgundy. Both added their *elogium*; the former even indicated that Bruno had been "very well known" to its monks.[137]

Bruno and his companions had left Sèche-Fontaine, not because Molesme was decadent—it was in its first fervor—but because they needed a more suitable hermitage for the implementation of their eremitic ideal. Unsuccessful elsewhere, they finally obtained the solitude of *Carthusia*, a wild expanse enclosed by high mountains and inhabited only by wild animals. Because of the rocky terrain and the cold climate it had only fruitless trees and offered little hope for a productive cultivation.[138] Here they constructed their hermitage. They built a chapel and around it, adjacent to a river, small separate cells connected by a closed passageway.[139] According to Guigo, the fifth prior of La Grande Chartreuse, "two lived (in a

---

136. "*In finibus autem Calabriae cum fratribus religiosis, et aliquot bene eruditis . . . eremum incolo ab hominum habitatione satis undique remotam.*" PL 152:421. Cf. ibid., 419, "*Morbidum gregem quorumdam vanissimorum laicorum ut pestem vitare.*"

137. "*Nostris versiculis, qui habitamus Molernium, addentes vobis, qui estis Turri, innotescimus, quod pro domino Brunone, patrono vestro, nostro autem familiarissimo, Missarum solemnia diebus triginta celebravimus, ejus etiam obitus anniversarium diem in catalogo fratrum nostrorum conscripsimus.*" PL 152:567. Cîteaux's entrance is found *ibid.*, 565.

138. "*Quaerebant vero locum eremiticae vitae congruum.*" PL 152:533. On bishop Hugh's intervention, see, PL 152:485f., 503f., 532ff. and 153:769. The place itself is described in PL 152:269ff., 505f. and 534. See also PL 156: 854.

139. "*Aedificare coeperunt ecclesiam necnon et parvas cellulas, non longe a dicta ecclesia distantes, circa quemdam fontem, qui usque in praesentem diem vocatur fons Brunonis, de se tamen invicem distinctas et aliquantulum separatas, ne alter alterius solitudinem impediret.*" PL 152:508. Cf. ibid., 535.

cell) in master Bruno's time."[140] They spent their time in prayer, contemplation, silence, reading and manual labor; the latter mostly involved the copying of books.[141]

The fact that Bruno accepted the place offered to him shows that he wished to give a stable organization to his fellow hermits and go beyond the father-son and master-disciple relationship. The soil could provide only for a limited number of religious, and the topography excluded any possibility of a local expansion. He utilized certain cenobitic features in the make-up of his organization. He brought the cells closer to each other than they had been in times of old in the vast deserts of Egypt, and connected them with a corridor. In the description of Guibert of Nogent, an early visitor: "though they had a cloister suited for cenobitic life they did not live claustrally, like the rest of the monks. For they have separate cells in a circularly built cloister, where they work, sleep and eat."[142] A later visitor, Peter the Venerable, observed that "they live in solitary cells for the rest of their lives, after the manner of the early Egyptian monks." In these cells, Peter the Venerable continued, "they devote themselves to silence, reading, prayer and manual labor."[143]

---

140. "*Bini quippe tunc per singulas inhabitabant cellas apud magistrum Brunonem.*" PL 153:770. Cf. also PL 152:535, "*In iis cellulis singulis bini fratres degebant.*" This, it seems, was not in imitation of Italian eremitic practices, as some believe, but simply the result of limited facilities. In any case, long before Guigo's time the Carthusians began to live alone in their individual cells. Cf. *Aux sources de la vie Cartusienne*, 174ff. and 187 and PL 156:854.

141. "*Ubi silentio, lectioni, orationi atque operi manuum, maxime in conscribendis libris jugiter insistebant.*" PL 152:508. Cf. ibid., 535, "*Silentio, orationi, lectioni, cordis puritati et rerum divinarum contemplationi vacabant, certis etiam horis operi manuum, praesertim conscribendis libris, incumbentes.*"

142. "*Tredecim sunt monachi, claustrum quidem satis idoneum pro coenobiali consuetudine habentes, sed non claustraliter, ut ceteri, cohabitantes. Habent quippe singuli cellulas per gyrum claustri proprias, in quibus operantur, dormiunt ac vescuntur.*" PL 156:854. Cf. *Aux sources de la vie Cartusienne*, 196f. See also ibid., 161ff., 165ff., 171, 179 and 187f.; W. Nigg, *op. cit.*, 187f.; Ian C. Hannah, *Christian Monasticism. A Great Force in History* (New York: The Macmillan Co., 1925), 118.

143. "*More antiquo Aegyptiorum monachorum, singulares cellas perpetuo inhabitant. Ubi silentio, lectioni, orationi, atque operi manuum, maxime in scribendis*

The Eleventh Century: New Religious Orders 209

It seems the first Carthusians said Matins and Vespers in common and recited the remaining canonical hours in their cells. On Sundays and certain feasts they had a community Mass, "after the manner of the ancient hermits."[144] Their liturgy was simple, differing from the Roman rite. Simplicity prevailed also in their chapel which had a wooden altar and only silver—i.e. less valuable—chalices.[145]

Having no abbots, the Carthusians were governed by priors. They considered Hugh of Grenoble as their abbot. He "was not lord or bishop to them, but a most humble associate and brother, always ready to help them, as far as it was in his power."[146]

To practice abjection, the Carthusians wore a coarse white habit.[147] Their diet was equally poor. On Mondays, Wednesdays and Fridays they fasted on bran bread—they never ate white bread—

---

libris, irrequieti insistunt." PL 189:945. According to Stephen of Obazine, who visited the Carthusians between the years a. 1032–1035, "*Habitatio eorum montaneis hyemalibus cingitur; cellulae ipsorum quinque cubitis a se invicem disterminatur.*" *Aux sources de la vie Cartusienne*, 192. Cf. ibid., 189 and 191. In this connection, Guibert also informs us that the Carthusians used sign language. "*Nusquam pene loquuntur, nam si quid peti necesse est, signo exigitur.*" PL 156:854. Cf. H. Workman, *op. cit.*, 251 and I. Hannah, *op. cit.*, 118.

144. "*Officium divinum, diurnum pariter et nocturnum, tam in ecclesia, diebus et horis illis quibus in eam conveniebant, quam per cellas, non perfunctorie, ut quidam, sed intentissime, oculis in terram demissis, cordibus vero in coelum fixis, devotissime persolvebant.... Diebus vero dominicis et certis sanctorum festivitatibus tantum antiquorum eremitarum more, ne ab aliis sacris operibus, licet dignitate inferioribus, impedirentur, missae sacrificium offerebant, quo omnes pariter conveniebant. Et ipsis diebus in refectorio simul ad ritum monachorum comedebant.*" PL 152:510. Cf. PL 156:854; PL 189:945 and *Aux sources de la vie Cartusienne*, 197.

145. PL 156:854; H. Löbbel, *op. cit.*, 123f.; M. Dmitrewski, *op. cit.*, 72; *Aux sources de la vie Cartusienne*, 198 and B. Bligny, "Les premiers Chartreux et la pauvreté," *loc. cit.*, 37.

146. "*Erat eis non ut dominus et episcopus, sed ut socius et frater humillimus, et ad cunctorum, quantum in ipso erat, obsequia paratissimus.*" PL 153:769f. Cf. H. Löbbel, *op. cit.*, 125. See also PL 156:854: "*Sub priore agunt, vices autem abbatis ac provisoris Gratianopolitanus episcopus vir plurimum religiosus exsequitur.*"

147. "*Fecerunt sibi vestes breves et angustas de grosso panno albo, vili et rudi quae eos contemptibiles intuentibus redderent et abjectos.*" PL 152:509. Cf. PL 156:854 and PL 189:944. See also B. Bligny, "Les premiers Chartreux et la pauvreté," *loc. cit.*, 41.

salt and water. On Tuesdays, Thursdays and Saturdays they had vegetables or fruits, and watered wine, and on Sundays, Thursdays and great feasts, eggs and some cheese. They never bought fish, but served it on non-lenten days if it was donated to them. On Sundays the procurator distributed their weekly supply of vegetables; they cooked in their own cells, as did the early Christian hermits. On Sundays and great feasts they had their meals in common: one after Sext, the other after Vespers.[148]

Bruno's ideal was, to use a contemporary expression, to follow the poor Christ in his destitution, on the narrow road which leads to heaven.[149] According to some authors, Bruno left Sèche-Fontaine and retired to the desert of *Cartusia* precisely because it excluded the danger of donations.[150] This would be in line with the early Carthusians' resolve to accept no possessions outside their enclosure and with their determination to limit their settlements to twelve monks, a prior, sixteen *conversi* and a few hired servants.[151] Poverty, however, was not an end in itself, as had been the case in other contemporary reforms; it was an instrument of the spiritual life which enabled the hermit to engage in undisturbed contemplation.[152]

---

148. PL 152:509; PL 156:854; PL 189:944f. See also H. Löbbel, *op. cit.*, 124 and 129 and *Aux sources de la vie Cartusienne*, 197.

149. "Ad perpetuam poenitentiam peragendam eremi deserta competentia quaerere, et ibidem relictis omnibus divitiis et deliciis et honoribus huius mundi, accipere singulas cruces suas et nudi nudum Christum sequi per arctam viam, quae ducit ad vitam." PL 152:485. Cf. *ibid.*, 1259.

150. J. Laurent, *op. cit.*, 1:126.

151. "Contra cupiditatem quae radix omnium malorum dicitur et avaritiam quae idolorum servitus nuncupatur, certos terminos juxta locorum suorum fertilitatem aut sterilitatem majores minoresve praefixerant, ita ut extra eos, etiamsi totus mundus eis offerretur, nec saltem, quantum pes humanus occupare potest, licet possidere. Certum etiam numerum, quem transgredi nullo modo liceret, animalibus et pecoribus imposuerunt. Et ut non esset eis quandoque necessarium, vel plus terrae quam dictum est possessioni suae addere, aut pecorum numerum augere, duodecim tantum monachos cum tertio decimo priore, ac sexdecim conversis paucisque mercenariis, nullo prorsus superaddito, in suis domibus esse perpetuo decreverunt." PL 152:509. Cf. PL 153:719f.; PL 189:944 and B. Bligny, "Les premiers Chartreux et la pauvreté," *loc. cit.*, 56.

152. B. Bligny, "Les premiers Chartreux et la pauvreté," *loc. cit.*, 55ff.

The Eleventh Century: New Religious Orders

In their cells, the Carthusians observed silence and devoted their time to prayer, spiritual reading and manual labor. At first they did not engage in farming, but worked only on the plots adjoining their cells. They also raised and sold animals. They transcribed books as a form of manual labor, partly to provide for their own needs, and partly to counter the charge that they did nothing tangible for the Church at large. Thus, to quote Guibert of Nogent: "While they are faithful in regard to all the other observances of poverty, they have accumulated a very rich library."[153]

It is reported that the founders of the *Cartusia* had "two laics" in their company whom they called *conversi*.[154] In his letter from Calabria, Bruno similarly mentions laybrothers.[155] This indicates that the Carthusians already had laybrothers between the years 1084 and 1090. Their task was to ensure a life of undisturbed contemplation for the hermits. They lived at a distance from the hermit community and followed, in view of their work, a somewhat different schedule. They were under the direction of the procurator.[156]

Since Bruno wrote no rule, his disciples at first simply followed his example. In time, however, they put their practices into writing. This was the work of Guigo, the fifth prior of the Grande Chartreuse, who codified the Carthusian usages at the request of the

---

153. "*Cum in omnimoda paupertate se deprimant, ditissimam tamen bibliothecam coaggerant.*" PL 156:854. Cf. PL 152:535, "*Vacabant certis etiam horis operi manuum, praesertim conscribendis libris incumbentes, tum ut suae inopiae consulerent, tum etiam ut ne quam darent occasionem illis qui quaerunt occasionem, sanctum eorum institutum calumniandi, quod nullam Ecclesiae Dei navarent operam, sed suis dumtaxat rebus studerent.*" Cf. also PL 156:855; *Aux sources de la vie Cartusienne*, 163; H. Löbbel, *op. cit.*, 128; W. Nigg, *op. cit.*, 196 and CMH 5:670.

154. "*Magister Bruno ... habebat autem socios ... duos laicos, quos appellamus conversos, Andream et Guarinum.*" PL 153:769.

155. "*De vobis, dilectissimis fratribus meis laicis dico: Magnificat anima mea Dominum.*" PL 152:418f.

156. "*Sunt infra montem illum habitacula laicos vicenarium numerum excedentes fidelissimos retinentia, qui sub eorum agunt diligentia.*" PL 156:855f. Cf. PL 153:747f.; H. Löbbel, *op. cit.*, 129 and E. Werner, *Pauperes Christi*, 198f. See also M. Heimbucher, *op. cit.*, 1:486.

superiors of the order.[157] How "Benedictine" were these usages? According to Mabillon, Bruno "proposed nothing beyond the Benedictine rule."[158] His view is supported to some extent by Guigo who stated that the Carthusian practices are based on the letters of St Jerome and the Rule of St Benedict,[159] and that "they—i.e. the Carthusians and the Benedictines—in the divine office have many things in common, especially in the psalmody."[160] The Carthusians also adopted the Benedictine way of taking the vows.[161] It is not surprising therefore that the acts of Bruno's canonization should call Benedict the father of the Carthusians and that the latter celebrated St Benedict's office in Mabillon's time, as well as in our own days.[162]

Boso, the nineteenth prior of the Grande Chartreuse (d. 1313), defended his order against the accusation that it had no rule of its own:

> It is clear from these (Guigo's) statutes—he pointed out—that the things described therein are either from the Rule of St Benedict or the letters of St Jerome, or else from the *Sayings of the Fathers,* the *Lives of the Fathers,* the books of Cassian and other holy doctors of the Church . . . . The Carthusian order could not simply adopt any of the aforesaid rules, for all are, or were, destined for the common and cenobitic life. As for eremitic life: there is the praiseworthy and hallowed rule composed and edited by Peter Damian in a most eloquent style; but even this the Carthusians would not or could not adopt, for, as we have shown above, the life of the Carthusians, although it must be

---

157. *Guigonis Carthusiae Prioris Quinti Consuetudines;* PL 153:635ff. Cf. M. Heimbucher, *op. cit.,* 1:484f.; L. Brockhoff, *op. cit.,* 184 and W. Nigg, *op. cit.,* 195ff.

158. "Non alia ab eo praeter Benedictinam proposita regula." *Annales Ordinis S. Benedicti,* 5:218.

159. PL 153:637f.

160. "*In [officio divino] cum caeteris monachis multum, maxime in Psalmodia regulari, concordes invenimur.*" PL 153:639f.

161. PL 153:685ff. Cf. also B. Bligny, "Les premiers Chartreux et la pauvreté," *loc. cit.,* 52f.

162. PL 152:296.

termed eremitic in its greater and worthier part, is a composite of solitary and community life.[163]

J. Leclercq saw Bruno's creation in this way:

> It is a solitary life, but cenobitism is not excluded; it is a return to the program of the Fathers of the desert, but it is not a copy of their way of life. Attention is given to tradition, to all the experiences accumulated by the Benedictine centuries.[164]

To the question whether Bruno wished to found a new order, the answer is probably, "No." He was a humble priest who left the world because he was concerned about his own salvation. He could have stayed and established his authority at Sèche-Fontaine, but left instead for the Grande Chartreuse. This indicates that he did not bind himself by the vow of stability, but wished to preserve his personal freedom. Also, when summoned to Rome, he simply left his foundation, a thing that would not have been possible had he been the head of a new order with precise rules. And in Rome itself he did not join a monastic community, but chose a solitary life instead. Yet after he was joined by disciples, he must have wished or felt the need to perpetuate the observances of the Grande Chartreuse.[165] Thus, as in other eleventh-century reforms, the initiatives of a religious leader produced a reform center which eventually developed into a new order based on Benedictine principles and the works of Jerome, Cassian and other Fathers of the Desert. Its members led a genuinely eremitic life in the best

---

163. "*Patet namque in eisdem statutis quod illa quae ibi scripta sunt, aut sunt de regula B. Benedicti, aut de epistolis B. Hieronymi, aut de collationibus Patrum seu de Vitis Patrum, vel etiam de libris Cassiani et aliorum sanctorum doctorum Ecclesiae. . . . Sed ordo Carthusiensis nullam potuit assumere de his praedictis, quia omnes, praedictae regulae sunt vel fuerunt de vita communi et coenobitica instituta; de vita vero eremitica invenitur regula laudabilis et devota a Petro Damiano stylo eloquentissimo edita et digesta, sed nec illam potuereunt et noluerunt Carthusiensis assumere, quia vita Carthusiensium, ut supra ostensum est, quamvis a majori et digniori parte sit eremitica judicanda, tamen est composita ex solitaria et communi.*" PL 152:302f.

164. *La spiritualité du Moyen Age*, 197.

165. H. Löbbel, *op. cit.*, 104ff. Cf. also *Aux sources de la vie Cartusienne*, 199.

tradition of the Egyptian anchorites, supplemented and strengthened by cenobitic forms. According to H. Löbbel, a late-nineteenth-century biographer of Bruno:

> Original in Bruno is only the blending of the two ways of life; the basic characteristic [of his reform] was eremitic life; but he was convinced that the individual will attain perfection only as a member of a greater unit; hence his aim to make the spiritual forces of community life available to the personal needs of the individual.[166]

The last question to be considered here is the architectural layout of the charterhouse. Did Bruno copy the canons' quarters in the city of Reims as his model? It is clear that in spite of undeniable similarities between the two, there are also a number of basic differences to be found in the physical plant of the Carthusians. The life in the desert was different and definitely stricter than in the residence of the canons who lived in the city and knew material wealth.[167] Nor did Bruno simply copy Camaldoli and its arrangements, for his means and resources in the desert of Chartreuse were very limited. Local conditions and the need for occasional, but regular, meetings were probably responsible for the fact that the cells were built close to each other and connected by a corridor.[168]

Bruno's contribution to monastic history was the application of cenobitic elements to eremitic monasticism. It was a successful formula which soon found its way across national boundaries and survived to the present, fully deserving the epithet: *"Numquam reformata, quia nunquam deformata,"* "Never reformed, because never deformed."[169]

---

166. *Op. cit.*, 237. Cf. *ibid.*, 117. According to C. Le Couteulx, "Bruno . . . sibi suisque sociis duo praecipue in Christo admiranda proposuit et elegit: unum est vitae austeritas, alterum arctissima solitudo." *Annales Ordinis Cartusiensis ab anno 1084 ad annum 1429* (Monstrolii: Typis Cartusiae S. Mariae de Pratis, 1887–1891), 1:4.

167. *Aux sources de la vie Cartusienne*, 195f.

168. *Ibid.*, 164f., 172, 177ff. Cf. H. Löbbel, *op. cit.*, 116ff.

169. W. Nigg, *op. cit.*, 183 and 193. For a reconstruction of Bruno's personality, see *Aux sources de la vie Cartusienne*, 389ff.

The Eleventh Century: New Religious Orders 215

To conclude, the new monastic foundations of the eleventh century, while displaying numerous and great individual variations, still had a number of common characteristics. These were not necessarily the result of a direct or indirect dependence, but simply grew out of the contemporary milieu—described, in some detail, in the preceding chapters—in a world well-prepared for such undertakings.

One of the most obvious features of the new institutions—both eremitic and cenobitic—was the cultivation of solitude, for a number of theological and ascetical reasons. This called not only for a secession from populous areas, *i.e.* a physical and pastoral withdrawal from society, but also implied a wholesale disengagement from the contemporary feudal world with all its implications.[170] It was a direct challenge to the Cluniac and similarly patterned establishments.

This challenge could hardly take effect without a very real shift from what may be called liturgical asceticism (*à la* Cluny) to a more physical and personalized asceticism. The latter was applied to practically every human need (food, clothing, sleep, etc.), and greatly stressed individual as well as communal poverty in landed property and in other possessions, including even sacred vessels and church furnishings.

The new poverty ideal, and certainly also the growing influence of Eastern monachism, hastened the introduction of the institution of lay brothers (*conversi*), in order to free the monks (and hermits)

---

170. A similar trend could also be observed within traditional monachism. Cf. Pope Nicholas II's privilege given to Desiderius, abbot of Monte Cassino, in 1059: "*Porro cupientes consulere monasticae religioni, quae peccatis exigentibus passim depravatur, et tantummodo diebus vitae tuae vicarium nobis ad correctionem omnium monasteriorum et monachorum ab ipso fluvio Piscaria, sicut influit in mare, scilicet per totam Campaniam, Principatum quoque, et Apuliam, atque Calabriam, assumere decrevimus, ita ut capitulum in eis habeas, et vice nostra indisciplinatos, cum adjutorio episcoporum ad quos monasteria ipsa pertinent, corrigas, et quae sunt emendanda, si potueris, secundum Dominum emendes, aut apostolicae sedis pontifici renunties ad perpetuam animae vestrae mercedem, et monasticae religionis emendationem et conservationem, pariter quoque ad tui cardinalatus dignitatem et sanctissimi Benedicti honorificentiam, ea gratia ut monasticus ordo corrigatur illis in partibus per te religiosum et prudentissimum successorem illius.*" PL 143:1309.

from field work and other temporal concerns, so that they could better concentrate on their prayer life. In view of the still strong appeal of the Cluniac *laus perennis* ideal, however, manual labor, though re-emerging and claiming its rightful place, did not reach "full growth" before the Cistercian solution (autarky).

Finally, there were undeniable attempts to define the organizational bonds linking the various houses of a particular reform or observance. Subsequent reformers were able to perfect these endeavors.

Since, in one way or another, the common features of the monastic reforms of the eleventh century were all present in the early Cistercian reform, it must again be pointed out that, contrary to previous thinking, Cîteaux was not a reform without antecedents.

MOLESME, THE HOME OF CÎTEAUX

THE NEW RELIGIOUS ORDERS which emerged in the second half of the eleventh century were not simply the creations of outstanding religious leaders, but also products of several other factors. These include a favorable monastic climate, the popularity of certain ideas and, in general, a definite readiness for contemporary answers in the question of monastic renewal. The same can be said about the beginnings of Molesme and Cîteaux. These monastic centers owe their existence not only to the brilliance and vision of a single spiritual and religious leader—St Robert of Molesme—but also to the interactions of a great many monastic, religious, ascetical, theological and sociological factors treated at length in the preceding chapters. Molesme and Cîteaux are products of these forces; hence a study of their origins will appropriately serve as a conclusion of our present investigation.

The pioneers of Cîteaux had not gathered by accident nor did they come from every direction of the horizon; they were all members of the renowned Burgundian abbey of Molesme, established in 1075. Their leader, St Robert, was the abbot and founder of Molesme. This in itself shows the importance of Molesme in the foundation of Cîteaux. Though they did not consider Molesme their "mother" in their system of filiation, the Cistercians always admitted that Molesme had generated Cîteaux "according to the flesh" or, in the words of their general chapter held in 1225, from it, "as though a sacred root, hailed the holy founders [of Cîteaux.]"[1] The consideration of Robert's life and of the pre-Cistercian history of Molesme is therefore indispensable for a right understanding—incomplete though it may be—of the motives and events which led to the foundation of Cîteaux at the close of the eleventh century.

The son of noble parents, Theodoric and Ermengarde, Robert was born around the year 1028 in the Champagne.[2] According to M. Chaume, he was a relative of the counts of Tonnerre and of Raynald, the viscount of Beaune—a fact of great importance in the foundation of Molesme and Cîteaux.[3] After devoting some time to the study of letters, Robert joined the abbey of Montier-la-Celle at Troyes, then governed by Abbot Bernard. There he led a life

---

1. "*Venerabili patri abbati Molismensi, de cuius domo tamquam de radice sancta prodierunt sancti patres, a quibus totius Ordinis religio pullulavit, conceditur . . .*" Josephus M. Canivez, *Statuta Capitulorum Generalium Ordinis Cisterciensis ab anno 1116 ad annum 1786* (Louvain: Bibliothèque de la Revue d'Histoire Ecclésiastique, 1934), 2:37. Cf. *ibid.*, 15f. and PL 157:1288.

2. The critical edition of Robert's life was produced by Kolumban Spahr, *Das Leben des hl. Robert von Molesme. Eine Quelle zur Vorgeschichte von Cîteaux* (Freiburg in der Schweiz: Paulusdruckerei, 1944). The *vita* is also found in PL 157:1268ff. and AS, Apr. 3:670ff. Further sources are Chrysostomus Henriquez, *Fasciculus sanctorum Ordinis Cisterciensis* (Bruxellis: apud J. Pepermann, 1623), 4ff.; Laurentius Surius, *De probatis sanctorum vitis* (Coloniae Agrippinae: apud Geruinum Calenium et haeredes Quentelios, 1570ff.); (Edouard Hautcoeur), *Vies de saint Robert et de saint Alberic premier et second abbés de Cîteaux* (Lérins: Imprimérie Marie-Bernard, 1875); Séraphine Lenssen, "Saint Robert Fondateur de Cîteaux," *Collectanea Ordinis Cisterciensium Reformatorum*, 4 (1937), 2ff., 81ff. and 161ff.; *idem, Le fondateur de Cîteaux, Saint Robert* (Westmalle: Imprimérie de l'Ordre Cistercien, 1937); Jean B. Van Damme, *Les trois fondateurs de Cîteaux* (Pain de Cîteaux, 29; Chambarand: Privately printed, 1966); Watkin Williams, "St Robert of Molesme," *Monastic Studies* (Manchester: Manchester University Press, 1938), 121ff.; Jean Lefèvre, "St Robert de Molesme dans l'opinion monastique du XIIe et du XIIIe siècles," *Analecta Bollandiana*, 74 (1956), 50ff.; E. Petit, *op. cit.*, 1:182ff.; J. Laurent, *op. cit.*, 1:146ff.; O. Ducourneau, *op. cit.*, 33ff.; J. Mahn, *op. cit.*, 40f.; *The Book of Saints*, 511; LTK 8:921f. See, in addition, the bibliography cited by K. Spahr, *Das Leben des hl. Robert*, XI-XIV. For an evaluation of Robert's *Vita* cf. *ibid.*, XV-XLVII and S. Lenssen, *op. cit.*, 7f.

3. "Born in the Champagne, St Robert was related—we do not know exactly how—to the counts of Tonnerre. Chaume concluded, Robert could have been related to Thierry of Champagne, bishop of Orleans (d. 1022),

wholly dedicated to God, with fasts and prayers spanning nights and days. Not earlier than 1053 he was appointed prior of the monastery at the express wish of the brethren. Soon after 1068, he became the abbot of Saint Michael of Tonnerre in the diocese of Langres. The abbey had been restored by William of Dijon around the year 980 and followed the usages of Cluny as they were interpreted by the abbey of Saint Benignus in the city of Dijon.[4] Robert, the fifth abbot of the place—after William of Dijon, Letbald, Hunald I and Hunald II (1057–1068)—was by this time a man well known for his sanctity. As it turned out, however, this proved insufficient to enforce his authority over the monks and to improve monastic discipline in general. Robert therefore returned,

---

brother of a certain Alberic, grandson of Thierry, lord of Château-Thierry, cousin of counts Milo and Renard of Tonnerre, etc. This kinship would best explain the establishment of Molesme on the territory of the counts of Tonnerre. The same kinship sheds also a better light on the foundation of Cîteaux. As lord of Cîteaux, Renard, viscount of Beaune, was one of the first benefactors of the New Monastery. This Renard (or Rainardus) was directly related to the ancient dukes of Burgundy, the lords of Vergy. His great-uncle, Agano or Azelin, was abbot of Moutier S. Jean en Tonnerrois; his great-grandmother, the viscountess of Ingola, was the owner of Ampilly near the Tonnerrois and the future abbey of Molesme." K. Spahr, *Das Leben des hl. Robert*, XLIV. Spahr refers to M. Chaume's letter on the subject, dated December 7, 1938; *ibid.*, n. 2. See also E. Petit, *op. cit.*, 1:183 n. 1. J. Laurent writes on this point, "Whenever he (Robert) is on a mission or makes a foundation, from Troyes to Tonnerre, at Molesme or at Cîteaux, he is protected and even aided by the prelates and the baronial descendants of the ancient house of Vergy, or the Milonides, or the Mainier; hence the Malignys, the viscounts of Beaune, the lords of Mont-Saint-Jean, and of Couches were all possibly cousins of the great abbot." *Abbayes et prieurés de l'ancienne France.* Tome douzième: *Province ecclésiastique de Lyon.* Troisième partie: *Diocèses de Langres et de Dijon* (Archives de la France Monastique, vol. 45; Paris: Librarie Picard, 1941), 299ff. See also C. Henriquez, *op. cit.*, 4; W. A. Parker Mason, "The Beginnings of the Cistercian Order," *Transactions of the Royal Historical Society,* New Series, 19 (1905), 169–207, esp. 182 n. 2.

4. Bruno Schneider, "Cîteaux und die benediktinische Tradition. Die Quellenfrage des Liber Usuum im Lichte der Consuetudines Monasticae," *Analecta Sacri Ordinis Cisterciensis*, 17 (1961), 107f. For Robert's stay at Tonnerre, see AS, Apr. 3:670; A. Manrique, *op. cit.*, 1:1f.; GCh 4:613f., 712ff.; DOR 1:921; E. Sackur, *op. cit.*, 1:262, 267 n. 2 and 268f.; R. Graham, "The Relation of Cluny to Some Other Movements of Monastic Reform," *loc. cit.*,

not later than 1072, to the monastery of his profession.[5] In his original monastery Robert led the life of a simple monk; but not for long. Around 1072 he became, by election or nomination, prior of Saint Ayoul[6] at Provins in the diocese of Sens. This monastery had recently been founded as a direct dependency of Montier-la-Celle, with the stipulation that a monastic community should take charge of the church of Saint Ayoul. Robert remained as its second prior for only a short time, i.e., between the years 1072 and 1074. Then, on papal orders—if the information of Robert's anonymous biographer from the early thirteenth century is correct—he assumed the leadership of hermits living in the nearby forest of Collan who needed an instructor in regular discipline. As his biographer further reports, Robert heeded the call because he could hope that his labors would not be in vain, since the hermits were of one mind in the rejection of earthly things and in the seeking of the things of heaven, and would therefore also have the right concept of obedience.[7] An additional factor was that Saint Ayoul was situated in a steadily growing city with lively markets and streets; a situation where the monks' exposure to the layman's world could hardly be avoided. Such surroundings and such a state of affairs could never satisfy

---

188; W. Parker Mason, "The Beginnings of the Cistercian Order," loc. cit., 171 n. 4; K. Spahr, Das Leben des hl. Robert, 8 n. 1, 9, XVI and XLIVf.; K. Hallinger, op. cit., 2:847; W. Williams, op. cit., 125 and L. Henri Cottineau, Répertoire Topo-bibliographique des abbayes et des prieurés (Mâcon: Frères Protat, 1935), 2:3170.

5. Cf. PL 66:134ff. and 148ff. See also K. Spahr, Das Leben des hl. Robert, XLIV.—There is a great similarity between this incident and the events recorded by St Gregory from the life of St Benedict, and it may create further questions about the real causes and circumstances of Robert's return to Montier-la-Celle. Perhaps his monks' refusal that he take charge of some seven hermits in the forest of Collan, situated between Tonnerre and Chablis, added its weight to Robert's decision.

6. On Saint Ayoul see, Mansi 19:629f.; Jean Godefroy, "L'histoire du prieuré de Saint-Ayoul de Provins et le récit des miracles du saint," Revue Mabillon, 27 (1937), 94ff. and 28 (1938), 84ff. and 112ff.; Cottineau, 2:2603; GCh 4: Instr. 25 and 12: Instr. 251; J. Laurent, op. cit., 1:206; and K. Spahr, Das Leben des hl. Robert, 10 n. 1, XVII and XLV.

7. K. Spahr, Das Leben des hl. Robert, 10f.

Robert's aspirations. "This is in all likelihood the reason why he left [Saint Ayoul] and began to look for a solitary place where, free from this bustle, he could lead a full and genuine monastic life."[8] It may be remarked here that, in the words of an extant summary of Robert's life, the envoys of Collan did not specify whom they wished for their master, but Robert, knowing his abbot's feelings and judging that he could be of service to the hermits, made himself available. By leaving to join the hermits of Collan, Robert clearly showed his preference for the latters' way of life. He aspired to a life of greater asceticism than was practiced in contemporary monasteries and sought therefore to join a community free of secular ties, a thing unheard-of in a monastic world so closely allied with feudalism.[9]

Collan[10] had been the property of Robert's relatives, the house of Maligny, a younger branch of the counts of Tonnere, which held a considerable part of the Tonnerrois in allodial tenure. (This may well have been a factor in Robert's secession to Collan and in the foundation of Molesme which was donated to Robert by the same relatives, the Maligny family.) The hermitage had originally been started by a priest who was soon joined by two brothers, converted, supposedly by Robert, after a duel, and then subsequently by four others. Their life, based on private ascetical practices, lacked all communal organization. After his takeover, Robert acquainted them with Benedictine life and monastic practices in general. His personal life, based on abnegation in imitation of the apostles in the early Church, greatly aided him in the undertaking. The result was that "they all accepted with equanimity the burden and heat of the day, as well as hunger and thirst, cold weather

---

8. J. Godefroy, "L'histoire du prieuré de Saint-Ayoul," *loc. cit.*, 99.

9. S. Lenssen, *op. cit.*, 22 and 37 n. 1.

10. PL 157:1257f.; DOR 1:921f.; E. Petit, *op. cit.*, 1:217; J. Laurent, *op. cit.*, 1:114; W. Williams, *op. cit.*, 125; K. Spahr, *Das Leben des hl. Robert*, XVIf. and XLV; U. Berlière, "Les origines de l'Ordre de Cîteaux," *loc. cit.*, 448 and Robert Folz, "Le problème des origines de Cîteaux," *Mélanges Saint Bernard* (XXIVe Congrès de l'Association Bourguignonne des Sociétés Savantes. VIIIe centenaire de la mort de S. Bernard; Dijon: Association des Amis de Saint Bernard, 1954), 284ff.

and destitution, fasting and prayer."[11] Robert's stay at Collan is attested by the cartulary of Molesme and the still extant remains of his cell, about one kilometer to the southeast of today's Collan.[12]

As time went on, more vocations arrived, among them—some say—Alberic, a prime mover in the Cistercian reform and Robert's successor as abbot of Cîteaux. By the time their number reached thirteen the place had become inadequate for their needs; this called for the transfer of the settlement to a more suitable location. Robert must have mentioned this to the Malignys, thus soliciting their assistance. The latter considered it a distinction to have a monastery on their grounds and to join the honorable ranks of those who made similar foundations. Accordingly they summoned their relatives, allies and vassals sometime during 1075 and with them conducted Robert and his companions to the forest of Molesme, a wooded and savage region in the eastern extremity of their holdings, which they had decided to donate to Robert and his monks.[13]

The original donors were Hugh, the lord of Maligny, his sisters, nephews, nieces, their respective husbands and wives, a knight named Raynald of Molesme, Hugh of Couteron and his wife Gersend, the lady of Chaceney, Gersend's sister, Odo of Fulvy and his wife, and Odo, son of Engebaut, and his wife. In common agreement they made their donation to Our Lady and the monks who proposed to serve her at Molesme. They renounced all ownership to their *alodium* at Molesme and gave up all seignorial rights with one minor exception: they retained some serfs and the manses cultivated by them, and a portion of the tithe received from the

---

11. *"In loco igitur qui nunc Colannus dicitur, Domino servientes in fame et siti, in frigore et nuditate, ieiunando et orando pondus diei et estus equanimiter tolerabant."* K. Spahr, *Das Leben des hl. Robert,* 11.

12. J. Laurent, *op. cit.,* 1:114 n. 8.

13. K. Spahr, *Das Leben des hl. Robert,* 11 and XVII. See also J. Laurent, *op. cit.,* 1:115; A. Manrique, *op. cit.,* 1:3; AS, Apr. 3:671; DOR 1:922; PL 157:1258; S. Lenssen, *op. cit.,* 20; W. Williams, *op. cit.,* 126; H. DeWarren, "Le monachisme à l'apparition de saint Bernard," *loc. cit.,* 61; K. Hallinger, *op. cit.,* 2:846. On the Celtic origin of "Molesme" see Pierre J. Bâcon-Tâcon, *Recherches sur les origines celtiques principalement sur celles de Bugey* (Paris: P. Didot l'Ainé, 1798), 2:418 and J. Laurent, *op. cit.,* 1:115 n. 2.

church of Pouilly. The document was signed by a great number of lords and knights invited for the ceremony. These notables included Achard of Chatillon, the seneschal of Burgundy, Tescelin the Red, the lord of Fontain-les-Dijon and father of St Bernard of Clairvaux, Hugh of Griselles, Bourdin and Guy, the lords of Larrey, Hugh of Eporves, and Raynald of Montfort. The date of the charter is given in general terms: "These were agreed upon while King Philip was ruling the Franks, while Robert headed the duchy of Burgundy, and Raynald governed the diocese of Langres."[14] As tradition has it, formal religious life began on the fourth Sunday of Advent, December 20th, 1075.[15] The monks dedicated the new establishment to the Blessed Virgin Mary, a custom practiced by the Cluniacs and adopted, later, by the pioneers of Cîteaux.[16] Although there is no extant documentary evidence of Robert's installation as first abbot of Molesme by the local ordinary, Bishop Hugh Raynard of

14. "*Ugo de Merlenniaco et sorores et nepotes et neptes sue cum maritis suis, et Rainaldus de Molismo et Odo Paganus et Wido, et Ugo de Curtiruno et uxor ejus Gersennis cum sorore sua Cacenniacensi et liberis ejus, et Odo de Furviaco et Odo filius Engelbaudi cum uxoribus suis . . . dederunt . . . omnes qui quicquam alodii ad Molismum attinentis habebant, illud Molismense alodium [Deo et] Beate Marie et fratribus eis in loco illo servituris, totum ita liberum et justitias et omnes redditus ejus et omnia consuetudinaria jura, et quicquid ad illud alodium adtinebat, ubicumque esset, sive in campis sive in pratis sive in nemoribus sive in aquis sive in molendinis, nichil sibi vel alicui ex [eo] et ex pertinentibus ad illos retinentes, nisi hoc decimationis quod quisque eorum accipiebat ab ecclesia Poliacensi. Quin etiam decimationis partes suas concesserant Beate Marie et servitoribus suis Rainaldus de Molismo et Odo filius Engelbaldi annuente uxore sua Sarra. Retinuerunt etiam sibi servos suos et mansos suos proprios. Mansos enim Beate Marie quos quasi proprios prius habuerant, dimiserunt ei et monachis ei servituris, nullusque eorum aliud aliquid excepit, excepta Gersenni et sorore sua, que plus quam alii servis suis usuarium nemoris et aquae tantummodo, nichilque aliud ex attinentibus toti Molismensi alodio, sibi retinuerunt. . . . Facta sunt hec Philippo rege Francorum regnante, Roberto vero ducatu Burgundie presidente, Rainardo autem diocesim Lingonensem gubernante.*" J. Laurent, *op. cit.*, 2:5f. Cf. *ibid.*, 1:115f. and 2:3. See also GCh 4:729, *ibid., Instr.* 147 and O. Ducourneau, *op. cit.*, 35.

15. "*Anno milleno quinto cum septuageno, Sub patre Roberto crevit domus haec in aperto;*" GCh 4:729 and *ibid., Instr.* 147f. Cf. PL 157:1258; PL 185bis:1399; PL 188:642; AS, Apr. 3:663; RHF 13:724 note; J. Laurent, *op. cit.*, 2:3; W. Parker Mason, "The Beginnings of the Cistercian Order," *loc. cit.*, 172 n. 1 and W. Williams, *op. cit.*, 126.

16. J. Laurent, *op. cit.*, 1:115.

Langres, the fact that Robert was the first abbot of Molesme is attested by a number of related documents.[17]

Life at early Molesme meant great hardships and extreme poverty. The monks, working with their own hands, used branches to build a small chapel and some cells. They sustained great privations in food and clothing. Often without bread, they contented themselves with vegetables.[18] At times Robert was even forced to send some monks begging. The pioneers of Molesme thus spent their first four or five years in privation and destitution; this was not deliberately sought but simply a consequence of their extreme poverty. Relief came when on a visit to Molesme Hugh, bishop of Troyes, became aware of their plight. He immediately decided to help them and called on the people of the neighborhood to do likewise. On another occasion, when learning that Molesme was without food and that Robert had dispatched some barefooted monks to Troyes to buy supplies without any money, he gave them new clothes and sent them home with a generous quantity of linen and bread.[19]

Helpful donations began to arrive with a steady flow, though somewhat slowly at the beginning. The first of them was, in all likelihood, the church and village of Marcenay, given to Molesme by Hugh I, duke of Burgundy, in 1076 or 1077. Around this time, too, Simon, count of Bar-sur-Aube, made over his property at

17. AS, Apr. 3:671; PL 157:1259 and GCh 4:729 and 731.

18. *"Robertus . . . assumptis fratribus in quoddam nemus cui Molismus nomen erat secessit; ubi propriis manibus laborantes ramos de arboribus exciderunt, ex eisdem domicilia in quibus possent quiescere construentes. Oratorium quoque simile scemate peregerunt . . . Qui cum panem non haberent quo post diuturnum laborem corpora possent reficere, tantummodo leguminibus utebantur."* K. Spahr, *Das Leben des hl. Robert*, 11ff. *Ibid.*, 13, we are also told that they went "nudis pedibus." Cf. *ibid.*, XLVI; J. Mabillon, *op. cit.*, 5:87f.; PL 188:642; DOR 1:922; J. Laurent, *op. cit.*, 1:148; M. Dmitrewski, *op. cit.*, 73f.; O. Ducourneau, *op. cit.*, 38.

19. K. Spahr, *Das Leben des hl. Robert*, XVII and 12f. Cf. J. Laurent, *op. cit.*, 1:116; PL 157:1275 n. 11; W. Williams, *op. cit.*, 126; Gregor Müller, "Gründung der Abtei Cîteaux," *Cistercienser-Chronik*, 10 (1898), 38 n. 21; Pius Gams, *Series Episcoporum Ecclesiae Catholicae quotquot innotuerunt a beato Petro Apostolo* (Leipzig: Verlag Karl W. Hiersemann, 1931), 643.

Molesme, the Home of Cîteaux

Grancey-sur-Aube to Robert and his monks. In 1079 Herbert Wifel donated the church of Senan. In the following year (1080) Raynald of Bar left Sèche-Fontaine to Molesme. In 1081 at the latest, Geoffrey II, the Elder, lord of Joinville, ceded the estate of Vaucouleurs to the new foundation. Also in 1081, Walter, castellan of the donjon of Brienne, offered Radonvilliers in free alms "to Our Lady of Molesme and its abbot named Robert." In 1083 the already mentioned Herbert Wifel added the church of Flacy to his previous donation.[20]

Since donations did not assume major proportions and in view of the continuing plight of the new foundation, the local ordinary, Bishop Raynard of Langres, a man always well-disposed toward Molesme, decided to make a direct appeal to his charges on behalf of the monastery in 1083. He solemnly called upon his vassals and clerics to make donations to Molesme and urged also the principal barons of his diocese—these included the duke of Burgundy, the count of Tonnerre, and the lords of Fouvent, Chacenay and Grancey—to do likewise.

The document reads, in part:

> I, Raynard, by the grace of God bishop of Langres, desirous of seeing the aforesaid church of Molesme grow stronger in honor of its mother [the diocese of] Langres [hereby declare]: If a cleric or *casatus* (i.e., lord enfeoffed with land on which he had built a house) of the diocese of Langres wishes to cede a church or part of his *casamentum* (land with house on it) to the aforementioned church [of Molesme], with the counsel and consent of the canons of Langres we consign it by this deed of ours to the monks dwelling in that place—saving the customary rights of the bishop [of Langres] . . . . These were acted upon in the year 1083 . . . during the reign of Philip, king of the Franks.[21]

---

20. AS, Apr. 3:671; PL 157:1259; J. Laurent, *op. cit.*, 1:80, 138, 148ff., 2:86, 134, 470f., 607 and 609; E. Petit, *op. cit.*, 1:395ff.; S. Lenssen, *op. cit.*, 26.

21. "*Ego . . . Rainardus, Dei gratia Lingonensis episcopus, premissam ecclesiam ad honorem sue matris Lingonensis ecclesie desiderans amplificare, quicumque clericus, quicumque Lingonensis ecclesie casatus sive ecclesiam sive aliquid de casamento seu pretitulate ecclesie velit concedere, salvis consuetudinariis episcopi redditionibus, consilio et laude canonicorum Lingonensium, dono nostro successorumque nostrorum monachis inibi degentibus concedimus optinere . . . Acta sunt hec Lingonis anno . . .*

The appeal, also the first public confirmation of Molesme, caused no resentment, as the ensuing flow of donations proved. The list of the donors is once more headed by the duke of Burgundy—by now Odo I—who was happy to relinquish the church of Louesme to Molesme. Next came Raynald, the lord of Choiseul, who presented the abbey with the church of Sts Peter and Gengulf at Varennes. This was followed by the donation of the churches of Saint Quentin and Saint Aignan, both in the region of Troyes, made respectively by count Odo III of Troyes and count William I of Tonnerre. Around 1090, duke Theobald of Lorraine gave a parcel of his lands outside the walls of Nancy to Molesme with the proviso that a church be constructed thereon. On June 17, 1095, Robert accepted the church of Lucheux in the county of Saint Pol, a gift of its count, Hugh of Candavene. Still in the same year Robert went to Abbéville, to take possession of the church of Authie, donated by Hugh the Poacher. From Abbéville Robert proceeded to Cohem and Blaringhem to accept donations in Flanders. Next he traveled to the castle of Aire, where count Robert of Flanders, flanked by his wife Constance, his marshal, the constable and castellan, gave additional lands at Cohem to Molesme. Between 1096 and 1097 Pibo, bishop of Toul, gave the church of Commercy and somewhat later Hugh, count of Troyes, donated that of Isle in the Champagne. Anseau, bishop of Beauvais, made his donation of the church of Nointel in the Isle-de-France shortly before the foundations of Cîteaux.[22]

---

millesimo LXXX. III., . . . regnante Philippo rege Francorum." J. Laurent, *op. cit.,* 2:7. Cf. also 1:3 and 1:127f. According to E. Petit, the bishop's favor may well have been additionally motivated by his desire to counterbalance the powerful abbey of Pothières, noted for its insubordination. *Op. cit.,* 1:184.

22. J. Laurent, *op. cit.,* 1:148. Cf. also 1:3, 19, 26f., 74, 84f., 93, 113, 125, 151, 175, 185, 190 and 2:7, 36f., 40f., 80, 89, 98f., 124, 160, 167, 172, 417, 433 and 453; GCh 4:731f.; PL 157:435f.; S. Lenssen, *op. cit.,* 26 and Jean Bouton, *Histoire de l'Ordre de Cîteaux* (Tirage-à-part des "Fiches cisterciennes" Westmalle: Imprimérie de l'Ordre, 1959), 51. On the benefactors of Molesme see J. Laurent, *op. cit.,* 1:113 and 132f.; GCh 4:732 and Émil Socard, "Chartes inédits extraits des cartulaires de Molesme, interessant un grand nombre de localités du départment de l'Aube," *Mémoires de la Société Académique d'agriculture, des science, arts et belles-lettres du départment de l'Aube,* 28 (1864), 164.

In a number of instances donations were made to the monastery with strings attached, i.e., for the reception of children as oblates, for one's acceptance in *praebendam,* i.e., in return for food, shelter and maintenance until death, for the privilege of becoming a monk *in extremis,* for obtaining a burial place in the monastery and for anniversary prayers said by the monks for the deceased relatives of the donors. It also happened that prospective crusaders sold part of their property to the monks and used the money received for their travel expenses.[23]

As can be seen from the instances listed, Robert accepted churches, revenues, tithes and villages for his monastery. This was considered legitimate, hence it was widely practiced by traditional monachism. As E. Petit remarked:

> Molesme shows us how a monastery, placed in favorable conditions and directed by an eminent man, was able to acquire an enormous influence in a short time, an influence others envied.[24]

And J. Laurent added:

> During the first half-century of its existence, but especially from 1075 to 1111, there was no baronial house in the southern Champagne, the diocese and seigneurie of Langres and the north of Burgundy that did not heap its favors on Molesme.[25]

The acceptance of donations was made possible through the influx of vocations which began soon after the foundation of the monastery. The early recruits comprised clerics and an even greater number of feudal lords and knights. The former included Stephen Harding and his friend Peter, Alberic—unless he already joined

---

23. J. Laurent, *op. cit.,* 1:14, 17, 21, 28, 33, 40f., 46, 53f., 78f., 88, 111, 126, 128, 132, 135ff., 138f., 146, 164, 176, 181, 197f., 203, 205, 209, 214, 219, 225, 227, 232, 238, 245, 251, 269, 272 and 2:48, 85, 94, 114, 125, 127, 177 and 214ff. See also E. Socard, "Chartes inédits extraits des cartulaires de Molesme," *loc. cit.,* 263 and J. Mabillon, *op. cit.,* 3:743.

24. *Op. cit.,* 1:249. Cf. also J. Laurent, *op. cit.,* 1:149 and *Aux sources de la vie cartusienne,* 114.

25. *Op. cit.,* 1:113.

Collan—another Peter, the future bishop of Tarantaise, Guy, the future abbot of Aulps, John and Ilbode, both from Arras, the future Cistercian envoys who will obtain the so-called *Roman Privilege* for the newly established abbey of Cîteaux, and a Norman by the name of William of Argues.[26]

In 1082 Molesme attracted a churchman of great renown, Bruno of Cologne. Leaving the world with two associates named Peter and Lambert, he came to Robert of Molesme and settled, with the latter's permission, at Sèche-Fontaine, a newly established dependent priory in the immediate vicinity of Molesme. The newcomers soon built a small oratory and led the life of hermits. When others joined and the question of transforming the hermitage into a *coenobium* arose, Bruno resolved to leave the place. He found a new home in the vicinity of Grenoble, and this became in 1084 the motherhouse of the Carthusian order. His decision to leave may have been hastened by the realization that the Burgundian forests, though far from the cities, offered no real escape from the world and little protection against curious people who wished to see the great Bruno. Be this as it may, Sèche-Fontaine still had its importance for Bruno's future life. It was here that the outlines of his reform, a unique combination of cenobitic and eremitic life, took concrete forms.[27] Also, by

---

26. J. Laurent, *op. cit.*, 1:119f. and 148ff.; K. Spahr, *Das Leben des hl. Robert*, 13. On Stephen Harding see, *Vita Sancti Petri Prioris Juliacensis*, PL 185:1259; William of Malmesbury, *Gesta regum Anglorum*, IV, PL 179:1287; Charles Oursel, "La genèse des manuscrits primitifs de l'abbaye de Cîteaux sous l'abbatiat de Saint Étienne Harding," *Mémoires de l'Académie des Sciences, Arts et Belles-Lettres de Dijon*, 114 (1957–1959), 47; Fernand Delehaye, "Un moine; Saint Robert, fondateur de Cîteaux," *Collectanea Ordinis Cisterciensium Reformatorum*, 14 (1952), 93; John B. Dailgairns, John H. Newman and Herbert Thurston, *Life of St Stephen Harding, Abbot of Cîteaux and Founder of the Cistercian Order* (Westminster, Md.: The Newman Press, 1942).

27. J. Laurent, *op. cit.*, 1:148; E. Petit, *op. cit.*, 1:246 note; J. Mabillon, *op. cit.*, 5:192; F. Delehaye, "Un moine; Saint Robert," *loc. cit.*, 93; B. Bligny, *L'Eglise et les ordres réligieux*, 259f.; *idem*, "Les premiers Chartreux et la pauvreté," *loc. cit.*, 52; J. Leclercq, *La spiritualité du moyen age*, 190; D. Knowles, *The Monastic Order in England*, 198; Alice Cooke, "A Study in Twelfth Century Religious Revival," *loc. cit.*, 146.

"turning towards eremitism, he was able to compare his own ideas with the poverty ideal then prevalent in contemporary spirituality."[28] Then, as G. Schreiber pointed out, there was the overriding importance of the diocese of Langres in the history of the medieval monastic reforms. He also noted the fact that "Bruno, the founder of the Carthusian order related to Cîteaux in so many instances, actually spent some time at Molesme (Sèche-Fontaine) where feudal law so strongly clashed with the new spirit which resolutely moved away from proprietary law." In Schreiber's view, this is still insufficiently appreciated by Bruno's (and Robert's) biographers.[29]

The lay recruits of Molesme formed an equally impressive list. It included Aimon the Red of Chatillon, Guervin of Mousson, Guy of Aprez, Guy of Chatel-Censoir, the second abbot of Molesme, Guy of Grancey, Hatto of Ricey, Herbert of Argenteuil, Hugh of Bourmont, Hugh of Montigny-Montfort, Lambert of Touillon, Lescelin of Maisey, Nivelon of Maligny and Raynald of Noyers.[30]

The greater monastic family of Molesme, headed by the abbot, consisted of monks, *conversi, praebendarii* and oblates. The abbot had as officials: the grand prior, the choir master, the secretary, the chamberlain, the cellarer, the sacristan, the almoner, the *pitanciarius*, the guest master, the cook, the overseer of the fisheries and the infirmarian. Of the early priors we know the names of Hugh, Walter, Alberic, Constans, Adam and Raoul. The office of the subprior, on the other hand, is mentioned only after 1099, after Robert's return from Cîteaux.[31]

The presence of *conversi* in early Molesme is attested by documentary evidence from the year 1095. According to K. Spahr, these *conversi* were classified as monks—as at Cluny. They worked in the

---

28. W. Lühe, *op. cit.,* 116.

29. *Gemeinschaften des Mittelalters,* 199 n. 185.

30. J. Laurent, *op. cit.,* 1:121ff. Cf. also 1:42, 44, 58, 60, 63, 70, 79, 91, 116, 156, 167, 180, 184, 216, 218, 224f., and 233.

31. *Ibid.,* 1:183ff. Cf. also 1:41f., 43, 46, 58, 60, 114f., 272 and 2:8, 55 and K. Hallinger, *op. cit.,* 2:847.

fields and in distant manors.[32] Other duties were carried out by all kinds of servants, called *famuli* as a group. Some of them found employment within the monastery, others—like the mayor, the forester, the seller and the overseer of the crops and vineyards—worked on the outside.

The *famuli abbatis* were the domestic servants of the abbot who also accompanied him on his journeys. We know some of Robert's *famuli* by name: Henry, Marinus, Raynald and William of Ponthieu. It seems officials like the prior and the chamberlain also had one *domesticus* each to assist them in their work.[33]

Moreover, in line with contemporary practices, the community had its oblates (*oblati*) i.e., children brought to the monastery to be raised as monks. Then, as mentioned, there were the so-called *praebendarii*, who in return for a donation to the monastery were allowed to stay with the monks and receive food and shelter without being obliged to take the monastic habit. In one instance a lord's only daughter was thus placed in the custody of the monks who received lands, forests, meadows and serfs for the favor.[34]

The influx of vocations and the generosity of its donors enabled Molesme to make foundations in quick succession, not only in Burgundy, but also in Bar, Lorraine, Picardy and Flanders. It had several priories during the first six years of its existence and erected some twenty-two additional ones from churches and other donations during the last decade of the century. According to E. Petit, by the year 1100, Molesme claimed some forty dependencies spread out in twelve dioceses, i.e., Arras, Autun, Auxerre, Beauvais, Chartres, Langres, Meaux, Metz, Rouen, Sens, Thérouanne, Toul and Troyes. These dependencies were, geographically:

32. K. Spahr, *De fontibus constitutivis primigenii juris constitutionalis Sacri Ordinis Cisterciensis*, 61; J. Laurent, *op. cit.*, 1:62, 198, 253 and 2:72, 236.

33. J. Laurent, *op. cit.*, 1:199ff., and 207.

34. "*Rogerius de Leesmo dedit Deo et Sancte Marie Molismensi omnem hereditatem suam de Leesmo et eam que pertinet ad Leesmum, ubicumque manet, in terris, in servis et ancillis, in silvis, in pratis. Ipse vero Rogerius, eo tempore quo hec facta sunt, habebat unam filiam, quam in custodiam Sancte Marie et monachorum posuit.*" J. Laurent, *op. cit.*, 2:125. Cf. also 1:79, 111, 126, 128, 135f., 181, 197f., 225, 230, 232, and 2:85, 125, 127, 164, 177 and 214.

Molesme, the Home of Cîteaux

establishment	territory	diocese	year of foundation
Collan	Tonnere	Langres	before 1075
Flacy	Sens	Sens	1079
Senan	Sens	Sens	1079
Vaucouleurs	Meuse	Toul	1081
Sèche-Fontaine	Lassois	Langres	1081
Radonvilliers	Brenois	Troyes	1081–1082
Louesme	Lassois	Langres	1083
Varennes	Langres	Langres	1084
Placy	Arcis	Troyes	1090
Bertignolles	Lassois	Langres	before 1090
Merrey	Lassois	Langres	before 1090
Bonne-Nouvelle	Roumois	Rouen	1090
Nancy	Port	Toul	1080–1090
St Quentin	Troyes	Troyes	before 1090
La Maison Dieu	Brie	Meaux	1093
Poissey	Pincerais	Chartres	before 1094
Nitry	Auxerre	Auxerre	1085–1095
Lucheux	Artois	Arras	1095
Cohem	Ternois	Thérouanne	1095
Montigny	Gatinais	Sens	1089–1096
St Aignan	Tonnerre	Langres	1089–1096
Nointel	Beaumont	Beauvais	1095–1096
Breuil-les-Commercy	Meuse	Toul	1096
Isle-Aumont	Troyes	Troyes	1097
Frolois	Duesmois	Autun	before 1098
Fouchères	Troyes	Troyes	before 1100
St Broin-les-Mains	Dijon	Langres	before 1100
Chambroncourt	Ornois	Toul	before 1100
Aube	Messis	Metz	before 1100
Lassicourt	Brenois	Troyes	1093–1100
Crisenon	Auxerre	Auxerre	before 1100
Buxereuilles-le-Chateaux	Bolenois	Langres	before 1100
Cirey-le-Chateaux	Barrois	Langres	before 1100

There was also, in 1097, the establishment of Aulps in the diocese of Geneva and, one year later, the foundation of Cîteaux, in the diocese of Châlon-sur-Sâone.[35]

35. J. Laurent, *op. cit.*, 1:208ff. Cf. also 1:3, 83, 126, 215, 224ff., 246f., 253ff., and 2:*passim*; E. Petit, *op. cit.*, 1:241f., CGh 4:730; PL 157:1259; S. Lenssen, *op. cit.*, 20f.; K. Hallinger, *op. cit.*, 2:758 and R. Graham, "The Relation of Cluny to Some Other Movements of Monastic Reform," *loc. cit.*, 193.

As the list of the monastic offices, the employment of the priory system, feudal involvements and some recorded contemporary monastic practices show, Molesme followed the Cluniac pattern in customs and organization. It may well be that Robert simply introduced the Clunaic practices of Tonnerre where he had stayed shortly before. An additional proof may be seen in the fact that the basic elements of the Cistercian reform were simply reactions to the Cluniac practices, for according to Ordericus Vitalis, the monks who were opposed to any change at Molesme argued:

> We have learned to preserve these rules from earlier monks who lived religiously, and we possess them as heirs to their order and profession. As long as we find the monks of Cluny and Tours (Marmoutier) and the other clergy maintaining these institutions, we shall not depart from them.[36]

Robert of Torigny, a Benedictine chronicler who died in 1186, similarly reports that the monks in question told their abbot:

> The customs observed by all the monasteries of the West are known to have been instituted by blessed Maur, the disciple of St Benedict, by blessed Columban, and—to come to the moderns —by St Odo, abbot of Cluny. They said that they could not abandon these customs.[37]

As in the case of traditional monachism, donations and foundations made contacts with the contemporary feudal world unavoidable. Accordingly Molesme, too, became the site of feudal gatherings. Its first cartulary actually mentions two such instances. On a Christmas Day, some time between 1081 and 1084, Odo I, duke of Burgundy, met with his barons at the monastery. His entourage included Anseric, the lord of Montreal; Miles of Chacenay, the lord of

---

36. *Historia Ecclesiastica*, III, viii, 25; PL 188:640. Cf. O. Ducourneau, *op. cit.*, 22f.; K. Hallinger, *op. cit.*, 2:846f.; R. Folz, "Le problème des origines de Cîteaux," *loc. cit.*, 286 and G. Müller, "Gründung der Abtei Cîteaux," *loc. cit.*, 38ff.

37. *De immutatione ordinis monachorum*, 1; PL 202:1309.

Grancey and his son Raynald; Bernard I, the lord of Montbard; Raynald of Chatillon, the seneschal of Burgundy; Hugh Godfrey, the lord of Duesme; and Aimon the Red of Chatillon.[38] A second reunion took place on April 5th, Easter Sunday, 1097, when Hugh, count of Troyes, arrived with his retinue. On this occasion he added to the donations made by his father, Theobald I, his mother Adelaide, and his brother count Odo III. Among the participants were Guy III, the lord of Vigny, and Dudo, the *vidame* of Châlons.[39]

The donations helped Molesme to wealth and prosperity which greatly affected its way of life. In the words of Robert's biographer, abundance in temporals led to discord, to vices and to a slowdown in things spiritual. Robert did not approve of a life based on riches; his aim was to live "in accordance with the institutes of St Benedict."[40] The situation therefore brought tensions and discord to the community. The abbot, seeing the futility of his efforts to end the disunion and fearing detrimental effects on his soul, left his monastery and joined a small, but fervent community of hermits at Aux, near Riel-les-Eaux.[41] This could only mean a temporary exodus—O. Ducourneau places it between the years 1090 and 1093[42]—for as abbot of Molesme he could not leave his monastery permanently, without formally renouncing his office, and making provisions for the election of a successor.

38. J. Laurent, *op. cit.*, 1:142 and 2:12.

39. *Ibid.*, 1:151. Cf. also 1:142 and 2:409 and 433.

40. *"Beatus autem Robertus cor suum divitiis affluentibus non apponens magis ac magis in Deum proficere conabatur, et secundum instituta sancti Benedicti iuste et pie et sobrie conversari."* K. Spahr, *Das Leben des hl. Robert*, 13. See also PL 157:1277; O. Ducourneau, *op. cit.*, 36; S. Lenssen, *op. cit.*, 15f.; W. Williams, *op. cit.*, 126f.; R. Folz, "Le problème des origines de Cîteaux," *loc. cit.*, 286

41. *"Orta igitur inter eos discordia recessit ab eis venitque ad locum qui vocatur Aux."* K. Spahr, *Das Leben des hl. Robert*, 14. Cf. *ibid.*, n. 3. See also AS, Apr. 3:671; PL 157:1277; J. Mabillon, *Annales*, 5:204 and 385; DOR 1:922; J. Laurent, *op. cit.*, 1:149 n. 9; O. Ducourneau, *op. cit.*, 36; W. Williams, *op. cit.*, 126; R. Folz, "Le problème des origines de Cîteaux," *loc. cit.*, 286 and Claude Courtépée, *Description générale et particulière du duché de Bourgogne* (Dijon: Frantin et Causse, 1775-1781), 7:197.

42. *Op. cit.*, 40.

At Aux Robert shared the life of the brethren. All worked with their own hands, prayed and kept constant vigils in their untiring service of God. In his biographer's description, Robert surpassed all others in virtue, but not at the expense of humility.[43] Not surprisingly then, he was elected abbot, or, perhaps, spiritual father of the group. As their leader he gave his special care to the weaker ones and encouraged the strong.[44]

Meanwhile the monks of Molesme began to feel the effects of Robert's departure. Filled with remorse for having offended Robert and realizing that their abbot's absence brought a substantial decrease in donations, a decline in monastic discipline and ruin to their economy, they appealed to papal authority to obtain Robert's return and thus remedy the situation. Their wish was granted, and Robert resumed his duties at Molesme.[45]

Back in his abbey, Robert is believed to have worked on the restoration of good order and regular life. In the wake of the latter came, once more, prosperity. The donation of churches, lands and the like resumed between 1094 and 1098, the year of Robert's next absence (in Cîteaux). At least nine priories and one abbey were set up under the auspices of Molesme or placed under its jurisdiction in this period. Hence, O. Ducourneau argues, the cause of Robert's secession to Aux could not have been a relaxation or lack of discipline. In S. Lenssen's view, things happened because Robert wished to introduce long-neglected but basic monastic practices—

---

43. *"Vixitque aliquamdiu inter eos laborans propriis manibus. . . . Vigiliis autem et orationibus incessanter insistens infatigabiliter Domino serviebat et cum in sanctitate cunctos excelleret omnibus serviens omnium se minimum reputabat."* K. Spahr, *Das Leben des hl. Robert*, 14.

44. Idem, *Das Leben des hl. Robert*, 14 and XLVI. Cf. also S. Lenssen, *op. cit.*, 8 n. 1.

45. K. Spahr, *Das Leben des hl. Robert*, XVII and 13ff. See also O. Ducourneau, *op. cit.*, 39; S. Lenssen, *op. cit.*, 27f.; J. Mahn, *op. cit.*, 41; J. Bouton, *op. cit.*, 51. The expression "papal authority" was used in the text, to avoid the difficulties caused by an all too frequent recourse to the Pope—Alexander II or Gregory VII—in Robert's *vita*. France had papal legates at this time, among them the great Hugh of Lyons, who were empowered to act with full authority.

such as manual labor—but did not succeed. Plausible as these views may be, they still do not give definite answers about the exact nature of Robert's difficulties.[46]

To the account of Robert's exodus to Aux his biographer adds the story of another secession, involving four monks advanced in the spiritual life, i.e., Alberic, Stephen Harding and two unnamed others, possibly John and Ilbode. "After learning the rudiments of claustral life, they longed for the singular battle of the desert." They left Molesme and retired to a place called Vivicus.[47] Modern historians give little credence to the report. In J. Laurent's view, there is no precise information in support of the historicity of the incident.[48] According to O. Ducourneau, the story is simply an invention.[49] For the secession—if it took place at all—was not the outcome of the violence done to Alberic as reported by the *Exordium Parvum*, but undertaken in search of eremitic life. Moreover, Alberic suffered hardships and beatings not in the early 1090's, but, according to the *Vita* (so it seems), after Robert's return from Aux. In any case it was in relation with the foundation of Cîteaux.[50] The *Vita Roberti* also informs us that the four remained

---

46. S. Lenssen, *op. cit.*, 27f. Cf. also J. Mabillon, *op. cit.*, 5:86; PL 157:1260; J. Laurent, *op. cit.*, 1:150 and 217ff.; K. Spahr, *Das Leben des hl. Robert*, 15; O. Ducourneau, *op. cit.*, 39f.

47. "*Erant autem inter illos quatuor viri spiritu fortiores, scilicet Albericus et Stephanus et alii duo, qui post claustralis exercitii rudimenta ad singulare certamen heremi suspirabant. Egressi igitur de monasterio Molismensi venerunt ad locum cui Vivicus nomen est.*" K. Spahr, *Das Leben des hl. Robert*, 15 and XLVI. A. Manrique mentions Peña's conjecture that the two unnamed brethren were Odo and John; *op. cit.*, 1:5. According to S. Lenssen, they may have been John and Ilbode who went to Pope Paschal to secure the *Roman Privilege; op. cit.*, 8 n. 1. See also AS, Apr. 3:671; J. Mabillon, *op. cit.*, 5:219; PL 157: 1260; DOR 1:925; J. Laurent, *op. cit.*, 1:149; O. Ducourneau, *op. cit.*, 50ff.; W. Williams, *op. cit.*, 128; W. Parker Mason, "The Beginnings of the Cistercian Order," *loc. cit.*, 173 n. 1; U. Berlière, "Les origines de l'Ordre de Cîteaux," *loc. cit.*, 450; G. Müller, "Gründung der Abtei Cîteaux," *loc. cit.*, 46 and H. DeWarren, "Le monachisme à l'apparition de saint Bernard," *loc. cit.*, 61.

48. *Op. cit.*, 1:223. Cf. K. Spahr, *Das Leben des hl. Robert*, XLVI.

49. O. Ducourneau, *op. cit.*, 51.

50. *Exordium Parvum*, IX; J. Van Damme, *op. cit.*, 10. Cf. O. Ducourneau, *op. cit.*, 50ff.

R

at Vivicus "for some time." Hypothetically speaking, this could mean from three to four years at the most, for in the convention drawn up in 1097 between Molesme and the newly established abbey of Aulps Alberic and Stephen Harding are explicitly mentioned.[51] In the biographer's account, the venture came to an end when, urged on by the monks of Molesme, the bishop of Langres threatened them with excommunication unless they returned to their abbey. "Compelled therefore to leave their place, they moved on to a certain forest which the neighboring population called *Cistercium*," the biographer added.[52] This information too is of a doubtful value. For the convention of 1097 clearly proves that Alberic and Stephen were at Molesme shortly before the establishment of Cîteaux. O. Ducourneau therefore concludes:

> This point of history remains rather obscure; one cannot absolutely prove its falseness, but there are good reasons for supposing that Alberic's and Stephen's exodus to Vivicus was a product of the imagination, to serve as a basis for the false representation of the Molesme tradition about the Cistercian origins, propagated among other Benedictines from the end of the twelfth century onward.[53]

In the meantime, while proclaiming at Clermont in 1095 a crusade to free the Holy Land from the Turks, Pope Urban II issued a bull of confirmation and papal protection for the abbey of Molesme, the first of its kind. Its provisions, while safeguarding the rights of

---

51. K. Spahr, *Das Leben des hl. Robert*, 15. On Aulps, see *below* nn. 57, 58 and 59.

52. "Quem [*locum, i.e., Vivicum*] *cum aliquanto tempore incoluissent, ad instantiam Molismensium a viro venerabili Joceranno Lingonensi episcopo, nisi reverterentur excommunicationis sententiam susceperunt. Compulsi ergo praefatum locum relinquere, venerunt ad quamdam silvam Cistercium ab incolis nuncupatam.*" K. Spahr, *Das Leben des hl. Robert*, 15. In connection with the reference to Jocerannus, K. Spahr remarks, "Not so, he was bishop of Langres 1113–1115; Gams 558." *Ibid.*, 15 n. 7.

53. O. Ducourneau, *op. cit.*, 51f.

the bishop of Langres, placed the monastery under apostolic protection, confirmed its holdings, and promised effective sanctions against anyone molesting it or doing violence to its possessions.[54]

With regard to regular life, the Pope ordained that no fraud or violence should be tolerated in the election of the abbot; it should rather be the outcome of a consensus or else the wish of the more mature part of the community. It must always be inspired by the fear of God and the ideals of the Rule of St Benedict. The person thus elected must then be blessed by the local ordinary, the bishop of Langres. Also, Urban II urged the monks to be faithful to their religious vocation:

> Therefore, Beloved Sons in Christ, always seek to have the fear and the love of God in your hearts, that the freer you are from the

---

54. "*Tam tuis et tuorum fratrum quam et reverendi fratris nostri Roberti Lingonensis episcopi postulationibus inclinati, coenobium Molismense, cui Deo auctore preesse dinosceris, per presentis decreti paginam sub tutelam apostolice sedis excipimus, salvo Lingonensis ecclesie jure et legitima defensione* . . . . *Apostolica auctoritate statuimus ut quicquid eidem cenobio supradictus episcopus vel ejus pre/de/cessor Rainardus contulerunt, et quecumque hodie juste possidet, sive in futurum concessione pontificum, liberalitate principum vel oblatione fidelium juste atque canonice poterit adipisci, firma tibi tuisque successoribus et illibata permaneant* . . . . *Decernimus ergo ut nulli hominum liceat eandem ecclesiam temere perturbare aut ejus possessiones auferre vel ablatas retinere, minuere vel temerariis vexationibus fatigare, sed omnia integra conserventur eorum pro quorum sustentatione et gubernatione concessa sunt usibus omnimodis profutura, salvo scilicet in omnibus jure et subjectione Lingonensis ecclesiae: ita tamen ut episcopo non liceat exactionis vel consuetudinis gravamen aliquod fratribus irrogare* . . . . . *Donationem illam, quam eidem monasterio bone memorie Rainardus et ejus successor Robertus, Lingonenses episcopi, consilio et assensu canonicorum suorum concesserunt, nos quoque presenti decreto firmamus, videlicet, ut quicumque clericus, quicumque Lingonensis ecclesie casatus cenobio vestro sive ecclesiam seu aliquid de casamento suo contulerit, salvis nimirum consuetudinariis episcopi redditionibus, monachis liceat optinere* . . . . *Si quis in crastinum archiepiscopus aut episcopus, imperator aut rex, dux, comes, vicecomes, judex aut ecclesiastica quelibet secularisve persona hanc nostre constitutionis paginam sciens contra eam temere venire temptaverit, secundo tertiove commonita si non satisfactione congrua emendaverit, potestatis honorisque sui dignitate careat reamque se divino judicio existere de perpetrata iniquitate cognoscat, et a sacratissimo corpore et sanguine Dei et domini Redemptoris nostri Jhesu Xristi aliena fiat, atque in extremo examine divine ultioni subjaceat.*" J. Laurent, *op. cit.*, 2:3f. Cf. also *ibid.*, 1:1 and 151, and J. Bouton, *op. cit.*, 53.

tumult of the world the better you strive to please God with every faculty of your mind and soul.⁵⁵

The document was issued "at Clermont, in the Auvergne . . . on November 29th, AD 1095, in the eighth year of Pope Urban II's pontificate."⁵⁶

A short time later, Molesme made Aulps, one of its cells in the diocese of Geneva, founded around 1090 by Guido and Guarinus, an abbey. On this occasion a convention was drawn up between Molesme and the monks of Aulps. Mentioned among the participants are Robert, the abbot of Molesme, Guido, the new abbot of Aulps, Alberic, the prior of Molesme, Ado, Walter, Hercelin, and Stephen, the secretary of Molesme, "by whose hand the deed was drawn up." The most important part of the document reads:

> Since the lands and tenements [of Aulps] had been given to our monastery some time ago and subjected to it as a cell, the brethren of that place, inspired by God, adhering more strictly to the precepts of our father St Benedict, heartened by the counsel of some religious, and enlightened by the authority of the same Rule, asked that we give them an abbot . . . . This was defined by the lord Robert, first abbot of Molesme, in the presence of . . . Alberic, the prior of Molesme . . . and the monk Stephen, by whose hand the deed was drawn up.⁵⁷

55. *"Nullus ibi qualibet surreptionis astutia seu violentia preponatur, nisi quem fratres communi consensu vel fratrum pars consilii sanioris secundum timorem Dei et beati Benedicti regulam elegerint. Electus autem a Lingonensi episcopo consecretur . . . . Vos igitur, filii in Xristo dilecti, Dei semper timorem et amorem in vestris cordibus habere satagite, ut quanto a secularibus tumultibus liberiores estis, tanto amplius placere Deo totis mentis et anime virtutibus haneletis [sic.]."* J. Laurent, *op. cit.*, 2:4.

56. *"Datum apud Clarum Montem Arvennie per manum Johannis sancte R. ecclesie diaconi cardinalis, III. kalendas decembris, indictione IIIa, anno dominice Incarnationis M°. XC° VI°., pontificatus autem domni Urbani secundi pape VIII°."* J. Laurent, *op. cit.*, 2:4.

57. *"Cum scilicet fundus ille olim nostre ecclesie collatus et per omnia subditus ut cella fuerit ipsius loci fratres, Deo inspirante sancti patris nostri Benedicti preceptis arcius inherentes, quorumdam religiosorum consilio animati, ipsius etiam regule auctoritate edocti, abbatem sibi a nobis donari petierunt. In qua peticione suppliciter in nostro capitulo perseverantibus, sic tandem annuimus, et ejusdem loci abbate obeunte, sicut hic primus, ita omnes ejus successores, a nostro loco expetiti atque collati, ₅uscipientes illius loci curam a nostro abbate ibidem substituatur. Eundem quoque abbatem nostrum, Molismensem scilicet, dum illuc venire contigerit, omnis ei*

The agreement, as can be seen, contains four basic provisions. (1) The monks of Aulps wished to observe the rule of St Benedict more strictly (*arcius*). (2) They turned to Abbot Robert, since Aulps was a dependency of Molesme. (3) They were encouraged in their resolve by some monks of Molesme. And, (4) they obtained Robert's agreement that Aulps become the daughter-abbey of Molesme.

Worthy of note is also the fact that all the prime movers of the Cistercian reform—Robert, Alberic, and Stephen—were present at this gathering. And what is more, the same principle—"to adhere more strictly to the precepts of our father, St Benedict"—guided both the erection of Aulps into an abbey and the foundation of the new monastery of Cîteaux. Last but not least, the same person is in charge on both occasions. It was Robert who authorized the elevation of Aulps, just as he was also in charge when Cîteaux was established.[58]

The document was drafted "in the ninth year of . . . Pope Urban II's pontificate." Since Urban's tenth year began on March 12th,

---

reverentia tam in sede quam in justiciis regulariter tamen peragendis exhibebitur. Si vero, quod absit! inter illos fratres ac suum abbatem discordie malum irresperit, ad hoc examinandum vel pacificandum noster abbas, non alia quelibet persona, advocabitur. Id quoque statutum est ut frater quilibet loci illius in aliquo scandalizatus ad nos confugerit vel de nostris quispiam ad eos itidem facere pertemptaverit, sine proprii abbatis permissu minime suscipiatur. Quod si forte illi fratres, quod Deus avertat! ab ipsa, quam arripuerunt, districtione ad usus secularium revertentes apostataverint, pristino more nobis ut cella locus ille restituetur. Diffinitum est hoc a domno Roberto Molismensium abbate primo in presentia subscriptorum, domni scilicet Widonis in eodem loco primitus in abbatem constituti, Alberici Molismensis prioris, Ade monachi, Walterii monachi, Liescelini mon., Stephani quoque mon. per cujus manum scriptum est." Abbatiae Alpensis Creatio, J. Van Damme, *op. cit.*, 3. Cf. also J. Mabillon, *Annales*, 5:663; GCh 4:730; PL 182:459; J. Laurent, *op. cit.*, 1:4, 7f., 151 and 112:7f.; W. Parker Mason, "The Beginnings of the Cistercian Order," *loc. cit.*, 175; *Aux sources de la vie cartusienne*, 138f.; G. Müller, "Gründung der Abtei Cîteaux," *loc. cit.*, 37; U. Berlière, "Les origines de l'Ordre de Cîteaux, *loc. cit.*, 449; Jean A. Lefèvre, "Que savons-nous du Cîteaux primitif?" *Revue d'Histoire Ecclésiastique*, 51 (1956), 19 and Charles Dereine, "La fondation de Cîteaux d'après l'Exordium Cistercii et l'Exordium Parvum," *Cîteaux*, 10 (1959), 147.

58. J. Lefèvre, "Que savons-nous du Cîteaux primitif?," *loc. cit.*, 19f. Cf. idem, "S. Robert de Molesme dans l'opinion monastique du XIIe et du XIIIe siècles," *loc. cit.*, 70. See also J. Laurent, *op. cit.*, 2:8, 1:7f. and S. Lenssen, *op. cit.*, 28.

1097, it must have been issued between this date and March 12th, 1096.[59]

The convention drawn up between Molesme and Aulps seems to indicate that the situation improved at Molesme after the abbot's return from Aux. This is also what Robert's biographer relates. "Given over to constant fasts and prayers—he writes—Robert was jealous for his charges with a divine jealousy, so that he reformed monastic discipline within a short time."[60] But not everyone was satisfied and, as a result of it, tensions remained. In need of help, Robert, Alberic, and the monks Odo, John, Stephen, Letald, and Peter—when traveling, the abbot was usually accompanied by a number of religious who could act as his chaplain, notary, chamberlain, etc.—personally journeyed to the papal legate, archbishop Hugh of Lyons. As they readily admitted, their problem centered around the manner of observing the Rule of St Benedict. They acknowledged that "in view of several hindering causes" they followed the Rule "poorly and neglectfully." Yet their ideal was to serve God "according to the Rule of St Benedict," not in the traditional manner, but "more strictly and more perfectly."[61] According to the *Exordium Magnum*, a longer account of the Cistercian origins written by Conrad of Eberbach and published after 1186, their concern was for "religious renewal," i.e., the restoration of a life based on a full-scale observance of the Rule of

---

59. "*Actum est hoc anno ab incarnatione Domini millesimo XCVII., indictione IIII, pontificatus domni Urbani secundi pape anno nono.*" J. Van Damme, *op. cit.*, 3. Cf. also J. Laurent, *op. cit.*, 2:8; J. Lefèvre, "S. Robert de Molesme dans l'opinion monastique," *loc. cit.*, 69; and J. Mabillon, *Annales*, 5:360.

60. "*Ieiuniis et orationibus incessanter intentus, emulatione Dei emulabatur subjectos sibi, ut in brevi observantiam in eis discipline monastice reformaret.*" K. Spahr, *Das Leben des hl. Robert*, 15.

61. This is evident from the legate's letter (written as a result of the encounter) in which he states, "*Notum sit omnibus . . . vos . . . molismensis cenobii fratres lugduni in nostra presentia astitisse ac regule beatissimi Benedicti quam illuc hucusque tepide ac negligenter in monasterio tenueratis arcius deinceps atque perfectius inherere velle professos fuisse. Quod . . . in loco predicto pluribus impedientibus causis constat adimpleri non posse.*" *Exordium Parvum*, II; J. Van Damme, *op. cit.*, 6. Cf. also J. Bouton, *op. cit.*, 53; R. Folz, "Le problème des origines de Cîteaux," *loc. cit.*, 289; D. Knowles, *The Monastic Order*, 209 and R. Duvernay, "Cîteaux, Vallombreuse et Etienne Harding," *loc. cit.*, 459.

St Benedict. For there existed a conflict between the Rule which they vowed to observe and their daily religious practices, a conflict which caused them fears of perjury.[62]

Such aspirations, however, threatened the internal stability of the monastery. As the legate was well aware, they could not be carried out peacefully at Molesme. Anxious to provide for the welfare of both parties, Hugh refrained from condemning those who favored the *status quo*. He saw the best solution in the establishment of two separate communities and issued a decree in this sense. He urged Robert and his companions "to persevere in their holy endeavor" and to leave Molesme with "others who properly and by likeminded consent have decided to join them." Divine Providence would point out a place for them where they will be able to serve the Lord "in a more wholesome manner." He made his decision official by attaching his seal to the document drawn up as a result of the meeting and thus provided the legal basis for a secession from Molesme.[63]

62. *Exordium Magnum*, XI; Bruno Griesser, *Exordium Magnum Cisterciense sive Narratio de initio Cisterciensis Ordinis auctore Conrado monacho Claravallensi postea Eberbacensi ibidemque abbate* (Romae: Editiones Cistercienses, 1961), 63. This is the critical edition of the *Exordium Magnum*.

63. "*Nos utriusque partis saluti, videlicet inde recedentium atque illic remanentium, providentes, in locum alium quem vobis largitas divina designaverit vos declinare, ibique salubrius atque perfectius domino famulari, utile decrevimus fore. Vobis ergo tunc presentibus Roberto abbati, fratribus quoque alberico, odoni, ioanni, stephano, letaldo, et petro, sed et omnibus quos regulariter et communi consilio vobis sociare decreveritis hoc sanctum propositum servare, et tunc consuluimus, et ut in hoc perseveretis precipimus, et auctoritate apostolice sedis per sigilli nostri impressionem in perpetuum confirmamus.*" *Exordium Parvum*, II; J. Van Damme, *op. cit.*, 6. Cf. also A. Cooke, "A Study in Twelfth Century Religious Revival and Reform," *loc. cit.*, 149.—This journey was not a unique contemporary occurrence, for we read in the life of Wederic, an itinerant preacher in Flanders and Brabant, that he and his followers "*magistrum pauperum pauperes sequuti sunt . . . arctioris vitae desiderio aestuantes.*" They eventually went to Anno, bishop of Cologne: "*absque mora Coloniam properantes, ad episcopum proveniunt, prioris vitae suae statum detestabliem per humilem confessionem aperiunt, ac deinde poenitentiae remedium secundum ipsius exquirunt arbitrium.*" Returning from Cologne, "*locum quemdam desertum, Afflegem dictum . . . anno videlicet incarnationis dominicae millesimo octuagesimo tertio convenerunt . . . . Illam terram desertam excolere coeperunt.*" PL 166:815.

Expressions like "we *then* advised" and "*then* present" in Hugh's letter suggest the possibility of either more than one trip to the archbishop, or the lapse of several days between the conversation and the issuance of the legatine decree.[64]

It may be asked here, why did Robert go to the papal legate when the local ordinary's authorization would have sufficed for a secession. According to W. Lühe, the "reformers" approached the papal legate—a man commanding respect on account of his religious zeal, prudence and determination"—only after Robert of Langres recoiled from dividing the community.[65] Thinking along similar lines, S. Lenssen moreover felt that such an action was dictated by prudence, since earlier Robert had taken charge of Collan and returned from Aux to Molesme upon the intervention of the highest ecclesiastical authority.[66]

Commenting on the legate's action A. Fliche writes:

> The intervention of the papal legate is worthy of note, for it proves that the papacy, the protectress of Cluny, did not discourage those who wished to separate themselves from it in order to lead a life of seclusion. It felt that there is room for both, for the rich Cluniac abbeys and for monasteries that did not want possessions. For both were able to contribute to the great work of reform which was the sole program of the papacy.[67]

What were the obstacles in the way to a better observance of the Benedictine Rule, alluded to, but not specified, by the legate? Authors of the seventeenth century, like C. Henriquez, A. Manrique and P. Le Nain believed that Molesme had become rich and decadent as a result of all the donations it had accepted. Hence they

---

64. G. Müller, "Gründung der Abtei Cîteaux," *loc. cit.*, 67. See also O. Ducourneau, *op. cit.*, 46 and R. Folz, "Le problème des origines de Cîteaux," *loc. cit.*, 289.

65. W. Lühe, *op. cit.*, 116.

66. *Op. cit.*, 38 n. 1. Cf. GCh 10:67; W. Parker Mason, "The Beginnings of the Cistercian Order," *loc. cit.*, 172 n. 4 and 177 and G. Müller, "Gründung der Abtei Cîteaux," *loc. cit.*, 67.

67. A. Fliche, *Le règne de Philippe Ier*, 467.

spoke of corruption, license, the disappearance of Benedictine regularity, and laxity.[68] More recent historians, however, strongly challenge such views. For abundance and even opulence do not automatically imply a relaxation of monastic discipline. In addition, there is no indication whatsoever of any aberration. In fact, J. Laurent, the editor of its cartulary, called Molesme "a model monastery," just as J. Mabillon before him stressed its fame under St Robert. Nor can it be said that while Robert's own renown spread, discipline sank to a low ebb in his monastery, for this would surely be a reflection on the abbot's personality as well. It may also be asked, how could a fervent community have declined in such a short time without any responsibility on the part of its abbot? Then, it must equally be considered that the founders of Aulps, Guarinus and Guido, turned to Molesme for recruits, and when Aulps became an abbey it wished to retain its allegiance to Molesme. Also, a community which included an impressive number of saintly men, like Robert, Alberic, Stephen Harding, Guarinus, and Stephen's friend Pro—the latter, it should be noted, remained at Molesme— and in which twenty-one religious opted for a more demanding life at Cîteaux, cannot simply be branded a place of corruption. This not even after the secession of its more fervent element to Cîteaux, for Molesme's sanctity continued to be attested by its contemporaries, among them by the early Cistercians who, one might think, would have listed deviations and precautions in their early statutes, if only by way of self-justification.[69]

68. A. Manrique, *op. cit.*, 1:6; PL 157:1259; U. Berlière, *L'ordre monastique dès origines au XIIe siècle*, 266; O. Ducourneau, *op. cit.*, 36 n. 2; S. Lenssen, *op. cit.*, 12ff.; C. Dereine, "Odon de Tournai et la crise du cénobitisme au XIe siècle," *loc. cit.*, 153.

69. *Exordium Parvum*, XII and *Exordium Cistercii*, I; J. Van Damme, *op. cit.*, 11 and 21. Cf. GCh 4:731; J. Mabillon, *op. cit.*, 5:414; PL 188:640; PL 202: 528, 599f., 601; MCH, SS 6:463; RHF 12:467, 13:459 and 673; J. Laurent *op. cit.*, 1:203, 254, 2:170, 262; O. Ducourneau, *op. cit.*, 43; A. Fliche, *Le règne de Philippe Ier*, 466; W. Williams, *op. cit.*, 127; S. Lenssen, *op. cit.*, 13, 16ff.; J. Bouton, *op. cit.*, 51; R. Folz. "Le problème des origines de Cîteaux," 288; *Aux sources de la vie cartusienne*, 114; J. Lefèvre, "Que savons-nous du Cîteaux primitif?," *loc. cit.*, 7; C. Dereine, "Odon de Tournai et la crise du cénobitisme au XIe siècle," *loc. cit.*, 153.

Yet, we know from Archbishop Hugh's letter that all was not quiet at Molesme and that efforts to introduce a more demanding observance were doomed to failure. This is also evident from Pope Urban's letter in which he told his legate that he learned from the brethren of Molesme that religious life had been upset in their monastery on account of Robert's departure to Cîteaux. The monks of Molesme spoke in similar terms when informing Hugh of Lyons that without Robert's return from Cîteaux they saw no possibility of restoring monastic life to its former state. Finally, one could also argue that the prevalence of great fervor would hardly have occasioned an exodus from Molesme. All this leads to the conclusion: while Molesme was no place of corruption, things were not perfect, in spite of the monastery's fame and its abbot's sanctity. If there is a fervent community, the secession of its abbot and of a number of monks does not, ordinarily, create turbulent conditions. Religious life, while not decadent, left room for improvements. In his letter to Pope Paschal II, Hugh of Lyons further specified this point, by stating: "In the observance of his (St Benedict's) Rule they have resolved to abandon the usages of certain monasteries."[70]

Riches, even if it brought no decadence to Molesme, still placed limits on monastic life. For one thing, it eliminated opportunities to practice greater fervor. In its early days Molesme had known poverty, manual labor and strict asceticism; now, as a result of seignorial munificence, poverty lost its original appeal and became practically impossible to observe. This in turn slighted the role of manual labor which ceased to be a necessity. As Robert of

70. *Exordium Parvum*, XII; J. Van Damme, *op. cit.*, 11. Cf. chs. II, VI and VII; *ibid.*, 6, 8f.—G. Coulton's remarks in this connection deserve to be quoted in full, "The abbey of Molesme, in Burgundy, was a great and respectable house; having made its mark, it had become rich and populous. There is no reason to suppose that it was below the average of other great houses; it was pretty certainly far above the average of the tiny 'cells' among which the monastic population was too often dispersed and which St Bernard frankly characterized as 'synagogues of Satan.' " Reference is made to St Bernard's *ep.* 78 and *ep.* 254, PL 182:191ff. and 459ff. See also S. Lenssen, *op. cit.*, 20 and A. Fliche, *op. cit.*, 8:449f.

Torigny stated: "Robert, scrutinizing the Rule of St Benedict to the letter, wished to persuade his monks that they should live from the labor of their hands."[71]

Also, as a popular recipient of donations, Molesme had accepted lands, churches, revenues from altars, tithes, villages, serfs and the like. Thus by 1098 it had some three dozen priories, manors, cells and even priories of women. But this ran counter to the contemporary ecclesiastical and monastic ideology of renewal which sought to eliminate contacts with and obligations to the feudal world of the eleventh century. Mention has already been made of how, in return for donations, feudal lords, *familiares, praebendarii*, pensioners, children and others were accepted by Molesme in a more or less convenient arrangement of a *quid pro quo*. It is true, of course, that in those days a monastery could hardly exist without generous patrons, usually blood relatives or feudal and other allies. These—i.e., kinsmen and allies—furnished, for instance, the main contingent of the monastic community of Molesme. But, as a rule, these noble lords—not always young in age—were hardly used to a disciplined and well-organized life; consequently, they showed little appreciation and docility in the field of obedience. Used to a life of ruling others, they joined the monastery with preconvinced attitudes so that they found it difficult to reconcile monastic discipline and abbatial rule with their impetuous, intemperate and domineering spirit. Since they, as a rule, brought gifts in exchange for their acceptance by the monastery, arrangements had to be made with them, with the result that Molesme developed more and more intimate bonds with the contemporary feudal world.[72] In the words of J. Laurent:

---

71. "*Robertus abbas . . . Regulam sancti Benedicti perscrutatus ad litteram, voluit persuadere discipulis suis ut labore manuum suarum viverent.*" *De immutatione ordinis monachorum*, I; PL 202:1309. Cf. also E. Petit, *op. cit.*, 1:41; U. Berlière, "L'ordre monastique dès origines au XIIe siècle," *loc. cit.*, 266; *idem*, "L'étude des réformes monastiques des Xe et XIe siècles," *loc. cit.*, 215 and R. Folz, "Le problème des origines de Cîteaux," *loc. cit.*, 286.

72. According to the editor of its cartulary, Molesme "offers a nearly continuous hospitality to the great and lesser lords of the region who all have relatives and friends at Molesme and by their noisy presence time and

Molesme took an active part in the private events of the feudal world; it even witnessed some manifestations of its public life. Our charters have transmitted to us the memory of four or five feudal courts held at the abbey between . . . 1081 and 1104 . . . under the . . . first abbot. There were also others.[73]

It is obvious, therefore, the same author goes on to say, that the benefactors of Molesme saw its *raison d'être* and its role in a completely different light than those of its monks who labored for a monastic renewal. In their mind the monastery's obvious function was to satisfy certain needs of contemporary society, and the rich lands of which they deprived themselves in favor of Molesme were intended to be in support of this social mission.[74]

According to G. Schreiber, Robert and his companions seceded from Molesme largely for this reason: they had enough of the feudalism of Molesme's and the Benedictines' *Eigenkirche* policy. In this connection the author remarks:

> It may be presumed that Stephen Harding, who left Molesme with Robert, perceived the dangers of the proprietary system even more clearly. For this future abbot of Cîteaux . . . was in all

---

again disrupt the peace and solitude which is the appanage of a place of prayer and recollection." J. Laurent, *op. cit.*, 1:113. Cf. also 1:118, 130, 148, 208ff. and 2: *passim*; E. Petit, *op. cit.*, 1:244f., 247; M. Dmitrewski, *op. cit.*, 73; S. Lenssen, *op. cit.*, 20ff.; J. Bouton, *op. cit.*, 50f.; K. Hallinger, *op. cit.*, 2:756; U. Berlière, *L'ordre monastique dès origines au XIIe siècle*, 266; idem, "L'étude des réformes monastiques des Xe et XIe siècles," *loc. cit.*, 450 and G. Müller, "Gründung der Abtei Cîteaux," *loc. cit.*, 36.

73. *Op. cit.*, 1:141.

74. J. Laurent writes in this connection, "From the outset, the regional feudal world treats the abbey as a collective foundation. By widely opening its doors, it [Molesme] acquaints them with the demands of the moral order, it makes them partners of its interests, of its whole life. Soon it sees knights renounce the world, hasten to it, and join the order of St Benedict or else end their days in a secular habit with a prebend that will shield them against the uncertainty of their personal resources; soon it even welcomes women anxious to live under the discipline of the famous Abbot Robert." *Op. cit.*, 1:113. Cf. E. Petit, *op. cit.*, 1:244; O. Ducourneau, *op. cit.*, 35f. and S. Lenssen, *op. cit.*, 21f.

likelihood by far the intellectual superior of the two. He had, in addition, the great organizational talent of the Anglo-Saxon.[75]

To understand such statements one must know that the Lingonie had been the citadel of the proprietary system and that Molesme was one of the most notable names connected with it. Cluniac in its organization, it had more churches and chapels than other well-known monasteries. Hence the reason for Robert's and his companions' departure from Molesme was simply to found a *different* monastery in the solitude of Cîteaux. As G. Schreiber concluded, "The spirit of the time had changed. The ideal of poverty asserted once more its creative force."[76]

This spirit generated or furthered the desire in some monks to observe the rule of St Benedict more perfectly in the monastery of Molesme. The great question however was not—as K. Spahr has demonstrated in opposition to practically all modern historians[77]— whether the Rule should be observed literally, but simply, whether Molesme should continue to follow the usages of Cluny.[78] For some of the more enlightened members of the community, imbued with the contemporary spirit of renewal, had come to favor an observance of the Rule in its—what they considered—basic demands. This is evident, for instance, from the cartulary of Molesme where the Rule of St Benedict is not mentioned in the

75. *Gemeinschaften des Mittelalters*, 199 n. 182.

76. *Ibid.*, 199 and 198. See also J. Laurent, *op. cit.*, 1:111, 146 and 2:353.

77. "Die Regelauslegung im Neukloster," *Festschrift zum 800-Jahrgedächtnis Bernhards von Clairvaux* (Wien: Verlag Herold, 1953), 22ff. Cf. O. Ducourneau, *op. cit.*, 42f.; R. Folz, "Le problème des origines de Cîteaux," *loc. cit.*, 287; A. Cooke, "The Settlement of the Cistercians in England," *English Historical Review*, 8 (1893), 626f.; U. Berlière, "Les origines de l'Ordre de Cîteaux," *loc. cit.*, 449; and *idem*, "L'étude des réformes monastiques des Xe et XIe siècles," *loc. cit.*, 216 on literalism. It must also be noted, however, that Benedict II, abbot of Chiusa and former monk of Carcassonne, insisted in his reform endeavors on a literal observance of the Benedictine Rule. PL 150: 1459ff., and DHE 8:200ff.

78. O. Ducourneau, *op. cit.*, 38; J. Bouton, *op. cit.*, 50; R. Folz, "Le problème des origines de Cîteaux," *loc. cit.*, 288; *Aux sources de la vie cartusienne*, 114 See also *above*, n. 36.

early documents, while it figures well in later donations.[79] It is also clear from the *Exordium Cistercii*—a possibly earlier Cistercian document than the so-called *Exordium Parvum*—according to which "men of great wisdom and insight had come to the realization that although life was holy and honorable at Molesme, they nevertheless observed the Rule which they had vowed to keep, to a lesser degree than was their desire and intention."[80] Moreover in his already cited letter, Hugh of Lyons recalled the admission of some of the brethren that the Rule of St Benedict had not been observed wholeheartedly and in every respect. In another letter, to Pope Paschal II, the archbishop further elaborated this point by stating that the Cistercian pioneers had left Molesme, "to lead a more rigorous and secluded life, following the Rule of St Benedict."[81] According to the Cistercian Caesarius of Heisterbach (d. 1240), "although they lived honorably in the said monastery [of Molesme], they did not sufficiently observe the Rule which they had professed [to observe]."[82] Even more specific is the *Exordium Magnum* when telling us:

> When the servants of God, hearing the daily readings of the Rule in the chapter room, came to see that the Rule prescribed one thing and the practices of the order called for something else,

79. J. Laurent, *op. cit.*, 1:200 and J. Bouton, *op. cit.*, 50.

80. "*Viri nimirum sapientes altius intelligentes, elegerunt pocius studiis celestibus occupari quam terrenis implicari negociis . . . simulque advertentes ibidem etsi sancte honesteque viveretur, minus tamen pro sui desiderio atque proposito ipsam quam professi fuerant regulam observari.*" *Exordium Cistercii*, I; J. Van Damme, *op. cit.*, 21. See also J. Lefèvre, "Que savons-nous du Cîteaux primitif?," *loc. cit.*, 7: "The Exordium Cistercii of 1119 is, chronologically, our earliest account about the Cistercian origins."

81. *Exordium Parvum*, XII; J. Van Damme, *op. cit.*, 11. Cf. also ch. 2, *ibid.*, 6 and D. Knowles, *The Monastic Order in England*, 209.

82. "*Quia divitiis virtutibusque diuturna non potest esse societas, viri nimirum sapientes et virtutum amatores, altius intelligentes, licet honeste in praefecto coenobio viverent, minus tamen ipsam quam professi fuerant regulam qualiter observant consiterantes.*" Caesarius Heisterbacensis, *Dialogus miraculorum* (Coloniae: J. M. Heberle, 1851), 1:1. See also Caesarius of Heisterbach, *The Dialogue on Miracles*, translated by H. V. E. Scott and C. C. Swinton Bland (London: George Rutledge & Sons, Ltd., 1929), 1:5f.; and W. Williams, *op. cit.*, 127.

they were greatly saddened realizing that they and the other monks had vowed to observe the Rule of [their] father Benedict by solemn profession, but that they did by no means live in accordance with his institutes.[83]

In their desire to observe the Rule more integrally, these monks "began to concentrate their thoughts on poverty which produces virtues."[84] Realizing that their monastery had been greatly blessed with possessions, and convinced that material wealth is not, as a rule, a regular companion of uprightness, they wished to devote themselves to heavenly matters rather than be implicated in the affairs of the world. Besides seeking a life of real poverty, they also wished to live "from the work of their hands, as the Rule prescribes," as Caesarius of Heisterbach tells us.[85] According to the *Exordium Magnum*, "with their beloved father Benedict, they preferred to be worn out by work rather than feel the relaxation induced by the comforts of this world."[86]

Convinced of the need of leading a life in strict accordance with the Rule of St Benedict, a life based on poverty, work and prayer, Robert set out to influence others in the same sense. His arguments, given in a talk addressed to the community, are recorded by Ordericus Vitalis. While the address itself may well be a product of Ordericus' imagination, it nonetheless expresses the basic points at issue.[87] Thus, according to Ordericus Vitalis:

> [Robert] studied carefully the Rule of St Benedict, and having also examined the writings of other holy fathers, he assembled the brethren, and thus addressed them: "My dear brethren, we

---

83. *"Servi Dei . . . dum cotidianas regulae lectiones in capitulo audirent et aliud regulam praecipere atque aliud consuetudines ordinis tenere perpenderent gravissime contristabantur videntes se ceterosque monachos regulam beati patris Benedicti solemni professione servaturos fore promisisse, sed secundum instituta eius nequaquam vivere."* Exordium Magnum, X; B. Griesser, *op. cit.*, 62.

84. *"De paupertate fecunda virorum cogitate ceperunt."* Exordium Cistercii, I; J. Van Damme, *op. cit.*, 21.

85. *"De opere manuum suarum, secundum Regulae praeceptum;"* Caesarius of Heisterbach, *op. cit.*, 1:1.

86. *"Malentes cum dilecto patre suo Benedicto pro Deo laboribus fatigari quam vitae huius commodis resolvi."* Exordium Magnum, XIII; B. Griesser, *op. cit.*, 64.

87. R. Folz, "Le problème des origines de Cîteaux," *loc. cit.*, 287.

have made our profession according to the Rule of St Benedict, but it appears to me that we do not observe it in its integrity. We follow many practices which are not found there, and we negligently omit many which it has enjoined. We do not labor with our hands as we read that the holy fathers did. If you do not believe what I say, my friends, read the acts of St Anthony, Macarius, Pachomius, and, above all, of the Doctor of the Gentiles, Paul the Apostle. We are supplied with an abundant maintenance in food and clothing from the tithes and obligations of the churches, and, either by address or violence, we receive what belongs to the priests. I therefore propose that we keep the entire Rule of St Benedict being careful to deviate from it neither to the right nor to the left. Let us procure what is necessary for food and raiment by the labor of our hands. Let us give up the use of underclothing, and linen and furs, and relinquish tithes and oblations which belong to the clergy who serve the parishes. Thus, treading in the steps of the father, we shall labor with zeal to follow Christ.[88]"

In this connection William of Malmesbury mentions the appointment of two members of the community "to discover the intention

88. "*Venerabilis Rotbertus abbas coenobium condidit et inspirante gratia Spiritus sancti, discipulos magnae religionis aggregavit, studioque virtutum in sancta paupertate, juxta usum aliorum coenobiorum, comiter instruxit, Post aliquo. annos, Sancti Benedicti regulam diligenter perscrutatus est, aliorumque sanctorum documentis Patrum perspectis, convocans fratres, six affatus est: 'Nos, fratres charissimi, secundum Normam sancti Patris Benedicti professionem fecimus. Sed, ut mihi videtur, non eam ex integro tenemus. Multa, quae ibi non recipiuntur, observamus, et de mandatis ejus plura negligentes intermittimus. Manibus nostris non laboramus, ut sanctos Patres fecisse legimus. Si mihi non creditis, o amici, legite gesta sanctorum Antonii, Macarii, Pacomii et ante omnes alios, doctoris gentium, Pauli apostoli. Abundantem victum et vestitum ex decimis et oblationibus ecclesiarum habemus, et ea quae competunt presbyteris, ingenio seu violentia subtrahimus. Sic nimirum sanguine hominum vescimur, et peccatis participamus. Laudo igitur ut omnino Regulam Sancti Benedicti teneamus, caventes ne ad dexteram vel ad sinistram ab ea deviemus. Victum et vestitum labore manuum nostrarum vindicemus. A femoralibus et staminiis, pelliciisque secundum Regulam abstineamus. Decimas et oblationes clericis, qui in dioecesi famulantur, relinquemus. Et sic, per vestigia Patrum, post Christum currere ferventer insudemus.'* " Historia Ecclesiastica, III, viii, 25; PL 188:637. English translation by Thomas Forester, in Ordericus Vitalis, *Ecclesiastical History of England and Normandy* (London: Henry G. Bohn, 1854), 39ff. See also J. Bouton, op. cit., 51ff. and P. Salmon, "L'ascèse monastique et les origines de Cîteaux," loc. cit., 275.

of the Founder's Rule; and when they had discovered it, to propound it to the rest."[89]

A majority of the monks of Molesme however saw no need for changing the relationship between the Rule and the monastic customs of the day. As Ordericus Vitalis further reports:

> The convent of monks did not agree to these proposals; they objected to innovations which would alter their usages, the examples and precepts of their predecessors . . . . They further replied, "As long as we find the monks of Cluny and Tours (Marmoutier), and other regulars maintaining these institutions we shall not depart from them; for we are unwilling to be condemned by our brethren, far and wide, as reckless innovators and inventors of novel practices.[90]

According to the oldest extant manuscript of the *Exordium Parvum*, there was no possibility of a compromise between the two groups, for to the pioneers of Cîteaux traditional monastic life was a deliberate violation of their monastic profession; in other words, perjury. To quote from the account:

---

89. "*Frequentibus ergo capitulis disputatio agitata hunc finem habuit, ut ipse abbas sententiam probaret, supersedendum superfluis, solam medullam regulae vestigandam. Ita duo fratres electi, in quibus scientia litterarum cum religione quadraret, qui, vicaria collatione, auctoris regulae voluntatem inquirerent, inquisitam aliis proponerent.*" Gesta Regum Anglorum, IV; PL 179:1288. English translation by John Sharpe, in *The History of the Kings of England and the Modern History of William of Malmesbury* (London: Longman & Co., 1815). Cf. also O. Ducourneau, op. cit., 42; W. Parker Mason, "The Beginnings of the Cistercian Order," loc. cit., 174; U. Berlière, *L'ordre monastique*, 266; J. Bouton, op. cit., 51.

90. "*Monachorum conventus non acquievit; imo praedecessorum quorum vita evidentibus miraculis insignita manifeste refulsit, exempla et instituta venerabilium vestigiis trita, virorum, moderatis novitatibus objecit. . . . Ad haec monachi responderunt . . . Quandiu Cluniacenses, sive Turonenses, aliique regulares viri ea nacti fuerint, non dimittemus; nec, ut temerarii, novitatum adinventores, a fratribus nostris longe lateque condemnari volumus.*" Historia Ecclesiastica, III, viii, 25; PL 188:637f. and 640. Cf. P. Salmon, "L'ascèse monastique et les origines de Cîteaux," loc. cit., 276f.; A. Cooke, "A Study in Twelfth Century Religious Revival and Reform," loc. cit., 145f. and 189 and U. Berlière, "L'étude des réformes monastiques des Xe et XIe siècles," loc. cit., 215.

S

252   The Eleventh-Century Background of Cîteaux

These men while still living in Molesme and inspired by divine grace, often spoke, complained about and lamented the transgression of the Rule of St Benedict, the father of monks, among themselves. They realized that they and the other monks, though they had promised to follow the Rule by solemn vow, had not observed it at all, and had therefore knowingly fallen into the crime of perjury.[91]

The *Exordium Magnum* saw the problem in the same light:

The aforementioned abbot and those of the brethren who were animated by the desire of renewing the monastic life, went to him—Hugh of Lyons—and humbly opened to him the ardent desire of their heart. They deplored the fact that the practices of the order differed too much from the Rule they had professed and sadly admitted that for this reason they had clearly and knowingly fallen into the sin of perjury.[92]

As for the problem of perjury, S. Lenssen believed that the last phrase, about perjury, was inserted by Conrad of Eberbach, the author of the *Exordium Magnum*, for reasons other than fairness.[93] Since then, however, older texts of the *Exordium Parvum* containing the crucial passage have been found. The passage may therefore be genuine; it seems to indicate that the author of the *Exordium Parvum*

---

91. K. Spahr, *De fontibus constitutivis primigenii juris constitutionalis Sacri Ordinis Cisterciensis*, 47f. Cf. Joseph Turk, "Cistercii Statuta Antiquissima," *Analecta Sacri Ordinis Cisterciensis* 4 (1948), 32 and 40 n. 8.

92. "*Hunc (Hugh of Lyons) ergo praedictus abbas et fratres, qui desiderio innovandae monasticae religionis flagrabant, adeunt, aestus et vota cordium suorum humiliter pandant, consuetudines ordinis a regula, quam professi erant, nimium discrepare conqueruntur et propterea manifeste periurii crimen se scienter incurrisse dolendo fatentur.*" *Exordium Magnum*, XI; B. Griesser, *op. cit.*, 63. Cf. also ch. X; *ibid.*, 62.

93. *Op. cit.*, 12. For the *Exordium Magnum* text see B. Griesser, *op. cit.*, 61: "*Monachi namque nigri ordinis, maxime in provinciis Germaniae degentes, ubicumque vel apud quoscumque possunt sacro ordini nostro derogare non cessant asserentes sanctos patres nostros cum scandalo et inobedientia contra voluntatem abbatis sui de Molismensi cenobio egressos fuisse. Quorum quam sit impudens mendacium, subsequentis narrationis textus rem gestam enucleantis pandens manifeste declarabit.*" See also Jacques Laurent, "Le problème des commencements de Cîteaux," *Annales de Bourgogne*, 6 (1934), 221.

is speaking in very plain terms, permitting no feeling of embarrassment or shame to cloud the issues. Puzzled by the phrase, "and for this reason," some however still feel that the passage is a later addition to the text.[94] This led J. Turk to conclude, "the pioneers of Cîteaux founded the New Monastery (Cîteaux) and the (Cistercian) order out of an erroneous conscience and fear of the formal sin of perjury." But because the passage could have embarrassed succeeding Cistercian generations and furnished arguments to their adversaries, it was deleted from the *Exordium Parvum* texts, a practice not unknown in those days.[95] Disagreeing with J. Turk, K. Spahr concedes the possibility that the compilers of a later *Exordium Parvum* edition may have omitted the passage in question so as not to offend the Black Monks with the allegation that the founders of Cîteaux, while observing the usages of the former at Molesme, considered themselves guilty of perjury. But, in his view, the omission was not made in fear of possible adversaries; it was undertaken for the purpose of conciliating souls.[96] K. Spahr also pointed out that the phrase "and for this reason they had knowingly fallen into the sin of perjury" was characteristic of the contemporary mentality and should not be seen, *à la* J. Turk, as a specifically Cistercian problem. For practically the same case figures also in the *Decretum de professione clericorum* and the *Decretum Gratiani*. And much earlier St Ambrose taught, "A lie is: to take the vows of a

---

94. K. Spahr, *De fontibus constitutivis primigenii juris constitutionalis Sacri Ordinis Cisterciensis*, 47f. See also J. Turk, "Cistercii Statuta Antiquissima," *loc. cit.*, 40 n. 8.

95. "*Sensus . . . verborum esset fundatores Cistercii ex conscientia erronea et ex formali peccato periurii Novum Monasterium et Ordinem condidisse.—Ex eisdem verbis etiam adversarii contra Cistercienses argumentum desumere potuissent. Ideo pro posteris petra scandali facta et ab iis ex metu adversariorum vel ex verecundia deleta sunt.*" "Cistercii Statuta Antiquissima," *loc. cit.*, 40 n. 8.

96. "*Concedi potest redactores posteriores recensionis EC* (i.e., of the *Exordium Parvum*, since Spahr uses a different terminology) *has voces praetermisisse, ne monachos nigros offenderent, si Cistercii fundatores eadem observantia Molisno viventes se periuros putavissent. Omissio non est facta metu adversariorum, sed magis ad conciliandos animos.*" *De fontibus constitutivis primigenii juris constitutionalis Sacri Ordinis Cisterciensis*, 48.

bishop, priest or cleric and do things contrary to this order."[97] The Cistercians, it seems, simply applied this text to the monastic profession, with the consequences just described.

The issues debated by the community of Molesme reveal a striking similarity with the main features of the early Cistercian reform. This raises the question about the latter's real "home." J. Laurent, the editor of its cartulary, saw in Molesme a halfway house between Cluny and Cîteaux; he believed that the Cistercian reform actually began at Molesme.[98] K. Spahr, who published the critical edition of Robert's *Vita*, agrees with this view. "It is clear—he writes—that the Cistercian monks while still at Molesme accurately conceived their future way of life; but they realized within a short time that it could not be carried out at Molesme."[99] These views were shared by A. Manrique; the editors who published Robert's life in the *Acta Sanctorum*; J. Mabillon; the anonymous late-nineteenth-century historian of Lérins; U. Berlière and Anselme LeBail. They based their judgment on the account of the so-called *Exordium Cistercii* and on the *Statutes of the Cistercian Monks who Departed from Molesme* which are contained in the *Exordium Parvum*. Some also find it important that Alberic, a leader of the Cistercian reform, had been at Molesme from its early days, possibly even at Collan.[100]

97. "*Mendacium est, episcopum, sacerdotum vel clericum se profiteri, et contraria huic ordini operari.*" Decretum Gratiani, II, xxii, V, xx; PL 137:1158. Cf. ibid., xix: "*Mendacium autem non solum in verbis, sed etiam in simulatis operibus esse probatur.*" See also Aemilius L. Richter (ed.), *Corpus Juris Canonici* (Lipsiae: Sumptibus Bernh. Tauchnitz Jun., 1839), 1:765f. and K. Spahr, *De fontibus constitutivis primigenii juris constitutionalis Sacri Ordinis Cisterciensis*, 49f. and 70 n. 28.

98. *Op. cit.*, 1:111f. Cf. A. Cooke, "A Study in Twelfth Century Religious Revival and Reform," *loc. cit.*, 145.

99. "*Constat monachos Cistercienses iam Molismi degentes futuram suae vitae formam accurate sibi proposuisse. Brevi tamen eis persuasum erat propositam vitae formam Molismi exequi nequisse.*" *De fontibus constitutivis primigenii juris constitutionalis Sacro Ordinis Cisterciensis*, 31.

100. A. Manrique, *op. cit.*, 1:23; AS, Apr. 3:671; J. Mabillon, *Annales*, 5:93; (E. Hautcouer), *op. cit.*, 21 and 28; U. Berlière, *L'ordre monastique des orgiines au XIIe siècle*, 247; idem, "L'étude des réformes monastiques dès Xe

O. Ducourneau called these views "suppositions without any justification." According to him, the documents dealing with early Molesme show no trace of an intention to found a new reform monastery or to have an observance different from that of other well-functioning contemporary monasteries. Besides, traditional monastic observances were passably strict; they formed the basis for monastic reforms during the preceding two centuries. Also, no contemporary viewed Molesme as an innovator, whereas Cîteaux faced accusations of this kind from its very beginning. Then, there is the testimony of Ordericus Vitalis stating that Robert, raised in the Cluniac tradition, simply introduced the traditional usages in his monastery without any indication that he was animated, as early as the mid-seventies of the eleventh century, by the ideals championed some twenty years later by the Cistercian pioneers.[101] To this S. Lenssen adds "that neither the letter nor the spirit of the *Statutes* has motivated the foundation of Molesme, even though the spirit resembled the ideals which inspired the establishment of Cîteaux." Molesme did not become a Cîteaux, however, since its ideals were not sufficiently crystallized. The founders of Cîteaux on the other hand were able to define their ideal in a very concrete manner: "Having learned from experience, and anxious to prevent the dangers stemming from extreme wealth, they . . . made a clear distinction between what is superfluous and what is necessary." We must, therefore, conclude: even if the idea of Cîteaux was not in evidence in the early years of Molesme, which accepted altars, tithes, etc., it was definitely taking shape before the exodus to Cîteaux; but there is no documentary evidence to suggest that its true author was St Robert himself.[102]

When trying to determine the authorship of the Cistercian idea, historians and modern manuals move in different directions, attributing the honor to Robert, or to one of his immediate successors, i.e., Alberic or Stephen Harding.

---

et XIe siècles," *loc. cit.*, 215f. and 229; S. Lenssen, *op. cit.*, 25f.; Anselme Le Bail, *L'ordre de Cîteaux* (Paris: Letouzey et Ané, 1947), 20f. Cf. also *Exordium Parvum*, III, IV and XII; J. Van Damme, *op. cit.*, 7 and 11.

101. *Op. cit.*, 37f.   102. *Op. cit.*, 26f. Cf. also 25.

In his already quoted passage Ordericus Vitalis credited Robert with the conception of the Cistercian reform:

> The venerable abbot Robert . . . studied carefully the Rule of St Benedict. . . . He assembled the brethren and thus addressed them: "My dear brethren, we have made our profession according to the Rule of St Benedict, but it appears to me that we do not observe it in its integrity. . . . I therefore propose that we keep the entire Rule of St Benedict, being careful to deviate from it neither to the right nor to the left. . . ." The convent of monks did not agree. . . . The abbot, persisting in his opinion, withdrew from them with twelve of the number who agreed with him, and it was a long time before he could find a suitable place for himself and his companions where they might observe the Rule of St Benedict to the letter, as the Jews kept the law of Moses.[103]

The Cistercian author of the *Dialogus inter Cluniacensem et Cisterciensem monachum* (composed a. 1170) seems to agree with Ordericus Vitalis; he writes:

> The founders of our order recorded their deeds. . . . These I relate in a brief summary. . . . The abbot of Molesme. . . and some of his brethren frequently spoke and complained among themselves about the transgression of the Rule. . . . This is why they came to this solitude (i.e., Cîteaux).[104]

---

103. "*Venerabilis Rodbertus . . . abbas . . . Sancti Benedicti regulam diligenter perscrutatus est, convocans fratres sic affatus est: 'Nos, fratres charissimi, secundum Normam sancti Patris Benedicti professionem fecimus. Sed, ut mihi videtur, non eam ex integro tenemus . . . Laudo igitur ut omnino Regulam Sancti Benedicti teneamus, caventes ne ad dextram vel ad sinistram ab ea deviemus. . . .' Monachorum chorus non acquievit . . . Abbas, in sua satis pertinax sententia, recessit ab eis, cum duodecim sibi assentientibus. Diuque locum quaesivit idoneum sibi suisque sodalibus, qui sancti decreverant Regulam Benedicti sicut Judaei legem Moysi ad litteram servare penitus.*" Historia Ecclesiastica, III, viii; PL 188:636f.

104. "*Auctores nostri Ordinis gesta sua scripserunt. . . . Eadem brevi summa refero. Molismensis abbas . . . et quidam fratres ejus saepius inter se . . . de transgressione Regulae . . . loquebantur, conquerebantur. . . . Propter hoc ad hanc solitudinem . . . veniebant.*" Edmond Martène and Ursin Durand, *Thesaurus Novus Anecdotorum* (Parisiis: F. Delaulne, 1717), 5:1593.

Robert of Torigny, a Benedictine chronicler, also stressed Robert's importance:

> Robert, having studied the Rule of St Benedict to the letter, wished to persuade his followers to live by the work of their hands.... But they, holding fast to the customs prevailing in the monasteries of the West . . . said that they could not renounce them. Robert, unyielding, left them, with twenty-one monks who agreed with him.[105]

These assertions, however, tend to exaggerate Robert's role, especially since neither the genuine documents of the *Exordium Parvum* nor any other early Cistercian writing single out Robert as the real originator of the Cistercian reform. Moreover, as the *Exordium Magnum* explicitly states, Robert heard about the reform plans only when their proponents came to him with their problems; he then joined them, "suddenly overcome by compunction."[106] The decision was thus not really his, nor was it the result of long reflection. Finally, there is the fact that none of the twelfth-century Cistercian authors include Robert in the catalog of the abbots of Cîteaux which was certainly not just done to express their misgivings about his return to Molesme. All this led S. Lenssen, a recent biographer of St Robert, to the conclusion: "Let us resign ourselves to the facts and refuse the authorship of Cîteaux to St Robert."[107]

---

105. "*Robertus abbas . . . Regulam sancti Benedicti perscrutatus ad litteram, voluit persuadere discipulis suis ut labore manuum suarum viverent. . . . At illi . . . nitentes consuetudinibus quae in occidui orbis monasteriis observabantur . . . dicebant se ab eis non recedere . . . Robertus . . . in sua sententia permanens, recessit ab eis cum viginti et uno sibi assentientibus.*" Tractatus de immutatione ordinis monachorum, I, 1; PL 202:309f.

106. "*Ad horam compunctus abbas ille propositum servorum Dei laudat.*" Exordium Magnum, X; B. Griesser, *op. cit.*, 63.

107. *Op. cit.*, 31. Cf. P. Salmon, "L'ascèse monastique et les origines de Cîteaux," *loc. cit.*, 276. It may be well to quote also D. Knowles who writes, "The history of Molesme and of the early days of Cîteaux would seem to show at least that his (i.e., Robert's) clarity of vision and talent for organization were not above those of previous reformers and that, if he had not attracted disciples of another temper, not only Molesme, but Cîteaux itself, would have gone

Should the honor of conceiving the Cistercian reform therefore go to Alberic? Both *exordia* answer the question in the affirmative. To quote the *Exordium Parvum*,

> They elevated a certain brother by the name of Alberic to be their abbot. He was a man of letters, well versed in both divine and human sciences, and a lover of the Rule and the brethren. For a long time he had served as prior in the community of Molesme as well as here (i.e., Cîteaux) and he had long urged the brethren to move from Molesme to this place, for which endeavors he had had to suffer many insults, prison and beatings.[108]

In our century Alberic found a strong champion in Gregor Müller, the founder and editor of the *Cistercienser-Chronik*. According to him:

> Alberic was appointed by Robert prior [of Molesmes].... The more he delved into the study of the Rule, and compared its prescriptions with life in the abbey, the more he realized that it was not in satisfactory harmony with it and the more vigorously he labored to bring this about.... But because he also wished

---

the way of similar ventures in the past." *The Monastic Order in England*, 198. O. Ducourneau is even more severe in his evaluation of Robert. "Robert was not of the stature to repress a revolt; he believed he could not triumph over the indocility of the recalcitrants; discouraged, in fear, trembling for his own virtue, the feeble abbot, as previously at Saint Michel, took the course of retreating." *Op. cit.*, 36. *Ibid.*, 50, he even speaks of "Robert's weakness of character and his pusillanimity."—But Robert has not only critics. Of the long list of admirers it will suffice to quote E. Petit: "His [Robert's] memory ought to be venerated in all the monasteries of Christendom.... By conferring the honor of sainthood on the greatest reformer of this age, it [the Church] has but ratified the sentiment of his contemporaries." 1:293. Cf. also J. Mabillon, *Annales*, 5:192, 379 and 448; *Aux sources de la vie cartusienne*, 139; B. Bligny, *L'Eglise et les ordres réligieux*, 319 and J. Lefèvre, "S. Robert de Molesme," *loc. cit.*, 50ff.

108. "*Viduata igitur suo pastore cisterciensis ecclesia convenit ac regulari electione, quendam fratrem albericum nomine in abbatem sibi promovit, virum scilicet litteratum in divinis et in humanis satis gnarum, amatorem regule et fratrum quique prioris officium et in molismensi et in illa diutius gerebat ecclesia, multumque diu nitendo laboraverat, ut ad illum de molismo transmigrarent fratres locum, et pro hoc negotio multa opprobria carcerem et verbera perpessus fuerat.*" *Exordium Parvum*, IX; J. Van Damme, *op. cit.*, 10. Cf. below, n. 119.

to suppress certain customs and usages . . . a storm broke loose. . . . Alberic wanted more than merely to remove abuses; his ideal was to secure full recognition to the prescriptions of the Rule... without any mitigation. . . . Some [of the monks] were ready to accept the plan the prior proposed to them. Particularly enthusiastic was the monk Stephen. . . . Since Alberic and Stephen realized that there could be no thought of realizing their plan at Molesme, they decided to implement it at another place. Now it was time to inform the abbot about their intention... After mature reflection . . . . Robert declared himself . . . ready to participate in its execution.[109]

In evaluating this conclusion one must now admit that it was drawn from documentary evidence which has since been proven debatable.[110] It is not possible then to conclude that the Cistercian reform depends on the inspiration of St Alberic alone.

Of Stephen Harding's role in the shaping of the Cistercian ideals, William of Malmesbury, Stephen's contemporary, writes:

It redounds to the glory of England to have produced the distinguished man who was the author and promoter of that order. To us he belonged, and in our schools he passed the earlier part of his life. Wherefore, if we are not envious, we shall delight in his good qualities more willingly as we know them to be more ours. . . . He was named Harding.[111]

Helinand of Froidmont, a Cistercian of the early thirteenth century, advocated views similar to those of William:

From the monastery of Molesme twenty-one monks went with . . . Robert to Cîteaux. . . . It is the glory of England to

---

109. *Vom Cistercienser Orden* (Bregenz: J. N. Teutsch, 1927), 9f.

110. J. Lefèvre, "Que savons-nous du Cîteaux primitif?," *loc. cit.*, 9ff.

111. "*Ejus diebus religio Cistellensis coepit, quae nunc optima via in coelum processus et creditur et dicitur. De qua hic loqui suscepti operis non videtur esse contrarium, quod ad Angliae gloriam pertineat, quae talem virum produxerit qui hujusce religionis fuerit et auctor et mediator. Noster ille, et nostra puer in palestra primi aevi tirocinium cucurrit. Quapropter, si non invidi sumus, eo illius bona complectimur gr:tiosius quo agnoscimus propinquius; simul et laudes ejus attollere mihi est animus, quia ingenua mens est si bonum in alio probes quod in te non esse suspires. Is fuit Hardingus nomine.*" *Gesta Regum Anglorum*, IV; PL 179:1286f.

have produced the man who was the founder and promoter of this order. He was Harding. . . . When told to observe certain things not mentioned by the Rule, he began to investigate their rationale and argued with one and another [of the monks], about certain superfluous customs at such length that he won over the abbot himself and twenty-two others to his opinion. This is how they came to Cistellae.[112]

The *Exordium Magnum*, besides excluding Robert from any initial influence in the conception of the reform, also points to Stephen's leadership in its execution. It states in unmistakable terms:

> Whenever there had been a discussion about the renewal of the order, Stephen worked with the utmost zeal, and, first among the first, vigorously urged that the place and the order of Cîteaux be established.[113]

William of Malmesbury's position that Stephen Harding was the originator of the movement which led to the foundation of Cîteaux may or may not be right. He was certainly influenced by the Sherborne version of the story since Sherborne, where Stephen Harding had spent his youth, was not far from Malmesbury. It will therefore be better—also in view of the great diversity of the answers—to leave the question of the authorship of the Cistercian reform somewhat as W. Parker Mason:

> Were William of Malmesbury the only authority, it might be supposed that Stephen was the prime mover in the whole matter. Probably this is merely an exaggeration of the truth. Robert was

---

112. "*Ex coenobio Molismensi viginti et unus monachi cum . . . Roberto Cistercium devenerunt . . . Pertinet . . . ad gloriam Angliae, quod talem virum genuit, qui hujus religionis auctor fuit et mediator. Is fuit Hardingus . . . Cum ei quaedam proponerentur observanda quae non erant de Regula, coepit eorum rationem inquirere, et tamdiu de quibusdam superfluis cum uno et alio disputavit, ut abbatem ipsum et alios 22 in suam sententiam induceret. Igitur Cistellas venere.*" *Chronicon*, XXXXVII; PL 212:990f. Stephen's argumentation is reproduced in William of Malmesbury, *loc. cit.*,; PL 179:1287f.

113. "*Cum verbum innovandae religionis in eadem domo motum fuisset, ipse primus inter primos ferventissimo studio laboravit ac modis omnibus institit, ut locus et ordo Cisterciensis institueretur.*" *Exordium Magnum*, XX; B. Griesser, *op. cit.*, 77.

almost certainly the older, his experiences, both religious and temporal, had been varied, and he was always a reformer at heart. But the very humility and gentleness that counted for so much in his saintliness were drawbacks and hindrances to the vigorous prosecution of reforms energetically resisted by comfortable recluses. Hence the whole idea may well have been Robert's, but probably Alberic and Stephen, both hard-headed, business like men, made it explicit, and as in William of Malmesbury's account, Stephen, it is likely enough, made, with Robert's approval, the actual proposal for a stricter adherence to the Benedictine rule.[114]

To determine the date of the secession from Molesme, one must consult the last document bearing Robert's name before his departure to Cîteaux; its date is April 5, 1097. On the other hand, the *Exordium Cistercii* tells us that Cîteaux became an abbey in 1098, "after many labors and great difficulties." The two dates and his belief that the legate's letter in the *Exordium Parvum* was not the *permissio abeundi* from Molesme, but Cîteaux's formal promotion into an abbey, led J. Lefèvre to the conclusion that Robert and his companions departed from Molesme some time during 1097; after Easter, to be more precise.[115] On this point J. Lefèvre differs from

---

114. *Op. cit.*, 173f. See also J. Lefèvre, "Que savons-nous du Cîteaux primitif?," *loc. cit.*, 41: "To whom attribute the fatherhood of the practical points of the reform? To Robert of Molesme alone? To Alberic, his successor? To the two first abbots conjointly, since the second continued what the first started? These passion-stirring questions are without an answer, and the Cistercian origins remain surrounded by numerous obscurities. The fact is that all the juridical documents in our possession refer to the second stage of the Cistercian reform: 1114–1120, i.e., to the time of the order. The first and most important [stage], that of 1098–1100, escapes us almost completely. One must simply admit: a thousand interpretations, no matter how ingeniously conceived, will never replace the documents we do not have."

115. J. Laurent, *op. cit.*, 2:122. Cf. *Exordium Cistercii*, II: "*Post multos labores . . . anno itaque ab incarnatione domini millesimo nonagesimo octavo . . . inventam heremum in abbatiam construere ceperunt.*" J. Van Damme, *op. cit.*, 22. See also J. Lefèvre, "Que savons-nous du Cîteaux primitif?," *loc. cit.*, 21: "An examination of the authentic sources undertaken without taking sides justifies the answer: the departure of the future Cistercians from Molesme took place spontaneously, without any recourse to the normal superior

the whole Cistercian and non-Cistercian historical and literary tradition, according to which the petitioners went to Hugh of Lyons in the early days of 1098, i.e., shortly before Cîteaux was established on March 21st, the feast of St Benedict, which was also Palm Sunday in that year.[116] He needs to explain the passage in the legate's document, "it would be expedient for you to retire to another place which the Divine Munificence will point out to you."[117] For, if the site of the new establishment is still unknown in the document, how can it be a decree of canonical erection into an abbey?

J. Lefèvre still contends that Robert and his companions left Molesme without the permission of the local ordinary; this, because the *Exordium Cistercii* mentions no such authorization in connection with the exodus from Molesme, while it does so when reporting the canonical elevation of Cîteaux into an abbey. On the other hand, when returning from Cîteaux to Molesme, Robert secured the permission of Walter of Châlons, the local ordinary. According to J. Lefèvre, this indicates that the seceders had no *permissio abeundi*, a fact which prompted the author of the *Exordium Parvum* to transpose Archbishop Hugh's letter. Given, originally, on the occasion of Cîteaux's elevation into an abbey, he made it into an

---

authority, in this case to the bishop of Langres, the ordinary of Molesme." Cf. also *ibid.*, 22f.

116. "*Anno igitur ab incarnatione Domini millesimo nonagesimo octavo . . . duodecimo Kalendas Aprilis, solemni scilicet die natalis sanctissimi Benedicti, quem geminata laetitia tunc celebrem reddiderat ob dominicam Palmarum, quae in ipsum occurrerat, laetantibus angelis, tabescentibus daemonibus Cisterciensis domus ac per hoc totius Cisterciensis ordinis religio per viros ad christianam philosophiam penitus expeditor exordium sumpsit.*" *Exordium Magnum*, XIII; B. Griesser, *op. cit.*, 64f. See also RHF 13:673; O. Ducourneau, *op. cit.*, 45; S. Lenssen, *op. cit.*, 40; Louis Lekai, *The White Monks* (Okauchee, Wis.: Spring Bank, 1953), 18; J. Bouton, *op. cit.*, 54 and G. Müller, "Gründung der Abtei Cîteaux," *loc. cit.*, 66.

117. "*Nos utriusque partis saluti, videlicet inde recedentium atque illic remanentium providentes, in locum alium quem vobis largitas divina designaverit vos declinare, ibique salubrius atque quietius domino famulari, utile duximus fore.*" *Exordium Parvum*, II; J. Van Damme, *op. cit.*, 6.

official justification of the Cistercians' illegal exodus from Molesme.[118]

The secession of Robert and the twenty-odd monks from Molesme was something unheard of in contemporary monastic circles; it was nothing short of a scandal, and this all the more since the abbot himself had joined. To correct this impression, the author of the *Exordium Parvum* inserted documentary evidence—eight original documents—into his account.[119]

Still, was the *transitus* authorized? To answer the question one must consult the *Exordium Cistercii* according to which the Cistercian pioneers obtained recognition as an abbey through

---

118. "Que savons-nous du Cîteaux primitif?," *loc. cit.*, 21ff. More on the problems raised in connection with the *Exordium Parvum* is found in A. Manrique, *op. cit.*, 1:5 and 112; W. Parker Mason, "The Beginnings of the Cistercian Order," *loc. cit.*, 176; G. Schreiber, *Gemeinschaften des Mittelalters*, 354; D. Knowles, *The Monastic Order in England*, 209; idem, *Great Historical Enterprises. Problems in Monastic History* (London: Thomas Nelson and Sons, 1963), 217f. and 220; K. Spahr, *De fontibus constitutivis primigenii juris constitutionalis Sacri Ordinis Cisterciensis*, 43ff. and 69 n. 10; idem, "Die Anfänge von Cîteaux," *loc. cit.*, 218 ; idem, "Neue Beiträge zur Ordensgeschichte," *Cistercienser-Chronik*, 58 (1951), 31; idem, "Cistercienser Bibliothek," *Cistercienser Chronik*, 70 (1963), 113; U. Berlière, "L'étude des réformes monastiques des Xe et XIe siècles," *loc. cit.*, 221; J. Lefèvre, "S. Robert de Molesme," *loc. cit.*, 52ff.; idem, "Le vrai récit primitif des origines de Cîteaux est-il l'Exordium Parvum?," *Le Moyen Age*, 61 (1955), 79ff. and 329ff.; Alain D'Herblay, "Le problèmes des origines cisterciennes," *Revue d'Histoire Ecclésiastique*, 50 (1955), 158ff.; François Masai, "Les études cisterciennes de J. A. Lefèvre," *Scriptorium*, 11 (1957), 119ff.; Jean Leclercq, "L'Exordium Cistercii et la Summa Cartae Caritatis sont-ils de Saint Bernard?" *Revue Bénédictine*, 73 (1963), 89ff.; Leopold Grill, "Der hl. Bernhard als bisher unerkannter Verfasser des Exordium Cistercii und der Summa Cartae Caritatis," *Cistercienser-Chronik*, 66 (1959), 43ff.; Jean B. Van Damme, "Autour des origines cisterciennes," *Collectanea Ordinis Cisterciensium Reformatorum*, 20 (1958), 78, 82ff., 137f., 148ff. and 155f.; C. Dereine, "La fondation de Cîteaux d'après l'Exordium Cistercii et l'Exordium Parvum," *Cîteaux*, 10 (1959), 126 and 131; Polykarp Zakar, "Die Anfänge des Zisterzienserordens," *Analecta Sacri Ordinis Cisterciensis*, 20 (1964), 113, 117ff., 129 and 134ff.

119. J. Lefèvre, "Que savons-nous du Cîteaux primitif?," *loc. cit.*, 22. Cf. R. Folz, "Le problème des origines de Cîteaux," *loc. cit.*, 288f.; R. Southern, *op. cit.*, 166 and G. Müller, "Gründung der Abtei Cîteaux," *loc. cit.*, 66. In view of the still unresolved controversies surrounding the *Exordium Parvum*, only the authentic letters are used for documentation in this study.

the advice and favor of such authorities as the papal legate, the bishop of Châlons and the duke of Burgundy.[120] Such a support would hardly have been forthcoming had the exodus from Molesme been irregular. However, at that time the question of a free *transitus* was frequently discussed by such authorities as Burchard of Worms, Anselm of Lucca and Ivo of Chartres. They painstakingly collected all available previous canonical legislation on the subject. The general consensus was that a fervent desire for a more perfect life should not be opposed.[121] The Fourth Council of Toledo had allowed a *transitus ad vitam arctiorem* without the superior's permission—a case also mentioned by Abbo of Fleury.[122] In fact, there was abundant contemporary legislation which allowed free passage to a stricter life. In 1085 the abbot of Saint Vannes in the city of Verdun and several of his monks had been expelled from their abbey by the imperial bishop, Thierry. They found refuge at Saint Benignus Abbey in Dijon. When after some time its abbot proposed that they change their vows to Saint Benignus, the question arose whether a second profession was legitimate in view of the vows—stability, etc.—made at Saint Vannes. To decide the issue all agreed to consult Hugh of Cluny[123] and archbishop Lanfranc of Canterbury. The latter, in favor of a *transitus*, reasoned this way:

> If I, Lanfranc, should vow with my own hand not to leave a certain monastery, but then see that I could not save my soul therein, I would leave without incurring the crime of perjury.

120. "*Anno itaque ab incarnatione domini millesimo nonagesimo octavo, venerabilis hugonis lugdunensis ecclesie archiepiscopi sedis apostolice tunc legati, et religiosi viri walterii cabilonensis episcopi, necnon et clarissimi principis oddonis burgundie ducis freti consilio, auctoritate roborati, inventam heremum in abbatiam construere ceperunt.*" Exordium Cistercii, II; J. Van Damme, op. cit., 22.

121. C. Dereine, "La fondation de Cîteaux d'après l'Exordium Cistercii et l'Exordium Parvum," loc. cit., 127f. For the references see ibid., 127 n. 11.

122. Mansi 10:631 and PL 139:487. Cf. C. Dereine, "La fondation de Cîteaux d'après l'Exordium Cistercii et l'Exoridum Parvum," loc. cit., 127.

123. Hugh of Flavigny, Chronicon; PL 164:342. Cf. C. Dereine, "La fondation de Cîteaux d'après l'Exordium Cistercii et l'Exordium Parvum," 128f.

For he who is bound to God because of God is not severed from him, unless he is severed in opposition to him.[124]

In another case, in 1098 Pope Urban II gave permission to the monks of St Hubert's in the diocese of Liége, harassed by the imperial bishop, Othbert, to move to another monastery, "if you are unable to live in your monastery according to the Rule of St Benedict and in fidelity to apostolic teaching."[125] This was in line with contemporary thinking that a distinction must be made between positive law (*lex publica*) and the law of one's own conscience (*lex privata*). According to the Pope, the Church's legislation on stability is based on the former and is given "because of transgressors." But it may not be invoked when the law of one's conscience (which is superior to it) urges a person to seek a more perfect life. For,

> those who act by the Spirit of God, are led by the law of God. Therefore, whoever is led by the Spirit of God, let him freely go with our authorization, even if his bishop should contradict.[126]

124. "*Si ego Lanfrancus manu propria me de aliquo monasterio non recessurum jurarem, viderem autem quod ibi animam meam salvare non possem, exirem nec periurii crimen incurrerem. Qui enim Deo propter Deum alligatur, non solvitur ab ipso nisi contra ipsum solvatur.*" *Ep.* 60; PL 150:549f.

125. "*Si in monasterio vestro secundum Beati Benedicti regulam et apostolicam veritatem vivere non valetis.*" Cf. C. Dereine, "La fondation de Cîteaux d'après l'Exordium Cistercii et l'Exordium Parvum," *loc. cit.*, 128 n. 16. The Pope's letter is found in PL 151:511. See also Edith Pásztor, "Le origini del'Ordine Cisterciense e la riforma monastica," *Analecta Cisterciensia*, 21 (1965), 126.

126. "*Urbanus papa secundus, Duae, inquit, leges sunt, una publica, altera privata; publica lex est quae a sanctis Patribus scripta est firmata, ut est lex canonum, quae quidem propter transgressores est tradita; verbi gratia, decretum est in canonibus clericum non debere de suo episcopatu ad alium transire, nisi commendatitiis litteris episcopi sui, quod propter criminosos sic statutum est . . . Lex vero privata, quod instinctum est sancti Spiritus, in corde scribitur, sicut de quibusdam dicit Apostolus, qui habent legem Dei scriptam in cordibus suis, et sibi et ipsi sancti sunt, lex. Si quis horum in Ecclesia sua sub episcopo suo proprium retinet et saeculariter vivti, si afflante Spiritu sancto in aliquo monasterio se salvare voluerit, quia lege privata ducitur, nulla ratio exigit ut a publica constringatur; dignior est enim privata lex quam publica. Spiritus quidem Dei lex est, et qui Spiritu Dei aguntur, lege Dei ducuntur. Et quis est qui possit spiritui sancto digne resistere? Quisquis ergo hoc Spiritu ducitur, et episcopo suo contradicente, eat liber nostra auctoritate.*" *Ep.* CCLXXVIII; PL 151:535. Cf. Mansi 20:714 and C. Dereine, "La fondation de Cîteaux d'après l'Exordium Cistercii et l'Exordium Parvum," *loc. cit.*, 128.

In later times, St Bernard of Clairvaux and Pope Innocent III wrote in the same sense. The latter allowed a *transitus* to a stricter monastery with and even without the authorization of the local ordinary. Applying the preceding to our point in question we must therefore conclude that Robert and his followers could thus leave Molesme to lead a more perfect life elsewhere without having to obtain the ordinary's permission. For a return to the basic demands of the Rule was an aspiration to a more perfect life, a *religo major* or a *religio altior,* which justified such a free *transitus.*[127]

In the account of the *Exordium Parvum,* the legate's permission to secede from Molesme extended to "Abbot Robert and the brethren Alberic, Odo, John, Stephen, Letald and Peter" who had journeyed to Lyons, and to all others who, after the former's return from Lyons, "properly and by unanimous consent have decided to join them."[128] Eventually, as the *Exordium Cistercii* testifies, the number rose to "twenty-one monks and the father of that monastery, Robert of blessed memory."[129]

According to J. Lefèvre, the secession took place in 1097, some time after Easter.[130] The site of the new establishment had not yet

127. For St Bernard, see ep. 253, PL 182:455ff.; for Innocent III cf. *Decretales Gregorii Papae,* IX, iii, XXXI, 18 in A. Richter, *op. cit.,* 554f. See also R. Folz, "Le problème des origines de Cîteaux," *loc. cit.,* 288 and 293; E. Pásztor, "Le origini dell'Ordine Cisterciense," *loc. cit.,* 125; and C. Dereine, "La fondation de Cîteaux d'après l'Exordium Cistercii et l'Exordium Parvum," *loc. cit.,* 128.

128. "*Roberto abbati, fratribus quoque alberico, odoni, joanni, stephano, letaldo et petro, sed et omnibus quos regulariter et communi consilio vobis sociare decreveritis.*" Exordium Parvum, II; J. Van Damme, *op. cit.,* 6.

129. "*Viginti et unus monachi una cum patre ipsius monasterii, beate videlicet memorie Roberto egressi.*" *Exordium Cistercii,* I; J. Van Damme, *op. cit.,* 22. Cf. also *Exordium Magnum,* XIII; B. Griesser, *op. cit.,* 64; RHF 14:381; Caesarius of Heisterbach, *op. cit.,* 1:1; O. Ducourneau, *op. cit.,* 47; L. Lekai, *op. cit.,* 18; J. Bouton, *op. cit.,* 53 (14); W. Parker Mason, "The Beginnings of the Cistercian Order," *loc. cit.,* 178 n. 1 and G. Müller, "Gründung der Abtei Cîteaux," *loc. cit.,* 68.

130. Cf. above, n. 115. For more details—real or legendary—of the exodus, see *Exordium Magnum,* XII; B. Griesser, *op. cit.,* 64f.; PL 157:1265; E. Petit, *op. cit.,* 1:248; O. Ducourneau, *op. cit.,* 53f.; G. Coulton, *op. cit.,* 1:280; R. Folz, "Le problème des origines de Cîteaux," *loc. cit.,* 287; J. Bouton,

been determined when Robert and his companions went to Lyons to negotiate with the papal legate, as the latter's expression "it would be expedient to retire to another place which the Divine Munificence will point out to you"[131] clearly indicates. The search was by no means an easy enterprise. According to the *Exordium Cistercii*, it was only "after many labors and great difficulties that . . . they finally came to *Cistercium* (Cîteaux)," which was at the time "a place of horror, and a vast solitude,"[132] in the diocese of Châlon-sur-Sâone. It had been given to them by Raynald, the viscount of Beaune. The notice announcing the foundation reads:

> Let it be known to all present and future Christians that to obtain remission of their own and their ancestors' sins, Raynard, viscount of Beaune, and his wife named Hodierna as well as their sons Hugh, Humbert, Raynard, Hagano and their sister Raimuldis, gave to the lord Robert and to the brethren who, together with him wished to observe the Rule of St Benedict more strictly and more faithfully than they had done heretofore, of their allod called *Cistercium* whatever they and their God-serving successors need for the construction of a monastery, the monastic workshops, the cultivation of the land, and every other need.[133]

op. cit., 51f.; W. Parker Mason, "The Beginnings of the Cistercian Order," *loc. cit.*, 65 and Joseph Canivez, "Le rite cistercien," *Ephemerides Liturgicae*, 63 (1949), 284.

131. *Exordium Parvum*, II; J. Van Damme, *op. cit.*, 6. Cf. also above, n. 117. The *Exordium Magnum's* account "*ad locum, quem proposito suo congruum iam ante per gratiam Dei praeviderant, id est heremum, quae Cistercium dicebatur, alacriter tetenderunt,*"—*Exordium Magnum*, XIII; B. Griesser, *op. cit.*, 65—is not necessarily in conflict with the *Exordium Cistercii*, especially if one sees the emphasis on the *heremus*, i.e., the quality of the place.

132. "*Post multos labores ac nimias difficultates . . . tandem . . . Cistercium devenerunt, locum tunc scilicet horroris et vaste solitudinis.*" *Exordium Cistercii*, I; J. Van Damme, *op. cit.*, 22. The name *Cistercium* indicates that the place was on this side of the third milestone—*cis tertium (lapidem milliarium)*—of the Roman road connecting Langres with Châlon-sur-Sâone. The stone itself was at Dijon, some fifteen miles to the north. Cf. A. King, *op. cit.*, 3ff. For other etymological explanations of *Cistercium*, see Gregor Müller, "Gründung der Abtei Cîteaux," *loc. cit.*, 74f. Cf. also *idem*, "Der Name Cistercienser," *Cistercienser-Chronik*, 17 (1905), 46ff. and 137.

133. "*Notum sit omnibus Christicolis presentibus atque futuris quod Rainardus Belnensis vicecomes et uxor ejus Hodierna nomine et eorum filii Hugho, Humbertus,*

At the New Monastery the Cistercian pioneers were at last able to put into practice "what they had unanimously conceived in their mind."[134] Though the extant documentary evidence is quite meager, it is possible—with the help of the *Exordium Cistercii* and the authentic letters of the *Exordium Parvum*—to trace the basic features of their reform. They are, briefly: a return to the strictness of the Benedictine Rule; solitude; poverty; the rejection of traditional monastic observances; and a strict fidelity. To elaborate, here is what the documents reveal:

In the renowned and prosperous abbey of Molesme a number of monks came to the realization that "although they lived in a holy and honorable manner, they obeyed the Rule they had vowed [to observe] less than was their desire and intention."[135] In the words of the papal legate, Hugh of Lyons, "they had observed the Rule of St Benedict poorly (*tepide*) and neglectfully in that monastery."[136] Perceiving this conflict between the prescriptions of the Rule on the one hand and their actual way of life on the other, "they began to talk among themselves how they ought to do justice to the words 'I shall render to you the vows which my lips uttered!' "[137]

Rainardus, Hagano eorumque soror Raimuldis, pro suorum peccatorum remissione antecessorumque suorum domno Roberto et fratribus qui cum eo Regulam sancti Benedicti artius atque fidelius quam illuc usque tenuerant, observare cupiebant, contulerunt de predio suo quod antiquitus Cistercium vocabatur, quantumcumque ipsis et eorum successoribus Dei famulis, ad monasterium et monasterii officinas construendas, ad arandum quoque, immo ad omnem usum necessarium fuerit." J. Marilier, *op. cit.*, 50 n. 23. More on Raynald is found in Maurice Chaume, "Les anciens vicomtes de Beaune et la fondation de Cîteaux," *Mémoires de l'Académie des Sciences, Arts et Belles-Lettres de Dijon. Bulletin de Mai 1923* (Dijon: Imprimérie Jobard, 1923), 112:73ff. Cf. also A. Manrique, *op. cit.*, 1:9.

134. "*Communi consilio communi perficere nituntur assensu.*" *Exordium Cistercii*, I; J. Van Damme, *op. cit.*, 22.

135. "*Advertentes etsi sancte et honeste viveretur, minus tamen pro sui desiderio atque proposito ipsam quam professi fuerant regulam observari.*" *Exordium Cistercii*, I; J. Van Damme, *op. cit.*, 21.

136. "*Regule beatissimi Benedicti quam illuc hucusque tepide ac negligenter in eodem monasterio tenueratis, arcius atque perfectius inherere velle.*" *Exordium Parvum*, II; J. Van Damme, *op. cit.*, 6.

137. "*Inter se tractant qualiter illum versiculum adimpleant Reddam tibi vota mea q(ae) d(istinxerunt) l(abia) m(ea).*" *Exordium Cistercii*, I; J. Van Damme, *op. cit.*, 22. Reference is made to Psalm 65:14.

They decided they must "serve God according to the Rule of Saint Benedict," not as their traditionalist contemporaries, but "more strictly and more perfectly."[138] The legate sanctioned "this holy endeavor;"[139] in his letter to Pope Paschal II, he again described it as "a more rigorous (*arcior*) and more holy life following the Rule of St Benedict which they had professed to observe."[140]

By the time of the Lyons meeting it had become evident, however, that "because of many hindering circumstances this aim could not be accomplished . . . in the aforementioned place."[141] With the legate's approval the reformers—"twenty-one monks, together with the father of that monastery, Robert of blessed memory"[142]— thereupon "left the community of Molesme," not for any worldly reason, but "because of the religious life."[143]

138. "*Hugo lugdunensis archiepiscopus et apostolice sedis legatus, Roberto molismensi abbati, et fratribus cum eo secundum regulam S. Benedicti deo servire cupientibus.*" Exordium Parvum, II; J. Van Damme, op. cit., 6. In the same letter the legate continues, "*Notum sit vos . . . Regule beatissimi Benedicti . . . arcius deinceps atque perfectius inherere velle.*" Ibid. On *arcior vita* see J. Mabillon, Acta Sanctorum Ordinis S. Benedicti, 5:62 n. 136.

139. "*Vobis . . . hoc sanctum propositum servare, et tunc consuluimus, et ut in hoc perseveretis precipimus.*" Exordium Parvum, II; J. Van Damme, op. cit., 6.

140. "*Sciatis autem eos . . . de Molismensi ecclesia cum abbate suo exeuntes, propter arciorem et sacratiorem vitam secundum regulam divi benedicti quam promiserunt tenendam.*" Exordium Parvum, XII; J. Van Damme, op. cit., 11. On the testimony of the following Cistercian generations see PL 182:1121; 183:379; 185:3, 111, 179, 379; 195:239–244; 608, 612; 211:583, 602, 614. C. Spahr mentions in this connection, "It must not be forgotten that in the course of time the Benedictine monks admitted various usages which mitigated the observance of the Rule and eventually acquired the force of law. These usages were by no means contrary to the Rule; still, they did not correspond to the purity of the Rule as championed by the first Cistercians. But it must be noted that the Cistercians were not the first ones who once again sought the purity and a stricter observance of the Rule. In the life of Benedict of Aniane we are told, "He devoted all his efforts to the restoration of the Rule." De fontibus constitutivis, 32.

141. "*Quod quia in loco predicto pluribus impedientibus causis constat adimpleri non posse.*" Exordium Parvum, II; J. Van Damme, op. cit., 6.

142. "*Viginti et unus monachi una cum patre ipsius monasterii, beate videlicet memorie Roberto, egressi.*" Exordium Cistercii, I; J. Van Damme, op. cit., 22.

143. "*A qua [Molismensi abbatia] religionis causa discesserant.*" Exordium Parvum, XI; J. Van Damme, op. cit., 10.

Preferring "to devote themselves to the study of heavenly things rather than become implicated in secular transactions,"[144] they migrated to Cîteaux, variously described as "a desert,"[145] "a wilderness [and] a wasteland of howling desert,"[146] far from frequented sites. Here they could "adhere to the Lord with greater benefit and more peacefully."[147] They "have left the broad roads of the world," Pope Paschal II himself attested, "in order to live in monastic tranquillity." Accordingly, he told them: "You must strive to keep always in your hearts the fear and love of God, so that the more free you are from the noises and pleasures of the world, the more you aim to please God with all the powers of your mind and soul."[148]

A secluded life alone, however, would not have ensured the success of their reform; an appreciation and cultivation of genuine

---

144. "*Elegerunt pocius studiis celestibus occupari, quam terrenis implicari negociis.*" Exordium Cistercii, I; J. Van Damme, op. cit., 21.

145. "*Inventam heremum in abbatiam Construere ceperunt.*" Exordium Cistercii II; J. Van Damme, op. cit., 8: "*Si fieri possit, abbas ille ab heremo ad monasterium reducatur. Quod si implere nequiveris, cure tibi sit, ut qui heremum diligunt conquiescant, et qui in ceniobo sunt regularibus disciplinis inserviant.*" According to J. Lefèvre, "It is evident, every diplomatic context proves it, that the word *heremum* cannot have the strict meaning of hermitage as juridically opposed to an abbey . . . It must be understood in the sense of a monastery established in solitude." "Que savons-nous du Cîteaux primitif?" 34.

146. "*Cistercium devenerunt, locum tunc scilicet horroris et vaste solitudinis.*" Exordium Cistercii, I; J. Van Damme, op. cit., 22. Reference is made to Deuteronomy 32:10.

147. "*Ibique salubrius atque quietius domino famulari.*" Exordium Parvum, II; J. Van Damme, op. cit., 6.

148. "*locum . . . inhabitandum pro quiete monastica elegistis.*" Exordium Parvum, XIV; J. Van Damme, op. cit., 12. Cf. ibid., "*Vos igitur filii in X° dilectissimi ac desiderantissimi meminisse debetis quia pars vestri seculares latitudines . . . reliquistis,*" and "*Dei semper timorem et amorem in cordibus vestris habere satagite, ut quanto a secularibus tumultibus et deliciis liberiores estis, tanto amplius placere deo totis mentis et anime virtuitbus anheletis.*" See also PL 157:1294; S. Lenssen, op. cit., 23; E. Werner, *Pauperes Christi*, 26; U. Berlière, "Les origines de l'Ordre de Cîteaux," loc. cit., 450; C. Dereine, "Odon de Tournai," loc. cit., 153; and B. Bligny, "Les premiers Chartreux et la pauvreté," loc. cit., 33. According to K. Hallinger, Cîteaux could adopt its ideal of seclusion either

poverty was also needed. The Cistercian pioneers were aware of this, for already at Molesme, a monastery "rich in possessions," these "lovers of virtue began to think about a fruitful poverty."[149] And in their new monastery they took "discipline and frugality"[150] so seriously that such an expert as Hugh of Lyons saw in them authentic *pauperes Christi*, "poor of Christ, having no wealth or power to defend themselves against their adversaries."[151]

---

from the missionary monks or else from the Italian eremitic movement. It "decided in favor of the Italian eremitic movement. The *world* was kept away from the solitude of the monastery as much as possible. The necessary contacts with the outside world were secured by the protective insulation of the new institution of laybrothers." "Woher kommen die Laienbrüder?," *loc. cit.*, 95. On the whole question of solitude and "desert," as applied to early Cîteaux, see also U. Berlière, *L'ordre monastique*, 283ff.; L. Bouyer, *op. cit.*, 6f.; H. DeWarren, "Le monachisme à l'apparition de saint Bernard," *loc. cit.*, 59; L. Champier, "Cîteaux, ultime étape dans l'aménagement agraire de l'Occident," *Mélanges Saint Bernard* (Dijon: Association des Amis de Saint Bernard, 1954), 254, 258, 261; Maurice Chaume, *Les origines du duché de Bourgogne* (Dijon: Librairie E. Rebourseau, 1925-1931), 3:592f.; R. Grand, *op. cit.*, 251; Jean Leclercq, "Problèmes de l'erémitisme," *Studia Monastica*, 5 (1963), 208ff.; S. Lenssen, *op. cit.*, 25; Ferdinand Lot and R. Fawtier, *Les institutions ecclésiastiques en France de la fin du Xe à milieu du XIIe siècle. Histoire des institutions francaises au Moyen Age* (Paris: Presses Universitaires, 1962), 3:127; J. Marilier, *Chartes et documents concernant l'abbaye de Cîteaux 1098-1182* (Roma: Editiones Cistercienses, 1961), V; idem, "Les débuts de l'abbaye de Cîteaux," *Les débuts des abbayes cisterciennes dans les anciens pays bourguignons, comtois et romands* (Dijon: Association des Sociétés Savantes, 1955), 73f., 76; P. Salmon, "L'ascèse monastique et les origines du Cîteaux," *loc. cit.*, 275f., 277 n. 2; G. Schreiber, *Gemeinschaften des Mittelalters*, 136; C. Spahr, *De fontibus constitutivis*, 46f.; E. Werner, *Pauperes Christi*, 40f.; W. Williams, *op. cit.*, 45 and Jacques Winandy, "Les origines de Cîteaux et les travaux de M. Lefèvre," *Revue Bénédictine*, 67 (1957), 65ff.

149. "*In episcopatu lingonensi situm noscitur esse cenobium nomine molismus . . . amplum possessionibus. . . . Mox virtutum amatores, de paupertate fecunda virorum cogitare ceperunt.*" Exordium Cistercii, I; J. Van Damme, *op. cit.*, 21.

150. "*In ea quam hodie observatis discipline ac frugalitatis observantia permanseritis.*" J. Lefèvre, "Que savons-nous du Cîteaux primitif?," *loc. cit.*, 18.

151. "*Paternitatem vestram humiliter et cum fiducia deprecamur, ut . . . eos et locum ipsorum ab hac infestatione et inquietudine liberando, auctoritatis vestre privilegio muniatis, utpote pauperes Xi (Christi) nullam contra emulos suos divitiis vel potentia defensionem parantes.*" Exordium Parvum, XII; J. Van Damme, *op. cit.*, 11. Cf. S. Lenssen, *op. cit.*, 24.

The return to a stricter observance of the Rule necessitated also a rejection of traditional monastic practices. The papal legate clearly had this feature of the early Cistercian reform in mind when informing Pope Paschal: "They left the community of Molesme with their abbot, in order to lead a more rigorous and secluded life following the Rule of St Benedict. In the observance of this Rule they have resolved to abandon the usages of certain monasteries maintaining that in their weakness they are unable to bear such a great burden."[152] These traditional monastic ways, originating in Benedict of Aniane's reform, had definitely altered the original provisions of St Benedict; hence they had to be discarded.[153]

This rejection sheds light on a further characteristic of the early Cistercian reform; J. Lefèvre calls it *intégrisme*, a term he does not however define. We may interpret it as a certain intransigence and purity in their fidelity to the Rule, producing a marked contrast between the Cistercian and traditional monastic ways. In his letter to Paschal II, Hugh of Lyons described this "otherness" in these terms: "The brethren from Molesme and some other monks of the neighborhood do not cease to annoy and disturb them, thinking that in the eyes of the world they are valued less and looked upon with contempt as the world takes notice of what an exceptional and new kind of monks are living in their midst."[154] This clear differentiation between traditional monasticism and this "exceptional and new kind of monk" is also evident from such expressions as "new

152. "*Sciatis autem eos esse de quodam loco qui novum monasterium vocatur, ad quem de molismensi ecclesia cum abbate suo exeuntes propter arciorem et sacratiorem vitam secundum regulam divi benedicti quam promiserunt tenendam habitandum venerunt, depositis quorundam monasteriorum consuetudinibus, imbecillitatem suam ad tantum pondus sustinendum imparem iudicantes.*" Exordium Parvum, XII; J. Van Damme, *op. cit.*, 11.

153. *Op. cit.*, 23ff.

154. "*Molismensis ecclesie fratres et quidam alii adiacentes monachi eos infestare et inquietare non desinunt, estimantes se viliores ac despectiores haberi apud seculum, si isti quasi singulares et novi monachi inter eos habitare videantur.*" Exordium Parvum, XII; J. Van Damme, *op. cit.*, 11. Cf. J. Lefèvre, "Que savons-nous du Cîteaux primitif?," *loc. cit.*, 37. See also Abelard's protest against Cistercian liturgical "innovations," *Ep.* X., PL 178:339.

monastery,"[155] "new cenobium,"[156] and "new monks,"[157] figuring prominently in the various documents of the *Exordium Parvum*. This special feature of the Cistercian reform can also be seen from Pope Paschal II's words to the early Cistercians, in the so-called *Roman Privilege:* "You must, therefore, remember, sons most beloved and dearest in Christ, that one part of you has left the broad roads of the world, another, the less strict paths of a laxer monastery.[158] . . . We decree that the place which you have chosen in order to live in monastic tranquillity, be secure and free and that an abbey may exist there forever and be particularly sheltered through the protection of the Apostolic See . . . as long as you remain in the observance . . . you now follow."[159]

These are the characteristic features of the Cistercian reform of 1098–1100. Since according to J. Lefèvre chapter XV of the *Exordium Parvum* is "a literary amplification of the *Instituta capituli generalis* I, IV, V, VI, VII, VIII and IX, i.e., of the second Cistercian

---

155. "*Dedimus etiam licentiam cum eo redeundi molismum omnibus illis de fratribus novi monasterii qui eum secuti fuerant.*" *Exordium Parvum*, VII; J. Van Damme, *op. cit.*, 9. Cf. ibid., "*[abbatia] quae novum monasterium dicitur.*" Cf., also "*de quodam loco qui novum monasterium vocatur*" (*Exordium Parvum*, XII; J. Van Damme, *op. cit.*, 11), and "*Venerabili alberico, novi monasterii abbati*" (*Exordium Parvum*, XIV; J. Van Damme, *op. cit.*, 12).

156. "*Interdicimus, ne cuiquam omnino persone liceat statum vestre conversationis immutare, neque vestri quod novum dicitur cenobii monachos sine regulari commendatione suscipere.*" *Exordium Parvum*, XIV; J. Van Damme, *op. cit.*, 12.

157. "*Molismensium fratres . . . eos infestare et inquietare non desinunt . . . si isti . . . novi monachi inter eos habitare videantur.*" *Exordium Parvum*, XII; J. Van Damme, *op. cit.*, 11.

158. "*Vos igitur filii in Xi (Christo) dilectissimi ac desiderantissimi meminisse debetis quia pars vestri seculares latitudines, pars ipsas etiam monasterii laxioris minus austeras augustias reliquistis.*" *Exordium Parvum*, XIV: J. Van Damme, *op. cit.*, 12.

159. "*Locum igitur illum quem inhabitandum pro quiete monastica elegistis, ab omnium mortalium molestiis tutum ac liberum fore sancimus, et abbatiam illic perpetuo haberi, ac sub apostolice sedis tutela specialiter protegi, quamdiu vos ac successores vestri in ea quam hodie observatis discipline . . . observantia permanseritis.*" J. Lefèvre, "Que savons-nous du Cîteaux primitif?," *loc. cit.*, 18. Cf. J. Turk, "Cistercii statuta antiquissima," *loc. cit.*, 43ff.

codification promulgated in 1152,"[160] it will not be considered here an authentic source of the early Cistercian reform. But even without the information furnished by the chapter in question, the reform program of the Cistercian pioneers has sufficiently been established and verified, not as "a reform of . . . a particular monastery—i.e., Molesme—but of traditional monastic observances"[161] as such. And this alone is a lasting testimony to the originality and greatness of the Cistercian founders.

---

160. J. Lefèvre, "Que savons-nous du Cîteaux primitif?," *loc. cit.,* 33.
161. *Ibid.,* 40.

CONCLUSION

THE STUDY OF EARLY CISTERCIAN HISTORY, begun in earnest around the turn of the twentieth century, received a powerful impetus after the second World War, largely on account of the discovery of hitherto unknown early Cistercian manuscripts and the ensuing investigations of Joseph Turk, Jean Leclercq, Jean B. Van Damme and, particularly, Jean Lefèvre. The labors of these experts yielded new knowledge and led to the advancement of untried and often conflicting theories and scholarly clashes. To end the confusion, Kolumban Spahr called for a critical edition of all relevant early Cistercian texts and for a determination of their exact chronological sequence. The validity of his argument is readily admitted by all authorities; still, it remains wanting and somehow incomplete as long as such hitherto neglected aspects of the Cistercian origins as the contemporary monastic *milieu* and what may be called the ideological background of Cîteaux are left unprobed.

It was of no small importance, therefore, to present the Cistercian origins in their full contemporary and historical context, i.e., to consider the monastic forerunners of Cîteaux, to examine such ideological inspirations as eastern and Celtic monachism, the aims of the Gregorian Reform, French conciliar legislation on monastic renewal and germane developments in the ascetico-theological field having a direct bearing on monastic life and on early Cistercian thinking, and to study the first decades of the Burgundian abbey of Molesme which produced and inspired the Cistercian pioneers.

The outcome of these labors, of this scrutiny of numerous, seemingly unrelated details and their assemblage into a more or less compact mosaic may well prove startling to those who either for reasons of piety or of unacquaintance with the facts still like to believe in a specific and original Cistercian *Weltanschauung*. For the preceding research has unmistakably demonstrated that practically every ideological, ascetical and organizational aspect of the Cistercian reform—fidelity to St Benedict and his Rule, poverty, seclusion, disengagement from the feudal world, liturgical simplicity, Marian devotion, intellectual activities and manual labor, economic self-sufficiency, regulations on food, drink, clothing and daily life, and such organizational features as the grange laybrotherhood, and, later, chapters and visitations—is hardly an exclusively Cistercian creation. Actually, all of these features are present, even if spread out, in a great many diverse contemporary or near-contemporary models, from Benedict of Aniane to the monastic and religious currents of the eleventh century. Still, this does not detract from Cîteaux's originality or greatness. In a world where traditional monachism had ceased to furnish universally adequate answers, its Founders were able to borrow and to wisely assimilate reform ideas from a wide range of sources, and produce a well-rounded system of their own which was eminently suited to satisfy contemporary as well as future needs. And this they accomplished without succumbing to the then prevalent and seemingly victorious trend of eremitism or to popular movements which eventually ended in heresy. To a century plagued by what Germain Morin called "the crisis of cenobitism" Cîteaux offered a solution which brought both reform and renewal and a decisive strengthening of Benedictine cenobitism.

BIBLIOGRAPHY*

1. Primary Sources

Adalbero, episcopus Laudensis. "Carmen ad Rotbertum regem Francorum." *Patrologia Latina* 141:771–786. Parisiis: J. P. Migne, 1880.
Albers, Paul Bruno (ed.). *Consuetudines Monasticae*. 5 vols. Stuttgartiae: Joseph Roth and Monte Cassino: Typis Montis Casini, 1900–1912.
Andreas abbas Strumensis. "Vita Joannis Gualberti." *Monumenta Germaniae Historica* Scriptorum tomus 30 (2): 1080–1104. Lipsiae: Impensis Karoli W. Hiersemann, 1934.
"Annales S. Benigni Divionensis." *Patrologia Latina* 141:875–898. Parisiis: J. P. Migne, 1880.
Anno archiepiscopus Coloniensis. "Vita." *Patrologia Latina* 143:1517–1584. Parisiis: J. P. Migne, 1882.
Anselmus Cantuariensis. "Carmen de contemptu mundi." *Patrologia Latina* 158:687–706. Parisiis: J. P. Migne, 1853.
Anselmus Havelbergensis. "Liber de ordine canonicorum regularium." *Patrologia Latina* 188:1091–1118. Parisiis: J. P. Migne, 1890.
Ardo seu Smaragdus. "Vita S. Benedicti Anianensis." *Patrologia Latina* 103: 353–384. Parisiis: J. P. Migne, 1864.
Atto. "Vita S. Ioannis Gualberti." *Patrologia Latina* 146:671–706. Parisiis: J. P. Migne, 1884.
"Auctarium Mortui Maris." *Patrologia Latina* 160:391–394. Parisiis: J. P. Migne, 1880.
Baldricus episcopus Dolensis. "Beati Roberti de Arbrissello Vita." *Patrologia Latina* 162:1043–1078. Parisiis: J. P. Migne, 1889.
Benedictus Anianensis. "Opera." *Patrologia Latina* 103:351–1420. Parisiis: J. P. Migne, 1864.
Bernard, Auguste, and Bruel, Alexandre (eds.). *Recueil des chartes de l'abbaye de Cluny*. 6 vols. Paris: Imprimérie Nationale, 1876–1903.
Bernardus abbas Claravallensis. "Apologia ad Gulielmum." *Patrologia Latina* 182:895–918. Parisiis: J. P. Migne, 1879.

*The following list includes also works describing the Burgundian background of Cîteaux.

――. "De praecepto et dispensatione." *Patrologia Latina* 182:859–894. Parisiis: J. P. Migne, 1879.

――. "Epistolae." *Patrologia Latina* 182:67–722. Parisiis: J. P. Migne, 1879.

Bernardus Cluniacensis. "Consuetudines Cluniacenses," in Hergott, Marquard. *Vetus disciplina monastica, seu Collectio auctorum ordinis S. Benedicti,* 33–364. Parisiis: Typis Caroli Osmont, 1726.

Bernardus Tironensis. "Vita." *Acta Sanctorum.* Aprilis tomus secundus, 220–254. Parisiis: Apud Victorem Palmé, 1865.

Bernoldus. "Chronicon." *Patrologia Latina* 148:743–1442. Parisiis: J. P. Migne, 1879.

Bligny, Bernard (ed.). *Recueil de plus anciens acts de la Grande Chartreuse (1086–1196).* Grenoble: Allier, 1958.

Bollandus, Ioannes, Henschenius, Godefridus, et al. (eds.). *Acta Sanctorum quotquot toto orbe coluntur, vel a Catholicis Scriptoribus celebrantur, quae ex Latinis et Graecis, aliarumque gentium antiquis monumentis collegit, digessit, notis illustravit Ioannes Bollandus Societatis Iesu Theologus.* Parisiis: Apud Victorem Palmé, 1863–1867.

Bouchel, Laurentius (ed.). *Decretorum Ecclesiae gallicanae libri octo.* Pariis: Sumptibus S. Cramoisy, 1621.

Bruno Carthusianorum institutor. "Acta." *Patrologia Latina* 152:9–632. Parisiis: J. P. Migne, 1879.

――. "Vita." *Acta Sanctorum.* Octobris tomus tertius, 491–786. Parisiis: Apud Victorem Palmé, 1868.

Bruno Querfurtensis. "Vita quinque fratrum." *Monumenta Germaniae Historica,* Scriptorum tomus 15(2):716–738. Hannoverae: Hahn, 1888.

Butler, Cuthbert (ed.). *Sancti Benedicti regula monachorum. Editio criticopractica.* Freiburg: B. Herder, 1912.

Caesarius Heisterbacensis. *Dialogus miraculorum.* Coloniae: J. M. Heberle, 1851.

Caesarius of Heisterbach. *The Dialogue on Miracles.* Translated by H. Von E. Scott and C. C. Swinton Bland. 2 vols. London: George Rutledge & Sons, Ltd., 1929.

Canivez, Joseph M. (ed.) *Statuta Capitulorum Generalium Ordinis Cisterciensis ab anno 1116 ad annum 1786.* 8 vols. Louvain: Bibliothèque de la Revue d'Histoire Ecclésiastique, 1933–1941.

(Carthusians). "Statuta antiqua ordinis Carthusiani." *Patrologia Latina* 153: 1123–1152. Parisiis: J. P. Migne, 1880.

Caspar, Erich (ed.). *Das Register Gregors VII.* Berlin: Weidmannsche Buchhandlung, 1920.

"Chronicon Affligemense." *Monumenta Germaniae Historica,* Scriptorum tomus 9:407–417. Leipzig: Karl W. Hiersemann, 1925.

"Chronicon Besuense, auctore Joanne monacho." *Patrologia Latina* 162: 861–1006. Parisiis: J. P. Migne, 1889.

"Chronicon S. Benigni Divionensis." *Patrologia Latina* 162:755–860. Parisiis: J. P. Migne, 1889.

D'Achery, Lucas (ed.). *Spicilegium sive collectio veterum aliquot scriptorum qui in Galliae bibliothecis delituerunt.* Nova editio. 3 vols. Parisiis: Apud Montalant, 1723.

De Clercq, Carolus (ed.). "Concilia Galliae A. 511–A. 695." *Corpus Christianorum* Series Latina 148A. Turnholti: Typographi Brépols, 1963.
"Exordium Cistercii cum 'Summa Cartae Caritatis' et capitulis," in Van Damme. . . . *Documenta pro Cisterciensis Ordinis*. Pp. 21–28.
Exordium Magnum Cisterciense sive Narratio de inito Cisterciensis Ordinis auctore Conrado monacho Claravallensi postea Eberbacensi ibidemque abbate. Ad codicum fidem recensuit Bruno Griesser. Romae: Editiones Cistercienses, 1961.
"Exordium Parvum," in Van Damme. . . . *Documenta pro Cisterciensis Ordinis* Pp. 5–15.
Gallia Christiana in provincias ecclesiasticas distributa, qua series et historia archiepiscoporum episcoporum & abbatum Franciae vicinarumque ditionum ab origine Ecclesiarum ad nostra tempora deducitur et probatur ex authenticis instrumentis ad calcem appositis. Opera et studio Domni Dionysii Sammarthani. Editio altera, labore et curis Domni Pauli Piolin recensita et aucta. Tomus Quartus complectens provinciam Lugdunensem. Parisiis: Apud Victorem Palmé, 1876.
Gaufridus Grossus monachus Tironiensis. "Vita beati Bernardi de Tironio." *Patrologia Latina* 172:1363–1446. Parisiis: J. P. Migne, 1895.
Geraldus Itherii Grandimontensis. "Vita S. Stephani." *Patrologia Latina* 204: 1005–1072. Parisiis: J. P. Migne, 1855.
Gerardus I Cameracensis episcopus. "Acta synodi Atrebatensis in Manichaeos." *Patrologia Latina* 142:1269–1312. Parisiis: J. P. Migne, 1880.
(Grandmont). "Annales Ordinis Grandimontis." *Patrologia Latina* 204:1071–1162. Parisiis: J. P. Migne, 1855.
Gregorius VII. papa. "Epistolae et diplomata pontificia." *Patrologia Latina* 148: 283–824. Parisiis: J. P. Migne, 1853.
Guibertus abbas S. Mariae de Novigento. "De vita sua libri tres." *Patrologia Latina* 156:837–1018. Parisiis: J. P. Migne, 1880.
Guignard, Philippe (ed.). *Les monuments primitifs de la règle cistercienne*. Dijon: Imprimérie Darantière, 1878.
Guigo Carthusiae Majoris prior quintus. "Consuetudines." *Patrologia Latina* 153:631–760. Parisiis: J. P. Migne, 1880.
Hallinger, Kassius (ed.). *Corpus Consuetudinum Monasticarum*. Tomus I. *Initia Consuetudinis Benedictinae. Consuetudines saeculi octavi et noni*. Siegburg: Apud Franciscum Schmitt, 1963.
Hefele, Charles-Joseph, and Leclercq, Henri (eds.). *Histoire des conciles d'après les documents originaux*. 8 vols. Paris: Letouzey et Ané, 1907–1921.
Helinandus monachus Frigidimontis. "Chronicon." *Patrologia Latina* 212: 990–1104. Parisiis: J. P. Migne, 1865.
"Herimanni Liber de restauratione monasterii Sancti Martini Tornacensis." *Monumenta Germaniae Historica*. Scriptorum tomus 14:274–327. Hannoverae: Impensis Bibliopolii Hahniani, 1883.
Herrgott, Marquard (ed.). *Vetus disciplina monastica seu Collatio auctorum ordinis S. Benedicti*. Parisiis: Typis Caroli Osmont, 1726.
Holstenius, Lucas, and Brockie, Marianus (eds.). *Codex regularum quas sancti patres monachis et virginibus sanctimonialibus servandas praescripsere*. 3 vols. Graz: Akademische Druck- und Verlagsanstalt, 1957–1958.

(Hugo abbas Cluniacensis). "Epitome vitae S. Hugonis abbatis Cluniacensis ab Ezelone atque Gilone monachis Cluniacensibus." *Patrologia Latina* 159: 909:928. Parisiis: J. P. Migne, 1903.

Hugo abbas Flaviniacensis. "Chronicon." *Patrologia Latina* 154:17–434. Parisiis: J. P. Migne, 1881.

Hugo Lugdunensis archiepiscopus. "Epistolae et Privilegia." *Patrologia Latina* 157:507–528. Parisiis: J. P. Migne, 1898.

Hümpfner, Tiburtius (ed.). *Exordium Cistercii cum Summa Cartae Caritatis et fundatio primarum filiarum Cistercii.* Vác: Kapisztrán nyomda, 1932.

Jaffé, Philippus, and Wattenbach, Gulielmus (eds.). *Regesta Pontificum Romanorum ab condita ecclesia ad annum post Christum natum MCXCVIII.* Lipsiae: Veit et comp., 1885.

"Joannes Gualbertus." *Acta Sanctorum.* Julii tomus 3:297–433. Parisiis: Apud Victorem Palmé, 1867.

John of Salerno. *St. Odo of Cluny.* Translated by Gerard Sitwell. New York: Sheed and Ward, 1958.

Jotsaldus monachus. "De vita et virtutibus sancti Odilonis abbatis." *Patrologia Latina* 142:897–940. Parisiis: J. P. Migne, 1880.

Labbé, Philippus, and Coleti, Nicholaus (eds.). *Sacrosancta Concilia ad regiam editionem exacta quae olim quarta parte prodiit auctior studio Philip. Labbei & Gabr. Cosartii . . . nunc vero integre insertis Stephani Baluzii & Joannis Harduini additamentis . . . curante Nicolae Coleti.* Venetiis: apud Sebastianum Coleti et Jo. Baptistam Albrizzi fil. Hieron., 1728–1733.

Laurent, Jacques (ed.). *Cartulaires de Molesme.* 2 vols. Paris: Alphonse Picard & Fils, 1907–1911.

Le Couteulx, Carolus (ed.). *Annales ordinis Cartusiensis ab anno 1084 ad annum 1429.* 8 vols. Monstrolii: Typis Cartusiae S. Mariae de Pratis, 1887–1891.

Loewenfeld, Samuel (ed.). *Epistolae Pontificum Romanorum ineditae.* Lipsiae: Veit & comp, 1885.

Ludovicus I et Lotharius. "Capitula." *Patrologia Latina* 97: 371–490. Parisiis: J. P. Migne, 1862.

Mabillon, Joannes (ed.). *Acta Sanctorum Ordinis S. Benedicti.* 9 vols. Parisiis: apud Ludovicum Billaine, 1668–1701.

———. *Annales Ordinis S. Benedicti occidentalium monachorum patriarchae.* 6 vols. Lucae: Typis Leonardi Venturini, 1739–1745.

Mansi, Joannes Dominicus (ed.). *Sacrosanctorum Conciliorum . . . collectio . . . ab initiis ad 1870.* Parisiis: H. Welter, 1901–1927.

Marianus Scottus. "Chronicon." *Patrologia Latina* 147:623–802. Parisiis: J. P. Migne, 1879.

Marilier, Jean (ed.). *Chartes et documents concernant l'Abbaye de Cîteaux 1098–1182.* Roma: Editiones Cistercienses, 1961.

Marrier, Martinus, and Quercentanus, Andreas (eds.). *Bibliotheca Cluniacensis in qua patrum abb. Clun. vitae, miracula, scripta, statuta, privilegia chronologiaque duplex, item catalogus abbatiarum.* Parisiis: R. Fouet, 1614.

Martène, Edmundus, and Durand, Ursinus (eds.). *Thesaurus novus anecdotorum,* 5 vols. Parisiis: Sumptibus Florentini Delaulne, 1717.

―――. *Voyage litteraire des deux réligieux Bénédictins de la Congregation de Saint Maur.* Paris: Florentin Delaulne, and Montalant, 1717–1724.

Meschet, Louis (ed.). *Privilèges de l'Ordre de Cisteaux recueilles et compilés de l'autorité du chapître général et par son ordre exprès, divisés en deux parties contenant les bulles des papes et les lettres patentes des rois et leurs règlements.* Paris: Denis Mariette, 1713.

Mittarelli, Joannes Benedictus, and Costadoni, Anselmus (eds.). *Annales Camaldulenses ordinis sancti Benedicti quibus plura interseruntur tum ceteras Italico-monasticas res, tum historiam ecclesiasticam remque diplomaticam illustrantia.* 9 vols. Venetiis: Aere Monasterii S. Michaelis de Muriano, 1755–1773.

Mombritius Boninus. *Sanctuarium seu Vitae sanctorum.* 2 vols. Parisiis: Apud Albertum Fontemoing, 1910.

Monumenta Germaniae Historica inde ab anno Christi quingentesimo usque ad annum millesimum et quingentesimum. Edidit Societas Aperiendis Fontibus rerum Germanicarum medii aevi. Hannoverae: Impensibus Bibliopolii Hahniani, 1876ff.

Munier, C. (ed.). "Concilia Galliae A. 314–A. 506." *Corpus Christianorum Series Latina* 148. Turnholti: Typographi Brépols editores pontificii, 1963.

(Nilus, S.). "De S. Nilo abbate Cryptae Ferratae in Agro Tusculano Italiae." *Acta Sanctorum.* Septembris tomus 7: 262–319. Parisiis: Apud Victorem Palmé, 1867.

Odilo, abbas Cluniacensis. "De vita beati Maioli abbatis libellus." *Patrologia Latina* 142: 943–962. Parisiis: J. P. Migne, 1880.

(Odo, abbas Cluniacensis). "Vita Sancti Odonis abbatis Cluniacensis secundi scripta a Joanne monacho ejus discipulo." *Patrologia Latina* 133:45–86. Parisiis: J. P. Migne, 1881.

Odorannus monachus. "Opuscula." *Patrologia Latina* 142:799–826. Parisiis: J. P. Migne, 1880.

Ordericus Vitalis, *Ecclesiastical History of England and Normandy.* Translated, with notes, and the Introduction of Guizot, by Thomas Forester. London: Henry G. Bohn, 1854.

―――. "Historia Ecclesiastica." *Patrologia Latina* 188:636–642. Parisiis: J. P. Migne, 1890.

Paschalis II papa. "Epistolae et privilegia." *Patrologia Latina* 163:31–448. Parisiis: J. P. Migne, 1854.

(Paulus Warnefrid). "Forilegium Casinense ex codice CLXXV. Commentarium Pauli Warnefridi Diaconi Casinensis in Regulam S. P. N. Benedicti." *Bibliotheca Casinensis* cura et studio monachorum ordinis S. Benedicti abbatiae Montis Casini. Tomus quartus. Monte Cassino: Ex typographia Casinensi, 1880.

―――. "Exposito Prologi Regulae sancti Benedicti." *Patrologia Latina* 95: 1581–1584. Parisiis: J. P. Migne, 1861.

Petrus Cellensis. "Epistolae." *Patrologia Latina* 202:405–636. Parisiis: J. P. Migne, 1885.

Petrus Damianus. "Opera." *Patrologia Latina* 144 and 145. Parisiis: J. P. Migne, 1867.

Petrus Diaconus, and Leo Marsicanus. "Chronicon Casinense." *Patrologia Latina* 173: 440-978. Parisiis: J. P. Migne, 1895.
(Petrus Juliacensis). "Vita Sancti Petri prioris Juliacensis puellarum monasterii et monachi Molismensis." *Patrologia Latina* 185bis:1257-1270. Parisiis: J. P. Migne, 1854.
Petrus Venerabilis abbas Cluniacensis. "De miraculis." *Patrologia Latina* 189: 851-954. Parisiis: J. P. Migne, 1890.
Prou, Maurice (ed.). *Recueil des actes de Philippe Ier, roi de France (1059-1108)*. Paris: Imprimérie Nationale, 1908.
Receuil des historiens des Gaules et de la France. Edited by Martin Bouquet, Leopold Delisle, et al. 23 vols. Paris: Victor Palmé, 1840-1894.
Richard, Carolus Ludovicus. *Analysis conciliorum generalium et particularium*. Venetiis: Typographia Balleonia, 1776-1780.
(Robertus de Arbrissello). "Vita beati Roberti de Arbissello." *Patrologia Latina* 162: 1043-1078. Parisiis: J. P. Migne, 1889.
———. "S. Roberti de Arbrissello vita." *Acta Sanctorum*. Februarii tomus 3: 598-621. Parisiis: Apud Victorem Palmé, 1865.
(Robertus Molismensis). "Vita." *Patrologia Latina* 157: 1255-1283. Parisiis: J. P. Migne, 1854.
———. "De sancto Roberto primo abbate Molismensi ac fundatore ordinis Cisterciensis." *Acta Sanctorum*. Aprilis tomus 3:670-685. Parisiis: Apud Victorem Palmé, 1866.
Robertus de Monte S. Michaelis (Thorigny). "Tractatus de immutatione ordinis monachorum." *Patrologia Latina* 202:309-310. Parisiis: J. P. Migne, 1855.
Rodulfus Glaber, "Historiarum sui temporis libri quinque." *Patrologia Latina* 142:611-698. Parisiis: J. P. Migne, 1880.
———. "Vita sancti Guillelmi abbatis Divionensis." *Patrologia Latina* 142:701-720. Parisiis: J. P. Migne, 1880.
Rupertus abbas Tuitiensis. "De divinis officiis." *Patrologia Latina* 170:9-334. Parisiis: J. P. Migne, 1894.
(Sauve-Majeure). "De S. Geraldo fundatore Silvae Majoris." *Acta Sanctorum*. Aprilis tomus 1:412-428. Parisiis: Apud Victorem Palmé, 1865.
Seherus, Arnulfus Spinalensis. "Primordia Calmosiacensia." *Monumenta Germaniae Historica*. Scriptorum tomus 12:325-347. Leipzig: Karl W. Hiersemann, 1925.
Séjalon, Hugo. *Nomasticon Cisterciense*. Solesmes: E. typographia S. Petri, 1892.
Sigebertus Gemblacensis. "Chronica." *Patrologia Latina* 160:9-546. Parisiis: J. P. Migne, 1880.
Spahr, Kolumban (ed.). *Das Leben des hl. Robert von Molesme. Eine Quelle zur Vorgeschichte von Cîteaux*. Freiburg, in der Schweiz: Paulusdruckerei, 1944.
(Stephanus de Mureto). "Vita." *Acta Sanctorum*. Februarii tomus 2: 205-213. Parisiis: Apud Victorem Palmé, 1864.
Surius, Laurentius. *De probatis Sanctorum vitis*. 7 vols. Coloniae Agrippinae: Apud Geruinum Calenium et haeredes Quentelios, 1570-1581.
Tabacco, Giovanni (ed.). *Vita beati Romualdi*. "Fonti per la storia d'Italia, n. 94." Roma: Istituto storico italiano, 1957.

Bibliography

Udalricus Cluniacensis monachus. "Antiquiores consuetudines Cluniacensis monasterii." *Patrologia Latina* 149:639–778. Parisiis: J. P. Migne, 1882.
Urbanus II Pontifex Romanus. "Epistolae et Privilegia." *Patrologia Latina* 151: 283–558. Parisiis: J. P. Migne, 1881.
Van Damme, Joannes-B. (ed.). *Documenta pro Cisterciensis Ordinis historiae ac juris studio.* Westmalle: Typis Ordinis Cisterciensis, 1959.
(Vaso of Liège). "Vita Vasonis." *Patrologia Latina* 142:725–764. Parisiis: J. P. Migne, 1880.
Willelmus monachus Clusiensis. "Vita V. Benedicti abbatis Clusiensis." *Patrologia Latina* 150:1459–1492. Parisiis: J. P. Migne, 1880.
Willelmus Godell monachus. "Ex Chronico Willelmi Godelli." *Recueil des historiens des Gaules et de la France.* Tome 13:671–677. Paris: Victor Palmé, 1869.
Willelmus Malmesburiensis. "De gestis regum Anglorum libri quinque." *Patrologia Latina* 179:859–1392. Parisiis J. P. Migne, 1899.
William of Malmesbury. *The History of the Kings of England and the Modern History.* Translated by John Sharpe. London: Longman, 1815.

2. Secondary Works

Albers, Bruno. "Die aeltesten Consuetudines von Vallombrosa," *Revue Bénédictine* 28 (1911) 432–436.
———. "Les plus ancien coutumier de Cluny," *Revue Bénédictine* 20 (1903) 174–184.
———. "Die Reformationssynode von 817 und das von ihr erlassene Kapitular," *Studien und Mitteilungen aus der Geschichte des Benediktinerordens und seiner Zweige* 28 (1907) 528–540.
———. *Untersuchungen zu den ältesten Mönchsgewohnheiten. Ein Beitrag zur Benediktinerordensgeschichte des X.-XII. Jahrhunderts.* München: Lentner'sche Buchhandlung, 1905.
Aux sources de la vie cartusienne. La Grande Chartreuse, 1960. (Mimeographed.)
Bacon-Tacon, Pierre J. J. *Recherches sur les origines celtiques, principalement sur celles de Bugey.* 2 vols. Paris: P. Didot l'Ainé, 1798.
Bardy, G. "Saint Bernard et Origène?," *Revue du Moyen Age Latin* 1 (1945) 403–421.
Becquet, Jean. "Les institutions de l'Ordre de Grandmont au Moyen Age," *Revue Mabillon* 42 (1952) 31–42.
———. "Le regle de Grandmont," *Bulletin de la Société archéologique et historique de Limousin* 87 (1958) 9–36.
———. "S. Etienne de Muret," *Dictionnaire de Spiritualité* 4 (1961) 1504–1514.
Beissel, Stephan. *Geschichte der Verehrung Marias in Deutschland während des Mittelalters. Ein Beitrag zur Religionswissenschaft und Kunstgeschichte.* Freiburg, i. B.: Herder'sche Verlagsbuchhandlung, 1909.
Bergeron, L. "Benoît d'Aniane," *Dictionnaire de Spiritualité* 1 (1937) 1438–1442.
Berlière, Ursmer. *L'ascèse bénédictine dès origines a la fin du XIIe siècle.* Paris: P. Lethielleux, 1927.

v

———. "Les coutumiers monastiques," *Revue Bénédictine* 23 (1906) 260–267.
———. "Les coutumiers monastiques de VIIIe et IXe siècles," *Revue Bénédictine* 25 (1908) 95–107.
———. "L'étude des réformes monastiques des Xe et XIe siècles," *Académie Royale de Belgique. Bulletin de la Classe des Lettres*, 5e Série 18 (1932) 137–156.
———. *L'ordre monastique dès origines au XIIe siècle; essai historique.* Paris: P. Lethielleux, 1924.
———. "Les origines de l'Ordre de Cîteaux et l'Ordre bénédictine au XIIe siècle," *Revue d'Histoire Ecclésiastique* 1 (1900) 448–471 and 2 (1901) 253–290.
Bernard de Clairvaux. Edited by Commission d'Histoire de l'Ordre de Cîteaux. Paris: Editions Alsatia, 1953.
Besse, Jean Martial. "Cisterciens," *Dictionnaire de Théologie Catholique* 2 (1905) 2532–2550.
———. "L'Ordre de Cluny et son gouvernement," *Revue Mabillon* 1 (1905) 5–40 and 2 (1906) 1–22.
Biron, Reginald. *St. Pierre Damien (1007–1072).* Paris: Victor Lecoffre, 1930.
Bishop, Edmund. "Cluniacs and Cistercians," *The Downside Review* 52 (1934) 48–70.
———. *Liturgica Historica. Papers on the Liturgy and Religious Life of the Western Church.* Oxford: Clarendon Press, 1918.
Blanchard, P. "Un monument primitif de la Règle cistercienne," *Revue Bénédictine* 31 (1914–1919) 35.
Bligny, Bernard. "Un aspect de la vie religieuse au Moyen Age. La concurrance monastique dans les Alpes au XIIe siècle," *Bulletin Philologique et Historique* Anneés 1951–1952, 279–287. Paris: Imprimérie Nationale, 1953.
———. *L'Eglise et les ordres réligieux dans le royaume de Bourgogne aux XIe et XIIe siècles.* Grenoble: Imprimérie Allier, 1960.
———. "Les premiers Chartreux et la pauvreté," *Le Moyen Age* 22 (1951) 27–60.
Bock, Colomban. *Les codifications du droit cistercien.* Westmalle: Imprimérie de l'Ordre (Cistercien), 1955.
Bonduelle, J. "Convers," *Dictionnaire de Droit Canonique* 4 (1949) 562–588.
Bouton, Jean de la Croix. *Histoire de l'Ordre de Cîteaux.* Tirage-à-part des "Fiches Cisterciennes." Westmalle: Imprimérie de l'Ordre (Cistercien), 1959.
Bouyer, Louis. *The Cistercian Heritage.* Translated by Elizabeth Livingstone. Westminster, Md.: The Newman Press, 1958.
Brémond, Henri, Gaudemet, Jean, et al. *L'empire chrétien et ses destinées en occident du XIe au XIIIe siècle. Essai sur les forces d'universalisme et de particularisme dans l'Europe du Moyen Age.* Paris: Librairie Générale de Droit et de Jurisprudence, 1944.
Brockhoff, L. E. D. *Die Kloster-Orden der heiligen katholischen Kirche.* Frankfurt: Verlag Gustav Bender, 1875.
Bultot, Robert. *Christianisme et valeurs humaines. La doctrine du mépris du monde. IV. Le XIe siècle. 1. Pierre Damien.* Louvain: Nauwelaerts, 1963.
———. *Christianisme et valeurs humaines. La doctrine du mépris du monde. IV. Le XIe siécle. 2. Jean de Fécamp, Hermann Contract, Roger de Caen, Anselme de Canterbury.* Louvain: Nauwelaerts, 1964.

Bibliography

Butler, Cuthbert. *Benedictine Monachism. Studies in Benedictine Life and Rule.* New York: Barnes & Noble, 1961.
Cacciamani, Giuseppe. *La reclusione presso l'Ordine Camaldolese.* Arezzo: 1960.
Canivez, Joseph-Marie. "Alberic," *Dictionnaire de Spiritualité* (1937) 276–277.
———. "Cîteaux," *Dictionnaire de Droit Canonique* 3 (1942) 745–795.
———. "Cîteaux," *Dictionnaire d'Histoire et de Géographie Ecclésiastiques* 12 (1953) 852–997.
———. "Le rite cistercien," *Ephemerides Liturgicae* 63 (1949) 276–311.
(Carthusians). *La Grande Chartreuse, par un Chartreux.* Grenoble: August Cote, 1884.
Casel, Odo (ed.). *Heilige Überlieferung. Ausschnitte aus der Geschichte des Mönchtums und des heiligen Kultes.* Festgabe Ildefons Herwegen. Münster in Westfalen: Aschendorffsche Verlagsbuchhandlung, 1938.
Chagny, André. *Cluny et son empire.* Lyon: E. Vitte, 1949.
Champier, L. "Cîteaux, ultime étape dans l'aménagement agraire de l'Occident," in *Mélanges Saint Bernard,* 254–261.
Chaume, Maurice. "Les anciens vicomtes de Beaune et la foundation de Cîteaux," *Mémoires de l'Académie des Sciences, Arts et Belles-Lettres de Dijon.* Bulletin de Mai 1923, 2, 73–77. Dijon: Imprimérie Jobard, 1923.
———. *Les origines du duché de Bourgogne.* 4 vols. Dijon: Librairie E. Rebourseau, 1925–1931.
Chenu, M. D. "Moines, clercs, laics au carrefour de la vie évangélique (XIIe siècle)," *Revue d'Histoire Ecclésiastique* 49 (1954) 59–89.
Cirot, de la Ville, *Histoire de l'Abbaye et congrégation de Notre Dame de la Grande-Sauve.* 2 vols. Paris: Mequignon, 1844–1845.
(Cistercian Order). *A Concise History of the Cistercian Order With the Lives of SS. Robert, Alberic, and Stephen.* London: Thomas Richardson, 1852.
(Cîteaux). *Histoire abrégé de l'Ordre de Cîteaux.* Par un moine de Thymadeuc. Saint-Brieuc: René Prud'homme, 1897.
Constable, Giles. *Monastic Tithes: From Their Origin to the Twelfth Century.* Cambridge Studies in Medieval Life and Thought; New Series, Vol. 10. Cambridge: University Press, 1964.
Cooke, Alice M. "A Study in Twelfth Century Religious Revival and Reform," *Bulletin of the John Rylands Library, Manchester* 9 (1925) 139–176. Manchester: University Press, 1925.
Cottineau, L. Henri. *Répertoire Topo-bibliographique des Abbayes et des Prieurés.* 2 vols. Macôn: Protat Frères, 1935.
Coucherat, François. *Cluny au onzième siècle. Son influence réligieuse, intellectuelle et politique.* Macôn: Académie de Macôn, 1951.
Coulton, George Gordon. *Five Centuries of Religion.* Vol. 1: *St. Bernard, His Predecessors and Successors, 1000–1200 A.D.* Cambridge: University Press, 1929.
Courtépée, M., and Beguillet, M. *Description générale et particulière du duché de Bourgogne.* 6 vols. Dijon: Frantin et Causse, 1775–1781.
Cousin, Patrice. *Précis d'histoire monastique.* Paris: Bloud & Gay, 1956.
Dailgairns, John Bernard, Newman, John Henry, and Thurston, Herbert.

Life of St. Stephen Harding, Abbot of Cîteaux and Founder of the Cistercian Order. Westminster, Md.: The Newman Press, 1942.

Daly, Lowrie. *Benedictine Monasticism. Its Formation and Development Through the 12th Century.* New York: Sheed and Ward, 1965.

Dammertz, Viktor. *Das Verfassungsrecht der benediktinischen Mönchskongregationen. Kirchengeschichtliche Quellen und Studien, begründet und geleitet von Heinrich Suso Brechter.* 6. Band. St. Ottilien: Eos Verlag, 1963.

Delahaye, Fernand. "Un moine: saint Robert, fondateur de Cîteaux," *Collectanea Ordinis Cisterciensium Reformatorum* 14 (1952) 83–106.

Déléage, André. *La vie rurale en Bourgogne jusqu'au debut du onziéme siècle.* 3 vols. Macôn: Protat Frères, 1941.

Delisle, Leopold. "Examen des treize chartes de l'Ordre de Grammont," *Mémoires de la Société des Antiquaires de Normandie* 20 (1853) 171–221.

Dereine, Charles. "La fondation de Cîteaux d'après l'Exordium Cistercii et l'Exordium Parvum," *Cîteaux* 10 (1959) 125–139.

———. "Odon de Tournai et la crise du cénobitisme au XIe siècle," *Revue du Moyen Age Latin* 4 (1948) 134–154.

———. "Vie commune, règle de saint Augustin et les chanoines réguliers aux XIe siècle," *Revue d'Histoire Ecclésiastique* 41 (1946) 365–406.

———. "La vita apostolica dans l'ordre canonial du IXe au XIe siècle," *Revue Mabillon* 51 (1961) 47–53.

Deutsch, S. M. "Cistercienser," *Realencyklopädie fur protestantische Theologie und Kirche* 4 (1898) 116–127.

DeWarren, Henry-Bernard. "Le monachisme à l'apparition de Bernard," in *Bernard de Clairvaux*, 45–63.

D'Herblay, Alain. "Le problème des origines cisterciennes," *Revue d'Histoire Ecclésiastique* 50 (1955) 158–164.

Dimier, Anselme, and Dumontier, P. "Encore les emplacements malsains," *Revue du Moyen Age Latin* 4 (1948) 60–65.

Dmitrewski, Michael von. *Die christliche freiwillige Armut vom Ursprung der Kirche bis zum 12. Jahrhundert.* Abhandlungen zur Mittleren und Neueren Geschichte, Heft 53. Leipzig: Walther Rothschild, 1913.

Dressler, Fridolin. *Petrus Damiani Leben und Werk.* Studia Anselmiana, fasciculus 34. Roma: Herder, 1954.

Ducourneau, Othon J. *Les origines cisterciennes.* Ligugé: Imprimérie E. Aubin et fils, 1933.

———. "Les origines cisterciennes," *Revue Mabillon* 22 (1932) 132–164, 233–252, and 23 (1933) 1–32, 81–111, 153–189.

Duvernay, Roger. "Cîteaux, Vallombreuse et Étienne Harding," *Analecta Sacri Ordinis Cisterciensis* 8 (1952) 379–494.

(L') *Eremitismo in Occidente nei secoli XI e XII.* Atti della seconda Settimana internazionale di studio Mendola, 30 agosto–6 settembre 1962. Miscellanea del Centro di Studi Medievali, 4 Milano: Societa Editrice Vita e Pensiero, 1965.

Evans, Joan. *Monastic Life at Cluny 910–1157.* Oxford: Oxford University Press, 1931.

Bibliography

Flach, Jacques. *Les origines de l'ancienne France.* 4 vols. Paris: Libraire de la Société du Recueil Sirey, 1886–1917.

Fliche, Augustin, and Martin, Victor. *Histoire de l'Eglise depuis les origines jusqu'à nos jours.* 26 vols. Paris: Bloud & Gay, 1934ff.

Fliche, Augustin. *La réforme grégorienne.* 3 vols. Paris: E. Champion, 1924–1937.

———. *Le règne de Philippe Ier, roi de France (1060–1108).* Paris: Société Française d'Imprimérie et de Libraire, 1912.

Folz, Robert. "Le problème des origines de Cîteaux," in *Mélanges Saint Bernard,* 284–294.

Franke, Walter. *Romuald von Camaldoli und seine Reformtätigkeit zur Zeit Ottos III.* Historische Studien, Heft 107. Berlin: Emil Ebering, 1913.

Fries, Heinrich (ed.). *Handbuch Theologischer Grundbegriffe.* 2 vols. München: Kösel-Verlag, 1962–1963.

Gams, Pius Bonifatius. *Series episcoporum Ecclesiae Catholicae quotquot innotuerunt a beato Petro apostolo.* Leipzig: Verlag Karl W. Hiersemann, 1931.

Gay, Jules. *Les papes du XIe siècle et la Chrétienté.* Paris: Librairie Victor Lecoffre, 1926.

Geanakoplos, Deno J. *Byzantine East and Latin West.* Oxford: B. Blackwell, 1966.

Gerards, Alberich. "Die ersten Cistercienser und die Handarbeit," *Cistercienser-Chronik* 59 (1952) 1–6.

———. "Wirtschaftliche Hintergründe zur Zeit der Gründung des Cistercienserordens," *Cistercienser-Chronik* 58 (1951) 65–79.

Gildas, F. M. "Cistercians," *Catholic Encyclopaedia* 3 (1913) 780–791.

Giseke, Paul, "Ueber den Gegensatz der Cluniacenser und Cistercienser. Ein Riss im Benediktinerorden,"*Jahrbuch des Pädagogiums zum Kloster Unserer Lieben Frauen in Magdeburg* 50 (1886) 1–41. Magdeburg: E. Baensch jun., 1886.

Godefroy, Jean. "L'histoire du prieuré de Saint-Ayoul de Provins et le récit des miracles du saint," *Revue Mabillon* 27 (1937) 94–107, and 28 (1938) 29–48, 84–98, and 112–117.

Gougaud, Louis. *Eremites et reclus. Études sur d'anciennes formes de vie religieuse.* Ligugé: Abbaye Saint-Martin de Ligugé, 1928.

———. "Essai de bibliographie érémitique (1929–1931)," *Revue Bénédictine* 45 (1933) 281–291.

———. *Gaelic Pioneers of Christianity. The Work and Influence of Irish Monks and Saints in Continental Europe (VIth-XII Cent.).* New York: Benziger, 1923.

———. "L'oeuvre des *Scotti* dans l'Europe continentale (Fin VIe-Fin XIe siècles," *Revue d'Histoire Ecclésiastique* 9 (1908) 21–37, 255–277.

———. "La Theoria dans la spiritualité médievale," *Revue d'Ascetique et de Mystique* 3 (1922) 381–394.

Gouillou, André. "Il monachesimo Greco in Italia meridionale e in Sicilia nel Medioevo," in *L'Eremitismo in Occidente nei secoli XI et XII.* 355–379.

Graham, Rose. "The Relation of Cluny to Some Other Movements of Monastic Reform," *Journal of Theological Studies* 15 (1914) 179–195.

Grass, Franz. "Neue Cistercienser-Literatur," *Zeitschrift der Savigny-Stiftung für Rechtsgeschichte, Kanonistische Abteilung* 46 (1960) 567–569.
Griesser, Bruno. "Die 'Ecclesiastica Officia Cisterciensis Ordinis' des Cod. 1711 von Trient," *Analecta Sacri Ordinis Cisterciensis* 12 (1956) 153–288.
Grill, Leopold. "Der hl. Bernhard als bisher unerkannter Verfasser des Exordium Cistercii und der Summa Cartae Caritatis," *Cistercienser-Chronik* 66 (1959) 43–57.
Grundmann, Herbert. *Religiöse Bewegungen im Mittelalter*. Hildesheim: Georg Olms Verlagsbuchhandlung, 1961.
Grützmacher, Georg. *Die Bedeutung Benedikts von Nursia und seiner Regel in der Geschichte des Mönchtums*. Berlin: Mayer & Müller, 1892.
———. "Mönchtum," *Realencyklopädie für protestantische Theologie und Kirche* 13 (1903) 225–226.
Guilloreau, Leon. "La vie monastique au declin du XIe siècle: les anachorètes dans le Maine," *Revue du Maine* 49 (1901) 113, and 52 (1904) 121.
Hallinger, Kassius. "Cluny," *Enciclopedia Cattolica* 3 (1949) 1883–1893.
———. *Gorze-Cluny*. 2 vols. Roma: Herder, 1950–1951.
———. "Klunys Bräuche zur Zeit Hugos des Grossen (1049–1109). Prolegomena zur Neuherausgabe des Bernhard und Udalrich von Kluny," *Zeitschrift der Savigny-Stiftung fur Rechtsgeschichte, Kanonistische Abteilung* 45 (1959) 99–140.
———. "Woher kommen die Laienbrüder?," *Analecta Sacri Ordinis Cisterciensis* 12 (1956) 1–104.
Hardick, L. *Cluny und Cîteaux*. Münster: Dissertatio Münster, 1949.
Hauck, Albert. *Kirchengeschichte Deutschlands*. 6 vols. Leipzig: J. C. Hinrichs'sche Buchhandlung, 1887–1920.
Haureau, Jean Barthelemy. "Sur quelques écrivains de l'Ordre de Grandmont, d'après le n° 17187 de la Bibliothèque Nationale," *Notices et Extraits des Manuscrits de la Bibliothèque Nationale* 24 (1876) 247–267. Paris: Imprimérie Nationale, 1876.
(Hautcoeur, Edouard). *Vies de saint Robert et de saint Alberic premier et second abbés de Cîteaux*. Lérins: Imprimérie Marie-Bernard, 1875.
Hauviller, Ernst. *Ulrich von Cluny, ein biographischer Beitrag zur Geschichte der Cluniacenser im 11. Jahrhundert*. Münster, i. W.: Heinrich Schöningh, 1896.
Heimbucher, Max. *Die Orden und Kongregationen der katolischen Kirche*. 3 vols. Paderborn: F. Schöningh, 1907–1908.
Hélyot, Hippolyte. *Dictionnaire des ordres réligieux ou Histoire des ordres monastiques, réligieux et militaires*. 5 vols. Paris: J. P. Migne, 1847–1859.
Henriot, Gabriel-Louis. *La vie et les légations d'Hugues, évêque de Die archévêque de Lyon*. Paris: École des Chartes, Position de thèses, 1904.
Henriquez, Chrysostomus. *Fasciculus sanctorum Ordinis Cisterciensis*. 2 vols. Bruxellis: Apud J. Pepermanum, 1623.
———. *Menologium Cisterciense notationibus illustratum, seorsim Regula, constitutiones et privilegia eiusdem Ordinis ac congregationum monasticarum et militarium quae Cisterciense institutum observant*. Antwerpiae: Officina Plantiana Balthasaris Moreti, 1630.
Hermans, Vincent. *Spiritualité monastique*. Rome: O. Cist. Ref., 1954. (Mimeographed).

Bibliography

Hilpisch, Stephanus. *Benedictinism Through Changing Centuries.* Translated by Leonard J. Doyle. Collegeville: St. John's Abbey Press, 1958.
———. "Chorgebet und Frömmigkeit im Spätmittelalter," in *Heilige Überlieferung. Auschnitte aus der Geschichte des Mönchtums und des heiligen Kultes. Festgabe Ildefons Herwegen.* Edited by Odo Casel. Münster, i. W.: Aschendorffsche Verlagsbuchhandlung, 1938.
———. *Geschichte des benediktinischen Mönchtums in ihren Grundzügen dargestellt.* Freiburg, i. B.: Herder & Co., 1929.
Hoffmann, Eberhard. "Die Entwicklung der Wirtschaftsprinzipien im Cisterzienserorden während des 12. und 13. Jahrhunderts," *Historisches Jahrbuch* 31 (1910) 699–727.
———. *Das Konverseninstitut des Cistercienserordens.* Freiburger Historische Studien. Freiburg: Otto Gschwend, 1905.
Hofmeister, Philipp. "Mönchtum und Seelsorge bis zum 13. Jahrhundert," *Studien und Mitteilungen zur Geschichte des Benediktinerordens und seiner Zweige* 65 (1955) 209–273.
Holtzmann, Robert. *Französische Verfassungsgeschichte von der Mitte des neunten Jahrhunderts bis zur Revolution.* München: R. Oldenbourg, 1910.
Homan, Helen Walker. *Knights of Christ.* Englewood Cliffs, N.J.: Prentice Hall, Inc., 1957.
Huckel, G. A. "Der bisher vermisste Teil des Exordium Magnum," *Cistercienser-Chronik* 2 (1908) 97–106.
———. "Les poèmes satiriques d'Adalberon," *Bibliothèque de la Faculté des lettres de Paris* 13 (1911) 129–167.
Ilarino da Milano. "Le eresie popolari del secolo XI nell' Europa occidentale," *Studi Gregoriani* 2 (1947) 43–89. Roma: Abbazia di San Paolo, 1947.
Janauschek, Leopoldus. *Originum Cisterciensium* tomus I. Vindobonae: Apud Alfredum Heelder, 1877.
Jemolo, Arturo Carlo. "Commenda," *Enciclopedia Cattolica* 4 (1950) 50–52.
King, Archdale. *Cîteaux and Her Elder Daughters.* London: Burns & Oates, 1954.
Knowles, M. David. *Cistercians and Cluniacs. The Controversy Between St Bernard and Peter the Venerable.* London: Oxford University Press, 1955.
———. *From Pachomius to Ignatius. A Study in the Institutional History of the Religious Orders.* Oxford: The Clarendon Press, 1966.
———. *Great Historical Enterprises. Problems in Monastic History.* London: Thomas Nelson & Sons Ltd., 1963.
———. *The Monastic Order in England; A History of Its Development From the Time of St Dunstan to the Fourth Lateran Council, 954–1216.* Cambridge: University Press, 1950.
Ladeuze, Paulin. *Étude sur le cénobitisme Pakhomien pendant le IVe siècle et la première moitié du Ve.* Frankfurt, a. M.: Minerva GMBH., 1961.
Lake, K. "The Greek Monasteries in Southern Italy," *The Journal of Theological Studies* 4 (1903) 345–368, 517–542, and 5 (1904) 22–41, 189–202.
Laprat, R. "Commende," *Dictionnaire de Droit Canonique* 3 (1942) 1029–1085.
Laurent, Jacques, and Claudon, Ferdinand. *Abbayes et prieurés de l'ancienne France. Recueil historique des archévêchés, évêchés et prieurés de France.* Tome

douzième: *Province ecclésiastique de Lyon*. Troisième partie: *Diocèses de Langres et de Lyon*. Archives de la France Monastique, vol. 45. Paris: A. Picard, 1941.

Laurent, Jacques. "Un fondateur," *Annales de Bourgogne* 12 (1940) 31–36.

———. "Le problème des commencements de Cîteaux," *Annales de Bourgogne* 6 (1934) 213–229.

Le Bail, Anselme. *L'Ordre de Cîteaux*. La Trappe. Paris: Letouzey et Ane, 1947.

———. "La paternité de Saint Benoît sur l'Ordre de Cîteaux," *Collectanea Ordinis Cisterciensium Reformatorum* 9 (1947) 110–130.

———. "Le règle de Saint Benoît dans l'Ordre de Cîteaux," *Mélanges publiés par les abbayes bénédictines de la Congregation belge à l'occasion du XIVe centenaire de la fondation du Mont Cassin, 529–1929*, 133–157. Maredsous: Abbaye de Maredsous, 1929.

Lecler, A. "Histoire de l'abbaye de Grandmont," *Bulletin de la Société Archéologique et Historique du Limousin* 57 (1907) 129–171.

Leclercq, Henri. *L'Ordre Bénédictin*. Paris: Les Editions Rieder, 1930.

Leclercq, Jean. "Une ancienne rédaction des Coutumes cisterciennes," *Revue d'Histoire Ecclésiastique* 47 (1952) 172–176.

———. "Un congrès sur l'érémitisme," *Studia Monastica* 4 (1962) 404–407.

———. "Contemplation," *Dictionnaire de spiritualité* 2 (1952) 1943.

———. "La crise du monachisme aux XIe et XIIe siècles," *Bolletino dell' Instituto Storico Italiano per il Medio Evo e Archivio Muratoriano* 70 (1958) 19–41.

———. "Documents pour l'histoire des chanoines réguliers," *Revue d'Histoire Ecclésiastique* 44 (1949) 556–569.

———. "Écrits monastiques sur la Bible aux XIe–XIIIe siècles," *Mediaeval Studies* 15 (1953) 95–106.

———. "Eremus et eremita. Pour l'histoire du vocabulaire de la vie solitaire," *Collectanea Ordinis Cisterciensium Reformatorum* 25 (1963) 8–30.

———. *Étude sur le vocabulaire monastique du moyen age*. Studia Anselmiana, 48. Roma: Herder, 1961.

———. "Études sur le vocabulaire monastique du moyen age," in *Studia Anselmiana philosophica-theologica*, fasciculus 48. Roma: Pontif. Instit. S. Anselmi, 1961.

———. "L'Exordium Cistercii et la Summa cartae Caritatis sont-ils de Saint Bernard?," *Revue Benedictine* 73 (1963) 89–99.

———. *The Love of Learning and the Desire For God*. Translated by Catharine Misrahi. New York: New American Library, 1960.

———. "Mediévisme et Unionisme," *Irénikon* 19 (1946) 6–23.

———. "On Monastic Priesthood According to the Ancient Medieval Tradition," *Studia Monastica* 3 (1961) 137–155.

———. "Origène au XIIe siècle," *Irénikon* 24 (1951) 425–439.

———. *Pierre le Vénérable*. Paris: Editions Fontenelle, 1946.

———. "Le poème de Payen Bolotin contre les faux ermits," *Revue Benedictine* 68 (1958) 52–86.

———. "The Priesthood For Monks," *Monastic Studies* 3 (1965) 58–85.

———. "Problèmes de l'érémitisme," *Studia Monastica* 5 (1963) 197–212.

———. "Textes cisterciens dans les bibliothèques d'Allemagne. Les Cisterciens

et Saint Benoît d'Anîane," *Analecta Sacri Ordinis Cisterciensis* 7 (1951) 46–70.
Leclercq, Jean, and Bonnes, Jean-Paul. *Un maître de la vie spirituelle au XIe siècle. Jean de Fécamp.* Paris: J. Vrin, 1946.
Leclercq, Jean, Vandenbroucke, François, and Bouyer, Louis. *La spiritualité du moyen age. Histoire de la spiritualité chrétienne,* 2. Paris: Aubier, 1961.
Lefèbvre, F. A. *Saint Bruno et l'Ordre des Chartreux.* 2 vols. Paris: 1883–1884.
———. "S. Robert de Molesme dans l'opinion monastique du XIIe et du XIIIe siècles," *Analecta Bollandiana* 74 (1956) 50–83.
Lefèvre, Jean A. "Que savons-nous du Cîteaux primitif?," *Revue d'Histoire Ecclesiastique* 51 (1956) 5–41.
———. "Les traditions manuscrites de l'Exordium Parvum," *Scriptorium* 10 (1956) 42–46.
———. "La véritable Carta Caritatis primitive et son évolution 1114–1119," *Collectanea Ordinis Cisterciensium Reformatorum* 16 (1954) 5–29.
———. "La véritable constitution cistercienne de 1119," *Collectanae Ordinis Cisterciensium Reformatorum* 16 (1954) 77–104.
———. "Le vrai récit primitif des origines de Cîteaux est-il l'*Exordium Parvum*?," *Le Moyen Age* 61 (1955) 79–120, 329–361.
Lefèvre, Placide. "Premontre, ses origines, sa première liturgie, les rélations de son code lègislatif avec Cîteaux et les chanoines du Saint-Sépulcre de Jerusalem," *Analecta Praemonstratensia* 25 (1949) 96–103.
Lekai, Louis J. *The White Monks.* Okauchee, Wis.: Spring Bank, 1953.
Lenssen, Seraphin. *Le fondateur de Cîteaux Saint Robert.* Extrait des *Collectanea Ord. Cist. Ref.* 4. Westmalle: Imprimérie de l'Ordre Cistercien, 1937.
———. "Saint Robert Fondateur de Cîteaux," *Collectanea Ordinis Cisterciensium Reformatorum* 4 (1937) 2–16, 81–96, 161–177.
Lesne, Emile, *Histoire de la propriete ecclesiastique en France.* Paris: H. Champion, 1910–1943.
———. "Les ordonnances de Louis le Pieux," *Revue d'Histoire de l'Église de France* 6 (1920) 161–175, 321–338, 449–493.
Letonnellier, Gaston. *L'abbaye exempte de Cluny et le Sanit-Siège. Étude sur le développement de l'exemption clunisienne dès origines jusqu'à la fin du XIIIe siècle.* Ligugé: Abbaye Saint-Martin, 1923.
Levison, Wilhelm. "Die Iren und die Fränkische Kirche," *Historische Zeitschrift* 109 (1912) 1–22.
Lialine, Clément. "Le monachisme oriental et le monachisme occidental," *Irénikon* 33 (1960) 435–459.
Löbbel, Hermann. *Der Stifter des Carthäuser-Ordens, der heilige Bruno aus Köln.* Kirchengeschichtliche Studien herausgegeben von Khöpfler, Schrörs, Sdralek, tom, 5, fasc. 1. Münster, i. W.: Verlag Heinrich Schöningh, 1899.
Lortz, Joseph (ed.). *Bernhard von Clairvaux Mönch und Mystiker. Internationaler Bernhardkongress Mainz 1953.* Wiesbaden: Franz Steiner Verlag, 1955.
Lucchesi, Giovanni. *Clavis S. Petri Damiani.* Faenza: Seminario Vescovile Pio XII, 1961.
Luddy, Ailbe John. *Centenary Life of St. Stephen Harding.* Dublin: M. H. Gill, 1934.
———. *The Order of Cîteaux.* Dublin: M. H. Gill, 1952.

Lühe, Wilhelm. *Hugo von Die und Lyon, Legate von Gallien.* Berlin: F. W. Jungfer, 1898.

Mahn, Jean-Berthold. *L'exemption et le gouvernement de l'Ordre cistercien aux XIIe et XIIIe siècles.* Paris: Ecole des Chartes, Position des thèses, 1935.

———. *L'ordre cistercien et son gouvernement dês origines au milieu du XIIIe siècle (1098-1265).* Paris: E. De Boccard, 1945.

Maisonneuve, Henri. *La morale chrétienne d'après les conciles des Xe et XIe siècles.* Analecta Mediaevalia Namurcensia, 15. Louvain: Editions Nauwelaerts, 1963.

Manrique, Angelus. *Annales Cistercienses. Cisterciensium seu verius ecclesiasticorum annalium a condito Cistercio tomus primus (-quartus).* 4 vols. Lugduni: Sumptibus haered. G. Boissat et Laurent Anisson, 1642-1657.

Marilier, Jean. "Les cisterciens," *Annales de Bourgogne* 29 (1957) 131-133.

———. "Les débuts de l'abbaye de Cîteaux," in *Les débuts des abbayes cisterciennes dans les ancient Pays bourguignons, comtois et romands.* Dijon: Association des Sociétés Savantes, 1955.

———. "Le vocable Novum Monasterium dans les premiers documents cisterciens," *Cistercienser-Chronik* 57 (1950) 81-84.

———. "La vocation," in *Bernard de Clairvaux,* 29-37.

Masai, Francois. "Les études cisterciennes de J. A. Lefèvre," *Scriptorium* 11 (1957) 119-123.

McLaughlin, Terence. *Le tres ancien droit monastique de l'Occident. Étude sur le développement général du monachisme et ses rapports avec l'église séculière et le monde laïque de saint Benoît de Nursie à saint Benoît d'Aniane.* Vienne: Abbaye Saint-Martin de Ligugé, 1935.

Mélanges Saint Bernard. XXIVe Congrès de l'Association Bourguignonne des Sociétés Savantes Dijon 1953. Dijon: Association des Amis de Saint Bernard, 1954.

Merlet, Lucien (ed.). *Cartulaire de l'abbaye de la Sainte-Trinité de Tiron.* 2 vols. Chartres: Imprimérie Garnier, 1883.

Molas, Clemente. "A propósito del *ordo diurnus* de san Benito de Aniano," *Studia Monastica* 2 (1960) 205-222.

Molin, Nicolas. *Historia Cartusiana.* 3 vols. Tornaci: Cartusiae S. Mariae de Pratis, 1903-1906.

Molitor, Raphael. *Aus der Rechtsgeschichte Benediktinischer Verbände.* 3 vols. Münster, i. W.: Aschendorffsche Verlagsbuchhandlung, 1928.

Morin, Germain. "Rainaud l'Ermite et Ives de Chartres: un épisode de la crise du cénobitisme au XIe-XIIe siécle," *Revue Bénédictine* 40 (1928) 99-115.

———. "Un traité de S. Guillaume Firmat sur l'amour du cloître et les saintes lectures," *Revue Bénédictine* 31 (1914) 244-249.

Mourre, Michael. *Histoire vivante des moines.* Paris: Éditions du Centurion, 1965.

Mulhern, P. F. "Origines des frères convers," *La Vie Spirituelle,* Supplement no. 22 (1952) 302-318.

Müller, Gregor. "Das Exordium Parvum," *Cistercienser-Chronik* 9 (1897) 311-315, 341-350, 371-378.

Bibliography

———. "Gründung der Abtei Cîteaux," *Cistercienser-Chronik* 10 (1898) 33–46, 65–76, 97–105.

———. "Der Name Cistercienser," *Cistercienser-Chronik* 17 (1905) 46–52, 137.

———. *Vom Cistercienserorden*. Bregenz: J. N. Teutsch, 1927.

Narberhaus, Josef. *Benedikt von Aniane. Werk und Persönlichkeit*. Beiträge zur Geschichte des alten Mönchtums und des Benediktinerordens. Heft 16. Münster i. W.: Aschendorffsche Verlagsbuchhandlung, 1930.

Niderst, René. *Robert d'Arbrissel et les origines de l'Ordre de Fontévrault*. Rodez: Imprimérie G. Subervie, 1952.

Nigg, Walter. *Vom Geheimnis der Mönche*. Zurich: Artemis-Verlag, 1953.

Noschitzka, Canisius. "Codex manuscriptus 31 Bibliothecae Universitatis Laibacensis," *Analecta Sacri Ordinis Cisterciensis* 6 (1950) 1–124.

Oursel, Charles. *Saint Étienne Harding abbé de Cîteaux*. Conférence aux Amis du Musée de Dijon. Dijon: Imprimérie Bernigaud et Privat, 1962.

———. "La genèse des manuscrits primitifs de l'abbaye de Cîteaux sous l'abbatiat de Saint Etienne Harding," *Mémoires de l'Académie des Sciences, Arts et Belles-Lettres de Dijon* 114 (1957–1959) 43–50.

Oursel, Raymond. *Les saints abbés de Cluny*. Paris: Éditions au Soleil Levant, 1960.

Parker Mason, W. A. "The Beginnings of the Cistercian Order," *Transactions of the Royal Historical Society*, New Series 19 (1905) 169–207.

Petit, Ernest. *Histoire des ducs de Bourgogne de la race capétienne avec des documents inédits et des pièces justificatives*. 8 vols. Dijon: Imprimérie Darantière, 1885–1905.

Philippeau, H. R. "Pour l'histoire de la coutume de Cluny," *Revue Mabillon* 44 (1954) 141–151.

Pignot, J. Henri. *Histoire de l'Ordre de Cluny depuis la fondation de l'abbaye jusqu'à la mort de Pierre le Vénérable (909–1157)*. 3 vols. Autun: M. Dejoussieu, 1868.

Plenkers, Heribert. *Untersuchungen zur Überlieferungsgeschichte der ältesten lateinischen Mönchsregeln*. München: C. H. Beck'sche Verlagsbuchhandlung, 1906.

Poncelet, Albertus. Review of *Die ersten Wanderprediger Frankreichs. I. Robert von Arbrissel* by Johannes von Walter, *Analecta Bollandiana* 23 (1904) 375–377.

Presse, Alexis. "La réforme de Cîteaux," *Discours de réception du Très Rev. P. Alexis Presse abbé de Tamié, Réponse de M. le Commandant Charrier, sécrétaire de l'Académie (des Sciences, Arts et Belles-Lettres de Dijon)*. Dijon: Imprimérie Bernigaud et Privat, 1932.

Quilici, Brunetto. "Giovanni Gualberto e la sua riforma monastica," *Archivio Storico Italiano* 99 (1941) 113–132, and 100 (1942) 45–99.

Ragon, M. F. *Précis de l'histoire de Bourgogne et de Franche-Comté*. Paris: L. Hachette, 1833.

Raison, L. "Souvenirs, culte et reliques du bien-heureux Robert d'Arbrissel," *Mémoires de la Société archéologique d'Ille-et-Vilaine* 51 (1923).

Raison, L., and Niderst, R. "Le mouvement érémitique dans l'ouest de la France a la fin du XIe siècle au debut du XIIe siècle," *Annales de Brétagne* 55 (1948) 1–46.

Richard, Jean. *Les ducs de Bourgogne et la formation du duché du XIe au XIVe siècle.* Paris: Société Les Belles-Lettres, 1954.

——. *Histoire de la Bourgogne.* Paris: Presses Universitaires de France, 1957.

——. "Le milieu familial," in *Bernard de Clairvaux,* 3–15.

Rony, A. "Hugues de Romans, légat pontifical," *Revue des Questions Historiques* 107 (1927) 287–303.

——. "La politique française de Grégoire VII," *Revue des Questions Historiques* 109 (1928) 5–34.

Sackur, Ernst. *Die Kluniacenser in ihrer kirchlichen und allgemeingeschichtlichen Wirksamkeit.* 2 vols. Halle: Max Niemayer, 1892–1894.

Salmon, Pierre. "L'ascèse monastique et les origines de Cîteaux," in *Melanges Saint Bernard,* 268–283.

——. "Monastic Asceticism and the Origins of Cîteaux," *Monastic Studies* 3 (1965) 119–138.

Schieffer, Theodor. *Die päpstlichen Legaten in Frankreich vom Vertrage von Mersen (870) bis zum Schisma von 1130.* Berlin: Verlag Emil Ebering, 1935.

Schmitz, Philibert. *Histoire de l'Ordre de Saint-Benoît.* 7 vols. Maredsous: Les Editions de Maredsous, 1948–1956.

——. "L'influence de saint Benoît d'Aniane dans l'histoire de l'Ordre de Saint-Benoît," in *Il monachesimo nell'alto medio evo e la formazione della società occidentale.* Spoleto: Settimane di Studio del Centro Italiano di Studi sull'Alto Medioevo, 1957, 401–416.

——. *La liturgie de Cluny.* Todi: Convegni del Centro di Studi sulla spiritualite medievale, 1960.

——. "S. Benoît d'Aniane," *Dictionnaire d'Histoire et de géographie ecclésiastique* 8 (1935) 178–188.

Schneider, Bruno. "Cîteaux und die benediktinische Tradition. Die Quellenfrage des Liber Usuum im Lichte der Consuetudines Monasticae," *Analecta Sacri Ordinis Cisterciensis* 16 (1960) 169–254, and 17 (1961) 73–114.

Schreiber, Georg. *Gemeinschaften des Mittelalters.* Münster: Regensberg, 1948.

——. *Kurie und Kloster im 12. Jahrhundert.* 2 vols. Stuttgart: Ferdinand von Enke, 1910.

——. "Religiöse Verbände in mittelalterlicher Wertung. Lateinischer Westen und griechischer Osten," *Historisches Jahrbuch* 62–69 (1949) 284–358.

Schwarz, Willi. "Der Investiturstreit in Frankreich," *Zeitschrift für Kirchengeschichte* 42 (1923) 255–328, and 43 (1924) 92–105.

Seebas, Otto. "Über das Regelbuch Benedikts von Aniane," *Zeitschrift für Kirchengeschichte* 15 (1895) 244–260.

Smith, Luch Margaret. *Cluny in the Eleventh and Twelfth Centuries.* London: Philip Allan & Co., 1930.

Société pour l'Histoire du Droit et des Institutions des anciens pays bourguignons, comtois et romands. *Les débuts des abbayes cisterciennes dans les anciens pays bouguignons, comtois et romands.* XXIVe Congrès de l'Association bourguignonne des Sociétés Savantes (Huitième centenaire de la mort de saint Bernard). Dijon: Faculté de Droit, 1953.

Spahr, Kolumban. "Die Anfänge von Cîteaux," in *Bernhard von Clairvaux Mönch und Mystiker*. Internationaler Bernhardskongress Mainz 1953. Wiesbaden: Franz Steiner Verlag, 1955.

――. "Cisterciensi," *Enciclopedia Cattolica* 3 (1950) 1737–1743.

――. *De fontibus constitutivis primigenii juris constitutionalis Sacri Ordinis Cisterciensis*. Romae: Lateran Thesis, 1953.

――. "Neue Beiträge zur Ordensgeschichte," *Cistercienser-Chronik* 58 (1951) 29–39, and 59 (1952) 6–17.

――. "Die Regelauslegung im 'Neukloster'," in *Festschrift zum 800-Jahrgedächtnis Bernhards von Clairvaux*. Wien: Verlag Herold, 1953.

Standaert, Maur. "S. Etienne Harding," *Dictionnaire de Spiritualite*, 4 (1961) 1489–1493.

Stevens, Paul. "Rectitudo Regulae," *Collectanea Ordinis Cisterciensium Reformatorum* 9 (1947) 131–142.

Sydow, Jürgen. "Cluny und die Anfänge der Apostolischen Kammer. Studien zur Geschichte der päpstlichen Finanzverwaltung im 11. und 12. Jahrhundert," *Studien und Mitteilungen zur Geschichte des Benediktinerordens und seiner Zweige* 63 (1951) 45–66.

Tellenbach, Gerd (ed.). *Neue Forschungen über Cluny und die Cluniacenser von Joachim Wollasch, Hans-Erich Mager und Hermann Diener*. Freiburg: Herder, 1959.

Thaner, Friedrich. "Ueber die Entstehung und Bedeutung der Formel 'Salva sedis apostolicae auctoritate' in den päpstlichen Privilegien," *Wiener Sitzungsberichte, Philosophisch-Historische Klasse* 71 (1872) 807–851.

Tomek, Ernst. *Studien zur Reform der deutschen Klöster im XI. Jahrhundert. Studien und Mitteilungen aus dem kirchengeschichtlichen Seminar der k.k. Universität in Wien*, Heft 4. Wien: Mayer & Co., 1910.

(Tuite, Francis). *The Cistercian Order. Its Object. Its Rule*. By a Secular Priest. Cambridge: The Riverside Press, 1905.

Turk, Joseph. "Cistercii statuta antiquissima," *Analecta Sacri Ordinis Cistercsiensis* 4 (1948) 1–159.

Università Cattolica del S. Cuore, Milano. *S. Bernardo. Pubblicazione commemorativa nell' VIII centenario della sua morte*. Milano: Società Editrice Vita e Pensiero, 1954.

Vacandard, Elphège. *Vie de Saint Bernard, abbé de Clairvaux*. 2 vols. Paris: Lecoffre, 1927.

Valous, Guy de. "Le domaine de l'abbaye de Cluny aux Xe et XIe siècles," *Annales de l'Académie de Mâcon*, Série 3, 20 (1920–1921) 299–481.

――. *Le monachisme clunisien dès origines au XVe siècle. Vie intérieure des monastères et organization de l'ordre*. 2 vols. Vienne: Abbaye Saint-Martin, 1935.

Van Damme, Jean-Baptiste. "Autour des origines cisterciennes," *Collectanea Ordinis Cisterciensium Reformatorum* 20 (1958) 37–60, 153–168, 374–390, and 21 (1959) 76–86, 137–156.

――. *Les trois fondateurs de Cîteaux*. Chambarand: Privately printed, 1966.

――. "Vir Dei Albericus," *Analecta Sacri Ordinis Cisterciensis* 20 (1964) 153–164.

Volk, Paulus. "Georg Schreiber, Gemeinschaften des Mittelalters. Recht und

Verfassung, Kult und Frömmigkeit," *Zeitschrift der Savigny-Stiftung fur Rechtsgeschichte, Kanonistische Abteilung* 35 (1948) 418–425.

Waas, Adolf. *Vogtei und Bede in der deutschen Kaiserzeit. Arbeiten zur deutschen Rechts- und Verfassungsgeschichte.* 2 vols. Berlin: Weidmannsche Buchhandlung, 1919–1923.

Walter, Johannes von. *Die ersten Wanderprediger Frankreichs. I. Robert von Arbrissel.* Studien zur Geschichte der Theologie und der Kirche, 9:3. Leipzig: Dieterich, 1903.

Wang, John J. *Saint Peter Damian the Monk.* New York: Fordham University (Ph.D.) Thesis, 1957.

Webster, Raymond. "Grandmont," *Catholic Encyclopaedia* 6 (1913) 725–726.

——. "Stephen of Muret," *Catholic Encyclopaedia* 14 (1913) 291.

Werner, Ernst. *Die gesellschaftlichen Grundlagen der Klosterreform im 11. Jahrhundert.* Berlin: Deutscher Verlag der Wissenschaften, 1953.

——. "Neue Texte und Forschungen zur Charta Caritatis," *Forschungen und Fortschritte* 29 (1955) 25–29.

——. *Pauperes Christi. Studien zu sozial-religiösen Bewegungen im Zeitalter des Reformpapsttums.* Leipzig: Koehler & Amelang, 1956.

Whitney, James Pounder. *Hildebrandine Essays.* Cambridge: University Press, 1932.

——. "Peter Damiani," *Cambridge Historical Journal* 13 (1925) 225–248.

Williams, Watkin W. "St. Benedict of Aniane," *The Downside Review* 54 (1936) 357–374.

——. *Monastic Studies.* Manchester: Manchester University Press, 1938.

Wilmart, Andre. "La chronique des premiers Chartreux," *Revue Mabillon* 16 (1926) 77–142.

Winandy, Jacques. "L'oeuvre monastique de saint Benoît d'Aniane," *Mélanges bénédictines publiés à l'occasion du XIVe centenaire de la mort de saint Benoît par les moines de l'abbaye de Saint-Jérôme de Rome.* St. Wandrille: Editions de Fontenelle, 1947.

——. "Les origines de Cîteaux et les travaux de M. Lefèvre," *Revue Bénédictine* 67 (1957) 49–76.

Workman, Herbert. *The Evolution of the Monastic Ideal From the Earliest Times Down to the Coming of the Friars. A Second Chapter in the History of Christian Renunciation.* London: Charles H. Kelly, 1913.

(Wulf, Alberic). *Compendium of the History of the Cistercian Order.* Trappist, Ky.: Privately printed, 1944.

Yepes, Antonio de. *Crónica general de la Orden de San Benito Patriarca de religiosos.* 7 vols. Navarra: por Matias Mares, 1609–1621.

Zakar, Polycarp. "Die Anfänge des Zisterzienserordens," *Analecta Sacri Ordinis Cisterciensis* 20 (1964) 103–138.

Zimmermann, Alfons M. *Kalendarium Benedictinum. Die Heiligen und Seligen des Benediktinerordens und seiner Zweige.* 4 vols. Metten: Verlag der Abtei, 1933–1938.

——. "Robert von Molesme," *Lexikon für Theologie und Kirche* 8 (1936) 921–922.

Zöckler, Otto. *Askese und Mönchtum.* 2 vols. Frankfurt: Heyden & Zimmer, 1897.

ANALYTIC INDEX

Aachen, council (789), 158, 160.
Aachen, council (816), 7, 158, 160.
Aachen, council (817), xiif., 8, 9ff., 22, 30f., 36, 37, 43, 114.
  see Benedict of Aniane; *Capitulare monasticum*; Carolingians; Louis the Pious.
Aachen, council (818), xii, 21.
Abelard, Peter, 153n92.
Abbo of Fleury, St, 97, 104, 264.
Abbots.
  and Camaldoli, 172; La Grande Chartreuse, 209.
  and the *Rule*, 128.
  as financial officers.
  canons concerning: Anselm of Lucca, 157; Burchard of Worms, 155f.
  capitulare monasticum's legislation concerning, 14, 25.
  criticized by monks, 103f.
  eleventh century conciliar legislation concerning, 119ff.
  illegitimate acquisition of office, 119ff.
  lay abbots, 10, 21, 115f.
  limitations placed upon by council of Poitiers (1100), 127.
  minimum age of, 120.
  murder of, 104ff.
  obedience to, xiii, 14f., 44f., 51, 98, 114, 156, 245. *see* Obedience.
  of Cluny, 69ff., 78, 79f., 88f., 90n155.
  reform of, 128f.
  unworthy, 97ff., 119ff. *see* Simony.
  use of *pontificalia,* 76, 127f.
  see Election.

Adalbero of Laon, 88f.
Advocati, 78, 109ff.
Aelred of Rievaulx, St, xvi, xviii.
Affective spirituality.
  Cîteaux, xviii, 61.
  Cluny, 60f., 87, 140.
  eleventh century, 140f., 152.
  laity, xvi.
  see Blessed Sacrament; Humanity of Christ; Lay spirituality; Mary, Virgin Mother of God.
Agapitus II, pope, 76.
Agde, council (506), 114.
Aigulfus, St, 104.
Alberic of Cîteaux, St., 91, 222, 227, 235f., 238ff., 240, 243, 254, 255, 266.
  his authorship of the Cistercian ideal, 258f., 261.
Albert of Marmoutier, 96.
Alcuin of York, Bl, xi, 7, 139
Alexander II, pope, 76, 157, 172, 176, 195.
Amalarius, 178n38.
Amalfi, council (1089), 125.
Ambrose, St, 139, 158, 178n38, 253f.
Andreas of Sturmi, 187n69.
Angers, council (453), 114.
Aniane, abbey, 2n3, 23n105, 131.
  foundation, 3.
  conversion to the *Rule,* 4f.
  imperial charter, 6.
  splendor of, 4f.
  influx of monks, 7.
  see Benedict of
Animchad, 137.
Anno of Cologne, St, 104.
Anse, council (1025), 117.

297

Analytic Index

Anselm of Bec and Canterbury, St, xvi, 139, 143f., 153n92, 155.
Anselm of Laon, 153n92.
Anselm of Lucca, St, xvi, 155, 156f., 264.
Anthony, St., 146, 168n3, 177, 204, 250.
Ardo (Smaragdus), 2n3, 3, 6, 7, 8, 9, 10, 11, 13n54, 15n67, 21, 24ff., 28n116, 138.
Asceticism, monastic.
  and eleventh century eremiticism, 146ff.; poverty, 144f.
  departures from at Cluny, 85ff., 94f.; in general during eleventh century, 101ff., 144f.
  influence of Cassian upon, 139.
  the new asceticism of the eleventh century, 90, 146ff., 215.
  of Benedict of Aniane, 2ff.; Camaldoli, 170f.; canons regular, 160f.; Cluny, 61, 82, 83f., 215.; Fonte Avellana, 181ff.; the early hermits, 146; Gerard of Brogne, 132; Gorze, 131f.; La Grande Chartreuse, 209; Grandmont, 199ff.; Molesme, 244; Peter Damian, 176f.; Robert of Molesme, 218f., 221; Romuald, 169f.; Vallombrosa, 190f.
  see Austerity; Discipline; Eremitical ideals and practices; Flagellation; Food and clothing; Manual labor; Poverty; Silence; Solitude.
Augsburg, council (962), 117.
Augustine, St, vii, xvii, 139, 140, 149, 153, 158, 160, 198.
Aulps, abbey, 236, 238ff., 243.
Austerity, monastic.
  at Cluny, 58, 61; Fonte Avellana, 181ff.; La Grande Chartreuse, 209f.; Grandmont, 199ff.; Vallombrosa, 190f.
  decline of at Cluny, 84f., 88f., 93ff.; in France, 96, 99, 101ff.
  of Benedict of Aniane, 2ff.; Bernard of Clairvaux, 56; the eleventh century, 215; Odo of Cluny, 61n70; Peter Damian, 99; Romuald, 168ff.

Autun, council (663–680), 114.
Autun, council (1094), 125.
Aux, hermitage, 233ff., 240, 242.
Aymard, 41, 71, 73.

Basil the Great, St, vii, 3, 60n68, 198, 204.
Baudry of Borgeuil, 153n92.
Baume, abbey, 1n1, 2n2, 40, 43.
Bec, abbey, 106, 126n42.
Bede, St, 77, 139, 178n38.
Benedict VIII, pope, 76.
Benedict IX, pope, 135.
Benedict of Aniane, St.
  and the *Rule* of St Benedict of Nursia, xiif., 1f., 3ff., 8, 9, 10–20, 24f., 28nn115, 116, 33f., 46, 63, 269n140, 272.
  contrasted with Benedict of Nursia, 1, 25n110, 29ff.
  evaluation of his work, 1f., 25n110, 29–39, 139.
  forerunner of Cîteaux, 1f., 35ff., 139, 275.
  influence on Cluny, xii, 1n1, 42, 43f., 48, 51n39, 53, 56, 68f., 77, 83, 139.
  life and deeds, xi–xv, 1–39, 134n16.
  see Aachen, council (817); Aniane; *Capitulare monasticum*; *Concordia regularum*; Euticius; Inde; Witiza.
Benedict II of Chiusa, 140n48, 247n77.
Benedict of Nursia, St and his *Rule*, vii, xiv, xviii–xix, 1, 10, 12, 16, 29ff., 32, 33, 38, 40, 46f., 53, 62f., 66f., 71, 84, 86, 89, 108, 118, 128, 134, 158, 172, 180, 183, 198, 203, 204, 212, 220n5, 232, 233, 237, 238, 244, 249, 250, 251, 262.
  see Rule of St Benedict of Nursia.
Berengar of Tours, 164.
Bernard of Clairvaux, St, xvi, xviii, xxi, 56, 165, 223, 244n70, 266.
Bernard of Cluny, 49f., 83, 85.
Bernard of Montier-la-Celle, 218.
Bernard of St Venant, 105.
Bernard of Tiron, St, 89, 151.
Berno of Baume, St, 1n1, 40ff., 44, 47, 48, 50, 58, 68f., 71, 73.

Bèze, abbey, 106.
Blessed Sacrament, monastic devotion to, 59, 60, 80.
Bobbio, abbey, 136.
Boethius, 139.
Boniface, St, ix, xf., 77.
Boso of La Grande Chartreuse, 212.
Bourges, council (1031), 115, 118.
Bruno of Cologne, St, xvi, xvii, 155, 228f.
  and the Carthusians, 203–214.
  see Grande Chartreuse, La.
Bruno of Querfurt, St, 175n26.
Burchard of Worms, 155, 264.

Caen, council (1061), 122.
Caesarius of Heisterbach, 248, 249.
Calabria, Greek monks of, 167.
Camaldoli, xvii, 137n37, 167, 187, 188, 197, 214.
  foundation and customs, 168–176.
  see Eremitical ideals and practices; Romuald.
Canon law.
  and monasteries, 155ff., 176n31.
  emergence of, 152, 155ff.
  influence of feudalism on, viiif.
  violation of, 116n15.
  see Anselm of Lucca; Burchard; Gratian; Ivo.
Canons regular, 7, 10, 13, 34, 96, 108, 166, 190, 198, 214.
  emergence of, 158–161.
Capitulare monasticum, xiif., xv, 8, 22, 24, 30f., 43, 48, 63n73, 84, 139.
  provisions of, 9–22.
  see Aachen, council (817); Benedict of Aniane.
Carlmann, ix, xf.
Carolingians and monastic reform, xff., 6ff., 20f., 36, 37, 43f.
Carthusians.
  see Grande Chartreuse, La.
Cassian, John, St, xiv, xvii, 47, 59, 64, 82n132, 132, 134n16, 139f., 141, 146, 147.
  influence on Benedict of Nursia, vii; Bruno of Cologne, 212; Romuald of Ravenna, 168, 173.
  see Desert; Eremitical ideals and practices.

Cassiodorus, vii, 139.
Cazaneuve, abbey, 23n105.
Celibacy, chastity, and continence of clergy, xi, 118, 119, 151, 152, 154, 156, 158.
Celleneuve, abbey, 23n105.
Celtic monasticism, xii, xiv, 19n91, 57f., 59, 136f., 147, 274.
  see Columbanus; Dunstan.
Centralization, monastic.
  Benedict of Aniane, 1f., 8, 21ff., 30, 34, 37, 83.
  Cîteaux, 1f., 37.
  Cluny, 47f., 68ff., 82, 84, 90n155, 97, 193.
  Vallombrosa, 193, 195.
  see Congregation; Priory system; Uniformity.
Chaise Dieu, La. abbey, 106, 133, 205.
Chalcedon, general council (451), 117, 121.
Charlemagne, 6, 21n99, 35, 86, 109.
Charles the Bald, 44.
Charter of Charity, 37, 118n21.
Christodulos, 58.
Chrodegang of Metz, St, xiv, 158.
Cîteaux, abbey, vii, 3, 57, 131, 155, 187n67, 194, 207, 216, 223, 226, 228, 229, 231, 235, 236, 243, 244.
  and Benedict of Aniane, 1f., 35ff.; Cluny, 40, 51n40, 71, 75, 90f.; eleventh century synodal enactments, 113, 118n21; Molesme, 217–273; Vallombrosa, 196.
  as the New Monastery, xviiif., 36, 37, 92, 247, 253, 268, 272f.
  authorship of its ideal, 254–261.
  desire to live *Rule* more strictly and correctly, xviiif., 36f., 71n99, 129f., 239ff., 247ff., 251ff., 268ff.
  establishment of, 261ff.
  ideals of, 268ff.
  necessity for a study of its antecedents, xxif., 274f.
  solitude of, xix, 137n37, 267, 270.
  see Alberic; Robert of Molesme; Stephen Harding.
Clerics, monks as, 87, 93, 100f., 102f., 108, 123, 125, 126f., 127ff.,

145, 156, 157, 160, 188, 190, 194f., 200.
Clermont, council (1095), 126, 236ff.
Cluny, abbey, xiv, xvii, 1, 3, 33, 34, 37, 39, 97, 106, 110, 117, 124, 131, 134, 138, 191f., 193, 215, 232, 242, 247, 251, 254.
  affective spirituality of, 60f., 87, 140; devotion to Mary, 51, 53, 56f., 59, 60, 80, 223.
  and Gregorian reform, 80f., 166.
  art, architecture, and ornamentation of, 55f., 56n54, 58f., 61n70, 99.
  Celtic monastic influence on, 58ff., 80.
  charter of, 41n3, 75.
  customs of, xviii, 1n1, 42, 44f., 45n16, 48–56, 61–69, 71, 83, 88, 101, 133, 191f., 219, 232, 247, 255, 271f.
  donations to, 73ff., 78, 85.
  eastern monastic influences on, 58ff., 80.
  foundation, spirit, and observances, 40–91.
  liturgy of, 46, 48, 52–57, 60, 64f., 68f., 80, 82, 83f., 85f., 95, 182n57, 191.
  modifications of the *Rule*, 48, 62–68, 94f.
  see Berno of Baume; Hugh; Majolus; Odilo; Odo of Cluny.
Clusa, abbey, 105.
Codex regularum, 9, 32n135.
Colan, abbey, xvii.
Collan, hermitage, 220ff., 231, 242, 254.
Collationes Patrum, 177.
Columbanus, St, xii, xiv, 58, 136, 232.
Concilium Germanicum (742), xf.
Concordances and compilations of monastic rules.
  see Capitulare monasticum; Codex regularum; Concordia regularum; Consuetudines antiquiores; Consuetudines cenobii Cluniacensis; Customs; Rule; Statuta Murbacensia.

Concordia regularum, 5, 31f., 43, 139.
Congregation, religious.
  and eleventh century reform, 216.
  Benedict of Aniane, 23, 30, 34, 68.
  Camaldoli, 172, 187.
  canons regular, 96, 159f.
  Cluny, 42f., 47, 57f., 68ff., 84, 87ff., 124.
  Fonte Avellana, 172, 187.
  La Grande Chartreuse, 213.
  Grandmont, 196ff.
  Poppo of Stavelot, 132.
  Vallombrosa, 188, 193f.
  see Centralization; Priory system; Uniformity.
Conrad of Eberbach, 240, 252.
Consuetudines antiquiores, 50ff., 101.
Consuetudines cenobii Cluniacensis, 49.
Contemplation.
  as an ideal, 141ff.
  at La Grande Chartreuse, 208; Grandmont, 199; Vallombrosa, 188f., 192, 195.
  see Silence; Solitude.
Conversi, 67f., 90n155, 173n22, 174, 181, 183, 196, 199, 202, 210, 211, 215, 229f.
  see Laybrothers; Manual labor; Serfs and servants.
Conversion of manners, 12, 15, 51f.
Cormery, abbey, 23n105.
Corneilly, abbey, 194.
Customs, monastic.
  and the *Rule*, xiii, xv, 10ff., 24f., 46, 48, 50f., 62ff., 133, 247, 269n140, 271f.
  compilation of, 10ff., 48ff., 137ff.
  ideal of *una consuetudo*, 33, 35, 37, 138f.
  legislation, xiiff., 7f., 10ff., 21f., 119, 123.
  model customs.
    Aniane, 6.
    capitulare monasticum, 10–20.
    Cluny.
      acceptance by other convents, 68f., 71, 219, 232, 247, 255; compared with customs of Benedict of Aniane, 45n16, 63; compared with customs of Cîteaux, 51n40; growth,

Analytic Index

48ff., 83; influence on Vallombrosa, 191f.; official books of customs, 48ff.; relation of abbot to customs, 88.
see Cluny.
Inde, 8, 20, 23f., 25ff.
see Centralization; Congregation; Uniformity.
observances of.:
Camaldoli, 170; Fonte Avellana, 180ff.; Fructuaria, 133; La Grande Chartreuse, 211ff.; Grandmont, 199ff.; Molesme, 232, 244, 247, 251, 253, 255, 258f., 260; Vallombrosa, 190ff.
rejection of contemporary customs by Cîteaux, 268, 271f.
uniformity of customs, 21f., 137ff.
see Asceticism; Austerity; Discipline; Eremitical ideals and practices; Flagellation; Food and clothing; Liturgy; Manual labor; Opus Dei; Silence.
Cyril of Scythopolis, 173.

De ordine eremitarum et facultatibus eremi Fontis Avellani, 180.
De suae congregationis institutis, 180.
Dead, care of.
burial of, 73, 74, 157, 190, 227.
monastic prayer associations, 36, 74, 82, 157, 227.
office of and prayers for, 16, 25, 28n115, 53, 54, 58, 60, 108, 157, 199.
processions for, 199.
Decanatus, 15, 71.
Desert, ideal of, xvii, 48, 58, 146ff., 167, 170ff., 178ff., 204, 213f., 235.
see Eremitical ideals and practices; *Fuga mundi*; Solitude.
Desert Fathers, xvi, 146, 161, 167, 170, 173, 185n63, 208, 212, 213.
see Anthony; Eastern monachism; Eremitical ideals and practices; Pachomius; *Verba seniorum*.
Déols, abbey, 44f.

Deusdedit, xvi.
Dialogus inter Cluniacensem et Cisterciensem monachum, 256.
Discipline, claustral.
at Camaldoli, 171; Cluny, 46f., 83, 84, 101f.; Fonte Avellana, 184; Molesme, 240, 243f.; Vallombrosa, 190, 191.
capitulare monasticum, 10, 12ff., 25.
efforts to improve through conciliar legislation, 114ff.
experience as necessary prerequisite for abbot's office, 116, 128.
relaxation of, 94, 97, 100, 101, 108f., 233f.
Dominic of Foligno, 146.
Dominicus Loricatus, St, 185.
Donations to monasteries, 73f., 78, 85, 87, 93, 107, 124, 144, 155, 210, 222f., 224ff., 230, 232, 233, 234, 242, 245.
see Poverty.
Dunstan, St, 132.

Eastern monachism's influence on the West, xii, xiv, 3f., 31f., 58ff., 66, 80, 107, 130n50, 135f., 146, 167, 168, 173, 190, 196, 203, 215, 274.
see Anthony; Basil; Cassian; Desert Fathers; Pachomius.
Eigenkirche, 32, 33, 42, 70, 74, 84, 90, 107, 110, 118, 126, 129, 152, 153, 161, 246.
definition of, ix.
see Feudalism and the Church.
Election, free, of abbots.
according to Burchard of Worms, 155; the council of Aachen (818), xiii, 21; Koblenz (922), 117; Reims (1049), 119f.
of Aniane, 6; Cluny, 41f.; Molesme 237; Vallombrosa, 192, 193.
sought for Frankish abbeys, 7.
Elne, council (1027), 115.
Elne, council (1050), 115.
Episcopal supervision and intervention, 10, 17, 41, 75f., 117, 119, 123, 124, 125, 126, 129, 155, 156, 157, 237.

Analytic Index

Eremitical ideals and practices in the West, xvif., 145-150, 167-187 195, 275.
   ideals and practices of Benedict of Aniane, xiif.; Bruno of Cologne, 204ff., 228f.; certain canons regular, 161; Peter Damian, 82, 178ff.; Robert of Molesme, 220ff., 233ff.; Romuald, 168ff., 181.
   influence of Cassian, xvif., 59, 139f., 147, 168, 173, 212.
   see Desert; Solitude.
Eusebius of Vercelli, St, 158.
Euticius (Benedict of Aniane), 2n2, 43.
Exordium Cistercii, 248, 254, 261, 262, 263f., 266, 267, 268.
Exordium Magnum, 240, 248f., 252, 257, 260.
Exordium Parvum, xviii, 36, 90, 235, 248, 251ff., 254, 257, 258, 261, 262f., 266, 268, 273.

Farfa, abbey, 131, 138.
Fécamp, abbey, 105, 132.
Feudalism and the Church, viiif.
   Benedict of Aniane and feudalism, 32f., 38.
   Cluny and feudalism, xvii, 41, 42, 52, 63, 69f., 74f., 77ff., 83, 85, 87, 90.
   feudal influences on monastic life, 107, 108ff.
   feudal obligations and concerns of monks, 12, 21, 29, 98, 104, 145.
   Inde and feudalism, 29.
   lay control and expropriation, x, xi, xiii, 10, 41, 115f.
   see Eigenkirche.
   Molesme and feudalism, 229, 232f., 245ff.
   movement to get away from a feudal Church, 148, 151, 153, 166, 215, 229, 245, 275.
      Camaldoli, 172; Cîteaux, 38f., 75; heresy, 162, 165, Grandmont, 203; Robert of Molesme, 221.
   see Donations; Serfs and servants of monks; Poverty.

Fingen, 136.
Firmatus, 102.
Flagellation, 184f., 186, 191.
Fleury, abbey, 132n8, 134, 136, 138.
Florus, 139.
Fonte Avellana, 167, 176, 177, 178n38.
   customs and life, 180-186.
   see Eremitical ideals and practices; Peter Damian.
Fontebuono, 174.
Food and clothing, monastic.
   Benedict of Aniane, 3, 4, 21.
   canons regular, 160.
   capitulare monasticum, 10, 13f., 16ff., 25, 31f.
   Cîteaux, 275.
   Cluny, xviii, 47, 62f., 68f., 82, 83, 84, 85, 89, 90, 95f.
   Déols, 44f.
   eastern influences on Cluny, 60.
   Fonte Avellana, 181ff.
   La Grande Chartreuse, 209f.
   Grandmont, 202.
   hermits, 148.
   Molesme, 224.
   Peter Damian at Fonte Avellana, 177.
   Romainmoutier, 45.
   Romuald and Camaldoli, 169, 170, 171.
   Rule, 116, 120, 123, 133, 137, 250.
   Statuta Murbacensia, 8n23.
   similarity among customs, 138.
   unmonastic magnificence of and care for, 89, 98, 103, 104, 156, 178n41.
   Vallombrosa, 190f., 192.
Fructuaria, abbey, 133.
Fuga mundi as a theme, 142ff.
   see Desert; Eremitical ideals and practices; Solitude.
Fulda, abbey, 137, 138.

Gand, abbey, 132n8.
Gandolf, 163.
Gelasius II, pope, 83.
Gellone, abbey, 23n105.
Geoffrey of Vendôme, 153n92.
Gerard of Brogne, St, 132.
Gerard of Cambrai, 152, 163.

Analytic Index

Gerard of Sauve-Majeur, St, 96, 133.
Gerard of Toul, St, 135, 136.
Gervasius of Reims, 160.
Gilbert of St Germaine, 106.
Glastonbury, abbey, 132.
Godfrey of Vendôme, 155.
Gorze, abbey, 131, 138.
Grande Chartreuse, La, xiii, xvii, 71, 167, 196, 197, 228.
   foundation and customs, 203–214.
   see Eremitical ideals and practices; Bruno of Cologne.
Grandmont, abbey, 71, 167.
   foundation and customs, 196–203.
   see Stephen of Thiers.
Gratian of Bologna, xvi, 119n25, 253.
Gregorian reform, 74, 80f., 112, 115, 131, 151ff., 187, 274.
   and monastic reform, 80f., 155ff.
   see Gregory VII.
Gregory I, St, pope, ix, 100, 146, 147, 178n38, 220n5.
Gregory V, pope, 76.
Gregory VII, St, pope, 76, 80f., 105, 151ff., 154, 158, 172, 187n67, 193, 203, 204.
Gregory of Tours, St, 146.
Guarinus of Aulps, 238, 243.
Guarinus of St Michael of Cuxa, 168.
Guests in monasteries, 12f., 17, 25, 44f., 82, 93f., 95f., 103, 114, 232f., 245.
   of hermits, 148, 183, 200.
Guibert of Nogent, 208, 211.
Guibert of St Peter at Gembloux, 132.
Guido of Aulps, 238, 243.
Guigo of La Grande Chartreuse, 207, 211, 212.
Guy of Aulps, 228.
Guy of Chatel-Censoir, 229.
Guy of Pomposa, St., 184.

Hadrian IV, pope, 199.
Hambye, abbey, xvii.
Haymo, 139, 178n38.
Helinand of Froidmont, 259.
Henry IV, emperor, 81.
Heresy, 149, 152, 161ff.
   Cathari, 162.
   Gandolf, 163.

Gnostics, 161.
   neo-Manichaeism, 150, 161, 162f., 165.
   Pataria, 153, 164.
Herman of Reichenau, Bl, 142.
Hilarion, St, 178, 204.
Hilary, St, 139.
Hermits.
   see Desert Fathers; Eremitical ideals and practices.
Hildebert of Lavardin, 153n92.
Hildebrand.
   see Gregory VII.
Hincmar of Reims, 139.
Hirsau, abbey, 50, 51n39, 66, 138.
Honau, abbey, 136.
Hrabanus Maurus, 139.
Hugh of Cluny (the Great), St, 41, 48, 57, 69, 70n98, 82f., 85, 88, 99, 106, 135, 155, 264.
Hugh of Die, 164.
Hugh of Grenoble, St, 155, 205, 207n138, 209.
Hugh of Lyons, 72, 105, 125, 204, 240ff., 244, 248, 252, 262, 264, 267, 268f., 271, 272.
   career, 154f.
Hugh of St Martin, 106.
Hugh of Silva Candida, 122n35.
Hugh of Troyes, 224.
Humanity of Christ, devotion to, xvi, 140, 152.
Humbert of Silva Candida, 151, 152.
Hunald I of St Michael in Tonnerre, 219.
Hunald II, 219.

Ilarino da Milano, 162.
Ilbode of Citeaux, 228, 235f.
Ile-Barbe, abbey, 23n105.
Immunity and independence, monastic, 7, 152.
   Aniane, 6.
   Cluny, 41, 42, 75ff., 78, 117.
   lack of, 10, 87ff., 115, 117, 155, 157.
   Molesme, 237.
   see Centralization; Congregation; Eigenkirche; Election; Episcopal supervision and intervention; Feudalism; Inspection; Priory system; Uniformity.

Inde (Cornelimünster), abbey, xiv, 23f.
  daily life, 25ff.
  model house, 7f., 20, 37.
  see Benedict of Aniane.
Innocent III, pope, 199, 266.
Inspection of monasteries, 36, 37, 96, 155, 157.
  abbot of Cluny's rights, 70, 71.
  abbot of Vallombrosa's rights, 193.
  Benedict of Aniane, xii.
  capitulare monasticum, xiiif., 8, 20f., 22, 23, 25, 30, 37.
  see Centralization; Congregation; Episcopal supervision and intervention; Immunity; Priory system; Uniformity.
Instituta Patrum, 177.
Intellectual activity in monasteries.
  Aniane, 6.
  Camaldoli, 171, 172.
  capitulare monasticum, 19.
  Cîteaux, 38, 275.
  Cluny, 60, 64f., 85, 87.
  eastern monastic aversion to, 135.
  Fleury, 134.
  Fonte Avellana, 178n38, 182.
  La Grande Chartreuse, 208, 211.
  illicit intellectual labors, 103, 178n41.
  liturgical work, 5n14, 38.
  monastic schools, 19, 25, 29, 32, 35, 54, 66, 87, 138.
  Peter Damian, 177f.
Investiture, lay, 121, 123, 125, 126, 127, 128, 129, 152, 154.
  see Eigenkirche; Feudalism; Gregorian reform.
Irish monasticism.
  see Celtic monasticism.
Isidore of Seville, St 139.
Itta of San Ellero, 188n71, 192.
Ivo of Chartres, xvi, 97, 102, 105, 139, 153n92, 155, 157, 160, 264.

Jarento of St Benignus, 104, 106, 155.
Jerome, St, xvi, 139, 178n38, 212, 213.
John of Cîteaux, 228, 235f., 240, 266.
John XI, pope, 42, 69, 76.
John XXII, pope, 199.

John Gualbert, St, xvii, 173n22.
  life and deeds, 187–196.
John of Fécamp, 99, 103, 142.
John of Salerno, 2n2, 43, 47n24.
John of Vandière, 131f., 134n16.

Kaddroe, St, 136.
Koblenz, council (922), 117.

Lambert, companion of St Bruno of Cologne, 205, 206n133, 228.
Lanfranc, Bl, xvi, 51n39, 128n47, 153n92, 264f.
Langres, diocese, 219, 223, 225, 229, 230, 231, 236, 237, 242, 262.
Lateran, abbey, 131.
Lateran, council (1059), 158.
Lay spirituality, xvff.
  and Cluny, 73f.; the New Monastery, xviiif.
  devotion to Mary, xvi, 56f.
Laybrothers.
  at Camaldoli, 173, 174; Cîteaux, 130, 275; Cluny, 60, 65, 67f.; La Grande Chartreuse, 211; Grandmont, 203; Monte Cassino, 67; Vallombrosa, 188, 192, 195, 196.
  see Conversi; Serfs and servants.
Leo I, St, pope, 139.
Leo IX, St, pope, 82, 109, 119.
Lérins, abbey, 96, 104.
Letald of Cîteaux, 240, 266.
Letbald of St Michael, 219.
Leuthard, 162.
Lillebonne, council (1080), 124.
Limoges, council (1031), 115, 119, 135.
Liturgy, monastic.
  Benedict of Aniane: early austerity 4, 37; outlook changes, 4f., 15, 34; views liturgy in relationship to monastic life, 28, 56.
  Cîteaux, 37f., 275.
  Cluny, 46f., 48, 52–57, 64f., 68f., 80, 82, 83f., 85f., 95, 182n57, 191; affective nature, 60f.; eastern influences on, 59f., 80.
  Déols, 44f.
  eleventh century, 93, 94, 107f.
  Farfa, 65n77.

Analytic Index

La Grande Chartreuse, 209.
  hermits, 149.
Inde, 25ff.
  legislation concerning, 10f., 15f., 25, 119.
  liturgical correction and composition, 5n14, 38.
Romainmoutier, 45.
Roman cursus, 11, 26, 119.
  uniformity of, 1, 11, 21f., 68f., 137.
  see Opus Dei.
London, council (944), 117n21.
Louis I (the Pious), xiif., 6ff., 20f., 23f., 37, 43.
  see Carolingians.
Luxeuil, abbey, 136.

Majolus, St, 41, 44, 53, 55, 57, 61n70, 69, 71, 73, 82, 99.
Malanum (Chézal-Benoît), abbey, 194.
Maligny (viscounts of Baume), family, 218, 219n3, 221, 222.
Manasses of Reims, 204.
Manual labor, monastic.
  Aniane, 4.
  Benedict of Aniane, 3.
  Camaldoli, 171.
  canons regular, 160.
  capitulare monasticum, 13, 18f.
  Cîteaux, 130, 216.
  Cluny, 52, 63ff., 82n132, 83, 85ff., 90.
  dissuetude of, 63ff., 93, 101, 107, 249, 250.
  Fonte Avellana, 182.
  La Grande Chartreuse, 208, 211.
  hermits, 82n132, 148, 149, 234.
  Inde, 29f.
  Molesme, 234f., 244f., 249, 250.
  Romuald, 168.
  Rule, viii, xviii, 8n23, 18, 29, 46, 52, 64, 85, 137, 245, 249ff.
  Sauve-Majeure, 133.
  Statuta Murbacensia, 8n23.
Marcenay, 224.
Marcigny, abbey, 72f., 135.
Marianus Scottus, 137.
Marmoutier, abbey, 23n105, 105, 106, 125, 138, 232, 251.
Martin of Tours, St, 158.

Mary, Virgin Mother of God, monastic devotion to, xviii, 3, 51, 53, 56f., 59, 60, 80, 187n68, 199, 222, 223, 275.
Massay, abbey, 23n105,
Maurilius of Fécamp, 105.
Maursmünster, abbey, 7.
Meaux, council (1082), 124f.
Ménat, abbey, 23n105.
Micy, abbey, 23n105.
Miles Christi, monk as, 58, 181.
Milo of Beneventum, 196, 197.
Molesme, abbey, xvii, 3, 36, 205, 206n133, 207, 217ff., 274.
  and Cîteaux, 272, 273.
  and the *Rule,* 240ff., 247ff.
  departures and secessions from, 233f., 235f., 241ff., 255, 256, 257, 258, 259f., 261ff.
  early donations to, 224ff.
  foundation, 222ff.
Monte Cassino, abbey, xviiif., 9n29, 34, 58, 134.
  see Benedict of Nursia.
Montier-la-Celle, abbey, 218, 220.
Montmajeur, abbey, 97.
Moyenmoutier, abbey, 152.
Mucheratus, 137.
Muret, hermitage, 197, 199.

Narbonne, council (1054), 115.
New Monastery.
  see Cîteaux.
Nicolaiticism, 79, 162, 166, 187.
Nicholas II, pope, 120, 159.
Nicholas of Myra, St 136, 196.
Nîmes, council (1096), 126.
Norigaud of Autun, 106.
Novices, 178n41, 181.
  Cluny, 85, 95.
  monastery is a novitiate for the hermitage, 179.
  Vallombrosa, 189f.
Nutriti, 65, 67.

Obedience, monastic, xiii, 14f., 98, 114, 156, 245.
  as opposed to Germanic fealty, xiii, 14f.
  of hermits, 220.
Oblates, 13, 157, 227, 229, 230, 245.

Analytic Index

Cluny, 60, 65f., 74, 101.
  schools for, 19, 29, 138.
Oda of Canterbury, 117n21.
Odilo of Cluny, St, 41, 49, 53, 57, 69, 73, 82, 88.
Odo of Cîteaux, 240, 266.
Odo of Cluny, St 41ff., 45ff., 53, 57, 61n70, 69, 71, 73, 102, 134, 232.
Odo I, duke of Burgundy, 226, 232.
Odo III, count of Troyes, 226, 233.
Opus Dei (Divine Office).
  and the *Rule*, viii, xviii, 11, 28f., 46, 52, 85, 114.
  Benedict of Aniane's views and contributions, 4f., 15, 28f., 34, 37, 56.
  Camaldoli, 171.
  canons regular, 160.
  Cîteaux, 140.
  Cluny, 49, 53ff., 82, 83f., 85f., 95f., 182n57, 191; eastern influences on, 52f.: expansion replaces manual labor, 52f.; expression of affective piety, 61.
  eleventh century, 108, 119.
  Fonte Avellana, 184.
  La Grande Chartreuse, 209, 212.
  Grandmont, 199.
  Greek, 135.
  Inde, 25ff.
  Irish influences, xiv.
  laus perennis, 145, 216.
  legislation concerning, 119.
  similarities in, 138.
  Vallombrosa, 191.
  see Liturgy.
Ordericus Vitalis, 119, 232, 249, 251, 255, 256.
Origen, 4, 31, 140.
Orleans, council (511), 113.

Pachomius, St, xiv, 59, 60, 250.
  influence on Benedict of Aniane, vii; Benedict of Nursia, xiii, 3, 37.
Palladius, St, 146, 168n3, 177.
Papalism.
  Cîteaux, 39.
  Cluny, 41, 75, 80ff., 84, 89, 90, 110.
Paschal II, pope, 67f., 89, 172, 244, 248, 269, 270, 271, 272, 273.

Paschasius Radbertus, St, 139, 178n38.
Paternus, 137.
Penal code, monastic.
  capitulare monasticum, 15.
  see Discipline.
Pepin the Short, ix, xf.
Peter of Tarantaise, 228.
Peter, companion of Bruno of Cologne, 205, 206n133, 228.
Peter, companion of Stephen Harding, 227.
Peter of Cîteaux, 240, 266.
Peter the Venerable, Bl, 48, 67, 73, 208.
Peter Damian, St, xvi, 54, 82, 97ff., 102, 139, 143, 161, 167, 168n2, 171, 195, 212.
  life and deeds, 176–187.
Philip I, 97, 105, 223.
Poitiers, council (1000), 115.
Poitiers, council (1078), 123, 126n42.
Poitiers, council (1100), 127f.
Poppo of Stavelot, St, 132, 184.
Pothières, abbey, 226n21.
Poverty, monastic, xviii, 114.
  and the crisis of cenobitism, 92, 144f.
  Benedict of Aniane, 4.
  capitulare monasticum, 13.
  legislation, 120, 157.
  new search for poverty of the eleventh century, 147f., 215, 245, 247.
  non-observance of, 116, 178n41, 233, 242, 244f.
  of Camaldoli, 171; canons regular, 158f., 160; Cîteaux, 91n156, 268, 270f., 275; Cluny, 51f., 58, 68, 81, 102, 150; Déols, 44f.; Fonte Avellana, 181ff.; La Grande Chartreuse, 210, 228; Grandmont, 200f., 203; hermits, 149; Molesme, 224, 242, 244f., 249; Romainmoutier, 45; Vallombrosa, 190f., 193.
  paupertas Christi as an ideal, xviif., 90, 150, 151, 210, 271.
  see Donations.
Prémontré, 57, 90f., 137n37.
Priory system.

of Cluny, xiv, 68ff., 78, 88, 90, 174; La Grande Chartreuse, 209; Molesme, 230ff., 234.
see Centralization; Congregation.
Prosper of Aquitaine, St, 178n38.

Ratherius, 152.
Raul Glaber, 100, 132.
Ravenna, 168, 173, 176.
Raynald of Baume, 218, 267.
Raynald of Melinais, 93, 103f., 145.
Raynard of Langres, 223, 225.
Reform, monastic.
 and French Councils, 115ff.
 and the Gregorian reform, 80f., 155ff.
 based on an ideal of unity, 138.
 differences between renewal and reform, vii, xv, xvii, xix.
 episcopal initiative, 117.
 of the tenth and eleventh centuries, 131ff.
 see Benedict of Aniane; Bruno of Cologne; Carolingians; Cîteaux; Cluny; John Gualbert; Peter Damian; Renewal; Robert of Molesme; Romuald; Stephen of Thiers.
Regino of Prüm, 184.
Reims, council (1049), 119.
Remigius, 178n38.
Remiremont, abbey, 136.
Renard of Baume, 219n3.
Renewal, monastic.
 at Cluny, 68; Molesme, 246, 247, 252.
 desire for, xvii, 240f., 245, 247.
 differences between renewal and reform, vii, xv, xvii, xix.
 in Italy, 167ff.
 of eleventh century, 131ff., 167-216.
 see Reform.
Richard of St Vanne, Bl, 132, 135.
Richard of St Victor (Marseille), 155.
Robert II (the Pious), 82.
Robert of Arbrissel, Bl, 151.
Robert of Chaise-Dieu, St., 96, 133.
Robert of Chartres, 105.
Robert of Langres, 206n133, 242.

Robert of Molesme, St, 96, 133, 155, 205.
 his authorship of the Cistercian ideal, 255ff., 260f.
 life and deeds, 217-273.
Robert of Torigny, 99, 232, 244f., 257.
Roger of Caen, 143.
Romainmoutier, abbey, 44, 45, 69.
Roman Privilege of Cîteaux, 228, 235n47, 273.
Roman synod (1059), 151.
Roman synod (1083), 126.
Roman synod (1096), 126n42.
Romuald of Ravenna, St, xvii, 82n132, 146, 167, 177, 180, 181, 184, 187, 195,
 life and deeds, 168-176.
Roscelin, 153n92.
Rouen, council (1059), 121.
Rouen, council (1072), 122.
Rouen, council (1074), 123.
Rudolph of Camaldoli, Bl, 170, 174n24.
Rufinus, 146.
Rule of Benedict of Nursia.
 and Aulps, 238ff.
 and Benedict of Aniane, xiiff., 1f. 3ff., 8, 9, 10-20, 24f., 28nn115, 116, 29ff., 33f., 46, 63, 269n140, 272,
 and Camaldoli, xvii, 169, 170f. 173, 174.
 and *capitulare monasticum*, 24f., 31.
 and Cîteaux, xviiif., 36f., 71n99, 129f., 239ff., 247ff., 251ff., 268ff.,
 and Cluny, 41ff., 68, 83, 84ff., 89, 94ff.
 and custom, xiii, xv, 10ff., 24f., 46, 48, 50f., 62ff., 133, 247, 269n140. 271f.
 and eleventh century religious orders, 167.
 and Fonte Avellana, 176, 180f., 185.
 and La Grande Chartreuse, xvii, 212f.
 and hermits, 149, 221.
 and Inde, 25ff.
 and Molesme, xvii, 244ff., 247ff.
 and Odo, 46ff.
 and Peter Damian, 180, 185, 187.

and reform of the Frankish church, xiff.
and Vallombrosa, xvii, 188ff.
as a monastic norm and a means of uniformity, 5, 6ff., 10ff., 36, 114. 116ff., 128f., 133, 134, 136.
departures from, xiiff., 71, 89, 94ff., 108, 111f., 131, 244, 248, 269n140.
desire to return and adhere more strictly to, xviiif., 36f., 71n99, 129f., 133, 166, 188ff., 238ff., 247ff., 251ff., 259, 268ff.
essence of, viif.
gaps in, 10f., 24f.
influences on, vii.
influences Rule of St Chrodegang, 158, 160.
knowledge and ignorance of in monasteries, xiii, 8n23, 11, 116.
mitigations of, 24f., 31, 34, 62f.
Moderation of suited to West, 4.
observation of in early tenth century, 40; in eleventh century, 131ff.; in Frankish abbeys, xiiff., 6ff., 10ff.
on solitude, 38, 158.
resistance to, xiiif., 3f.
role of manual labor, viii, xviii, 8n23, 18, 29, 46, 52, 64, 85, 137 245, 249ff.
role of *Opus Dei*, viii, xviii, 11, 28f., 46, 52, 85.
role of private reading, viii, xviii 11, 29, 52, 85, 249.
rule for beginners (chap. 73), 3, 11f., 137, 172, 180.

St Ayoul, abbey, 220f.
St Benignus, abbey, 105, 106, 138, 219, 264.
St Bertin, abbey, 105.
St Clement, abbey, 136.
St Eloi, convent, 106.
St Emmeram, abbey, 138.
St Fare, convent, 106.
St Gall, abbey, 136.
St Giles, abbey, 105.
St Hubert, abbey, 265.
St Magloire, abbey, 105.
St Martial, abbey, 105.

St Martin (Autun), abbey, 1n1.
St Martin (Cologne), abbey, 136, 137.
St Maur-des-Fossés, abbey, 105.
St Maximilian, abbey, 138.
St Michael (Cuxa), abbey, 168, 173.
St Michael (Tonnerre), abbey, 133, 219, 232, 258n107.
St Pantaleon, abbey, 137.
St Peter at Gembloux, abbey, 132.
St Pierre de Lagny, abbey, 105.
St Prisca di Luca, abbey, 174.
St Savin, abbey, 1n1, 23n105.
St Vannes, abbey, 137, 264.
St Vincent (Laon), abbey, 105.
Salve Regina, xviii.
San Apollinare, abbey, 168.
San Miniato, abbey, 188.
Sauve-Majeure, abbey, 133.
Savigny, abbey, xvii.
Sèche-Fontaine, hermitage, 205, 206n133, 207, 210, 213, 225, 228.
Seguin of La Chaise Dieu, 205, 206.
Serfs and servants of monks, 4, 29, 65, 67, 86f., 101, 171, 210, 230, 245.
see Manual labor.
Serlo of Bayeux, Bl, 103.
Silence, monastic, xviiif., 98, 103.
and the *Rule*, 123, 127.
at Camaldoli, 171, 174; Cluny, 46f., 68, 82, 84, 95; Fonte Avellana, 182; La Grande Chartreuse, 208; Grandmont, 200; Inde, 27; Vallombrosa, 190, 192.
capitulare monasticum, 14, 19n91.
of Peter Damian, 180; Romuald, 170.
sign language, 47, 86, 95.
see Asceticism; Austerity; Solitude.
Simeon, 135, 146.
Simony, 79, 80, 97, 103, 118, 119ff., 128, 152, 154, 162, 166, 175, 187, 188, 192, 194f.
Soissons, council (744), xi.
Social involvement of Cluny, 82, 84.
Solitude, monastic, 31.
according to Benedict of Nursia, 38.
as understood by Cîteaux, 38, 137n37, 275.

Analytic Index

Benedict of Aniane, 1f., 5, 7, 33, 38.
capitulare monasticum, 12f., 31.
eastern ideal of, 135.
eleventh century ideal of, 90, 147, 148, 158, 215.
factors limiting, 92ff.
flight away from, 102f., 104, 116.
  see Stability.
of Camaldoli, 137n37, 170ff.; Celtic monks, 137n37; Cîteaux, xix, 137n37, 267, 268, 270, 271; Cluny, 48, 58, 82, 83, 137n37; La Grande Chartreuse, 207ff.; Grandmont, 200; hermits, xvif., 149; Peter Damian, 82, 180; Prémontré, 137n37; Romuald, 168ff.; Vallombrosa, 189, 190, 195.
  see Desert, Eremitical ideals and practices; *Fuga mundi*.
Statuta Murbacensia, 7f., 31.
Stavelot, abbey, 132.
Stephen IX, pope, 176.
Stephen of Lissac, 199.
Stephen of Thiers, St, 196–203.
Stephen Harding, St, 91, 227, 235f., 238ff., 243, 246f., 255, 266.
his authorship of the Cistercian ideal, 259ff.
Sulpicius Severus, 177.
Synods, French provincial, 113ff.
  see Aachen, council; Carolingians.
Sytria, hermitage, 169, 171.

Tescelin the Red, 223.
Theodoretus, 146.
Theoria, 141f.
Thierry of Orleans, 218n3.
Tiron, abbey, xvii.
Tithes, monastic.
  acquisition of, 107, 125, 128, 129, 201, 227, 245, 250.
  capitulare monasticum, 19f.
Tonnerre, county and counts of, 133, 218, 219, 220n5, 221, 225, 226, 231.
La Torre, charterhouse, 206, 207.
Toulouse, council (1056), 120, 164.
Toulouse, council (1068), 122.

Tours, council (1060), 121f.
Transferal of monks, 23, 119, 129.
  see Stability.
Trosly, council (909), 115f.
Truce of God, 82, 90.
Udalric (Ulric), 49ff., 55, 57, 60, 66, 83, 85, 101.
Uniformity, monastic.
  Benedict of Aniane's work and influence, 1f., 6ff., 21ff., 33f., 35ff.
  Cîteaux, 118n21.
  Cluny, 68.
  evaluation of, 30.
  lack of before end of the eighth century, 22.
  of one set of customs, 21f., 137ff.
  Vallombrosa, 193.
Urban II, Bl, pope, 67, 76, 126, 160, 193, 206, 207, 236ff., 244, 265.
Ursus, 136.

Vallombrosa, abbey, xvii, 167, 187n67.
  foundation and customs, 188–196.
Vannes, council (between 461–491). 114.
Venerius, 146.
Verba Seniorum, 146.
Verdun-sur-les-Doubs, council (1016), 115.
Victor II, pope, 188, 192.
Vienne, council (1060), 121.
Vitalis of Savigny, 151.
Vivarium, abbey, 131.
Vivicus, hermitage, 235f.

Waulsort, abbey, 136.
Wazo, 152.
William of Aquitaine, 40, 44, 75, 78.
William of Argues, 228.
William of Champeaux, 153n92, 160.
William of Dijon, St, 132f., 219.
William of Hirsau, Bl, 50, 66.
William of Limoges, 105.
William of Malmesbury, 250, 259, 260f.
William of St Thierry, Bl, xvi.
Witiza (Benedict of Aniane), 2.
Women and monks, 13, 93f., 102, 115, 156, 245, 246n74.

Laus tibi Christi

CISTERCIAN FATHERS SERIES

Under the direction of the same Board of Editors as the CISTERCIAN STUDIES SERIES, the CISTERCIAN FATHERS SERIES seeks to make available the works of the Cistercian Fathers in good English translations based on the recently established critical editions. The texts are accompanied by introductions, notes and indexes prepared by qualified scholars.

CF1 Bernard of Clairvaux, vol. 1: Treatises I
   Introductions: Jean Leclercq OSB

CF2 Aelred of Rievaulx, vol. 1: Treatises, Pastoral Prayer
   Introduction: David Knowles

CF3 William of St Thierry, vol. 1: On Contemplating God, Prayer, Meditations
   Introductions: Jacques Hourlier OSB

CF4 Bernard of Clairvaux, vol. 2: On the Song of Songs I
   Introduction: Corneille Halflants OCSO

CF5 Aelred of Rievaulx, vol. 2: On Spiritual Friendship
   Introduction: Anselm Hoste OSB

CF6 William of St Thierry, vol. 2: Exposition on the Song of Songs
   Introduction: J.-M. Déchanet OSB

CF7 Bernard of Clairvaux, vol. 3: On the Song of Songs II
   Introduction: Jean Leclercq OSB

CF8 Guerric of Igny: Liturgical Sermons I
   Introduction: Hilary Costello OCSO and John Morson OCSO

CF12 William of St Thierry, vol. 4: The Golden Epistle
   Introduction: J.-M. Déchanet OSB

CF32: Guerric of Igny: Liturgical Sermons II